ACTING LITURGICALLY

Nicholas Wolterstorff is Noah Porter Professor Emeritus of Philosophical Theology, Yale University. He is the author thirty books, fellow of the American Academy of Arts and Sciences, and former president of the American Philosophical Association.

T0355186

ACTING LITURGICALLY

PHILOSOPHICAL REFLECTIONS ON RELIGIOUS PRACTICE

NICHOLAS WOLTERSTORFF

OXFORD

UNIVERSITY PRESS

OXFORD

UNIVERSITY PRESS

Great Clarendon Street, Oxford, OX2 6DP,
United Kingdom

Oxford University Press is a department of the University of Oxford.
It furthers the University's objective of excellence in research, scholarship,
and education by publishing worldwide. Oxford is a registered trade mark of
Oxford University Press in the UK and in certain other countries

First published 2018
First published in paperback 2021

Published in the United States of America by Oxford University Press
198 Madison Avenue, New York, NY 10016, United States of America

British Library Cataloguing in Publication Data
Data available

Library of Congress Cataloging in Publication Data
Data available

ISBN 978–0–19–880538–0 (Hbk.)
ISBN 978–0–19–289422–9 (Pbk.)

Printed and bound by
CPI Group (UK) Ltd, Croydon, CR0 4YY

Contents

Preface

My interest in liturgy was first sparked by serving as a member of my denomination's Liturgical Revision Committee in the mid-1960s. I never learned why I was appointed to the committee, at the time I knew nothing about liturgy; but the mandate given the committee looked interesting, so I accepted the appointment. I took my assignment seriously and began to read widely in the history and theology of liturgy. I found it fascinating.

It wasn't long before I began to sense a lack, however. The historians and theologians had interesting things to say; but I, as a philosopher, had interests and questions they did not address, or addressed only obliquely. My fellow philosophers were of little help; few of them exhibited any interest in liturgy as a topic for philosophical reflection. The few who did show some interest focused their attention almost exclusively on the ontology of the Eucharist. I set out on my own to reflect philosophically on liturgy.

The talks I gave and the essays I wrote, beginning in the late 1960s, were initially for popular audiences and periodicals. Reading them now, I realize that they were as much theological as philosophical in the questions raised and the terminology employed.[1] Though that is not, in my judgment, a bad thing, it shows that I had not yet learned to employ the distinct resources of philosophy in my reflections on liturgy. It was not until 1990 with my essay, "The Remembrance of Things (Not) Past," that I felt I had succeeded in doing that.[2] But for a good many years I did not follow up that essay with others in philosophy of liturgy; I was occupied with other topics.

In April 2006 I participated in a panel at the annual convention of the Central Division of the American Philosophical Association on the topic, "Philosophy of Religion in the 21st Century." I concluded my talk by first noting that the near-exclusive focus of analytic philosophers of religion on philosophical theology and the epistemology of religious belief had yielded

---

1. Five of them are included in Wolterstorff (2011a).
2. Wolterstorff (1990).

truly impressive results over the forty or so prior years, and then declaring that it was time to expand the scope of our inquiries. I said, "My hope for the field [of philosophy of religion] is that ten years from now there will be, for example, a body of truly impressive philosophical reflections on liturgy."

In the question period afterwards one of the young philosophers in attendance asked, with a puzzled look on his face, what sorts of questions philosophers should ask about liturgy. I mentioned a few, and then said that, beyond those, I didn't know, adding that it would be for young philosophers such as himself to discover the right questions. I was not being fully candid. It was true, at the time, that I did not know what sorts of questions philosophers should be asking about liturgy, apart from the few I had mentioned; but I had no intention of leaving the field exclusively to young philosophers. I fully intended, if life allowed, to contribute to creating a new subfield within philosophy of religion, namely, philosophy of liturgy.

Why bother? Why not leave the study of liturgy to historians, theologians, and students of ritual? My answer is that it has been my experience, when thinking about the issues I discuss in this volume, that the tradition and literature of philosophy suggest questions about liturgy that scholars from other academic disciplines are not raising, and that addressing these questions illuminates aspects of liturgy that receive scant attention from other scholars. Conversely, it has been my experience that liturgy offers to philosophers an extraordinarily rich field for philosophical inquiry.

This has proved the most difficult to write of all the books I have written, partly because liturgical activity is among the most complex forms of human activity, partly because I have almost no predecessors in the project of reflecting philosophically on liturgy. It has been a long struggle to make the right distinctions, to settle on the best terminology, to ask the right questions, to find the correct answers to the questions, to achieve the right balance between abstraction and concreteness, generalization and specificity. My hope is that all signs of struggle have been eliminated and that the distinctions drawn seem obvious, the terminology employed, felicitous, the questions asked, the right ones, the answers proposed, correct.

As my subtitle suggests, my main target audience is my fellow philosophers. But I have tried to write in such a way that those who are not philosophers will find the discussion accessible. Chapter 11, which delves into some of the intricacies of philosophical theology, will prove the most challenging to those not schooled in the way philosophers think and write.

Over the past decade or so I have benefited greatly, in my struggle to get it right, from discussions with a small group of philosophers and liturgical theologians. In 2007 Sarah Coakley, Terence Cuneo, Reinhard Hütter, Peter Ochs, James K. A. Smith, and I met at the University of Virginia as a small seed group—funded by the Calvin Institute for Christian Worship—to discuss work that we were doing on liturgy and how to "jump start" the subfield of philosophy of liturgy. The following year, 2008, the Calvin Institute for Christian Worship sponsored a conference on liturgy at Calvin College at which those of us who had met in Virginia, along with a number of other scholars, presented papers on liturgy. Then in the summer of 2009 Terence Cuneo and I led a three-week seminar on liturgy at Calvin College with fifteen participants.

I thank the Calvin Institute and Calvin College for sponsoring those events, and I thank those who participated in the 2008 conference and the 2009 seminar for their stimulating presentations and discussions, especially Howard Wettstein, who was a visiting presenter in the 2009 seminar.

I must single out two people for special mention. One is John Witvliet, head of the Calvin Institute for Christian Worship. John, a former student of mine, is a liturgical scholar without peer: he knows the history of liturgy, he knows the theology of liturgy, he is comfortable around philosophers. I am immensely pleased to see how he has flourished as a scholar and how the Calvin Institute for Christian Worship, which he founded twenty years ago and of which he is the director, has prospered under his leadership. John organized a small group at Calvin College to discuss my manuscript in the fall of 2015 and the spring of 2016. The group consisted of himself along with Cornelius Plantinga, David Smith, and Ronald Rienstra; their comments were extremely helpful. I thank them all warmly.

The other person whom I must single out for special mention is Terence Cuneo, also a former student. Terence has been my constant companion in the project of "jump starting" the subfield of philosophy of liturgy. Over the past several years he has published a number of very insightful essays on liturgy that have now been collected in *Ritualized Faith: Essays on the Philosophy of Liturgy*.[3] Terence read the complete manuscript of this present volume and gave me very helpful comments; I thank him warmly.

3. Cuneo (2016b).

Introduction

In recent decades there has been an extraordinary surge of interest in philosophy of religion within the analytic tradition of philosophy. Those who have participated in this movement—myself included[1]—have focused almost all of their attention on just four topics: the nature of God, the epistemology of religious belief, the nature of religious experience, and the problem of evil. If someone who knew nothing about religion drew conclusions about the religious mode of life from this literature she would come to the view that, apart from the mystical experiences of a few people, the religious life consists of believing things about God. She would have no inkling of the fact that liturgies and rituals are prominent within the lives of most adherents of almost all religions, including the religion dominant in the West, namely, Christianity.[2] Between the priorities of analytic philosophers of religion and the priorities of most religious adherents there is a striking discrepancy. My hope is that the philosophical reflections on liturgy in this book will contribute to diminishing this discrepancy.[3]

Why the neglect of liturgy by philosophers of religion?

It's easy to understand why the topics mentioned have drawn the attention of contemporary philosophers of religion. Disputes about the Trinity and

1. See Wolterstorff (2010a) and Wolterstorff (2010b).
2. Charles Taliaferro, in "Ritual and Christian Philosophy," remarks, "It is regrettable that mainstream, contemporary philosophy of religion has largely ignored the role of ritual in Christian life and practice....A neglect of this terrain results in an excessively intellectual or detached portrait of religion." Taliaferro (2004), 238.
3. In addition to Schilbrack (2004), two other books of philosophical reflections on liturgy have recently appeared: Terence Cuneo (2016b), and James K. A. Smith (2013).

the Incarnation that arose early in the history of Christianity, and conciliar pronouncements declaring certain positions on those topics to be orthodox and the others heretical, combined to make believing the right things about God prominent in Christianity. The so-called Athanasian Creed (*Quicunque vult*), probably originating somewhere in the West in the sixth century, opens with the awesome words, "Whosoever will be saved, before all things it is necessary that he hold the catholic faith; which faith except every one do keep whole and undefiled, without doubt he shall perish everlastingly." What then follows is a rather elaborate statement concerning the Trinity and the Incarnation. The prominence in contemporary philosophy of religion of discussions about the nature of God reflects the prominence within Christianity of claims and disputes about God.

The epistemology of religious belief was placed on the agenda of modern philosophers by John Locke;[4] the presence of religious diversity in the Western world has kept it on our agenda. For us, the topic is unavoidable. The prominence of discussions about religious experience seems to me due primarily to the influence of Schleiermacher and his fellow Romantics. As for discussions of the problem of evil, those go back into both Jewish and pagan antiquity.

In short, the fact that analytic philosophers of religion have concentrated their attention on the four topics mentioned is a reflection of their theological and philosophical heritage. Apart from reflections on the ontology of the Eucharist, we have no rich heritage of philosophical reflections on liturgy.

Philosophers are quite capable of going beyond their intellectual heritage, however. So though their heritage explains why contemporary philosophers of religion have discussed the four topics mentioned, it does not explain why they have not *also* attended to liturgy. Given the prominence of liturgy and ritual in the lives of religious people generally, why the near-total neglect of liturgy?[5]

Some would say it's because of the nature of Christianity and its prominence in the West. On the continuum from orthopraxic to orthodoxic

4. On this see Wolterstorff (1996).
5. Schilbrack (2004) gives as the reason for the neglect, "the assumption [by philosophers] that ritual activities are thoughtless. That is, rituals are typically seen as mechanical or instinctual and not as activities that involve thinking or learning" (1). I rather doubt that philosophers make that assumption.

religions,[6] Christianity, so it is often said, is on the orthodoxic end. This is the understanding of Christianity that the ritual theorist, Catherine Bell, claims is dominant in religious studies departments. Reflecting on her own experience of teaching the subject of ritual to undergraduates she says:

> Students know they may be at a disadvantage when they step into one of my classes if their own previous coursework addressed Christianity, but I think the disadvantage is quite different from what they imagine. It is not of knowledge but of perspective. Christianity is the religious tradition least likely to be taught with reference to its key rituals. In most religious studies departments, undergraduate courses on Judaism or Islam naturally discuss some of the main ritual components of these traditions, often presented as more orthopraxic in orientation than Christianity.... Yet courses on Christian history or theology that refer to the liturgical expression of key doctrinal ideas will do so without ever examining what these liturgical expressions mean to anyone.[7]

I have no reason to doubt Bell's report of how Christianity is understood and taught in most religious studies departments. But it's a distorted understanding. Though it's true that having the right beliefs about God is prominent in Christianity, from this it does not follow that Christians regard participation in enactments of their liturgies as unimportant. I know of no branch of Christianity in which such participation is, in fact, regarded as unimportant.[8]

A related reason for this not being the correct explanation for the neglect of liturgy by philosophers is the following. As a rough and ready generalization, liturgy is more important, and right belief less important, in present-day Orthodoxy and Catholicism than in evangelicalism and confessional Protestantism. So if it were Christianity's relatively heavy emphasis on right belief that accounted for the fact that analytic philosophers of religion pay little attention to liturgy, one would expect those philosophers who identify themselves as Orthodox or Catholic to pay more attention to liturgy than those who identify themselves as evangelicals or confessional

---

6. "Orthopraxic" comes from the Greek for *right practice*, "orthodoxic" from the Greek for *right belief*.
7. Bell (2007), 187. I thank Terence Cuneo for calling this passage to my attention.
8. I will be using the term "enactment" as a quasi-technical term. An enactment of a liturgy is a performance of that liturgy. I prefer the term "enactment" because of the misleading connotations of the term "performance." Some liturgical enactments are almost entirely performances: the people watch and listen to what is happening up front on the stage. But that is not true in general. Richard D. McCall titles his book on liturgy, *Do This: Liturgy as Performance* (2007). But he remarks, "to avoid the theatrical overtones of the word [performance], I often refer to the *enactment* of the liturgy" (6).

Protestants. But that's not how it is. Liturgy suffers from near-neglect by all philosophers, no matter what their religious identification.

Some would say it's Descartes's fault that philosophers of religion have neglected liturgy. Descartes is to blame for the obsessive preoccupation of philosophers of the modern period with the mind, so he's to blame for the fact that philosophers of religion have talked a great deal about religious belief and experience and hardly at all about liturgy. Liturgy, after all, involves the body.

Whether or not it was because of Descartes's influence, the extent to which philosophers of the early modern period focused on the mind is indeed striking. Review the titles of the classics of the period: *Essay Concerning Human Understanding, Inquiry into the Human Mind, Critique of Pure Judgment, Critique of Practical Judgment*; the list could easily be extended. Even a classic whose title suggests something more, Hume's *Treatise Concerning Human Nature*, is in fact not about human nature in general but about the nature of the human mind.

The focus on the mind in early modern philosophy cannot, however, be the explanation for the neglect of liturgy by philosophers of religion. Political philosophy has flourished in the modern period; more recently, philosophy of language has flourished. None of these is about the mind. If Descartes's influence has not prevented philosophers from reflecting on politics and language, why suppose it has deterred them from reflecting on liturgy?

Might the neglect of liturgy by philosophers in the contemporary analytic tradition be due to the fact that the skill set of the typical analytic philosopher doesn't fit the study of liturgy? Up front center in analytic philosophy are analysis of concepts, proposals concerning criteria for the application of concepts, and analysis of the logical relationships among propositions. So it's no surprise that in essays by analytic philosophers on religion one finds extensive discussions on the conditions for the application of the concept of justification to religious beliefs and extensive discussions on how the concepts of divine omniscience, omnipotence, immutability, eternity, and so forth are to be analyzed. Such topics are the bread and butter of the typical analytic philosopher. Participants in liturgical enactments do, of course, employ concepts and assert propositions, but they do much more than that. They eat bread, drink wine, put money in baskets, etc. So might it be that analytic philosophers neglect liturgy because they lack the skills for dealing with this "more"?

I think not. There is a rich body of work in philosophy of art by analytic philosophers. Some of this is philosophy in the traditional analytic style: analysis of concepts such as *work of art, representation, expression, aesthetic excellence*, and the like. But much of it deals directly with art rather than with propositions and concepts; it's phenomenology of a certain sort.

I do not understand why analytic philosophers of religion have neglected liturgy. I find the neglect inexplicable. Some readers might be thinking that liturgy has been neglected because it offers little of interest to philosophers. In this book I hope to show that liturgy poses a multitude of fascinating issues for philosophical reflection; liturgical participation proves to be among the most complex forms of human activity.

My discussion will take the form of phenomenology of a certain sort, resembling, in that respect, recent philosophy of art.[9] The phenomenology will employ concepts and distinctions from the analytic tradition whenever those prove helpful. But my overarching goal is not to analyze concepts or discern logical relations among propositions but to understand, at a deep level, what is done in liturgical enactments.

A common distinction in discussions about liturgy by non-philosophers is between the *expressive* function of liturgy and the *formative* function: liturgical activity as expressive of the beliefs, commitments, habits, emotions, and so forth of the participants, and liturgical activity as formative of those.[10] The focus of my discussion will not be on the expressive and formative functions of liturgical activity but on *what is done* in liturgical enactments. Call this the *performative* dimension of liturgy. Insofar as liturgical activity is expressive and formative, it's what is done that is expressive and formative. What is done is basic.[11] My goal is to understand, at a deep level, the performative dimension of liturgy.

9. When I say that it takes the form "phenomenology of a certain sort," I mean to suggest that it is descriptive, in a certain way, of the phenomena. I do not mean to suggest that my discussion is an example of the philosophical movement known as "phenomenology," of which Husserl and Merleau-Ponty were prominent representatives.

10. A line of interpretation that was popular for almost a millennium, from the fourth to the fourteenth centuries, was the so-called *mystagogical* interpretation, according to which almost all of the prescribed movements and gestures of the liturgical leaders were interpreted as symbolic, mostly of actions by God or Christ. The mystagogical line of interpretation has everywhere fallen out of favor.

11. Emma O'Donnell (2015) notes that a great deal of liturgical theology focuses on meaning and then says this: "Recognizing that the search for meaning can sometimes obscure the essentially performative nature of liturgy, much liturgical theology in recent decades has expressed a preference for what liturgy 'does' rather than what liturgy 'means'" (23). O'Donnell declares that she is a participant in this recent trend. Her phrase, "the performative nature of liturgy,"

A full discussion of liturgy would analyze not only its performative
dimension and its expressive and formative functions but also the liturgical
significance of the environment within which the liturgy is enacted: the
architectural environment, the environment of light, shadow, and darkness,
the sensory environment of smells and colors, sound and silence, the artistic
environment of images and banners. Important and fascinating as all that is,
it lies beyond the scope of this book.

Liturgical theology and ritual studies

Though philosophers have neglected liturgy, theologians have not; there is
a long and rich tradition of *liturgical theology*. In this book I will now and
then interact with this body of thought.[12] The interactions will not be
deep and sustained, however, in part because the tool-kit of theologians is
significantly different from that of philosophers—different questions, different
concepts, different ways of arguing, different literature—but also because the
main interest of liturgical theologians is not in what is done in liturgical
enactments but the theological significance of what is done. And for reasons
that elude me, liturgical theologians typically conduct their discussions at a
very high level of generality, only infrequently referring to specific liturgical
actions and specific passages from liturgical texts; in my discussion I will
attend to the fine texture of liturgical enactments.

There is also a rich body of *ritual theory*, some composed by theorists
whose home field is anthropology, some by theorists whose home field is
religious studies. I will now and then interact with this body of theory as
well. In this case too, however, the interactions will not be deep and sustained,
mainly because most ritual theorists are no more interested in understanding
in depth the performative dimension of liturgical enactments than are
theologians. In *Ritual Theory, Ritual Practice*, Catherine Bell presents a helpful
survey of developments in ritual theory over the prior several decades. Most
of the theories she surveys focus either on the social functions of ritual or

makes it sound as if she too is interested in what I call the "performative dimension" of liturgy.
She is not. It's significant that she speaks of what *liturgy* does, not of what *we* do when participating in a liturgy enactment. Her interest is in the formative function of liturgy—what liturgy
does to us. Specifically, she is interested in how liturgical participation orients us in time.

12. The liturgical theologians whom I have found most helpful are the Russian Orthodox theologian
Alexander Schmemann and the Swiss Reformed theologian Jean-Jacques von Allen.

on the causal efficacy that participants in ritual activity attribute to their actions. Those ritual theorists who do not think of ritual activity in these functional terms mostly think of it as "symbolic or expressive activity (i.e., communicative in some way)."[13] They think of ritual activity as "depicting, modeling, enacting, or dramatizing what are seen as prior conceptual ideas and values."[14]

When congregants follow the script for the beginning of the Episcopal liturgy and say, "Blessed be [God's] kingdom, now and forever," their action may or may not have certain social and personal effects and they may or may not be expressing "prior conceptual ideas and values." But if they are doing what the script prescribes, they are blessing God's kingdom. It's their liturgical act of blessing God's kingdom that interests me.

The Archetypal Actions of Ritual, by Caroline Humphrey and James Laidlaw, appeared a few years after Bell's *Ritual Theory, Ritual Practice* and explicitly distances itself from prior ritual theory by placing ritualized action itself at the center of attention, rather than its purported functions, arguing that such action is a special way of doing things that, for the most part, can be done in non-ritualized ways as well. Describing their approach in the Introduction, they say:

> We suggest ... that ritual is a distinctive way in which an action, probably any action, may be performed. Thus a "theory of ritual" is an account of the transformation of action by ritualization. There is no point in trying to frame generalizations about the social function, or whatever, of all rituals, because ritualization can happen to anything. The proper focus of theoretical attention is therefore the distinctive quality which action, performed in this way, comes to have.[15]

My project in this book is not to develop a theory of liturgy or ritual but, to say it again, to understand at a deep level what is done in liturgical enactments. In conducting my analyses I will, unavoidably, employ theory; some of the theory I employ is similar to the theory Humphrey and Laidlaw articulate. (I will discuss their theory in some detail in Chapter 2.) But I do not have what could be called "a theory of liturgy."

An implication of what I have been saying is that there is almost no ready-made readership for this book. Liturgical theologians and ritual theorists who happen to pick it up and dip into it will find its philosophical style strange, perhaps off-putting. The concepts used, the questions raised, the

13. Bell (1992), 71.   14. Bell (1992), 43.   15. Humphrey and Laidlaw (1994), 3.

literature engaged, the modes of analysis and argumentation employed, will be unfamiliar to them. One liturgical scholar who read some of the chapters wrote, "Reading your text, I often felt as if I was overhearing a conversation, say between urban planners, about the house I grew up in. I know the object the conversation centers on intimately, but the lens through which my home is looked at is different from what I know of this, my house." Philosophers of religion will find the style familiar, of course; but the terrain covered will be new and unfamiliar to them: topics are discussed that they have never thought about and perhaps don't know how to think about.

My examples

Since it is Christian liturgies I know best, it will be those liturgies that I analyze. I realize that much of what I say about Christian liturgies applies to the liturgies and rituals of other religions as well, especially to those of Judaism; but I will leave it to those whose knowledge of those other liturgies and rituals is deeper and more comprehensive than mine to make the relevant applications and generalizations.

My examples will be drawn from the liturgies of mainline denominations. My reason is not that I regard only these as having liturgies. Whenever Christians assemble on Sundays they enact a liturgy. There may be nothing printed out, the cues may consist entirely of "audibles" voiced by one or more leaders, and the participants may be strongly opposed to the claim that they have a liturgy; the term suggests to them the "ritualism" they abhor. They speak instead of "the order of worship." But as I will explain in Chapter 1, their order of worship is an example of what I call a "liturgy." My usage on this point accords with that of most scholars who write about liturgy.

My reason for drawing my examples from Catholic, Orthodox, and mainline Protestant liturgies is that the principal components of these liturgies are easily accessible in published texts whereas the alternative contemporary liturgies of free church Protestants are not accessible in that way. To gain access to them I would have to do field research. I think it's important that some scholars go out into the field; but that's not for me.[16]

---

16. Some scholars have begun to do liturgical field research, for example, Melanie Ross (2014).

I draw more examples from the Orthodox liturgy than from any other, not because I know it best—I do not—but because, unlike the liturgies of the West, the Orthodox liturgy has never been subjected to what one might call "rationalization." In Western liturgies the thought has been simplified, the language clarified, complexity reduced, hyperbole diminished, metaphors eliminated. The Orthodox liturgy is prolix, poetic, excessive, wild, hyperbolic, highly metaphorical, complex, often obscure, much of it clearly the production of poets rather than theologians.[17] For philosophers reflecting on liturgy it offers more challenges to analysis than any Western liturgy that I know of, and many more vivid and arresting examples.

17. Richard D. McCall's description of the Gallican liturgies of the tenth century in McCall (2007) makes clear that they resembled the Orthodox liturgy in these respects. He describes their language as "expansive and poetic" (17), and says that they exhibit "the desire for lush poetry and dramatic expression" (16). Rome succeeded in taming the liturgical impulses of the Gallicans.

PART
I

Liturgy, enactments, and scripts

I

What is liturgy?

Our project is to reflect philosophically on liturgy, so let's begin with the most basic question: what is liturgy? Putting the question that way suggests there is some single thing called "liturgy," when in fact there are only *liturgies*, plural. So let's be more precise: what are liturgies? What differentiates liturgies from other things? Where, on the ontological map, are liturgies located?

When I speak of liturgies it is liturgies in the strict sense of the term that I have in mind, the liturgies of religious communities. Books and essays have been written on the liturgies of football games, the rituals of shopping, etc. There's nothing wrong with using the terms "liturgy" and "ritual" in those analogically extended ways. But liturgies in the strict sense are sufficiently fascinating and baffling to keep us occupied for a long time; no need to include analogous phenomena in the scope of our inquiry.

As for liturgies in the strict sense, a point made in the Introduction bears repeating. Whenever Christians assemble on Sundays (or Muslims on Fridays or Jews on Saturdays) there is a liturgy they follow. They may resist calling it a "liturgy," preferring to call it "the order of worship" or something similar. But there will be actions that are to be performed and, usually, an order in which they are to be performed; and that is their liturgy. This is true even for the meetings of Quakers on the Eastern seaboard of the United States. Each person is to meditate in silence until he or she feels moved by the Spirit to say or sing something; the others are then to listen attentively.[1]

Different meanings of "liturgy"

I have on my shelves a volume titled *The Orthodox Liturgy*, published by Oxford University Press in 1982. The volume contains two texts bound together: the English text for the liturgy of St John Chrysostom and the English text for the liturgy of St Basil the Great. Each of these is a text for the enactment of that liturgy, specifying words to be said or sung by the participants, and gestures and movements to be made, for a correct enactment of that particular liturgy to take place. The use of the term "liturgy" to refer to a text of a certain sort is common.

In describing these texts as a text as *for a correct enactment* of the liturgy of St John Chrysostom and a text *for a correct enactment of* the liturgy of St Basil the Great, I was using the term "liturgy" for something other than a text. That which one enacts is not a text but a type of act, or a type of sequence of act-types. This use of the term "liturgy," to refer to that which is enacted when a liturgical text is followed, is also common. To make matters yet more confusing, the term is also commonly used to refer to particular enactments of liturgies.[2]

I will confine my use of the term "liturgy" to refer to that which is enacted—not, for example, to the text for enacting the liturgy of St John Chrysostom, and also not to any particular enactment of that liturgy, but only to that type of sequence of act-types that is enacted when that particular liturgical text is faithfully followed.[3]

---

1. For an interesting discussion of the theology underlying Quaker "liturgies of silence" see Dandelion (2005).
2. Recall that I am using "enactment" as a quasi-technical term for a performance of a liturgy, for a "doing" of it.
3. This explanation of how I will be using the term "liturgy" will be qualified later when I explain that a liturgical text never specifies more than part of what I call the *script* for a liturgical enactment, and that it is the script that determines the identity of the liturgy which is enacted.

Fundamental to the discussion that follows in this chapter and several others is the distinction I have just now employed between *types* of acts and *instances* of types. I will use terminology familiar to philosophers and call the former of these entities, *act-types*, and the latter, *act-tokens*. Most act-types are universals; they can be multiply instantiated, their instantiations being particulars. To use alternative terminology, they can recur.

No doubt some readers will be mystified by my comment that *most* act-types are universals; they assume that if something is a type, then necessarily it can be multiply instantiated and is, therefore, a universal. But not so. An example of an act-type that cannot recur, and hence is not a universal, is *the act of first setting foot on the moon*. The act-token, *Neil Armstrong's setting foot on the moon*, is an instance of that act-type and there can be no others. There *could have been* a different instance of this act-type than the one that is in fact the instance. Armstrong's companion, Buzz Aldrin, might have been the first to set foot on the moon, in which case the act-token, *Buzz Aldrin's setting foot on the moon*, would have been an instance of the act-type of *first setting foot on the moon* and there could subsequently be no others. (I concede that to call an entity of which there can be only one instance a *type* is not entirely felicitous.)

Let me approach my answer to the question, what sort of entity is a liturgy, by first characterizing the acts that constitute an enactment of some liturgy, and then using that characterization to explain what sort of entity a liturgy itself is.

Scripted activity

Those who participate in enacting some liturgy do so by following what I shall call a *script*, the result being *scripted activity*.[4] To participate in the enactment of some liturgy is to engage in scripted activity. Scripted activity is by no means confined to liturgical enactments; it is to be found throughout our ordinary lives. It will aid our understanding of scripted liturgical activity if we first look at some other examples of the genus.

---

4. One can aim to follow a script without actually following it in every detail; one may make mistakes. In this book I will often speak of *following* a script when what I mean, strictly speaking, is *aiming* to follow it.

Scripted activity is a species of activity for which there are prescriptions in force. At every moment in the life of every conscious human being who has emerged from infancy there are prescriptions in force: moral prescriptions, legal prescriptions, linguistic prescriptions, and so forth. These prescriptions identify certain act-types and specify either when and where one is *required* to perform an instance of that act-type or when and where one is *permitted* to do so. Most requirements and permissions are conditional on some aim that one has set for oneself—the aim of speaking English correctly, for example. Moral requirements and permissions are not conditional. Among the moral prescriptions in force for all of us is the prescription, always refrain from committing acts that consist of *abusing someone*. By reference to prescriptions for action, act-tokens can be judged as correct or incorrect.

Prescriptions for action vary enormously with respect to the generality and specificity of what they require and what they permit. Rules for games are prescriptions. So consider, for example, the rules for chess. The rules specify which moves are allowable and which are required in playing the game; by reference to the rules, moves are correct or incorrect. The rules, for the most part, are highly general; millions of different playings of the game are correct at every point. The rules for American football are likewise highly general; they too allow for a vast number of different playings of the game each of which is correct at every point.

Suppose, now, that on a team's first possession of the football the quarterback decides that the first play will be Play #9 in the team's playbook. The description and diagram of Play #9 in the playbook identify with relative specificity what each player is required to do when Play #9 is called. Their actions are what I shall call *scripted*. And in general, when the prescriptions that are in force for some activity identify with relative specificity a certain act as required, I will say, when the prescriptions are followed, that the act is *scripted*, and I will call the prescription for that act, the *script* for it. *Relative specificity* is, obviously, a vague concept; there are borderline cases.

In the example just given, the quarterback's choice of Play #9 as the first play was not scripted; it's the acts the members of the team are required to perform when the quarterback calls Play #9 that are scripted. But suppose that, rather than allowing the quarterback to choose the first play, the coach has drawn up a game-plan in advance which prescribes that on the team's first possession, the first play the quarterback is to call is Play #9. Then, though the quarterback's calling of that play is not scripted by the rules for football, it is scripted by the coach's game-plan.[5]

With an eye on our subsequent discussion of liturgy let me call attention to five features of this example that are typical of scripted acts in general. The quarterback can perform the act of calling Play #9 for the first play of the team's first possession whether or not his calling of that play is scripted. When we ask whether the team members can likewise perform the actions specified by Play #9 whether or not their doing so is scripted, the sheer unlikelihood of their doing so brings to light one of the fundamental reasons for there being scripts: scripts, in many cases, are very nearly indispensable for acting together.

Second, what the script created was not the possibility of the players performing the specified acts but the possibility of their performing them *correctly or incorrectly*. When the script is in force, what the players do is infused with normativity, in the sense that what they do is correct or incorrect by reference to the script.[6] In the absence of a game-plan, the calls the quarterback makes will be better or worse but not correct or incorrect.[7] Of course, by no means everything that the players do in executing Play #9 can be evaluated in terms of correctness and incorrectness. Much of it is just good or bad, better or worse, not correct or incorrect.

Third, when the players aim to follow the playbook and the game-plan with respect to the actions specified they suspend acting on their own judgments as to what would be good to do and instead follow the script. For the sake of some good to be achieved by acting together they suspend for a time the exercise of their own autonomy and together submit to the script. The self-image assiduously cultivated by many contemporary writers is that

5. Suppose the game-plan that the coach draws up specifies that the quarterback is to choose between plays #7, #8, and #9 on the team's first possession; then the quarterback's choice of one or the other of those three is required, but not his choice of any particular one of the three. Is the requirement in this case "relatively specific"? I would say that it is; but nothing in what follows will hang on that judgment call.

6. Sociologists and anthropologists employ a different concept of *script* from that which I am employing, one that does not involve correctness and incorrectness of performance. The anthropologists Caroline Humphrey and James Laidlaw define a script as "a stereotyped sequence of events which the actor knows and uses as a guide to understanding and performance, for example, 'going to the theatre'.... [T]he idea of the script was developed in attempts to give cognitive descriptions of routine, everyday events like a visit to a restaurant or a trip to the dentist." Humphrey and Laidlaw (1994), 111.

7. Unless the social practice of American football determines that certain plays in certain situations, though allowed by the rules, are just "the wrong play."

of the autonomous self. We are all, in fact, *rule-submissive* and *script-submissive* selves; nobody is a purely autonomous self. We all act heteronomously.

Fourth, an important point I did not take note of when describing the example is that the description and diagram of Play #9 in the team's playbook do not specify all the acts that the players are to perform in executing Play #9; the description and diagram could not possibly specify them all. Taken for granted is what the players have been taught and trained to do by their induction into the local version of the social practice of American football. The full script for Play #9 consists of the prescriptions that the description and diagram specify plus those embedded in the social practice.

Last, an enactment of the script for Play #9 has a beginning and an end. It is bounded, set off from the ebb and flow of the rest of the game and from life in general.[8]

Another example

In the discussion that follows we will not only need the concept of a particular act being scripted by the prescriptions in force but also the concept of a whole sequence of acts being scripted, call it *scripted activity*. Let's have an example.

Suppose one is attending an evening event put on by the local high school and that, when one arrives, one is handed a printed program. The program specifies actions that are to take place and the order in which they are to take place. Perhaps it specifies that the head of the institution is to begin the event by extending a welcome to the audience, after which the school orchestra is to play a brief number. Perhaps it also specifies some responses that members of the audience are to voice.

In following the program the participants engage in scripted activity, their acts exhibiting the same five features that I highlighted in the football example: the script enables the participants to act together; the script's being in force brings it about that the acts of the participants are norm-infused; in following the script the participants suspend acting on their own judgments as to what would be good to do and together submit to the script for the sake of the good to be achieved thereby; the full script consists not just of the prescriptions specified in the printed program but includes, as well,

---

8. Some writers use the term "framed" instead of "bounded."

those that are implicit in the relevant social practice plus those given orally on the spot; and enactments of the script are bounded.

When the school orchestra follows the program and performs the musical work specified at the point where the program says it is to do so, its act of performing the work at that point is scripted. But so too, its act of *following the score* for the work is scripted; following the score is scripted activity.

Rather than pointing out that each of the five features of scripted activity I highlighted in the section "Scripted activity" are present when the orchestra follows the score, let me just take note of the fact that the notations in a score never completely specify what the performers are to do. The composer, when creating his score, could not possibly notate all the prescriptions; always he does and must take for granted various prescriptions embedded in the social practice of musical performance—embedded in the social practice of violin-playing, for example. What I call the *script* for a musical perform-ance is the total set of prescriptions holding for that performance, both those specified in the score and those embedded within the relevant social practice (along with those, if any, that are given orally on the spot). Or in case the work was not composed and scored but emerged organically within the musical culture of the society, the script is the set of prescriptions embedded within the musical practice of that society.

It will now be clear, if it was not before, that I am stretching the ordinary meaning of the word "script." Usually what is called a "script" consists of instructions written down in words. What I am here calling a "script" is, instead, the complete set of prescriptions for the performance of certain acts. Often some of those prescriptions are specified by notations of some sort—words, diagrams, musical notations, and the like. But never are all of them specified by notations, and sometimes none of them is.

A new point: when the school orchestra follows the prescriptions notated in the score plus those embedded in musical practice, it does something else as well; it performs a certain musical work, specifically, the work for which that score is the score. What is that musical work? It's the type of sequence of act-types prescribed by the script—the type of sequence of act-types enacted when the script is faithfully followed.[9] That type of sequence of act-types can be enacted in different places and at different times. It is, thus,

9. In saying that a musical work is a type of sequence of act-types, I am assuming that it is performances of the work that instantiate the work. One could also think of a musical work as a type of sequence of sound-types. When a musical work is so conceived, instantiations of the work are not sequences of act-tokens but sequences of sound-tokens.

a universal. Works of music are universals. And they can be performed correctly or incorrectly. They are performed correctly when the script for the work is faithfully followed.

Play #9 in the team's playbook is to be thought of along the same lines. The play itself, in distinction from the script for the play, is that type of sequence of act-types that is enacted when the script for Play #9 is faithfully followed. Since that type of sequence of act-types can be enacted in different places and at different times, it is a universal. Likewise the program for the evening's event, in distinction from the script, is a universal; specifically, it is that type of sequence of act-types that is enacted when the script for what is to take place is faithfully followed.

Liturgy

Liturgical enactments are a species of the genus: scripted activity. Participants enact the liturgy of St John Chrysostom by together aiming to follow the script for that liturgy and being relatively successful in doing so. The fact that a script is in force brings it about that their actions are norm-infused: some are correct, some are incorrect. Part of the script, but only part, is specified by the text for that liturgy. In addition to the prescriptions speci- fied by the text there are those that are embedded in the Orthodox social practice of enacting their liturgies (plus any that may be specified orally on the spot).

When the members of a Christian congregation assemble to enact their liturgy they come prepared to suspend for a time acting on their own judg- ments as to what would be good to do and instead follow the liturgical script. For the sake of some good to be achieved by together submitting to the script they suspend for a time the exercise of their own autonomy. They act heteronomously. Of course, there is still room for micro-autonomy; by no means is everything that they do scripted, any more than everything in the execution of a game-plan or in the performance of some work of music. The liturgical script does not prescribe how energetically they are to sing the hymns nor how loudly they are to recite the creed. But on the matters to which the script does speak, the congregants conform their acts to the script rather than deciding for themselves what to do.[10]

10. This claim will be qualified in Chapter 5; what I say here is true only for those congregants who fully conform to the script.

This tells us what it is to enact a liturgy. What is the thing enacted, the liturgy itself? Given some liturgical script, the liturgy itself is the type of sequence of act-types prescribed by the script. It's that type of sequence of act-types that is instantiated when the script is faithfully followed. Such a sequence can be enacted in different places and at different times. Liturgies are universals.

Bell's alternative

An influential book in the field of ritual studies is Catherine Bell's 1992 publication, *Ritual Theory, Ritual Practice*. Liturgy is a species of what Bell has in mind by ritual.[11] After explaining that she much prefers the concept of *ritualized activity* to that of *ritual*, Bell then explains the nature of ritualized activity as follows:

> Viewed as practice, ritualization involves the very drawing, in and through the activity itself, of a privileged distinction between ways of acting, specifically between those acts being performed and those being contrasted, mimed, or implicated somehow. That is, intrinsic to ritualization are strategies for differentiating itself—to various degrees and in various ways—from other ways of acting within any particular culture. At a basic level, ritualization is the production of this differentiation. At a more complex level, ritualization is a way of acting that specifically establishes a privileged contrast, differentiating itself as more important or powerful. Such privileged distinctions may be drawn in a variety of culturally specific ways that render the ritualized acts dominant in status.[12]

Nowhere does Bell offer a general account of what it is about ritualized activity that differentiates such activity from other activities; she gives examples of ritualized activities that are set off from somewhat similar activities that are not ritualized and lets it go at that. It appears that she finds generalization impossible.

I find this unsatisfactory. It's true, of course, that ritualized activity is set off from non-ritualized activity. But that's true for many other forms of

---

11. By the term "ritual" some writers have in mind not scripted activity of a certain sort but activity in accord with social conventions. That is how the term is used, for example, in Seligman et al. (2008). On occasion the writers use the term "convention" rather than "ritual" (e.g., on p. 24).
12. Bell (1992), 90.

activity as well—play, for example. Play is set off from non-play. And if it be said, in response, that though play is set off from non-play, it is not set off as "more important or powerful," then how about warfare? Warfare is certainly set off from other activities as more important and powerful.

Bell misses what seems to me the heart of ritualized activity. Ritualized activity is scripted activity and is thus norm-infused in the way that scripted activity in general is norm-infused. It would be a mistake to identify ritualized activity with scripted activity; that would have the counter-intuitive consequence that a musical performance is an instance of ritualized activity. Ritualized activity is a species of the genus: scripted activity. To overlook the fact that ritualized activity is scripted activity, and thereby norm-infused, strikes me as overlooking its defining genus.[13]

Liturgical enactments occur within social practices

Above I remarked that only part of the script for an enactment of the liturgy of St John Chrysostom is specified in the text for that liturgy; much of it is embedded within the Orthodox social practice of enacting that liturgy. The same is true for all other liturgical enactments: the script for enacting a particular liturgy is never fully specified by a text, nor by a text supplemented by oral directives. Always some of the prescriptions constituting the script are embedded within the social practice of that particular religious community for enacting its liturgies.

It's a social practice among Christians to participate in liturgical enactments, as it is among Jews, Muslims, and others. Participation in liturgical enactments is not a one-off thing. When a congregation enacts its liturgy by following the script for that liturgy it is employing a social practice for following that script and others like it. Typically that practice is shaped both by dynamics internal to that congregation and the religious tradition to which it belongs and by dynamics in society generally.

Alasdair MacIntyre's analysis of social practices in *After Virtue* is now classic.[14] Since his discussion is well known, and since I judge it to be substantially correct, I will refrain from summarizing it and will instead confine myself

---

13. In the course of her discussion, Bell does now and then remark that ritualized activity is norm-infused. But norm-infusion does not enter into her theory of ritualized activity.
14. The discussion of social practices is to be found in MacIntyre (1981), 175–81.

to highlighting those aspects of social practices that are especially relevant for understanding liturgical practices.[15]

A social practice is a way of performing actions of a certain type. The term "a way" is ambiguous in this formulation. The phrase "a *way* of performing actions of type *X*" can be used to refer to a means for bringing about tokens of act-type *X*. For example, one way or means of sharpening a pencil is using an electric pencil sharpener, another way or means is using a sharp knife. The phrase can also be used to refer to *how* the actions are performed: quickly, thoughtfully, with abandon, etc. Social practices are typically ways of performing actions of a certain type in both senses of the term "way."

For one's way of performing actions of a certain type to be the exercise of a practice, one must be in the habit of performing such actions in that way. But that's not enough for it to be the exercise of a *social* practice. For a practice to be a social practice, a number of people must be in the habit of performing actions of that sort in that way. And practitioners must be aware of other practitioners and thereby aware of the fact that other people see some good in that activity just as they do; lacking such awareness of others, it would not be a social practice but the happenstance of a number of people being in the habit of doing things of the same sort in the same sort of way. And not only are practitioners aware of other practitioners. Typically they observe how others perform the actions in question, exchange advice, discuss better and worse ways of engaging in the practice, imitate others, and so forth. The shared practice is a focus of social interactions.

Social practices are social in yet another way: the knowledge, the attitudes, the forms of attentiveness that go into performing actions of that sort in that sort of way are handed on from those who are already practitioners, or capable of being practitioners, to those who are not yet capable. Let me save breath by calling all that is handed on, the *know-how*. Intrinsic to social practices is the phenomenon of *handing on the know-how*: the know-how of the present practitioners is handed on to the would-be practitioners. Some of the handing on takes place by explicit instruction; much of it takes place by modeling.

Social practices are thus spread out in both time and space. They have, or they *are*, traditions. Novices are inducted into the tradition of the present practitioners and their predecessors. As MacIntyre remarks, "To enter into a practice is to enter into a relationship not only with its contemporary

---

15. In Wolterstorff (2015a), 83–106, I discuss social practices more fully than I do here.

practitioners, but also with those who have preceded us in the practice, particularly those whose achievements extended the reach of the practice to its present point. It is thus the achievement, and *a fortiori* the authority, of a tradition which I then confront and from which I have to learn."[16]

In that last sentence, MacIntyre is alluding to the fact that it is typical of social practices for those who engage in the activity, along with those who teach it, to regard some performances as better than others. They employ standards of excellence whereby some people are judged to figure-skate better than others, whereby some are judged to play the oboe better than others, and so forth. Sometimes they employ rules for correctness as well; this will perforce be the case if the practice is for the performance of scripted activity.

These standards of excellence and criteria for correctness are handed on as part of the know-how so that, in this respect too, the activity is social and the practice has a tradition. As MacIntyre puts it in another passage, a social practice "typically involves standards of excellence and obedience to rules.... To enter into a practice is to accept the authority of those standards and the inadequacy of my own performance as judged by them. It is to subject my own attitudes, choices, preferences, and tastes to the standards which currently and partially define the practice.... If, on starting to listen to music, I do not accept my own incapacity to judge correctly, I will never learn to hear, let along to appreciate, Bartok's last quartets."[17]

MacIntyre overstates the point a bit in this passage. It's true that if the learner is to acquire the capacity to listen well to music she has to accept her own "incapacity to judge correctly." But she does not have to accept every-thing her teachers tell her; she does not have to treat them as the final authority on all relevant matters and she does not have to conform to all the rules they lay down. To some extent, it's open to her to come up with her own views on these matters.

A connected point is that often there is disagreement on the standards of evaluation and the criteria for correctness to be employed when engaging in the practice. Furthermore, in most practices the dominant standards and criteria will have changed over the course of history, sometimes subtly, sometimes dramatically. In the course of the history of a practice new goods emerge as candidates for guiding the aims of practitioners while goods once aimed at lose their attraction. Such changes typically call forth new know-how;

16. MacIntyre (1981), 181.   17. MacIntyre (1981), 177.

and the new know-how often suggests new standards of excellence and new criteria for correctness. Changes in aims, innovations in know-how, and innovations in standards and criteria, evoke and nurture each other; among them there is a circular process of discovery and innovation. Practices expand and alter our human ways of achieving excellence and correctness.

These observations about social practices in general apply to liturgical enactments. Full participation in some liturgical enactment requires practical know-how: knowing how and when to perform the scripted actions. It's not a know-how one is born with, nor is it a know-how one acquires automatically as one matures. It's a learned know-how. Some of it can be learned by reading the text for the liturgy being enacted. But sometimes there is no text. And even if there is a text, the text, as we have noted, never specifies the full script for an enactment of the liturgy; many of the prescriptions have no other "location" than in the social practice for enacting that liturgy and others like it. To acquire the relevant know-how one has to be inducted into the social practice. Liturgical know-how is a shared know-how, shared both with one's fellow participants, making it possible to participate together, and with those who preceded one in enactments of that liturgy and others like it.

The verbal and gestural acts prescribed by liturgical scripts are mostly not prescribed for their own sake

Our question in this chapter is, where on the ontological map are liturgies located? The answer proposed thus far is that a liturgy is a type of sequence of act-types, and that essentially associated with a liturgy is a script for correctly enacting that liturgy. But the same is true, as we have seen, for a play in football, for a program for an evening's event, and for a work of music. So let's move on to differentiate liturgies from other members of the genus.

An important contribution of speech-act theory has been calling to our attention the fundamental role in human life of the phenomenon of one act *counting as* another.[18] Raising one's hand at a certain point in an auction

18. The classic presentation of speech-act theory is Searle (1969).

counts as placing a bid on the item being auctioned; smashing a bottle of champagne against the hull of a newly minted ship and pronouncing a name for the ship, when done by a duly authorized official, *counts as* christening the ship; uttering in the appropriate context the sentence, "Rain is predicted for tomorrow," *counts as* asserting that rain is predicted for tomorrow. In each case, the agent's performance of some perceptible behavioral act—raising his hand, smashing a bottle of champagne, uttering some words—counts as his performance of an imperceptible non-behavioral act: placing a bid, christening a ship, making an assertion. When one act counts as another, let me speak of the former as a *counting-as act* and the latter as a *counted-as act*. And let me say that the former has *count-as significance*.

The way in which I used the term "count as" in the preceding paragraph has to be distinguished from another use of the same term. Suppose someone says he's not sure that Pluto counts as a planet. Obviously he is not expressing his doubt that one act counts as another. What he means is that he's not sure the definition of the term "planet" fits Pluto. Or suppose that the contestants in a folkdance contest are each required to perform a jig and that one of the judges says to another, about one of the performances, "I'm not sure that counts as a jig." What he means is that he's not sure that the definition of the term "jig" fits the performance. The idea of the definition of a term fitting something is very different from the idea of one act counting as another act by virtue, say, of some convention being in effect. When I say that uttering the sentence "Rain is predicted for tomorrow" counts as asserting that rain is predicted for tomorrow, I do not mean that the definition of the phrase "asserting that rain is predicted for tomorrow" fits the act of uttering that sentence. It does not fit it. Uttering a sentence is a perceptible bodily act; making an assertion is not.

When a play is executed in a football game none of what is done has any count-as significance; the behavior of the players is the whole thing. So too a musician's performance of some passage in a work of instrumental music normally has no count-as significance, exceptions being program music and passages containing certain musical motifs. By contrast, all of the words that a liturgical script prescribes to be said or sung, and most of the movements and gestures prescribed, are prescribed for the purpose of the participants thereby performing certain counted-as actions. The text for The Holy Eucharist of the Episcopal Church prescribes that the first words spoken by the people shall be, "Blessed be [God's] kingdom, now and forever." The text prescribes the saying of these words for the purpose of the people thereby blessing God's kingdom. Their saying those words is to *count as* their blessing God's kingdom.

Henceforth, when speaking of liturgical enactments, let me call the saying and singing of words, *verbal acts*, the making of movements and gestures, *gestural acts*,[19] and acts of listening, *auditory acts*. The fact that all of the verbal acts prescribed by liturgical scripts and most of the gestural acts are not prescribed for their own sake but for the sake of some other acts that the verbal and gestural acts are to count as makes liturgical enactments complex in ways that plays in most games and performances of most musical works are not.

In many of us there is a strong tendency, when thinking about the scripted acts performed in an enactment of some liturgy, to focus primarily if not exclusively on the verbal acts of speaking and singing. When we do that, we soon notice that most of the counted-as actions performed thereby are acts of address: the people addressing God in praise, thanksgiving, petition, and so forth, and ministers, priests, and readers addressing the people. On a view that I share with others, not only do the human participants perform acts of address but God does so as well by way of the speech of ministers, priests, and readers. So it's tempting to think of the counted-as actions of liturgy as primarily mutual address between God and the people.[20] It's a temptation to which I have myself succumbed in the past. The temptation must be resisted.

Of course, a great deal of speaking and singing does take place in liturgical enactments, and most of this does indeed have the count-as significance of address. But liturgically scripted acts are extraordinarily diverse; they include much more than speaking and singing and much more than address. Participants keep silence, play musical instruments, stand, sit, kneel, bow, prostrate themselves, process, dance, get out of their seats and walk forward, return to their seats, cross themselves, fold their hands, raise their hands, close their eyes, drop money into a container, distribute bread and wine, eat bread and drink wine, sprinkle with water, immerse in water, rub with oil,

19. I am thinking here of the Latin *verba et gesta*.
20. Cf. Graham Hughes (2003), 160–1: "It is a commonplace that the liturgy is a dialectic in its structure: '[I]n its actual celebration the liturgy is truly a dialogue between God and his people'." The passage Hughes quotes is from A. G. Martimort. He quotes a number of other writers making the same claim.

wash themselves, wash the feet of others, shake hands, embrace, spit, wave palm branches, light candles, and more besides.[21]

The scripted acts just now mentioned are all gestural acts. Many of them have count-as significance when they are performed, but not all. The prescribed act of sitting down after the singing of a hymn does not. The congregants sit down; that's all. Their sitting down does not count as doing something else. And of those gestural acts that do have count-as significance, that significance is not always address. Performing the scripted act of arising to sing a hymn counts as paying due honor to God but is not a case of addressing God.

The species: liturgies are for being directly engaged with God

We have still only identified the genus to which liturgies and liturgical scripts belong. Liturgical scripts prescribe verbal and gestural acts primarily not for their own sake but so that the participants can thereby perform certain counted-as actions; that differentiates liturgical scripts from scripts for moves and plays in games and from scripts for musical performances. But it does not differentiate liturgical scripts from typical programs for events, nor does it differentiate them from scripts for dramatic performances; these also prescribe actions that, when performed, have count-as significance.

Liturgy is a species of ritual. Some rituals have to do with God, some do not; some have to do instead with persons and events important in the history of a people. Liturgy, as I understand it, has to do with God. More specifically, when enacting a liturgy the participants *orient* themselves toward God. In our lives in the everyday we orient ourselves toward the natural world, toward cultural artifacts, and toward our fellow human beings. Those are the direct object of our actions. When we assemble to enact a liturgy, we turn around and orient ourselves toward God.

The heavenly bodies manifest God's wisdom and power, so when I look at the starry heavens I engage God in a certain way. But my engagement of God is indirect and implicit; the direct object of my action is the stars at which I am looking. My fellow human beings bear God's image, so when

---

21. In no liturgical enactment do the participants do all of these things; not even in any one Christian tradition do they do all of them.

I deal with them I also engage God in a certain way. But in this case, too, my engagement with God is indirect and implicit; the direct object of my actions is my fellow human beings.

When we orient ourselves toward God by enacting a liturgy we engage God directly and explicitly. When we kneel, there is no creature before whom we are kneeling; we are kneeling before God. When we stand with hands upraised, there is no creature before whom we are standing with hands upraised; we are standing with hands upraised before God. When we sing hymns of praise, there is no creature whom we are praising; we are praising God.

A common view in the Christian tradition is that by way of the reading of Scripture and the preaching of a sermon or homily, God addresses the people; another common view is that by way of the people's reception of the bread and wine of the Eucharist, Christ imparts himself to them. These views imply that liturgical enactments are not only for the people to engage God but also for God to engage the people. In the heading of this section I put it like this: liturgical enactments are for being directly engaged with God.[22]

Not everything that the participants do in a liturgical enactment is an instance either of the participants directly engaging God or of God engaging them. The participants also engage each other at certain points—when they pass the peace to each other, for example, and when the presider says to the people, "Let us pray." But such interpersonal engagements are ancillary and subordinate to being engaged with God. Being directly engaged with God is what liturgical enactments are *for.*

Up to this present section my discussion in this chapter has been theistically neutral; everything I have said could be affirmed both by those who believe that God exists and by those who do not. Not so when I say that in a liturgical enactment the people orient themselves toward God so as to be directly engaged with God. I could have remained theistically neutral even at this point by saying that the participants *see themselves* as oriented directly toward God and *see themselves* as being directly engaged with God. Something along those lines is what I would say if I were describing the liturgy of some aboriginal tribe. But it would be artificial for me to speak that way here.

22. In Chapter 3 and Chapter 10 I take note of the conviction expressed in many liturgies, and deeply embedded in Christian Scripture and tradition, that God enables our worship of God. God is active liturgically not only when God engages the people but also when the people engage God.

The purpose of Christian liturgical enactments

Consider those liturgical acts in which the people or their leaders directly engage God—not those in which God engages them but those in which they engage God. Is there some common purpose underlying this quite wide variety of actions?

From the history of religion it's clear that human beings directly engage God for a number of quite different reasons, prominent among those being to placate God and to keep God favorably disposed toward the participants. The idea is that God takes delight in what transpires in liturgical enactments and that this placates God or keeps God well disposed. Reading between the lines of some of the prophetic literature of the Hebrew Bible/Old Testament, we learn that this idea was common in ancient Israel. Here is an example. The speaker is God:

> I hate, I despise your festivals,
>   and I take no delight in your solemn assemblies.
> Even though you offer me your burnt offerings and grain offerings,
>   I will not accept them;
> and the offerings of well-being of your fatted animals
>   I will not look upon.
> Take away from me the noise of your songs;
>   I will not listen to the melody of your harps.
> But let justice roll down like waters,
>   and the doing of what is right like an everflowing stream.
>
> (Amos 5: 21–4)[23]

The traditional view concerning Christian liturgy is that the people engage God liturgically not to placate God or to keep God well disposed toward them but to worship God. Is that traditional view correct? It's not obvious that it is.

I take worship to be, at heart, adoration.[24] Worship of God is adoration of God. In the case of Christian worship, worship is adoration of God for God's unsurpassable excellence. Is the liturgical confession of sin an instance of adoration of God? It is an implicit acknowledgment of God's excellence, in particular, of God holiness and authority. But is it adoration? I would say it is not. Is petitioning God an instance of adoration? It is an implicit

---

23. I will be using the NRSV translation of Scripture.
24. I develop and defend this view in Wolterstorff (2015b), 21–40.

acknowledgment of God's excellence, in particular, of God's love and power. But is it adoration? I would say it is not. Liturgical acts of listening likewise seem to me not to be adoration: listening to the opening greeting, listening to the absolution, listening to the reading of Scripture, listening to the preaching of the sermon, listening to the closing benediction.

If the concept of worship or adoration does not cover everything that the people and their leaders do when directly engaging God in their liturgical enactments, is there some other concept that covers everything? It appears to me that the concept I employed in the preceding paragraph almost does the work: Christian liturgical enactments are for the purpose of acknow-ledging the excellence of who God is and what God has done. What has to be added is that they are also for the purpose of *learning* who God is and what God has done. Christian liturgical enactments are for the purpose of learning and acknowledging the excellence of who God is and what God has done.

That's a mouthful. So in what follows I will often use the term "worship" as a synecdoche. When I say that Christian liturgical enactments are for the purpose of worshipping God, what I mean, speaking strictly, is that they are for that range of liturgical actions that consist of learning and acknowledging the excellence of who God is and what God has done.

In his first letter to the Corinthians (chapter 14) St Paul several times over makes the point that the assemblies are for "building up" the participants in the faith; he criticizes various things taking place in the Corinthian assemblies on the ground that they do not contribute to building up the participants. So building each other up in the faith is also a purpose for assembling to enact the liturgy. But being built up in the faith results from the participants learning and acknowledging the excellence of who God is and what God has done; it does not result from their doing something other than that. Learning and acknowledging the excellence of who God is and what God has done is basic.

In conclusion

Here is my proposal concerning the location of liturgies and of liturgical enactments on the ontological map. An enactment of a liturgy consists of the participants together performing scripted verbal, gestural, and auditory actions, the prescribed purpose of their doing so being both to engage God directly in acts of learning and acknowledging the excellence of who God is and what God has done, and to be engaged by God. And the liturgy itself is that type of sequence of act-types that is enacted when the participants do what the script prescribes.

An extant liturgy offers to us a certain type of sequence of act-types for directly engaging God in worship and for being engaged by God. Rather than having to devise such a sequence for ourselves, we can join with others and follow the script. In following the script we suspend for a time the exercise of our own autonomy with respect to the matters prescribed by the script and together submit to the script. Liturgical action is communal heteronomous action.[25]

---

25. Bruce E. Harbert (2008) questions whether the term "liturgy" should be confined to communal enactments. The important substantive point he makes is that a great deal of scripted worship of God is individual rather than communal. I see no harm in following the common practice and confining the term "liturgy" to communal enactments. Much of what I have to say about communal enactments holds also for individual enactments.

2

On following a liturgical script

In Chapter 1 I first explored what it is to enact a liturgy and then used what we learned about the nature of liturgical enactments to explain the nature of liturgy. The order of explanation reflects the order of importance. A liturgy is an abstract entity, a universal; a liturgical enactment is a form of activity. Those abstract entities that are liturgies have no importance in themselves; it's enactments of liturgies that are important.[1]

We learned from our analysis that to enact a liturgy is to follow a liturgical script. I analyzed the phenomenon of following a liturgical script in no more detail than was necessary for understanding the nature of liturgy. The project of this present chapter is to dig deeper. That done, I will close with some observations about the good of joining with others in such activity.

How to determine what is prescribed by a liturgical script

A liturgical script resembles the score for a work of music in being a script for actions of a certain sort. But whereas most of the verbal and gestural acts prescribed by liturgical scripts are prescribed for the purpose of the participants thereby performing various counted-as actions, the actions prescribed by the scores for most works of instrumental music are not prescribed for that purpose; the actions the musicians perform in following the score have no count-as significance.

Normally when one speaks one chooses what to say and the words with which to say it. When one follows a liturgical script one does not choose

---

1. I am here echoing the insistence of Catherine Bell, noted in Chapter 1, that *ritualized activity* is more important than *ritual*.

one's own words; the words are prescribed. Nor does one choose what saying or singing the words is to count as. The script, along with the linguistic conventions in force, determine the count-as significance of one's words.

A novice participating in a liturgical enactment may find himself unsure at certain points as to the verbal and gestural actions to be performed. That may happen because the prescriptions at certain points are not specified but remain implicit in the liturgical practice and the novice is not familiar with the practice, or it may happen because, though the prescriptions are specified, the novice doesn't understand the specifications. Perhaps they are formulated in a language he doesn't understand. What the novice typically does in such a situation is take note of what the initiates are saying and doing and imitate them as best he can.

Initiates as well as novices may find themselves with a quite different sort of uncertainty: they may know which verbal and gestural acts are to be performed but be uncertain as to what those actions are to count as. Let's have an example. Enactments of the Orthodox liturgy of St John Chrysostom are to begin with the deacon saying, "Master, give the blessing," whereupon the priest is to say, "Blessed is the kingdom of the Father, and of the Son, and of the Holy Ghost, now and forever, world without end."[2] Obviously the priest is to say those prescribed words so as thereby to bless the kingdom of the Trinity. Perhaps some of the people don't know what it is to bless the kingdom of the Trinity. No problem. It's the priest who is to bless the kingdom of the Trinity by saying those words; presumably he knows what it is to do that.

After the priest has blessed the kingdom of the Trinity the deacon is to say, "In peace let us pray to the Lord." What then follows in the text are sentences prescribed for the deacon to use for bidding the people to offer specific petitions. The deacon's first sentence is, "For the peace from on high, and for the salvation of our souls, let us pray to the Lord." No problem there. The deacon is bidding the congregants to join in praying for the peace from on high and for the salvation of their souls; most of the participants will have a good idea of what it is to pray for those.

The text of the ninth bidding spoken by the deacon reads, "That we may be delivered from all tribulation, wrath, danger, and necessity, let us pray to the Lord."[3] Now it is far from clear what the deacon is bidding the congregants

2. The text I am quoting from is *The Orthodox Liturgy* (1982).
3. The same bidding to prayer occurs at a later point in the liturgy.

to do. They are to pray, that's clear. But for what? They know what it is to be delivered from danger. But what is it to be delivered from tribulation, wrath, and necessity? What is the deacon referring to with these words? Familiarity with their meanings in ordinary English doesn't help; clearly a distinct idiom is in play.

Since it was the deacon who spoke the words, one could ask him afterwards what he was referring to. But suppose he says that he himself doesn't really know? Or if he does claim to know, is his view on the matter decisive?

But if not to the deacon, where then does one turn? It might help to consult a different English translation. As it happens I have on my shelf another translation that reads, "For our deliverance from affliction, wrath, danger, and want, let us in prayer ask of the Lord."[4] This helps, assuming that it's not a "dumbing down" translation. We know what affliction and want are. But we're left wondering what "wrath" refers to.

Do we try to find out what the person who long ago composed this part of the text for the Orthodox liturgy had in mind? Scholars tell us that we don't know with any certainty who that was—or whether there was anyone who, strictly speaking, composed this text. It's quite possible that these prayer biddings just emerged and that, after being used and passed around for some time, someone wrote them down. But even if someone did compose them, and we knew who that was, it's irrelevant to try to find out what he had in mind. Let's see why that is.

Why authorial-discourse interpretation is irrelevant

In *Divine Discourse* I argued that what I called "authorial-discourse inter-pretation" is the dominant mode of interpretation employed by all of us when interpreting texts and verbal utterances, and that it *should be* the dominant mode of interpretation. The background to my argument was the following.

In the 1930s so-called New Criticism emerged as an influential theory and practice of interpretation, especially of poetry. The New Critics argued that, when interpreting a poem, one should ignore both the author and the

---

4. *The Orthodox Liturgy* (1974).

context in which it was written and concern oneself solely with the words, their meaning in the language, and their interrelationships within the poem. Interpretation, they said, should aim at discovering the sense of the poem, that being a function of the meaning of its words in the language and of their relation to each other within the poem. Hence the slogan, "the death of the author." They acknowledged that interpretation, so practiced, would often leave one with ambiguities. But ambiguity, William Empson famously argued, is a hallmark of good poetry.[5] He assumed, as did his fellow New Critics, that the ambiguities would usually occur within the context of an otherwise clear and stable sense.

I interpret the deconstructionists of the 1970s and 1980s as taking Empson's celebration of ambiguity and running with it. They affirmed the dictum of the New Critics that we should stick with the text and not bring author and context into the picture. But texts, they argued, have no fixed sense. Ambiguity is all. Derrida proposed what he called "a play of interpretation." I side with the deconstructionists in their claim that a text, as such, has no fixed sense.

But suppose one accepts the understanding of discourse proposed by speech-act theory, namely, that we utter or inscribe sentences primarily so as thereby to perform such illocutionary acts as make assertions, ask questions, express wishes, and so forth. We do so for other reasons as well, as we shall see shortly. But primarily we perform locutionary acts so as thereby to perform illocutionary acts. Accordingly, in most cases the natural thing to do when presented with a trace of some locutionary act—that is, with an inscribed or uttered sentence—is to ask what was the illocutionary act that the writer or speaker performed with his locutionary act. An indispensable step in arriving at an answer to this question is determining what the words the writer wrote or the speaker uttered meant and referred to in his use of them. I called such interpretation, *authorial-discourse* interpretation. I noted that even those theorists who espouse deconstructionism do in fact engage in authorial-discourse interpretation, especially when it comes to interpretation of their own writings.

Authorial-discourse interpretation is not to be identified with determining what the speaker *intended* to say. Speakers and writers do not always say what they intend to say and sometimes say what they did not intend to say. Authorial-discourse interpretation aims at discerning what the speaker

5. Empson (1957).

or writer actually did say, not at what he or she intended to say. Normally, aspects of a speaker's or writer's intentions contribute to determining what he or she said; but what one says is not identical with what one intended to say.

Back now to liturgy. Though authorial-discourse interpretation is the mode of interpretation of texts and verbal utterances that all of us employ most of the time, it's irrelevant to determining what the deacon in the Orthodox liturgy is bidding the people to pray for when he says, "That we may be delivered from all tribulation, wrath, danger, and necessity, let us pray to the Lord." That's because, in the relevant sense of "author," liturgical texts have no author. (I will qualify this claim for hymns in the section "The exception of hymn" in this chapter.)

Though it's not known how much of the text of the Orthodox liturgy of St John Chrysostom was actually composed by John, if any, we do know that Thomas Cranmer compiled and composed the text of the original liturgy of the Anglican Church. When Cranmer compiled and composed the texts for the prayers and the blessings in his liturgical composition he compiled and composed them *for* praying and *for* blessing by the participants when the liturgy was enacted. He may also himself have been praying and blessing when compiling and composing the texts. But to compile and compose texts *for* praying and *for* blessing by liturgical participants is not the same as oneself praying and blessing by compiling or composing some text. By contrast, when John Donne wrote the sonnet that begins with the words, "Batter my heart, three person'd God," he was almost certainly performing the illocutionary act of enjoining the three person'd God to batter his heart; that's what makes it appropriate to employ authorial-discourse interpretation when interpreting the sonnet. Cranmer was not doing that sort of thing when he compiled and composed texts *for* liturgical praying and *for* liturgical blessing. That's why authorial-discourse interpretation is irrelevant to what he did.

The New Critics and the deconstructionists argued that we should treat a text *as if* it had no author. Even if someone did compose and inscribe the text in order to say something (perform some illocutionary act), we are to ignore what that person said. Cranmer's liturgical text, and liturgical texts in general, represent the dream come true of the New Critics and the deconstructionists. No need to treat these texts *as if* they have no author. They have no author, not in the relevant sense of "author." To compile or compose a text for liturgical use is not to perform some illocutionary act thereby. Authorial-discourse interpretation is irrelevant because there is no authorial discourse to interpret!

Compare the greeting cards for sale in a card shop. Though someone composed the words of greeting on the cards, they did not themselves greet someone by so doing. They designed the cards *for* use by purchasers to greet friends and relatives. Purchasers do so use them when they buy them, sign them, and send them off.

When an author creates a text so as to say something thereby—to perform certain illocutionary acts—one can, if one wishes, engage in a play of interpretation. But ordinarily we use what the author said as a sort of "anchor" for interpretation. We interpret the text for the illocutionary acts that the author performed. Is there anything that similarly anchors interpretation of a liturgical text? Or in this case is there truly nothing but play—a play of interpreting the meaning of the words in whatever way we wish, provided the rules of the language allow it, and a play of performing whatever illocutionary actions we wish, provided the illocutionary conventions in force allow it? When the Orthodox deacon says, "That we may be delivered from all tribulation, wrath, danger, and necessity, let us pray to the Lord," are the people free to give those words whatever meaning and reference they wish, provided the rules of the language allow it, and are they free to pray for deliverance from whatever they understand tribulation, wrath, and necessity to be, provided the illocutionary conventions in force allow it?

They are not. A script creates a way of doing things correctly or incorrectly. If it were open to each of us to interpret the script as we wish, within the limits of linguistic rules and illocutionary conventions, it would be, at best, by one's own private interpretive lights that one acted correctly or incorrectly.

What then is relevant?

In 1549 the English Parliament exercised its authority over the English churches by requiring them to use Cranmer's composition as their liturgical text. God was to be worshipped in the English churches by the participants performing the verbal, gestural, and auditory acts that Cranmer's text specified—with due allowance for options. When Parliament, in the context of the liturgical practice of the day, prescribed this text for use by the English churches, the members of Parliament would have had in mind certain meanings and references for the words. So too they would have had in mind the acts of worship to be performed by performing the prescribed verbal, gestural, and auditory actions: God was to be praised by singing these words here; God was to be petitioned by saying those words there; and so forth. Call those prescribed acts of worship, the *authorized worship-function* of the prescribed verbal, gestural, and auditory acts. And call the meanings and references that the members of Parliament had in mind for the words they prescribed, the *authorized meanings* of those words.

An explanatory qualification is in order. Just as an author may use words without having a clear understanding of what they mean, so too the members of Parliament might have prescribed words without having a clear understanding of what they mean—or different members might have had different understandings. And just as it may not be entirely clear to an author what he is saying with his words, so too it might not have been entirely clear to Parliament just which acts of worship they were prescribing—or different members might have had somewhat different acts in mind. This qualification should be kept in mind in what follows.

What Parliament did with Cranmer's text is an example of how it always goes. For every liturgical enactment, some person or body of persons with authority over this particular enactment has determined the verbal, gestural, and auditory acts to be done and the acts of worship to be performed thereby. Up to this point in my discussion I have referred to the prescriptions for liturgical enactments without ever ascribing any of those prescriptions to anyone, other than remarking that some are embedded within the relevant liturgical practice. Readers may have wondered whether liturgical prescriptions exist out in the ether somewhere, not issued by anyone. That makes no sense. It was Parliament that prescribed the use of the 1549 *Book of Common Prayer* for the liturgical enactments of the churches over which it had authority; it was the General Convention of the (American) Episcopal Church that prescribed the use of the 1979 *Book of Common Prayer* for the liturgical enactments of the churches over which it had authority. In my copy of the Catholic Missal it says that it was "published with the approval of the Committee on Divine Worship of the United States Conference of Catholic Bishops."

Authority to prescribe the verbal, gestural, and auditory acts to be performed in a particular liturgical enactment is always divided. It comes close to being undivided in those non-denominational congregations where the pastor has sole authority to prescribe the liturgy for the day. But even he is operating within a certain liturgical social practice and is subject to its authority. In Eastern Orthodoxy, liturgical authority comes close to being undivided in the opposite direction; almost everything that is to take place in Orthodox liturgical enactments is prescribed by the particular branch of the Orthodox Church of which the congregation is a member. However, the priest of the local congregation does have the authority to skip certain parts of the liturgy designated for the day. In Catholicism and mainstream Protestantism, officials of the local congregation, unlike Orthodox priests, have the authority to select many of the psalms and hymns to be sung.

How do we discover the authorized worship-function of the verbal, gestural, and auditory actions prescribed in a particular liturgical enactment? We do so in essentially the same way that we discover authorial discourse. To identify authorial discourse we try to discover relevant features of the context in which the author did his writing, the meanings of the words in his particular use of them, what he was referring to with the words he used, etc. To identify the authorized worship-function of the verbal, gestural, and auditory acts prescribed for some particular liturgical enactment we try to discover what those with authority over this particular liturgical enactment meant by the words and what they had in mind as the reference of the words.

An important difference between authorial discourse and authorized worship-function is that whereas the former cannot change, the latter can change. If an author did in fact perform such-and-such an illocutionary act by writing certain words, it remains true for all time that he performed that act. But in the case of a liturgical text, the prescribed verbal, gestural, and auditory acts may remain the same while their authorized meaning and worship-function changes over time. The 1979 General Convention of the Episcopal Church passed the resolution requiring the use of what is now known as the 1979 *Book of Common Prayer*; thereby the Episcopal Church itself authorized the use by its member congregations of that edition of the *Book of Common Prayer*. Whereas the 1979 General Convention is now several decades in the past, the Episcopal Church authorizes, on a continuing basis, the use by its member congregations of the 1979 *Book of Common Prayer*. It's quite possible that the authorized meaning and worship-function of some of the words and gestures has changed over the intervening years.

The exception of hymns

The texts for Orthodox liturgies include the texts of the psalms and hymns to be sung. For the most part, the texts for Catholic and traditional Protestant liturgies do not; instead they include such rubrics as the following from the text for the Catholic Order of Mass: "The Communion Psalm or other appropriate chant is sung while Communion is given to the faithful. If there is no singing, the Communion Antiphon is said." The fact that the text for the Catholic liturgy contains only this rubric and not any actual hymn text makes it easy to overlook the fact that the liturgical scripts for Catholic liturgical enactments, as for Protestant enactments, are like Orthodox enactments in that they always include the singing of specified psalms and hymns. For each liturgical enactment, someone with the relevant local authority has specified the psalms and hymns to be sung.

A question that suggests itself here is whether the prescribed hymns have authors, in the relevant sense of "author." In Chapter 6 I will have something to say about the reading and singing of psalms in liturgical enactments; here let me speak only about hymns.

Isaac Watts composed for congregational singing the hymn that begins with the words, "Joy to the world! the Lord is come." Martin Luther composed for congregational singing the hymn that begins with the words, in English translation, "A mighty fortress is our God, a bulwark never failing." The texts for these hymns are like the text for the liturgy of St John Chrysostom and like the text for Cranmer's liturgy in that they were for congregational use.

One cannot help but ask, however, whether Watts and Luther did something more than compose a text for congregational singing. When Watts wrote the words, "Joy to the world! the Lord is come," was he thereby himself exclaiming, *Joy to the world, the Lord is come*? When Luther wrote the words, "A mighty fortress is our God, a bulwark never failing," was he thereby himself declaring, *Our God is a mighty fortress, a never-failing bulwark*? If so, then both of these hymn texts have authors, in the relevant sense of "author," and both are candidates for authorial-discourse interpretation.

It seems to me likely that Watts was making that exclamation and that Luther was making that declaration. If that is correct, and if Watts and Luther are typical of hymn writers, the function of hymns is complex in that it combines the function of liturgical texts with the function of lyric poems. A hymn text functions, and was intended to function, as a text for a congregation's worship of God; at the same time the inscription of the text is likely to have functioned as an instrument of authorial discourse. These two functions can pull apart. The authorized meaning of some of the words, in a particular liturgical enactment, may differ from the meaning of the words in the author's use of them, with the result that what the congregation says by singing the words differs from what the author said by inscribing them.

The words not always specified

I have described the script for a liturgical enactment as prescribing the verbal, gestural, and auditory acts to be performed and prescribing the counted-as acts of worship to be performed thereby. This description has to be qualified. There are many liturgical scripts for which this description fits only part of the script. Sometimes the counted-as action is specified but not the words; this is true especially for the prayers in many Protestant churches. For example, the worship book of the Evangelical Lutheran Church, *Evangelical Lutheran Worship*, instructs the minister who is leading the intercessory prayers to invite the assembly to pray "with these or similar words: 'With the whole people of God in Christ Jesus, let us pray for the church, those in need, and all of God's creation'."[6] It then specifies the general content of the prayer but not the words: "for the church universal, its ministry, and the mission of the gospel; for the well-being of creation; for peace and justice in the world."

In the same year (1549) that it prescribed the use of Cranmer's text in the English churches the English Parliament passed an Act of Uniformity that enjoined the abolition of most traditional rituals and ceremonies. These two acts of Parliament provoked an uproar that lasted for more than a century. A prominent party in this uproar consisted of those who agreed with the Act of Uniformity in its proscription of most traditional liturgy and ritual but went further and also objected to the imposition of Cranmer's liturgy. They insisted that the words used in public prayer, as well as those used in private prayer, should flow spontaneously from the one praying. In 1644 Parliament, now under the control of the Puritans, forbade the use of the *Book of Common Prayer* and prescribed instead the use of the *Directory for*

---

6. *Evangelical Lutheran Worship* (2007), 105.

the Publique Worship of God, a document produced by the Westminster Assembly of Divines.

After some instructions on how the congregants were to conduct themselves when entering the assembly ("in a grave and seemly manner, taking their places without adoration or bowing"), the *Directory* prescribed how the service was to begin:

> The Congregation being assembled; the Minister, after solemne calling on them to the worshiping of the great name of God, is to begin with Prayer;
>
> *In all Reverence and Humility acknowledgeing the incomprehensible Greatness and Majesty of the Lord, (in whose presence they doe then in a speciall manner appeare) and their own vileness and unworthiness to approach so neare him; with their utter inability of themselves, to so great a Work: and humbly beseeching him for Pardon, Assistance, and Acceptance in the whole Service then to bee performed; and for a Blessing on that particular portion of his Word then to bee read: and all, in the Name and Mediation of the Lord Jesus Christ.*[7]

Though no words are prescribed, the content of the prayer that the minister is to offer is prescribed in considerable detail. Words are used to specify the content; how else could the content be specified? But the minister is free to choose his own words. Ironically, however, the prescribed content is stated in such detail that, with just a slight change of grammar, the words specifying the content can be used by the minister for praying. In place of the words in the *Directory*, "humbly beseeching him [God] for pardon," the minister can say, "We humbly beseech thee for pardon."[8]

Clearly two conflicting impulses were operating here. Though Parliament was opposed to prescribing the words of the prayers, it did not want to give ministers free rein to pray as they felt moved. So it adopted this uneasy compromise.

On performing the prescribed actions without knowing what those are

One can do as the Orthodox deacon bids one to do, namely, pray for deliverance from tribulation, wrath, and necessity, without knowing what the terms "tribulation," "wrath," and "necessity" refer to. To understand how

---

7. Quoted by Branch (2006), 53.   8. Lori Branch makes this point in Branch (2006).

that can be, consider an analogy. Suppose I say to my wife, after reading a report in the newspaper about the results in 2012 of an experiment at the CERN complex in Switzerland, "Physicists have discovered the Higgs boson." I have only the vaguest idea of what the Higgs boson is; I don't know what it is. All I know is that it is a subatomic particle named after the physicist, Peter Higgs, and that physicists had for some time been trying to detect it. Knowing those things falls far short of knowing what the Higgs boson is. If my wife asks me to explain what kind of subatomic particle the Higgs boson is, there is nothing I can say. Have I nonetheless referred to the Higgs boson when I said, "They've discovered the Higgs boson"? I have indeed. I referred to the Higgs boson and said of it that physicists have discovered it.

There is a passage in an essay by Hilary Putnam, "The Meaning of 'Meaning'," that illuminates how one can refer to the Higgs boson without knowing what it is.[9] Putnam points out that, for many of our terms, there is what he calls a "division of linguistic labor" in how we use them. He uses the metal gold and the word "gold" to explain the idea.

> Gold is important for many reasons.... Consider our community as a "factory": in this "factory" some people have the "job" of *wearing gold wedding rings*, other people have the "job" of *selling gold wedding rings*, still other people have the "job" of *telling whether or not something is really gold*. It is not at all necessary or efficient that everyone who wears a gold ring... engage in buying and selling gold. Nor is it necessary or efficient that everyone who buys and sells gold be able to tell whether or not something is really gold in a society where this form of dishonesty is uncommon... and in which one can easily consult an expert in case of doubt. And it is *certainly* not necessary or efficient that everyone who has occasion to buy or wear gold be able to tell with any reliability whether or not something is really gold.[10]

This "mundane division of labor," as Putnam calls it, engenders a corresponding division of linguistic labor:

> Everyone to whom gold is important for any reason has to *acquire* the word "gold"; but he does not have to acquire the *method of recognizing* if something is or is not gold. He can rely on a special subclass of speakers. The features that are generally thought to be present in connection with a general name— necessary and sufficient conditions for membership in the extension, ways of recognizing if something is in the extension ("criteria"), etc.—are all present

---

9. Reprinted in Putnam (1975).   10. Putnam (1975), 227.

in the linguistic community *considered as a collective body*; but that collective body divides the "labor" of knowing and employing these various parts of the "meaning" of "gold".[11]

Putnam generalizes from the example to propose what he calls the "hypothesis of the universality of the division of linguistic labor":

> Every linguistic community exemplifies the sort of division of linguistic labor just described: that is, possesses at least some terms whose associated "criteria" are known only to a subset of the speakers who acquire the terms, and whose use by the other speakers depends upon a structured cooperation between them and the speakers in the relevant subsets.[12]

There are members of the scientific community who know what a Higgs boson is. When I say to my wife, "Physicists have discovered the Higgs boson," the term "the Higgs boson" stands for whatever it is that the experts refer to when they use the term. There is a division of linguistic labor between me and those experts in the use of the term "the Higgs boson."

There is likewise a division of linguistic labor among those who are members of a particular liturgical tradition. Within a liturgical tradition there are some who are "experts" in the meanings and references of the words used in the liturgical enactments of the tradition. When those of us who are not experts follow a liturgical script from the tradition, the words we say or sing have the meanings and references they have when the liturgical experts use them. Within the Orthodox tradition there are those who know what the deacon is referring to when he uses the words "tribulation," "wrath," and "necessity." Whatever those are, it is those things that the people pray to be delivered from when they respond in prayer to the deacon's bidding. Liturgical traditions and their corresponding communities are paradigmatic examples of the division of linguistic labor. That makes it possible to perform acts of worship while having only the vaguest idea of what those acts are.

It's easy for those who participate regularly in liturgical enactments to overlook how different liturgical language is from the language used in ordinary affairs: special words are used, and ordinary words are used with special meanings. In ordinary affairs we don't speak of blessing God, of being delivered from tribulation, wrath, and necessity, of someone descending into hell, of someone or something as ineffable, of seraphim and cherubim—I could

11. Putnam (1975), 227–8.   12. Putnam (1975), 228.

go on. Liturgical language is a special idiom, shaped in good measure by Christian Scripture and by Christian theology in one or another of its traditions. To identify the authorized worship-function of the words prescribed for some liturgical enactment one has to learn the idiom, namely, the authorized meanings of the words.

For any traditional liturgy, a good many of those who participate in enacting the liturgy never do fully learn the authorized idiom; they would be at a loss if asked to explain just what it is they are doing by saying or singing those words and by making those movements and gestures. What must be added, however, is that those who participate regularly in the liturgical enactments of some tradition usually find that their understanding of what they are doing gradually deepens and expands. Initially they have little if any idea of what they are doing by performing the prescribed verbal and gestural acts; later they have a vague idea; eventually, if all goes well, they understand. They grow into the liturgy.

On performing the prescribed acts without enacting the intention to do so

The phenomenon of performing some prescribed verbal act and thereby performing the prescribed act of worship even though one doesn't know what the words mean or refer to is closely related to another phenomenon, namely, performing some prescribed verbal or gestural act and thereby performing the prescribed act of worship without intending to perform that act of worship. Suppose, for example, that though one knows what it is to bless God's kingdom one is distracted on a particular Sunday and absent-mindedly says the words "Blessed be God's kingdom forever and ever" without the thought of blessing God's kingdom ever crossing one's mind.[13] Even though one did not enact the intention to bless God's kingdom, one has nonetheless done so. The script has, as it were, taken over.

13. *The Catecheses of Cyril of Jerusalem* (c.350) include this instruction: "You then respond [to the words 'Lift up your hearts' by saying], 'We turn them to the Lord.' You thus give your assent, you assert your agreement. Let no one, then, stand there and say with his lips only, 'We turn them to the Lord,' while his mind remains absorbed by the cares of life. We ought to be constantly mindful of God, but if that is not possible because of human weakness, then at this moment above all we must make the effort to have him before us." Deiss (1979), 285.

This phenomenon of the script taking over is central to the theory of ritual action proposed by Caroline Humphrey and James Laidlaw in their book, *The Archetypal Actions of Ritual: A Theory of Ritual Illustrated by the Jain Rite of Worship*. "We suggest," say the authors, "that ritual is a distinctive way in which an action, probably any action, may be performed. Thus a 'theory of ritual' is an account of the transformation of action by ritualization. There is no point in trying to frame generalizations about the social function, or whatever, of all rituals, because ritualization can happen to anything. The proper focus of theoretical attention is therefore the distinctive quality which action performed in this way, comes to have.... Ritual is a quality of action, and not a class of events or institutions."[14] The authors note that "a study of ritualization as a mode of action [is] relatively new in anthropology."[15] Readers will discern the affinity between my approach to liturgy and the approach of Humphrey and Laidlaw to ritual.

The central thesis of Humphrey and Laidlaw is that what is definitive of ritualized action is that the relation that prevails in ordinary life between one's intentions and the identity of one's actions is fundamentally altered in ritual. "'Ritualization begins with a particular modification of the normal intentionality of human action. Action which has undergone this modification is ritual action."[16] In ordinary life, they say, the identity of what one does is determined by one's intention in acting as one did. If one's intention in tossing a newspaper onto someone's doorstep was to deliver the daily newspaper to a customer, then what one did was *deliver the daily newspaper to one of one's customers*. If one's intention was instead to annoy one's neighbor, then what one did was *try to annoy one's neighbor*.[17] So "when we attempt to understand what another's action is, to succeed in this we must grasp his or her intention in acting."[18]

"*It is one of our central claims in this book*," say the authors, "*that when an action is ritualized, this is not the case*.... Under ritualization, the relation which normally exists between intention and act is transformed."[19] "The *identity* of

14. Humphrey and Laidlaw (1994), 3.
15. Humphrey and Laidlaw (1994), 88. They note, "The idea that ritual is essentially communicative and expressive is almost a social compact in anthropology" (73).
16. Humphrey and Laidlaw (1994), 71.
17. The newspaper example comes from Humphrey and Laidlaw (1994), 93.
18. Humphrey and Laidlaw (1994), 94. "If we do not see a person's conduct as the intentional doings of an agent but merely as physical movement—then we have no grounds for distinguishing actions: no more grounds than a person who hears speech in an unknown language has for distinguishing words" (93).
19. Humphrey and Laidlaw (1994), 94. Emphasis in original.

a ritualized act does not depend, as is the case with normal action, on the agent's intention in acting."[20]

If it is not the enacted intention that determines the identity of a ritualized action, what then determines its identity? The script determines its identity, say the authors. I take their thought to be the following. If a participant in some liturgical enactment performs the prescribed verbal and gestural actions, then no matter what the participant's intentions or other states of mind, she has in fact performed the acts of worship that the script prescribes to be performed by those verbal and gestural acts. If the script prescribes that at a certain point the participants are to kneel as an indication of humble devotion, then, if a participant kneels, she has indicated humble devotion no matter what her state of mind. She may have knelt to get off the painfully uncomfortable pew for a few minutes. No matter. The script determines that she has also performed the act of *kneeling as an act of humble devotion*. So too, if the script prescribes that at a certain point the participants are to say the words "Blessed be God's kingdom for ever and ever" so as thereby to bless God's kingdom, then if a participant says those words, she has blessed God's kingdom no matter what her state of mind.

Here is their theory in their own words:

> Ritualized acts in liturgical traditions are socially prescribed and present themselves to individuals actors as "given" and external to themselves.[21]
>
> The important sense in which ritual is "prescribed"...is not that there are rules restricting what people do, but that what their action *can be* is "prescribed." The kinds of acts they can be counted as being are prescribed, we shall say, by *ontological* stipulation.... The ritual practitioner finds his or her acts already separated out, constituted, and named, for they are stipulated in the rules for performing the ritual. Thus the ontology of ritualized action (the range of essential entities of which it is composed) is ready-made and precedes the conduct of those who come to perform the ritual.[22]

The essence of ritualized activity consists in the fact that if one engages in the prescribed behavior, then one has performed the prescribed acts of worship no matter what one is thinking, feeling, or intending; one's mental

---

20. Humphrey and Laidlaw (1994), 89.
21. Humphrey and Laidlaw (1994), 5.
22. Humphrey and Laidlaw (1994), 96. Cf. this passage: "The ritual act [is] something separated, constituted, and awaiting, as it were, apprehension by the actors. It is for this reason that ritual can posit a transcendence of ordinary functional action" (12).

states are irrelevant to the identity of one's acts. When one participates in some liturgical enactment, one surrenders for the duration one's "intentional sovereignty."[23]

Assessing the theory of Humphrey and Laidlaw

I agree, of course, with the claim of Humphrey and Laidlaw that following a script belongs to the essence of participating in ritual and liturgical enactments. And I agree that a worshipper can, for example, cross herself without having the concept of crossing herself and hence without forming and acting on the intention to cross herself, and that her saying certain words may count as blessing God even though she does not form and act on the intention to bless God. Contrary, however, to the central thesis of Humphrey and Laidlaw, such phenomena are not unique to ritualized and liturgical action. Conversely, the state of mind of participants in ritual or liturgical enactments is not as irrelevant to determining what they have done as the authors suggest.

As to the first of these points, whenever rules or conventions are in force we find the same phenomenon as that which Humphrey and Laidlaw hold to be definitive of ritual: the rules or conventions may determine what one has done rather than one's intentions. Uttering certain words may count as asserting something even though one did not intend to make that assertion. Raising one's hand at an auction may count as bidding on the item being auctioned even though one did not intend to bid on it. A beginner's pass in soccer may be offside even though he has no concept of an offside pass. And so forth.

---

23. Humphrey and Laidlaw (1994), 99. Here is another passage in which Humphrey and Laidlaw summarize their theory: "Action is ritualized if the acts of which it is composed are constituted not by the intentions which the actor has in performing them, but by prior stipulation. We thus have a class of acts in which the intentions which normally serve to identify acts, that is to say, intentions in action, are discounted . . . A set of constitutive rules is accepted as determining the kinds of acts which he or she will perform. In adopting the ritual stance one accepts, that is, that in a very important sense, one will not be the author of one's acts" (97–8).

Humphrey and Laidlaw recognize that the possibility of doing things correctly or incorrectly is essential to ritual and liturgical activity. They say, "ritualization does require that people feel that somewhere there are rules telling you what to do and that the question of what is the correct thing to do can be settled by consulting them (however this might be done) . . . Ritual is prescribed action; you have to get it right" (128). However, the fact that an essential feature of ritualized conduct is that it is either correct or incorrect does not enter into their theory of ritual.

Conversely, the identity of liturgical actions is not as purely script-determined as Humphrey and Laidlaw claim. Suppose someone from abroad who knows how to pronounce English words but knows nothing of Christian worship wanders into a church some Sunday and says "Blessed be God's kingdom, now and for ever" when the text specifies that those words are to be said. Has he blessed God? I think not. Suppose the visitor gets down on his knees when the others do. Is his kneeling a sign of humble devotion? I think not. Though one can perform an act of worship without forming and acting on the intention of performing that act, one cannot do so if one has no idea of what is going on. Worship requires cognitions and intentions of some sort. Which sort, I am not able to say. Humphrey and Laidlaw declare, "the intentions and thoughts of the [ritual] actor make no difference to the *identity* of the act performed."[24] That unqualified claim seems to me not true.

In Chapter 5 I will analyze what those who lack faith are doing when they engage in liturgical enactments. I will argue that if, at a certain point, such a person performs the prescribed verbal or gestural action with the intention that he *not* thereby perform the prescribed count-as action, then he has not in fact performed that action. His intention determines that he has *not* performed that act of worship rather than the script determining that he *has* performed that act of worship. By performing some verbal or gestural act one can perform some act of worship without intending to do so; but if one performs that verbal or gestural act with the intention of *not* thereby performing that act of worship, one has not done so. Negative intentions play a decisive role in determining what one has done.

Is following a script a case of submitting to authority?

A question that comes naturally to mind here is whether following a liturgical script is a case of submitting to authority. Humphrey and Laidlaw quote the anthropologist, Roy Rappaport, as saying, "Since to perform a liturgical order, which is by definition a relatively *invariant* sequence of acts and utterances *encoded by someone other* than the performer himself, is to

---

24. Humphrey and Laidlaw (1994), 5. Emphasis in the original.

conform to it, authority or directive is *intrinsic* to liturgical order."[25] Is Rappaport right about this? Is following a liturgical script a case of submitting to authority?

That depends on which form of authority one has in mind. To follow a liturgical script is to submit to certain forms of authority and not to others. A form of authority that pervades society is the authority to govern what certain persons do by issuing authoritative directives to them; call it, *governance-authority*. The authority of the US government over its citizens is an example. In an earlier writing of mine I described as follows what it is for the employees of a firm to regard the owner as having authority over them to govern what they do while at work.

> For the employees to treat as authoritative some directive of the owner to perform some action is for them to regard the owner's having directed them to perform that action as generating in them an obligation to perform that action. The employees may believe they know better than the owner what would be good or right to do; they may think he's making a mistake. Nonetheless they defer to his enunciated will, allow his enunciated will to direct their will, doing so not just because they think that would be a good thing to do but because they believe that his enunciation of his will has generated in them [a *prima facie*] obligation to act as directed... To treat some directive of the owner as authoritative is to regard it as generating in one a *prima facie* obligation to comply.[26]

I went on to distinguish between treating the owner's directives as authoritative and treating them as wise:

> Deferring to the will of the owner in this way is to be distinguished from deferring to his judgment. The employees may do what the owner directs them to do because they want to do what's best to do and they believe that the owner has a better grip on that than they do. That is not to treat the owner's directives as authoritative but as wise.[27]

If this analysis is correct, of what it is to treat someone's directives as authoritative, then there is an obvious similarity between doing that and following a liturgical script: in both cases one suspends acting on one's own judgment as to what would be good to do and instead defers—defers to someone's directives in the former case, defers to the script in the latter case. In both cases, one acts heteronomously, to use Kant's term.

There is, nonetheless, a decisive difference. Those who resolve to follow a liturgical script are not thereby *obligated* to do what the script prescribes. By reference to the script there are correct and incorrect ways of acting. But if one acts incorrectly at a certain point, one is not, on that account, violating one's obligations. If one declines to sing one of the hymns because one is not in the mood for singing, that would be a case of acting incorrectly vis-à-vis the script but not of failing in one's duties. Of course, if one has promised to follow the script faithfully, then failure to sing the hymn constitutes violating an obligation. But then it's the promise that generates the obligation, not the resolution to follow the script.

In most liturgical enactments there is a point at which the priest, the minister, or some other leader follows the script and says, "Let us pray." Isn't that a case of exercising governance-authority? Aren't the people then obligated to pray? I think not. Without moral fault one can fail to follow the injunction to pray. In short, though following a liturgical script and submitting to governance-authority are alike in that both are cases of heteronomous action, the heteronomy is distinctly different.

There are other forms of authority, however, such that in following a liturgical script one is submitting to authority. The most obvious of these is that whoever it was that authorized this particular script for this particular liturgical enactment, by following the script one accepts or submits to their authority to do so. In Orthodoxy, to follow the script for some liturgical enactment is to submit to the authority of some branch of the Orthodox Church to determine the script for this particular enactment. In free-church Protestantism, to follow the script for some liturgical enactment is to submit to the authority of the pastor to determine the script for the enactment. One may be opposed to the pastor's having such authority. Nonetheless, by following the script one is perforce submitting to his authority to determine the script.

There is another form of authority as well to which one is submitting when following a liturgical script. In Chapter 1 I argued that an enactment by a religious community of its liturgy is never a one-off thing but always an exercise of the social practice of enacting its liturgies. Now recall a passage that I quoted from Alasdair MacIntyre's analysis of social practices: "To enter into a practice is to enter into a relationship not only with its contemporary practitioners, but also with those who have preceded us in the past, especially those whose achievements extended the reach of the practice to its present point. It is thus the achievement, and *a fortiori* the authority, of a tradition which I then confront and from which I have to learn."[28]

By being inducted into the social practice of musical performance a young would-be musician is confronted with what MacIntyre calls "the authority of a tradition." When she then exercises her induction into the practice by following a score in accord with how she was taught, she perforce submits to the authority of the tradition. So too for liturgy. To be inducted into the tradition of Catholic liturgical practice is to be confronted with the authority of that tradition. When someone who has been inducted into that tradition then participates with others in an enactment of the Catholic liturgy, she is perforce accepting the authority embedded in Catholic liturgical practice. She is submitting to its authority.

So, yes, to follow a liturgical script is to submit to authority: to the authority of whoever it was that authorized this script and to the authority of the relevant liturgical practice. To this it is important to add, however, that for many of those who follow the script it doesn't feel like submitting to authority. In a study of the second-century rabbi known as "Rabbi Nathan" the author writes, "The ideal sage is a man who is fully constituted through the Torah such that his most basic impulses are structured in accord with rabbinic laws and ideals. He attains this state by allowing himself to be trained, molded, planted, conquered, or governed by the tradition."[29] "The inner comes to reflect the outer, not the other way around."[30]

The good of liturgical enactments

Let me conclude with some reflections on the good of following liturgical scripts. What is the good of worshipping God by joining with others in performing the prescribed verbal, gestural, and auditory actions and thereby performing the prescribed acts of worship?

If one is to worship God together with others, and not just at the same time and in the same place, there has to be a script that most of the participants

---

28. MacIntyre (1981), 181.
29. Quoted by Jonathan Schofer in Seligman et al. (2008), 36.
30. Seligman et al. (2008), 36.

follow more or less closely; otherwise chaos erupts. This point was amusingly made in a mock catechism published in Glasgow in 1720:

Q: *Why do not the Presbyterians say the Creed and the Doxology?*

A: Because they are not, Word by Word, in Scripture.

Q: *Why do they not say the Lord's Prayer?*

A: Because it is, Word by Word, in Scripture.

Q: *Wherefore do not the Presbyterians sing Glory to God on high?*

A: Because that was a Song of Angels, made upon *Yool-Day*, and they are not for *Christmas Carols*.

Q: *Have the Presbyterians any Set Forms at all?*

A: Yes, they have a Form of Godliness, but deny the power thereof.

Q: *What is the sad Effect of the Want of a Form in a Church?*

A: It is just as it was said of the Earth, *Gen. i. The Earth was without form, and void, and Darkness was upon the Face of the Deep.*[31]

If people are to worship together there has to be a script. But is this pragmatic consideration the end of the matter? I think not. Let me divide the question. There are not only scripts for communal worship but also scripts for private devotions. Let us reflect first on the good of submitting to a script for worshipping God, be it a script for private devotions or a script for communal worship, and then on the good of following a script for worshipping God together with others.

What is lost if one puts away all scripts and, worshipping alone, says and sings whatever comes to mind and makes whatever movements and gestures seem appropriate? Why worship God by following a script? Why not renounce heteronomy and worship with full and complete autonomy?

It will help to look, once again, at the analogous case of music. If musicians are to play together they have to follow a script of some sort. But why play together with others? Why not be content to play the piano by oneself? And when playing by oneself, why not improvise rather than follow a score? What is the good of submitting to a musical script? Why not be autonomous?

Well, suppose one does follow a score and that the work for which it is the score has been well-crafted by someone with considerable musical imagination. Then, for most of us, a good reason to follow the score rather than improvise is that the music one makes by following the score is much

---

31. From *A Short Catechism, for the Instruction of Young and Old,* by R.C. *Philo-Presbyt.* Quoted in Branch (2006), 35.

better than the music one would make if one improvised. Most of us have little gift for improvising. The situation is different, of course, if it's a bad piece of music. Then it would be better not to follow the score; following the score might even prove damaging.[32]

There are additional goods to be obtained from following a well-crafted score by someone with considerable musical imagination, and these additional goods are experienced not only by those who have no gift for musical improvisation but also by those who are themselves gifted at improvising. Assuming that one has not oneself composed the score, following the score puts one in touch with the trace of a musical imagination distinct from one's own. In following the score for a Bach partita one apprehends a trace of Bach's musical imagination; in following the score for a Brahms intermezzo one apprehends a trace of Brahms's musical imagination. One's musical universe is expanded beyond what one has oneself imagined, beyond what one could imagine. One breaks out of the confines of one's own musical imagination and enters the musical universe of humankind. Often we do not fully understand, on first acquaintance, those works that we did not ourselves imagine. They hold mysteries that are revealed only by returning to them again and again, dwelling with them. Such revelation is also a good.

The good of following a liturgical script, be it a script for private devotions or a script for liturgical enactments, is much like the good of following a musical script. For most of us, the praise we offer by singing hymns from the treasure-house of the church is far better than the praise we offer when we extemporize. Even the average among those hymns have a richness, an eloquence, a poetry, a profundity, beyond the capability of most of us. So too, the confessions and petitions that we offer when following a well-crafted script are far better than those we offer when we extemporize. Our own words are clumsy and prosaic by comparison, cliché-ridden. In following a well-crafted script our confessions and petitions are enhanced and elevated, as befits worship of God.

What the script also does is put us in touch with traces of liturgical imagination distinct from our own. We are presented with ways of praising God that never occurred to us, ways of petitioning God that never crossed our mind. We are released from the confines of our own liturgical imagination

32. This is a point that David Smith called to my attention.

and put in touch with traces of the liturgical imagination of the church at large. Our liturgical universe is expanded.

Sometimes the things we find ourselves saying when following a script are things we delight in saying; sometimes the things we find ourselves saying are things we would prefer not to say. Over and over in the Lenten liturgies of the Orthodox Church the participants express contrition for their sinfulness with an intensity and insistence that many of us find excessive. In the matins for two Sundays before the beginning of Lent the people (choir) sing, "O Lord, I have sinned as no other man before me, I have transgressed more than any man: before the day of judgment comes, be merciful to me in Thy love for mankind."[33]

The enhancement and expansion of worship that ensues from following a well-crafted liturgical script that we did not ourselves compose forms and shapes us. A liturgical script is a template for the worship of God. Over time, conforming one's worship to such a template shapes how one thinks of God, shapes how one thinks of oneself in relation to God, shapes how one thinks of the world, shapes how one praises God, shapes how one petitions God. One is reminded of facets of the Christian story that one had forgotten.

Often we do not fully grasp the meanings and references of the words we are voicing, the significance of the images and metaphors, the meaning of the gestures we make, with the result that we do not fully understand the acts of worship we are performing. To understand, we have to live with the words we speak, with the psalms and hymns we sing, with the gestures we make. By living with them we eventually grow into them. That too is a good. Nathan Mitchell makes the point vividly: "The church's liturgy has long relied on a seat-of-the-pants principle: 'Bring your body, your mind will follow.' That is, if believers get themselves to church regularly, repeatedly, the light will slowly dawn. Understanding and change result from repeated action; people act their way into new ways of thinking; they don't think their way into new ways of acting.... Liturgical acts first address the body, the sensorium, not the neocortex. *Caro cardo salutis*, wrote Tertullian; 'the flesh is the hinge of salvation'."[34]

---

33. *Lenten Triodion* (1984), 154. Very nearly the same words are repeated later in the same liturgy— "I have transgressed as no other man on earth"—and in a number of the other liturgies in the *Triodion*.
34. Mitchell (2006), 27.

But why do it together with others? Why not find some well-crafted scripts for private devotions and follow them alone at home? What is the good brought about by following a liturgical script together with others?

The question has a certain artificiality about it. Adherents of almost all religions assemble together on fixed occasions to enact their liturgies and rituals. Evidently there is some deep human impulse at work in this. It seems strained and artificial to ask what is the good achieved. Those who assemble do not have some good in mind that they aim to bring about; they assemble because they feel impelled to do so.

When Christians assemble on Sundays to enact their liturgies they do so in celebration of Christ's resurrection. And when, in the course of enacting their Sunday liturgies, they celebrate the Eucharist, they do so as a memorial of Jesus and his last supper. I like what Schmemann says about assembling to celebrate.

> The very concept of celebration implies both an event and the social or corporate reaction to it. A celebration is possible only when people come together and, transcending their natural separation and isolation from one another react together as one body, as indeed one person to an event (e.g., the coming spring, a wedding, a funeral, a victory, etc.) And the natural miracle of all celebration is precisely that it transcends, be it only for a time, the level of ideas and that of individualism. One truly loses oneself in the celebration and one finds the others in a unique way.[35]

---

35. Schmemann (1969), 81.

3

With one accord

The communal dimension of liturgical action

In Chapter 2 we explored the fact that participating in a liturgical enactment requires relating to the script for that enactment in a certain way. The word I used for that relationship was "following"; the participants *follow* the script. We took scarce note of the fact that those who participate in a liturgical enactment do so *together*: *together* they sing a hymn of praise, *together* they confess their sins. In order for that to happen, each participant's intentions must interlock and mesh with those of the others; and that requires that each participant respond and adjust to what the others are doing. Participating in a liturgical enactment requires not only that one relate to the script in a certain way but also that one relate to one's fellow participants in certain ways. Liturgical participation requires dual tasking, as does performing a musical or dramatic work together with others.

Our project in this chapter is to explore the communal dimension of liturgical enactments. We will begin by analyzing the phenomenon of liturgical participants *together* enacting their liturgy. That will lead naturally into consideration of a couple of additional modes of togetherness prescribed by traditional liturgical scripts.

Philosophers on acting together

There has been a good deal of discussion by philosophers of the phenomenon of *acting together*; it proves not easy to understand. Some call it "collective action," some call it "shared agency"; I will call it both "joint action" and "collective action."

Let's have an example of joint action. In his essay, "Collective Intentions and Actions," John R. Searle invites us first to imagine members of a group acting individually, and then to imagine members of a group acting collectively while behaving in exactly the same way as the members of the first group.

> Imagine that a group of people are sitting on the grass in various places in a park. Imagine that it suddenly starts to rain and they all get up and run to a common, centrally located, shelter. Each person has the intention expressed by the sentence "I am running to the shelter." But for each person, we may suppose that his or her intention is entirely independent of the intentions and behavior of others. In this case, there is no collective behavior; there is just a sequence of individual acts that happen to converge on a common goal. Now imagine a case where a group of people in a park converge on a common point as a piece of collective behavior. Imagine that they are part of an outdoor ballet where the choreography calls for the entire *corps de ballet* to converge on a common point. We can even imagine that the external bodily movements are indistinguishable in the two cases; the people running for shelter make the same types of bodily movements as the ballet dancers. Externally observed the two cases are indistinguishable, but they are clearly different internally.[1]

I know of no philosopher who denies that there is the phenomenon Searle calls "collective behavior"; the challenge is to understand what it is that makes action or behavior collective rather than individual.

A common view, which I share, is that the difference lies in the distinct character of the intentions of the agents.[2] Among those who share that view there is, as one would expect, considerable disagreement as to the precise character of those intentions. I endorse the analysis articulated by Michael E. Bratman in his essay "Shared Agency."[3] Bratman highlights the basic structure of his proposal by contrasting it with Searle's analysis. So before I present Bratman's analysis, let us briefly consider Searle's.

For any intention, we can distinguish between the *act* of intending and *what it is* that is intended, that is, the *content* of the intention. In the case of ordinary individual intentions, the structure of the intention is, *I intend that I do X*. Everyone who writes on these matters agrees that in the case of

---

1. Searle (1990), 403–4.
2. Searle (1990), 404, notes that another common view is that the difference lies not in the character of the intentions but in the nature of the beliefs that accompany the intentions. He offers what seem to me compelling objections to this view.
3. Bratman (2009).

intentions constitutive of joint action, "*we*" replaces "*I*" in the content of the intention; the intention is *that we do X together*. Searle's proposal is that "*we*" also replaces "*I*" in the act of intending: *We intend that we do X together*.[4] Searle calls such an intention, a "we-intention." As Bratman puts it in stating Searle's view, "we-intentions are not just ordinary intentions with a special *content*, a content that involves the activity of a 'we'. We-intentions are, rather, a special intending *attitude*, to be distinguished from the ordinary attitude of intending involved in individual agency."[5]

A parenthetical comment is in order here. For the members of some group to share the intention *that we do X together* they must experience or regard themselves as "*we*." In *Self and Other* Dan Zahavi offers a perceptive analysis of what is required for, in his words, "a *we* to emerge."[6] It would be interesting to apply his general remarks on the topic to the specific case of the formation of a liturgical "*we*." We will have to forgo doing that in this volume.

Searle does not explain what a we-intention is. He notes that some philosophers, to explain collective action, appeal to group minds; he rejects that appeal as "at best mysterious and at worst incoherent."[7] Intentions, including we-intentions, exist only in the minds of individual agents. "We simply have to recognize [as a primitive phenomenon which cannot be analyzed] that there are intentions whose form is: We intend that we per-form act A; and such an intention can exist in the mind of each individual agent who is acting as part of the collective."[8]

But if a we-intention is not the intention of a group mind, what then is it? Or to put the question somewhat differently: when Searle says that the structure of the intentions constitutive of joint action is *we intend that we do X together*, what is the force of the "we intend"? If its force is not, "Our group mind intends," what then is its force? Might its force be, "We each intend"? Surely not. If we each intend, then I individually intend, you individually intend, and so forth for all the members of our group. There is no distinct we-intention, only a set of individual intentions whose content, in each case, is *that we do X together*.

So what then is the force of "we intend" in Searle's formula? I have no idea. I find his proposal inscrutable.

4. Searle (1990), 407.   5. Bratman (2009), 43.
6. Zahavi (2014) 241–50. Zahavi summarizes his analysis in Zahavi (2015), 154–9.
7. Searle (1990), 404.   8. Searle (1990), 407.

Whereas on Searle's view the intentions constitutive of collective actions are non-ordinary we-intentions, the view I share with Bratman is that they are ordinary individual intentions with a distinct content. In "shared agency," as Bratman calls it, each participant has an intention of the form, *I intend that we do X together*—that is, *I intend that you and I do X together* (where "you" refers to all the members of the group). The joint activity, the doing-it-together, is an element in each person's intention; "the content of my intention refers to the role of your intention, and vice versa."[9]

Bratman speaks of intentions related in this way as *interlocking*, in the sense that each party "intends that the shared activity go in part by way of the relevant intentions of each of the other participants."[10] Call intentions whose content is of the form, *that you and I do X together, joint-action intentions*. And when two or more people each have the intention that they perform a certain act together, let us say that they *share* the joint-action intention.

The existence of intentions whose contents interlock presupposes, quite obviously, that each party believes that the other party has the relevant intention: I believe that you intend to do X together with me and you believe that I intend to do X together with you. If I did not believe that you intended to do X together with me, I would not intend that you and I do X together.

An issue that Bratman raises at this point is whether, if I intend that you and I do X together, I not only believe that you have the corresponding intention but also *intend* that you have that intention. "When I intend that we go to NYC, do I thereby intend both that I go (by way of my intentions) and that you go (by way of your intentions)"?[11] He observes that "sometimes we intend something that involves a certain pre-condition but do not intend that pre-condition. I might intend to respond to your threat or to your offer, but not intend your threat or your offer. Your threat or offer is only a pre-condition of what I intend, not itself something I intend."[12] In shared agency, does one intend that the other parties have the relevant intention?

It's likely some readers will wonder whether it's possible to intend that someone else have a certain intention. Is this the sort of thing one can intend? A bit of reflection shows that one can. In various ways one can aim to bring it about that someone intend to do a certain thing: one can offer

9. Bratman (2009), 48.   10. Bratman (2009), 47–8.
11. Bratman (2009), 49.   12. Bratman (2009), 49.

them reasons, tempt them, threaten them, and so forth. One doesn't have to stand by and hope the other person will form the relevant intention on his or her own.

Bratman's answer to the question raised is that, in shared agency, I do intend that you have the relevant intention. "My intention that we go to NYC does not see your contribution to our joint activity as merely an expected pre-condition of our going." It is, rather, "a part of what I intend."[13] I am dubious. If I believe you do not have the relevant intention, then I will form and enact the intention that you have it. But if I believe you already have the relevant intention, then I will not form and enact the intention that you have it; my belief that you already have that intention will function simply as a pre-condition of my intention. As Bratman himself notes, one intends to do X only if one believes that X would not obtain if one did not so intend.[14]

Though it is a necessary condition of shared agency that the intentions of the participants interlock, interlocking is not sufficient for shared agency. The example Bratman gives to make the point is this: suppose you and I each intend to go to New York City together with the other, but I intend to go together with you by car whereas you intend to go together with me by train. What the example shows is that, for there to be shared agency, not only must our intentions interlock but our *sub*-intentions must *mesh*, "in the sense that they are co-realizable."[15] Typically such meshing is the result of negotiations, revisions, assistance, and the like; Bratman calls it "mutual responsiveness."[16] He notes that mutual responsiveness may be required not only in planning shared activity but also in the course of performing the shared activity. What mutual responsiveness presupposes, of course, is that each party has knowledge of the intentions and sub-intentions of the other.

In concluding this section, let me raise a question that neither Searle nor Bratman raises in the essays I have been discussing. When you and I go together to New York, I go together with you and you go together with me. But is that the end of the matter: two individuals going together to New York? Might it also be the case that *we together* go to New York—that is, the pair of us, that small group whose members are you and I? Does the ontological furniture of the universe include groups in addition to individuals,

---

13. Bratman (2009), 49.   14. Bratman (2009), 52.
15. Bratman (2009), 48. What I call "sub-intentions," Bratman calls "sub-plans."
16. Bratman (2009), 53.

and do those groups do things by way of their members doing things? Can a group go to New York? If so, one way for the group to go would be for each member of the group to go together with the others in the way explained above.

It's my view—for which I have no argument that an ontological reductionist would find persuasive—that the ontological furniture of the universe does include groups and that groups do things; in particular, groups do things by way of their members acting together in the way explained above. Let me use the term "corporate" activity for the actions of groups.[17]

Acting together in the liturgy

Let us now apply what we have learned about acting together to liturgical activity. Bratman's terms, "interlocking," "meshing," and "mutual responsiveness," will prove helpful in our analysis.

Participants in liturgical enactments often perform only some of the prescribed actions—some but not all of the prescribed verbal, gestural, and auditory actions, some but not all of the prescribed counted-as actions. They are inattentive at certain points, they deliberately refrain from performing certain actions, or whatever. Their actions do not fully conform to the script. As we now analyze the phenomenon of together enacting a liturgy let us, for the sake of convenience, set off to the side participation that does not fully conform to the script. Formulating the analysis in such a way that it would be true for all forms of participation would be too convoluted.

Begin with this question: though much liturgical activity is obviously joint activity, aren't some of the actions prescribed by liturgical scripts purely individual? When a priest follows the script for the Episcopal liturgy and begins the service by saying, "Blessed be God: Father, Son, and Holy Spirit," isn't that an individual act on his part? When later he says, "Let us pray," isn't that an individual act on his part? Isn't the offering of gifts by the congregants, nowadays usually in the form of money, coordinated individual actions rather than joint action?

17. Neither Searle nor Bratman uses the term "corporate" in the essays referred to. Searle speaks of *collective* activity, Bratman, of *shared agency*, by which they clearly mean not what I call "corporate activity" but individuals acting together.

Perhaps some liturgical actions are purely individual, but fewer, I think, than one might suppose. An example of joint action that Searle gives is useful for seeing why. Suppose Jones and Smith are together preparing a hollandaise sauce: Smith slowly pours in the ingredients while Jones stirs. We could say that in the performance of this joint action there are two roles, that of pourer and that of stirrer; Smith plays the former of these roles, Jones the latter.

Searle argues that Smith does not intend two distinct things, *that he pour the ingredients* and *that he and Jones together make hollandaise sauce*, the former being an individual act and the latter, a joint act. Smith intends just one thing: *that he make hollandaise sauce together with Jones by pouring the ingredients.*[18] Similarly for Jones; he intends *that he make hollandaise sauce together with Smith by stirring the ingredients.* These two intentions are both similar and different; each has a joint dimension and an individual dimension. I think this analysis is correct.

Every liturgy has a role-structure. Liturgies are like dramatic works in this regard; in no liturgy does everybody do everything. There's the role of priest or minister, the role of deacon, the role of reader, the role of preacher, the role of Eucharistic celebrant—and, of course, the role of the people. When a liturgy is enacted, different persons play different roles. Though it's possible for a priest or minister to play all the roles, that would be a very aberrant enactment. In all ecclesiastical traditions it would be frowned on; in some, it is expressly forbidden.

Back now to the Episcopal liturgy. The two most prominent roles in the Episcopal liturgy are that of the person called "the celebrant" and that of those called "the people." When the person playing the role of celebrant follows the script and opens the service with the words, "Blessed be God: Father, Son, and Holy Spirit," he or she is not simply intending the individual act, *that he bless God by saying, "Blessed be God: Father, Son, and Holy Spirit."* Nor is he or she intending that individual act along with the additional joint act, *that together we enact the liturgy.* He or she is intending the complex act: *that he enact the liturgy together with the other participants by saying "Blessed be God: Father, Son, and Holy Spirit" and thereby blessing God.* So also, I suggest, for most if not all of the other prescribed actions.[19]

18. Searle (1990), 410–11.
19. Searle's analysis suggests an answer to a question raised by liturgical practice in the late middle ages in the West. Here is how the liturgical scholars, R. C. D. Jasper and G. J. Cuming, describe the practice: "the active participation of the laity virtually disappeared, the eucharist becoming

Joint action requires that the participants agree with each other over what to do.[20] The agreement may emerge effortlessly. One party may learn what the other party intends to do and then say, "I'll join you." Or one party may say, "Let's take the next train to New York," whereupon the other immediately agrees. Alternatively, the agreement may be achieved laboriously by protracted back-and-forth negotiations, by promises, by threats, and the like.

When the participants in some liturgical enactment act together they don't do any such thing as *come to agreement with each other* over their actions. Joint action automatically results from each participant intending to fill his or her role in together following the script. Shared joint-action intentions that interlock emerge automatically. No need for "coming to agreement" with each other.

But as we saw when discussing joint action in general, it's not sufficient for acting together that the shared joint-action intentions of the parties interlock. Their sub-intentions must mesh. It's at this point that jointly intending to follow the script is no longer sufficient for securing joint action and that mutual responsiveness enters the picture.

Always, when a liturgy is enacted, there will be one or more participants filling the role of presider, sometimes named as such. The presider is, as it were, the conductor or director of the enactment; he or she prescribes to the other participants when and how they are to perform such-and-such actions. Let us call prescriptions issued on the occasion by the presider (or presiders), "audibles."[21] Some of the audibles issued by the presider are prescribed for him or her; for example, traditional scripts specify that at

a spectacle, overlaid with ceremonies and symbolism unknown to the early Church: communion itself became a rare occurrence, being supplanted by the elevation and adoration of the consecrated elements" (Jasper and Cuming [1987], 177). Richard D. McCall calls this late medieval practice "a piety of seeing" (McCall [2007], 24 and *passim*). The question raised by this way of enacting the liturgy is whether, in any significant sense, a layperson was acting together with other laypersons and with the clergy in enacting the liturgy. He did not pray together with others, did not sing together with others, did not say the creed together with others. His participation was very different from the participation of laypersons in present-day enactments of the Catholic liturgy. Nonetheless, medieval laypersons did have a role to play in enacting the liturgy together with others. Together they were to observe the actions of the clergy, insofar as those actions could be seen, together they were to listen to the singing and speaking of the clergy, insofar as those could be heard, together they were to receive the host at least once a year, and so forth.

20. When henceforth I say "joint action," I mean that as short for "joint action and action with a joint dimension."

21. A particular prescription may both be specified by the text for the liturgy and be issued on the occasion by the leader. The text may specify that hymn #296 is to be sung at a certain point, and at that point in the enactment the leader may say, "Let us now sing hymn #296."

a certain point the presider shall issue the audible, "Let us pray." Many are not prescribed; liturgical scripts do not prescribe exactly when some particular liturgical enactment is to begin nor how quickly one liturgical act is to follow another. Presiders are needed if the people are to enact the liturgy together.

But even the faithful following of the audible of presiders falls short of achieving the mesh required for together enacting the liturgy. Sooner or later the participants have to go beyond prescriptions and adjust what they are doing to what the others are doing; sooner or later they have to engage in mutual responsiveness. Together following the script is not sufficient for together enacting the liturgy. If one person, for example, says the creed very slowly and another says it very quickly, they are not saying the creed *together*.

It would be possible for the presider to say the creed loudly and for the people to follow his or her lead. The presider's saying the creed at that pace would then function as a directive; no mutual responsiveness would be required. Though possible, this is certainly not usual. Normally the acting together that occurs in liturgical enactments is achieved by a blend of following the script and mutual responsiveness. When it comes to the people singing together in harmony, prescription necessarily falls short; mutual responsiveness is unavoidable.

In Stacy Horn's book, *Imperfect Harmony: Finding Happiness Singing with Others*, there is a fascinating discussion of the mutual adjustment required for choral singing. Here is a passage in which she describes her experience of singing in a choir; everything in her description has its analogue in liturgical singing.

> You make a contribution of sound waves and airwaves, and something more complex, something you couldn't possibly produce on your own, comes back to you. You constantly adjust your contribution.... It requires more concentration than if you were producing sound or singing on your own, say, in the shower, and thus you really do get lost—in the sense that you can't worry about anything else in your life at that moment.... I've loved being able to listen to individual voices singing right next to me on parts other than my own. It's both energizing and stabilizing to be surrounded by all four parts.... After all, there aren't too many chances in ordinary life to be in perfect cooperation with other people. Singing fulfills that need.[22]

22. Horn (2013), 120–1.

Good congregational singing requires the same sort of mutual responsiveness that Horn experienced in singing in a choir. The theologian David Ford makes the point well in a chapter that he calls "Communicating God's Abundance: A Singing Self": "The specific contribution of music to [the] building up of community in worship includes its encouragement of alertness to others, immediate responsiveness to changes in tone, tune and rhythm, and sharing in the confidence that can come from joint singing. Singing together embodies joint responsibility in which each singer waits on the others, is attentive with the intention of serving the common harmony."[23]

Ignatius of Antioch describes beautifully the result of such mutual responsiveness in singing:

> Therefore in your agreement and harmonious love, Jesus Christ is sung. Become a choir, one by one, so that being harmonious in love, taking up the song of God in unison, you may sing to the Father with one voice through Jesus Christ, so that he may both hear you and perceive, because of what you do, that you are the members of the Son.[24]

The togetherness of speaking for each other

Let us move on to a mode of liturgical togetherness quite different from the togetherness that consists of together enacting the liturgy. The togetherness I have in mind is the togetherness that consists of participants speaking for their fellow participants as well as for themselves.

In the contemporary Catholic liturgy there are several options for the act of confession. In one of them the priest summons the people to confession with the words, "Brothers and sisters, let us acknowledge our sins, and so prepare ourselves to celebrate the sacred mysteries." The people then confess with these words:

> I confess to almighty God
> and to you my brothers and sisters,
> that I have greatly sinned,
> in my thoughts and in my words,
> in what I have done and in what I have failed to do.

23. Ford (1999), 122.   24. Quoted in McGowan (2014), 117.

What then follows is a brief dialogue between priest and people:

PRIEST: Have mercy on us, O Lord.
PEOPLE: For we have sinned against you.
PRIEST: Show us, O Lord, your mercy.
PEOPLE: And show us your salvation.[25]

Notice the shift from the first-person singular pronouns "I" and "my" in the confession to the first-person plural pronouns "we" and "us" in the dialogue. The participants each confess their own sins; they say, "*I* confess," "*I* have greatly sinned," "*my* thoughts," and so forth. But in the dialogue following the confession they do not say, "*I* have sinned." They say, "*we* have sinned." And they do not say, "Show *me* your mercy and your salvation." They say, "Show *us* your mercy and your salvation."

How is this shift from singular to plural to be understood? How else but that, after each participant has confessed her own sins, each then speaks for the others as well? Each declares that her fellow congregants have sinned along with her: *we each* have sinned. Each declares that her fellow congregants plead for salvation along with her: *we each* plead that you [Lord] show *us* your salvation.

Note the difference between speaking for one's fellow congregants in this way and the priest speaking on behalf of the congregants by saying, "We all have sinned." This latter is the sort of thing that happens in a public meeting when someone rises and, pointing an accusing finger at a city official, says, "I speak on behalf of everyone here when I say this injustice must stop at once." In the passage quoted from the Catholic liturgy the priest does not speak on behalf of the congregants; rather, each congregant speaks both for herself and for her fellow congregants by declaring that *we* have sinned. Rather than one person speaking on behalf of everybody, everybody speaks for everybody.

Whereas this use of "we" and "us" is to be found here and there in many liturgical scripts, in the Orthodox liturgy it is pervasive. By my count it occurs at least twenty-five times in the English translation that I have of the Orthodox liturgy of St John Chrysostom:[26] "we ascribe glory," "we beseech thee," "we bless thee," "we hymn thee," "we give thee thanks," "we have seen the resurrection," "we have seen the true light, we have received the heavenly Spirit, we have found the true faith, we worship the undivided

25. *Sunday Missal* (2011), 12–13.   26. *The Orthodox Liturgy* (1982).

Trinity," and so forth.[27] There are a few cases in which the priest or deacon speaks on behalf of the people, using first-person plural pronouns. Much more often, what is prescribed is that the people speak for their fellows as well as for themselves using "we" and "us."

What is one to make of speaking not only for oneself but also for one's fellow worshippers by using first-person plural pronouns in this way? It is one thing to prescribe that each participant confess his or her own sins by saying, "I confess." Each can then decide whether or not to say the prescribed words; and if she does decide to say the words, she can then decide whether to confess her sins thereby or to just try out this part of the liturgy.[28] It is quite another thing to prescribe that each participant say, "We have sinned," each thereby (implicitly) declaring that their fellow participants have sinned along with them. It is one thing to prescribe that each participant say, "I give thee thanks," each thereby performing the act of giving thanks to God. It is quite another thing to prescribe that each participant say, "We give thee thanks," thereby each (implicitly) declaring that their fellow participants give thanks along with them.

At first glance it appears that what is prescribed to be said in such cases is either presumptuous or known to be false. Who of us is in a position to presume what our fellow congregants are doing when we assemble together for some liturgical enactment? Those who believe that all human beings are sinful will have no problem saying, "we have all sinned," thereby declaring that we all have sinned. But what about saying, "We give thee thanks"? Is it not presumptuous on my part to say those words and thereby perform the prescribed act of declaring that we give God thanks? Who am I to speak for the others? For all I know, some of those present are not giving God thanks.

Or suppose I know, as a matter of fact, that some of those present have not come to worship God but only to try out liturgical participation. Then when I say the words, "we give thee thanks," thereby declaring that we give God thanks, what I say appears to imply what I know to be false. I know there are some among us who are not giving God thanks. The point is even sharper when I say, "we have found the true faith." Am I not

---

27. It also occurs frequently in *The Lenten Triodion* (1978) of the Orthodox Church. Over and over, for example, the people (choir) sing, "We praise, bless, and worship the Lord" (232, and *passim*).

28. I will discuss "trying out" the liturgy in Chapter 5.

either speaking presumptuously or saying what I know to be false when I say those words?

In short, what are we to make of this characteristic feature of liturgical scripts, that they not only prescribe the performance of certain acts of worship by the performance of certain verbal and gestural acts but also prescribe, concerning many of those acts of worship, that the participants declare that *we* perform those acts—not each declare that he or she performs those acts but each declare that *we* perform those acts? Are we not either speaking presumptuously or prevaricating?

I think not. I suggest that the clue to how this feature of liturgical scripts is to be understood lies in who it is that the terms "we" and "us" are being used to refer to. If they are being used to refer to all who are present, then to say those things is indeed either presumptuous or implies what one knows to be false. But that need not be how the pronouns are being used. If an angry speaker says to a city official in a public meeting, "We insist that you put a stop at once to this injustice," the "we" need not refer to everyone in the room; often it does not.

Rather than understanding the "we" and the "us" in liturgical scripts as referring to all present, I suggest that they be understood as referring to all who are fully conforming to the script. It is unity among these participants that is expressed by sentences containing the prescribed "we" and "us."

Perhaps there is another way of understanding at least some occurrences of the liturgical "we" that we should take note of before we leave the topic. Perhaps the "we" can sometimes be understood as referring to that corporate body which is the congregation, or to that corporate body which is the church. Recall some of the "we" language that I quoted from the Orthodox liturgy: "we ascribe glory," "we bless thee," "we hymn thee," "we have seen the resurrection," "we have seen the true light, we have received the heavenly Spirit, we have found the true faith, we worship the undivided Trinity." I think these can be interpreted as "the church ascribes glory," "the church has seen the resurrection," "the church has found the true faith," and so forth. Perhaps this is a somewhat less natural interpretation than the interpretation suggested above; but I don't think it can be ruled out. The two interpretations are compatible. Perhaps the congregants should be understood as declaring both that they have each found the true faith and that the church as a corporate body has found the true faith.

Every liturgy assigns a role to what is typically called "the people." Who fills this role? Is it the individual congregants who fill this role? Or is it, sometimes at least, that entity which is the congregation? Perhaps sometimes it is both at once. Perhaps sometimes the term "People" in the liturgical text can be replaced both by "The Congregants" and by "The Congregation."

Prescribing the manner in which liturgical acts are to be performed

There is a third mode of liturgical togetherness that is worth taking note of. To get at this third mode, we must first consider a feature of liturgical scripts that, thus far, I have said nothing about, namely, liturgical scripts often prescribe not only the acts to be performed but *how* they are to be performed. The *Catecheses* traditionally attributed to Cyril of Jerusalem (*c.*349–86) give the following instructions concerning the reception of the Eucharistic elements:

> When you approach...hollow your palm and receive the body of Christ, saying after it, "Amen."...Then...approach also the cup of his blood. Do not stretch out your hands, but, bowing and saying "Amen" in a gesture of adoration and reverence, sanctify yourself by partaking of the blood of Christ.[29]

In the English translation I have of the Orthodox liturgy of St John Chrysostom the text specifies, at seven different points, that the deacon is to bid the people to pray with the words, "In peace let us pray to the Lord."[30] At another point he is to bid them to pray with the words, "Let us all say with our whole soul and with our whole mind."[31] He is to introduce the recital of the Nicene Creed with the words, "Let us love one another that with one mind we may confess."[32] Immediately after the recital of the creed he is to say, "Let us be upright, let us stand with fear, let us take heed to present the holy offering in peace."[33] And the priest is to dismiss the people with the words, "Let us depart in peace."[34]

What is prescribed in these passages is not just that the congregants perform certain acts but that they perform them in a certain way. They are to pray in peace, to recite the creed with the one mind that comes from

---

29. Jasper and Cuming (1987), 87.
30. *Orthodox Liturgy* (1982), 35, 38, 39, 55, 56, 57, 80.
31. *Orthodox Liturgy* (1982), 50.   32. *Orthodox Liturgy* (1982), 68.
33. *Orthodox Liturgy* (1982), 71.   34. *Orthodox Liturgy* (1982), 97.

loving each other, to stand with fear, to take heed to present the holy offering in peace, to depart in peace.

Those who authorized the liturgy of St John Chrysostom for use in the Orthodox churches did not assume that it is in the power of the people themselves to perform, in the prescribed way, the actions that the deacon and the priest direct them to perform. At one point the priest prays, "Grant us with one mouth and one heart to glorify and praise thy sublime and wondrous name, of the Father, and of the Son, and of the Holy Ghost; now, and forever: world without end."[35] The people must be empowered by God to glorify and praise God with one mouth and one heart.

Can we infer that when the people are enjoined to pray to God in peace, they are also implicitly being enjoined to pray that God will empower them to pray in peace? Can we infer that when they are enjoined to have the love for each other that empowers them to recite the creed with one mind, they are also implicitly being enjoined to pray that God will evoke in them that love for each other? And so forth? I think we can infer that.[36]

Though injunctions to the congregants that they perform the prescribed acts in certain ways occur more frequently in the Orthodox liturgy than in any other that I know of, they commonly occur in other liturgies as well, as do prayers that God empower the congregants to perform the prescribed acts in the prescribed ways. Consider some examples from The Holy Eucharist: Rite One of the Episcopal Church.

Almost immediately after the opening of the service the celebrant prays, "Cleanse the thoughts of our hearts by the inspiration of thy Holy Spirit, that we may perfectly love thee, and worthily magnify thy holy name."[37] The intercessions of the people include the prayer, "that with meek heart and due reverence we may hear and receive thy holy Word."[38] The celebrant's exhortation to the congregants to confess their sins includes the words, "Draw near with faith, and make your humble confession to Almighty God, devoutly kneeling."[39] In the Reformed churches it is especially in the celebration of the Eucharist that the people are enjoined to participate in certain ways.

---

35. *Orthodox Liturgy* (1982), 80.
36. This is a point made by Terence Cuneo in "The Significance of Liturgical Singing." Cuneo (2016b), 126–44.
37. *Book of Common Prayer* (1979), 323.
38. *Book of Common Prayer* (1979), 329.   39. *Book of Common Prayer* (1979), 330.

A noteworthy feature of the Episcopal liturgy is that, at certain points, rather than the priest directing the people to perform some act of worship in a certain way the people are to *declare that they are* performing that act of worship in a certain way. In their confession they declare, "we do earnestly repent, and are heartily sorry for these our misdoings."[40] In their prayer of thanksgiving after communion they declare, "we most heartily thank thee for that thou dost feed us" and "we humbly beseech thee, O heavenly Father,... to assist us with thy grace."[41]

"In peace let us pray"

These comments, about the fact that liturgical scripts often prescribe not only the acts to be performed but how they are to be performed, were introduced as preparation for taking note of a third prescribed form of liturgical togetherness. The Episcopal liturgy that I cited prescribes that the people *worthily magnify* God's holy name, that they hear and receive God's holy word with *meek heart and due reverence*, and that they kneel *devoutly*. Each of these ways of performing the act of worship in question is something to be done by individual participants, albeit together with the others. Together with the others, each participant is to worthily magnify God's name, to hear and receive God's word with meek heart and due reverence, to kneel devoutly.

In many liturgies, but especially in the Orthodox liturgy of St John Chrysostom, a way of performing certain acts of worship is prescribed that is not something each participant can do on his or her own along with others. It's a way of performing the prescribed acts that requires that they *already be related* to each other and to God in a certain way.

Seven times the Orthodox deacon says, "In peace let us pray to the Lord." All by itself this sentence could be interpreted as meaning, *let us each pray to the Lord with an untroubled heart*. I judge that we should probably hear an echo of that meaning; I will take up the point in the final section of this

---

40. *Book of Common Prayer* (1979), 331.
41. *Book of Common Prayer* (1979), 339. Form VI for the prayers of the people in the Episcopal liturgy opens with the leader saying, "In peace, we pray to you, Lord God" (392). In this case the grammar forces one to conclude that the leader is implicitly saying that the people are in fact praying in peace.

chapter ("'My peace I give to you'"). But that individualistic meaning is not, I think, its primary meaning. When the sentence is read in the context of the liturgy as a whole it becomes clear that praying in peace is not each person praying with an untroubled heart together with others who are likewise praying with an untroubled heart. To pray in peace the people must be united with each other and with God in peace. To distinguish this form of peace from the peace of an untroubled heart let me call it *concord*. The Orthodox priest begins one of the prayers with the words, "O Thou who hast given us grace with one accord to make our common supplications."[42]

Though the printed text of the Orthodox liturgy refers and alludes to the peace of concord more frequently than any other text that I know of, in most enactments of traditional Christian liturgies there are references and allusions to concord. This will not always be evident if one looks only at printed liturgical texts. But recall that the psalms and hymns to be sung are also part of the script for an enactment; a good many of these contain references and allusions to concord. One of many examples is the following versification of Psalm 133:

> How good and pleasant is the sight
> When brethren make it their delight
> To dwell in blest accord;
> Such love is like anointing oil
> That consecrates for holy toil
> The servants of the Lord.[43]

And here is another, this one a versification of Psalm 134:

> O bless our God with one accord,
> Ye faithful servants of the Lord,
> Who in his house do stand by night,
> And praise him there with all your might.[44]

In short: those who have assembled to worship God are not just to perform together the prescribed acts of worship but they are to do so in the context of the peace of concord. Worshipping God in concord is a fundamental aspect of the communal dimension of liturgical enactments.

---

42. *Book of Common Prayer* (1979), 40.
43. The versification is without attribution in *Psalter Hymnal* (1959), 278.
44. The versification is in *Psalter Hymnal* (1959), 280, and is attributed to Lambertus J. Lamberts (1928). It is commonly sung to the tune of "Old Hundredth."

What is concord?

What is the sort of peace that I am calling "concord"? Christianity is like most religions in that its members both participate together in liturgical enactments and regard certain scriptures as sacred. The scriptures do not exist side by side with the liturgical enactments in the life of the community; the two interact with each other in multiple ways. The scriptures shape the liturgical enactments and how those are understood, and the liturgical enactments invoke and interpret the scriptures. I will be developing the point in detail in Part II of this volume.

The Septuagint is a translation of the Hebrew Bible into Greek that was completed by the end of the second century BCE. The term *shalom* occurs often in the Hebrew Bible. In the Septuagint it was usually translated with the Greek term *eirenê*. The same term, eirenê, occurs often in the New Testament. This suggests a continuity of meaning between eirenê in the New Testament and shalom in the Hebrew Bible. (Of course, context may in some cases indicate otherwise.) In English translations of the Old and New Testaments, shalom and eirenê are both regularly translated as "peace."

In the Greek text of the liturgy of St John Chrysostom the term translated into English as "peace" in the sentence, "In peace let us pray to the Lord," is eirenê. This linguistic continuity between the Greek text of the liturgy and the Greek text of the New Testament and Septuagint strongly suggests that we should understand what the deacon says as an allusion to biblical shalom/eirenê. So too when the priest says, in Form VI for the prayers of the people in the Episcopal liturgy, "In peace, we pray to you, Lord God," we should understand "peace" as an allusion to biblical shalom/eirenê.

Elsewhere I have analyzed in some detail what the term "shalom" refers to in the Hebrew Bible/Old Testament.[45] Here let me briefly summarize. Shalom requires peace as that is commonly understood, namely, absence of hostility. But shalom is not merely the absence of hostility. Shalom is harmony. Shalom is present in a community only if its members live in harmony in all dimensions of their existence: with God, with each other, with themselves,

---

45. Wolterstorff (1983), 69–72.

with nature. Harmony is to be understood here as ethically infused. The harmony of shalom requires that the members of the community seek the good of each other and treat each other justly. Additionally it requires that they do so not to fulfill what they perceive to be an onerous duty but because they find delight in doing so. In short, shalom is present in a community insofar as its members live in generous, just, and joyful harmony with God, with each other, with themselves, and with nature.

I judge that the English word that comes closest to capturing the idea is "flourishing." Shalom is present in a community insofar as its members flourish in all dimensions of their existence. When the Orthodox deacon says, "In peace let us pray to the Lord," and when the Episcopal priest says, "In peace, we pray to you Lord," the peace they are referring to is the peace of shalom.

And what is the force of the "in"? I have been taking its force to be, *in the context of*. The people are to offer their prayers in the context of their shalom. In his essay, "The Significance of Liturgical Singing,"[46] Terence Cuneo suggests an additional meaning. When the people pray in peace, they not only pray in the context of shalom but they also enact and enhance shalom/eirenê. "The injunction to pray in peace is not, in the first instance, a directive to pray *for* peace or to *be at* peace with oneself when one prays. Nor, for that matter, is it [just] a directive to pray *from* a state of peace. Rather, it is a directive that the assembled pray in a shalom-enacting and enhancing way."[47] Worship of God is a component of shalom. In offering prayers to God in the right spirit we here and now enact and enhance shalom.

When the people pray to God in peace they enact that dimension of shalom which consists of living and acting in right and joyful harmony with God and with each other. Can that dimension of shalom which consists of living and acting in right and joyful harmony *with the natural world* also be enacted within the assembly? It can be enacted outside the assembly. Can it be enacted by following a liturgical script?

It can indeed. In that same essay, "The Significance of Liturgical Singing," Cuneo writes the following: think "of the various actions of the liturgy in which the people interact with elements of (or products of) the natural world, such as when the priest blesses the people with water or the assembled kiss

---

46. Included in Cuneo (2016b).   47. Cuneo (2016b), 134.

a cross of wood at the conclusion of the liturgy. When they perform these actions, these elements or products of the natural world are treated not with indifference but with reverence."[48] Many other examples of the same sort can be cited: in baptism, water is treated with reverence; in the Eucharist, bread and wine are treated with reverence; in singing, sound and air are incorporated into shalom.

The reverence for the natural world that is to be enacted in the liturgy is expressed wonderfully in the anaphora to be found in the *Apostolic Constitutions* (late fourth-century church order from Syria, possibly Antioch):

> It is truly fitting and right to praise you before all things.... You made water for drinking and cleansing, lifegiving air for breathing in and out, and for the production of sound through the tongue striking the air, and for hearing which is aided by it to receive the speech which falls upon it.
>
> You made fire for comfort in darkness, for supplying our need, that we should be warmed and given light by it.
>
> You divided the ocean from the land, and made the one navigable, the other fit to be trodden by our feet; you filled the one with creatures great and small, the other tame and wild; you wove a crown of varied plants and herbs, you beautified it with flowers and enriched it with seeds....
>
> You filled the world and adorned it with sweet-smelling and healing herbs, with many different living things, strong and weak, for food and for work, tame and wild, with hissing of reptiles, with the cries of variegated birds, the cycles of the years, the numbers of months and days, the order of the seasons, the course of rain-bearing clouds for the production of fruits and the creation of living things....
>
> For all things, glory be to you, almighty Lord.[49]

---

48. Cuneo (2016b), 134.
49. Jasper and Cuming (1987), 104–8. I thank John Witvliet for calling this passage to my attention. Jeffery Rowthorn, in his essay "Water in the Book of Common Prayer," observes that whereas there is an abundance of references to water in the psalms, there is a "dearth of references to water in the prayer and praise of the Episcopal Church"—except when those psalms are used—and he asks why this is (Rowthorn [2015], 5). He suggests that it is part of a general failure, in the liturgies of Christians in the West, "to celebrate both the Creator and the creation he has brought into being" (Rowthorn [2015], 5), which has led, in turn, "to a divorce between the staples of daily existence and their sacramental use in worship. A communion wafer has nothing in common with the crusty bread on our table;...a handful of baptismal water does not suggest being washed clean all over.... By failing to use these elements of daily life liturgically in an immediately recognizable form, we diminish the close relationship between our sacramental worship and the created world we live in. This can lead to indifference to the material universe that impoverishes our worship and diminishes our sense of responsibility for the creation entrusted to us" (Rowthorn [2015], 5–6).

"My peace I give to you"

It would be a mistake to conclude our discussion of the third mode of liturgical togetherness without coming back to a point we have mentioned, namely, that though the primary meaning of "peace" in the Orthodox liturgy and others is concord or shalom, we should probably hear an echo of another meaning as well, namely, that of *untroubled hearts*. Strictly speaking, of course, the person whose heart is troubled is not fully flourishing, not fully experiencing shalom. But my primary reason for thinking we should probably hear an echo of this other meaning is that this is the meaning of "peace" (eirenê) in a passage in the Gospel of John that has undoubtedly influenced Christian liturgies. I refer to the use of the term by Jesus in what has come to be called his "farewell discourse" to his disciples. Jesus said:

> Peace I leave with you; my peace I give to you. I do not give to you as the world gives. Do not let your hearts be troubled, and do not let them be afraid. (14: 27)

Might Jesus have meant by "peace" here what I have been calling *concord* and which, so I have argued, is to be understood as shalom? I think not. The peace of which Jesus speaks here is bestowed on his disciples so that their hearts may not be troubled.

Jesus has just told his disciples that shortly he will be leaving them. They are understandably disturbed. They have followed him in the conviction that God was working through him in some special way, a way that they grasped in part, but only in part. Now he says he is going where they cannot follow. They are disturbed. So he speaks words meant to give them courage and confidence. Twice over he says, "Do not let your hearts be troubled" (14: 1; 14: 27). To this he adds, "I will not leave you orphaned; I am coming to you" (14: 18). He concludes with the words, "I have said this to you, so that in me you may have peace. In the world you face persecution. But take courage; I have conquered the world" (16: 33). Dark words. But clearly this peace is not shalom.

It was the practice of the ancient church, at a certain point in the liturgy, for the people to pass the so-called kiss of peace to each other. Though the practice gradually fell out of use, the rubric "Kiss of Peace" sometimes remained in the liturgical text (the Orthodox liturgy is an example). As part of the liturgical revival that took place in the twentieth century the practice was revived in most Christian traditions. Typically the leader says to the people, "The peace of the Lord be with you," whereupon the people pass the peace to those around them with the same or similar words, usually accompanied by a handshake or hug.

The words typically used to introduce the passing of the peace, "The peace of the Lord be with you," are an allusion to what Jesus said in his farewell discourse to his disciples. The allusion is made explicit in the contemporary Catholic liturgy. The priest introduces the "sign of peace" with the words, "Lord Jesus Christ, who said to your Apostles: Peace I leave with you; my peace I give you....Let us offer each other the sign of peace."[50] I suggest that when the congregants do then pass the peace to each other, the peace of concord is in the background and what they are primarily doing is saying, "May you experience the peace that Christ bestowed on his disciples."

---

50. *Sunday Missal* (2011), 73.

4

On bended knee

The bodily dimension of liturgical action

Christians worship God with their bodies, as do the adherents of most other theistic religions. Let me repeat the list I gave in Chapter 1 of what participants in Christian liturgical enactments do. They play musical instruments, stand, sit, kneel, bow, prostrate themselves, process, dance, get out of their seats and walk forward, return to their seats, cross themselves, fold their hands, raise their hands, close their eyes, drop money into a container, distribute bread and wine, eat bread and drink wine, sprinkle with water, immerse in water, rub with oil, wash their hands, wash the feet of others, shake hands, embrace, spit, wave palm branches, light candles, and more. And of course they also use their vocal cords to read aloud from books, sing, and speak. My project in this chapter is to reflect on the bodily dimension of Christian liturgical action.

Though no liturgical enactment includes all the actions mentioned, enactments of the Orthodox liturgy include many of them, more than do the enactments of any other liturgical tradition. At the opposite end of the spectrum are the worship services of some contemporary Protestants: the people do little more than sit in their seats observing and listening to what musicians and ministers are doing and saying up front.[1]

Almost always when a liturgical enactment takes place there are some people present who do not speak or sing because they cannot, some who do not stand or kneel because they cannot, some who do not raise their hands because they cannot. This does not imply that their participation is deficient, defective, deviant, imperfect, incorrect, or anything else of the sort.

---

1. In that way their participation is much like that of the people in enactments of the liturgy of the Mass in late medieval Western Europe, described in footnote 20 in Chapter 3.

The reason it does not have that implication is that the verbal, gestural, and auditory actions prescribed by liturgical scripts are to be understood as implicitly conditional: stand *if able*, kneel *if able*, say *if able*, sing *if able*. So understood, the person who can stand but does not when the text says "All stand" is failing to follow the script, whereas the person who does not stand because she cannot is not failing to follow the script. Hence it is that no stigma is attached to her not standing. The words "All stand" mean "Stand if able."[2]

My project in this chapter is to reflect on those verbal, gestural, and auditory actions that are prescribed to be done if one is able.

Ascending to the Supreme Being

Let's begin with a sharp contrast. The situation in Plato's *Symposium* is that Socrates is summarizing the speeches given at a banquet where the participants agreed that they would offer eulogies of the god Love (*eros*). Each speech proves more elevated than its predecessor. Finally we arrive at Socrates' report of the speech he himself gave.

Socrates reports that he began his eulogy with the declaration that love always has an object, that object being something the lover regards as good and beautiful and which he loves because of some lack in himself: "In general, all who feel desire feel it for what is not provided or present; for something they have not or are not or lack; and that sort of thing is the object of desire and love."[3] Socrates then reported that in the remainder of his speech he rehearsed what he once heard a woman named Diotima say on the topic of love. Socrates reported Diotima as urging an ascent of the mind from beautiful things to Beauty Itself.

The lover begins with love of some beautiful body. He then notices that the beauty of that body is "cognate" to the beauty of other bodies. Having noticed this, it would be "gross folly not to regard as one and the same the beauty belonging to all" bodies. "Having grasped this truth, he must make

---

2. I am told that those who cannot stand nonetheless find that they can do something that they describe as "standing in spirit." Accordingly, they would prefer that the rubric say "Stand in body or spirit" rather than "Stand if able." People who think seriously about participation by the handicapped often come up with ingenious suggestions concerning ways in which participation by the handicapped can be enhanced and enabled.

3. *Plato, with an English Translation* (1946), 171.

himself a lover of all beautiful bodies, and slacken the stress of his feeling for
one by con[d]emning it and counting it a trifle." "His next advance will
be to set a higher value on the beauty of souls than on that of the body."
That should lead him, in turn, "to contemplate the beautiful as appearing in
our observances and laws." From there "he should be led on to the branches
of knowledge, that there also he may behold a province of beauty." By
looking on "beauty in the mass" in this way, he "may escape from the mean,
meticulous slavery of a single instance,... and [turn] rather toward the main
ocean of the beautiful." He now "descries a certain single knowledge connected with a beauty which has yet to be told."

What is that beauty yet to be told? "When a man has been thus far
tutored in the lore of love, passing from view to view of beautiful things, in
the right and regular ascent, suddenly he will have revealed to him as he
draws to the close of his dealings in love, a wondrous vision beautiful in
its nature." Beauty itself is "the final object of all those previous toils." It is
ever-existent and does not change. It is not beautiful in one respect and
lacking in beauty in another respect. And to one who has achieved this vision
it is presented as "existing ever in singularity of form independent by itself,
while the multitude of beautiful things partake of it." By "ever climbing
aloft," the lover of beauty has arrived at "the Beautiful Itself and that alone;
so that in the end he comes to know the very essence of beauty."[4]

This famous passage on the ascent of the mind, culminating in a purely
intellectual contemplation of the eternal, has had a profound impact on
Christian theology and philosophy, both in the East and the West. The
image of *ascent* pervades the writings of Pseudo-Dionysius. Near the beginning
of *The Divine Names* the author writes:

> The Good... generously reveals a firm, transcendent beam, granting enlight-
> enments proportionate to each being, and thereby draws sacred minds upward
> to its permitted contemplation.... What happens to those that rightly and
> properly make this effort is this. They do not venture toward an impossibly
> daring sight of God, one beyond what is duly granted them. Nor do they go
> tumbling downward where their own natural inclinations would take them.
> No. Instead they are raised firmly and unswervingly upward in the direction
> of the ray which enlightens them. With a love matching the illuminations
> granted them, they take flight, reverently, wisely, in all holiness.[5]

4. The quotations above are from *Plato, with an English Translation* (1946), 203, 205, 207.
5. *Pseudo-Dionysius: The Complete Works* (1987), 50. Cf. the opening of *The Mystical Theology*:
"Timothy, my friend, my advice to you as you look for a sight of the mysterious things is to

The image of *ascent* is likewise prominent in Augustine's *Of True Religion*, written around 390 at the end of his philosophical meanderings and the beginning of his theological career. "Let us see," he says, "how far reason can advance from visible to invisible things in its ascent from temporal to eternal things."[6] What then follows is an ascent of the mind starting from the unity to be found in perceptible things and moving up by stages until finally it arrives at that by reference to which all judgments of unity are ultimately made and which is thus above the rational mind itself. "We must not have any doubt that the unchangeable substance which is above the rational mind is God."[7] God is absolute unity, the source and criterion of all partial unities. "It is with the mind that we see true unity."[8] "Many stop with what delights men and are unwilling to rise to higher things."[9]

Assemble, not ascend

To enact their liturgies Christians assemble on foot and in wheelchairs to worship God with their bodies, not to enact an ascent of the mind to the Supreme Being. Perhaps some who join the assembly have been practicing the Platonic type of ascent during the week. If so, they leave that practice behind and come on foot or in wheelchair to worship God with their bodies along with others who likewise worship God with their bodies.

In many traditional liturgies, the Great Thanksgiving Prayer which begins the Eucharist includes this dialogue, or one very much like this:

CELEBRANT: The Lord be with you.

PEOPLE: And also with you.

CELEBRANT: Lift up your hearts.

PEOPLE: We lift them up to the Lord.

CELEBRANT: Let us give thanks to the Lord our God.

PEOPLE: It is right to give God thanks and praise.

---

leave behind you everything perceived and understood, everything perceptible and understandable, all that is not and all that is, and with your understanding laid aside, to strive upward as much as you can toward union with him who is beyond all being and knowledge. By an undivided and absolute abandonment of yourself and everything, shedding all and freed from all, you will be uplifted to the ray of the divine shadow which is above everything that is." *Pseudo-Dionysius: The Complete Works*, 135.

6. Augustine (1959), 49.   7. Augustine (1959), 53–4.

8. Augustine (1959), 58.   9. Augustine (1959), 56.

What then follows is not an ascent of the mind by the people to intellectual contemplation of God but the presider using his tongue and vocal cords to lead the congregants in giving God thanks and praise.

In the Orthodox liturgy of St John Chrysostom the people sing the so-called Hymn of the Cherubim:

> We, who mystically represent the cherubim and sing the thrice-holy hymn to the life-giving Trinity, let us lay aside the cares of life that we may receive the king of all.[10]

What then follows is not an ascent of the mind by the congregants to intellectual contemplation of the Trinity but the singing of hymns and the voicing of prayers, the latter including prayers for the lives of the congregants and for the world: "For things good and profitable to our souls, and peace for the world, let us entreat the Lord."[11]

In the Form for the Celebration of the Lord's Supper that was included in the 1566 edition of the Dutch Psalter by Petrus Dathenus the celebrant says to the congregants, just before he distributes the bread and wine, "let us not cling with our hearts unto the external bread and wine but lift them up on high in heaven, where Christ Jesus is, our advocate, at the right hand of his heavenly father."[12] What then follows is not an ascent of the mind by the congregants to intellectual contemplation of Christ enthroned in heaven but the celebrant's distribution of bread and wine and the congregants eating the bread and drinking the wine.

In short, though Christian liturgies employ the metaphors of ascent and of leaving behind our earthly cares, they are relentlessly bodily.[13] Rather than leaving their bodies behind as they ascend to the purely intellectual contemplation of God the participants enlist their bodies into their worship of God. They do not lift up their hearts to God *instead of* speaking and singing and chewing and drinking. They lift up their hearts to God *in* speaking and singing and chewing and drinking. They do not lay aside all earthly

---

10. *Orthodox Liturgy* (1974), 31.   11. *Orthodox Liturgy* (1982), 67.
12. *Psalter Hymnal* (1959), 95.
13. There have nonetheless been Platonizing interpretations of the Christian liturgy. Here, for example, is Clement of Alexandria's interpretation of the Eucharistic prayer: "We raise our heads, we extend our hands up toward heaven, and we stand on tiptoe at the final acclamation in our prayer, as we direct the thrust of our minds toward the Intelligible Substance. By attempting through words to raise our bodies above the earth, and by raising up our souls to which a longing for heavenly things have given wings, we force them to advance toward the Sanctuary, for we scorn the bonds that still link us to the flesh." Quoted in Rordorf et al. (1978), 105.

cares *instead of* voicing prayers for their lives and for the world; they pray for their lives and for the world as they lay aside all earthly cares. They worship God with their bodies. Marilyn Adams writes, "We *are* by nature *embodied* persons, personified matter, enmattered spirit; both poles are brought together in our very selves.... [T]he attempt somehow to detach or abstract the personal from the material in human being and bring the personal to God while leaving the material behind would constitute a betrayal of the human vocation."[14]

That we worship God with our bodies is expressed with childlike simplicity in the Eucharistic prayer of the ancient liturgy of Addai and Mari:

> It is right that every mouth should glorify
> and every tongue give thanks.
> With open mouth and faces unveiled
> we present you with praise and honor.[15]

Worshipping God with our bodies

What Norman Mitchell calls the "orthodox consensus" among ritual theorists of the 1970s and 1980s fails us most decisively when reflecting on the bodily dimension of liturgical actions. The orthodox consensus held that the main goal of ritual theory is to identify the "meaning" of rituals, both the meaning of rituals in general and the meaning of particular rituals. The consensus, says Mitchell, was "that 'ritual' is essentially a way to regulate social life; to shape personal and corporate identity; to review and renew values; to express and transmit meaning in symbolic word and act; to preserve tradition; and to insure cultural cohesion and to guarantee social continuity. This prevailing, 'orthodox consensus' further assumed that rituals are not 'utilitarian,' but characteristically symbolic in structure."[16]

From this description it's clear that ritual theorists of the 1970s and 1980s had no interest in getting clear on what it is that those who participate in rituals and liturgies are actually doing, no interest in getting clear on what I call the "performative dimension" of liturgical activity. Whatever it is that ritual and liturgical agents do, theorists wanted to know what it *means*.

---

14. M. Adams (2006), 287.   15. Deiss (1979), 160, 163.
16. Mitchell (2006), 48. The quotes within quotes are quotations by Mitchell from an earlier book of his.

Sociologists and anthropologists wanted to uncover the social meaning; Christian liturgical scholars the theological meaning.

Mitchell rejects this search for "the meaning" of ritual activity. He does so by making heavy use of Roland Barthes's book, *Empire of Signs*, in which Barthes describes various aspects of Japanese life and argues that, to understand what is done, one should attend to the gesture itself and not search for its meaning. Mitchell argues that we in the West should do the same when trying to understand ourselves. We should rid ourselves of "our neurotic habit of finding meanings where there are none or putting them where they don't belong. Paradoxically, our Western impulse to overfeed symbols, to load them with stacks of meaning they cannot sustain, makes us miss their real power to reveal and disclose the new, the unexpected, the *other*."[17] Applying to liturgy Barthes's diatribe against meaning, Mitchell declares that "the purpose of liturgical rites is *not* to 'produce meanings.' Liturgy's goal isn't meaning but *meeting*," specifically, meeting God, setting aside our preconceptions and allowing God to meet us as God wishes.[18]

This sounds promising. Don't look for meanings in the liturgy but attend to the gesture. Attend to what is done. But as it turns out, in his discussion of meeting God liturgically Mitchell pays no more attention to what is actually done than do "orthodox" ritual theorists. His view appears to be that, when participating in the liturgy, we should not focus on what we are doing but let God "enter,"[19] "*let* God come toward us in a gracious—indeed, kenotic—movement of self-donation."[20]

In the chapter of *Meeting Mystery* titled "The Book of the Body" Mitchell emphatically makes the point that "The most basic language liturgy speaks is *the body itself*." But at no point does he look closely at how we "meet God" with our bodies when we participate in liturgical enactments. What he does instead is discuss various attitudes toward the body: attitudes toward the body in early Christianity; the gradual emergence of a distinctly Christian anthropology; "the modern retrieval of the body as a 'theological site'"; and so forth.[21] It may be that the presence of positive attitudes toward the body among Christians helps explain why they worship God with their bodies.

---

17. Mitchell (2006), 53.   18. Mitchell (2006), 59.
19. We should learn "the art of *letting*: letting *go* of our compulsion to control or master people, places, and things; *letting enter* the God who is moving toward us..." Mitchell (2006), 67.
20. Mitchell (2006), 68.   21. Mitchell (2006), 185.

But being cognizant of those positive attitudes does not illuminate how they do that.

The speech-act theory I have employed throughout our discussion comes to our aid at this point. When I use my tongue and vocal cords to utter the words "Thanks be to God," I thereby perform the illocutionary act of thanking God. My act of thanking God is imperceptible, not itself a bodily act. But I perform that act by using my tongue and vocal cords to utter the words, "Thanks be to God." My uttering of the words does not *cause* my thanking God; my act of thanking God is outside the causal order. My uttering of the words *counts as* my thanking God. My act of uttering those words and my act of thanking God are joined together so that the former counts as the latter. It's by virtue of that joining together that I thank God with my body. The situation is not that my bodily act of uttering those words is infused with *meaning*; rather, that bodily act is conjoined with the act of thanking God. I can also thank God silently, in my mind; then there is no bodily act on my part that counts as thanking God. But when I follow some liturgical script and utter the words "Thanks be to God," I thank God with my body and mind conjoined. I enlist my body together with my mind into thanking God. And when I eat bread, drink wine, wave palm branches, kiss an icon, I not only enlist my body into worship of God but I enlist items and substances from the material world as well. I enlist my body, along with items and substances from the material world, into worshipping the one who is not to be found among the bodies, the items, and the substances of the material world.

The ability to do this is uniquely human. Though angels can praise God, they cannot praise God by using their mouths and vocal cords to sing their praise. Though birds can sing, they cannot perform the illocutionary act of praising God by doing so.[22]

If this sort of joining together of body and mind were not so common we would find it utterly amazing. How can it be that one's performance of some bodily act can count as one's performance of some imperceptible illocutionary act outside the causal order? How can it be that by virtue of uttering certain words I am to be credited with having thanked God and

---

22. See my discussion in Wolterstorff (2016b). Though birds and other non-human creatures cannot perform illocutionary acts, the psalmist thinks that they can, nonetheless, in some sense praise God. The opening ten verses of Psalm 148 are an extended injunction to non-human creatures to praise the Lord: "Wild animals and all cattle, creeping things and flying birds, praise the Lord" (v. 10).

with having all the rights and responsibilities pertaining thereto? How can this be? Amazing.

It would be difficult to find a postmodernist text in which the terms "signifier" and "signified" are not employed. The terms were taken over from the Swiss linguist, Ferdinand Saussure. Among those who employ them there is a good deal of variation as to what they regard as signified by verbal signifiers. Sometimes one finds them falling back on the expressionist theory of language favored by the nineteenth-century Romantics according to which words, along with other "symbols," are basically a means "of communication by which we humans share emotions, thoughts, ideas, plans, and dreams."[23] Employing this conceptuality in thinking about liturgy makes it impossible to recognize what speech-act theory enables us to recognize, namely, that those who participate in liturgical enactments worship God with their bodies.

If the words and gestures of the liturgy are signifiers, what do they signify? What do the words "Thanks be to God" signify when spoken by someone in a liturgical enactment? Do they signify the participant's act of thanking God? One can only signify what there is; one cannot bring something into existence by signifying it. So how, on this view, did that act of thanking God come about—not the act of uttering the words "Thanks be to God" but the act of thanking God? The conceptuality of signifier/signified gives us not a clue as to how that act came about.

Might the words "Thanks be to God" signify the participant's thankful thoughts toward God? They might. The participant might well have such thoughts; if so, those thoughts are candidates for being signified or expressed. But then the point to be made is that having and expressing worshipful thoughts about God is not to be identified with worshipping God. One can do the former without doing the latter. I can express my worshipful thoughts about God to my wife; I have not, by so doing, worshipped God. Or suppose I express my worshipful feelings about God by saying to God, "Oh God, I have worshipful feelings for you." Would that be to worship God? It would not. Suppose I say to God, "Oh God, I have petitionary thoughts and feelings for you." Would that be to perform the act of petitioning God? It would not.

Let's pause for a moment to let the point sink in. Those who employ the concepts of signifier and signified in their analysis of liturgy are ineluctably

---

23. Mitchell (2006), 149. He presents this as his own view.

forced away from understanding the purpose of liturgy as worshipping God toward understanding its purpose as signifying or expressing worshipful thoughts about God. Employing the signifier/signified conceptuality blocks from view the performative dimension of liturgy—blocks from view the fact that liturgy is for performing acts of worship with one's body and mind conjoined, not for signifying or expressing worshipful thoughts. Liturgy is for praising God, not for signifying or expressing praiseful thoughts about God; liturgy is for thanking God, not for signifying or expressing thankful thoughts about God; liturgy is for petitioning God, not for signifying or expressing petitionary thoughts about God. The awkwardness of the language indicates something profoundly wrong about the signifier/signified analysis of liturgical enactments. Liturgy is not for signifying or expressing worshipful thoughts and feelings about God. Liturgy is for worshipping God with mind and body conjoined.

Why worship God with our bodies?

There is no lack of contemplative practices in the Christian tradition, nor is there any lack of treatises describing and recommending those practices. For some ascetics, those practices have taken the place of participating in liturgical enactments. And there are some Christians who prefer to engage God by taking meditative walks in the woods rather than following a liturgical script. Most Christians, however, participate in liturgical enactments. Evidently they feel intuitively that there is something important about worshipping God with one's body and mind conjoined, not just with one's mind, and doing so in company with others.

Before we explore what that is, it's worth noting that, influential though Plato's presentation of the ascent of the mind in the *Symposium* (and corresponding passages in the *Republic* [VI.509]) has been, many if not most Christian practices of meditation differ in a significant way from Plato's ascent. They do not try to transcend the powers and capacities of the body in the way that Plato's philosopher does.

Plato's philosopher is to ascend stage by stage to the point where he no longer makes use of images. "The summit of the intelligible world is reached in philosophical discussion by one who aspires, through the discourse of reason unaided by any of the senses, to make his way in every case to the essential reality and perseveres until he has grasped by pure intelligence the very nature of Goodness itself."[24]

Compare that to this passage from the *Life of Christ* by the German Carthusian, Ludolph of Saxony (*c.*1295–1378), in which the author urges his reader to imagine, as vividly as possible, events in the life of Jesus. (Ignatius of Loyola had read Ludolph's *Life* before he composed his own enormously influential *Spiritual Exercises.*)

> If you wish to derive fruit from these meditations, set aside all your worries and cares. With the affections of the heart make present to yourself, in a loving and delectable way, everything the Lord Jesus said and did, just as present as if you were hearing it with your ears and seeing it with your eyes. Then all of it becomes sweet because you are thinking of it and, what is more, tasting it with longing. And even when it is related in the past tense, you should consider it all as if it were occurring today. . . . Go into the Holy Land, kiss with a burning spirit the soil upon which the good Jesus stood. Make present to yourself how he spoke and went about with his disciples and with sinners, how he speaks and preaches, how he walks and rests, sleeps and watches, eats and performs miracles. Inscribe into your very heart his attitudes and his actions.[25]

Ludolph does not employ the image of ascent. Rather than *ascending* to the eternal we are to *go back* in our imagination to the time when Jesus lived. And far from urging the employment of pure imageless intelligence, Ludolph urges his readers to cultivate images of Jesus' life on earth.

Back to the question: why worship God with our bodies? The Platonic type of ascent ends not in acts of worship but in contemplation of the Supreme Being. But it's possible to perform acts of worship—praising, thanking, petitioning, and so forth—without performing bodily acts that count as acts of worship. One can perform such acts silently, immobile, with eyes closed and ears stopped. So why worship God with our bodies?

"Why not?" someone might reply. But that would be to miss the point. The question is, why it is that for almost two millennia Christians have assembled to worship God with their bodies?

In Chapter 3 I noted that Christian Scripture and Christian liturgical enactments interact: Scripture shapes liturgical enactments and liturgical enactments invoke and interpret Scripture. So a thought that comes to mind is

---

24. Plato (1945), 252.   25. Quoted in von Balthasar (1982), 377–8.

that in worshipping God with our bodies we are expressing or reflecting the positive attitude toward the body that one finds in Scripture.

In *Meeting Mystery*, Nathan Mitchell quotes a sentence from Rudolph Bultmann that nicely captures how Scripture understands human existence: *human existence is somatic existence.*[26] The theologian David Kelsey is getting at the same point when he speaks of human beings as "personal bodies."[27] The biblical writers do distinguish the body from other aspects of the self— mind, spirit, soul, etc.; but they never do so in order to declare that the body is inferior to some other aspect.[28] Given that it was God who created human beings as personal bodies, and given the Incarnation, how could Christians think the body is inferior?

Is it because of the influence of the positive attitude of Scripture toward the body that Christians have persisted in worshipping God with their bodies? Most likely that has been a factor. But it cannot be the entire explanation, since a good many Christians have had a negative attitude toward the body, in spite of what Scripture says, while nonetheless continuing to worship God with their bodies. If assembling together with others to worship God with one's body can coexist with negative attitudes toward the body, then attitudes toward the body do not fully explain why Christians find it important to worship God with their bodies. Something more is at work. What might that be?

Let's perform a thought experiment. Imagine an assembly of Christians in which nobody performs any verbal or gestural act that counts as an act of worship, nor any that counts as God saying or doing something. The participants may utter certain words and make certain gestures, and some of those verbal and gestural acts may have count-as significance. But none of them has the count-as significance of the agents thereby worshipping God or of God thereby saying or doing something. The participants do worship God. But their worship is disembodied, purely mental, purely internal. There is a script for them to follow that's printed out. To get the people to proceed through the script more or less simultaneously the leader indicates when they are to move on to the next liturgical act.

---

26. Mitchell (2006),163. The five words in the text are excised by Mitchell from Bultmann's longer sentence.
27. Kelsey (2009), *passim.*
28. Karl Barth develops the point at length in *Church Dogmatics* III/2. David Kelsey develops the point in chapters 6 and 7 of *Eccentric Existence.*

What would be lost if worship were disengaged from the body in this way? A lot. For one thing, the people would not be worshipping God *together*; their worship, though more or less simultaneous, would be individual. Their worship would be no different from what it would be if they were each seated in a separate room and the leader's voice, indicating when they were to move on to the next liturgical act, was piped in. Indeed, it would be no different from what it would be if they all stayed home and the leader's voice was piped into their separate living rooms. The communal dimension of liturgical enactments, discussed in Chapter 3, would be entirely missing. A point I did not make when discussing the communal dimension was that worshipping God together requires that we worship God with our bodies.

There would be no sacraments. Disembodied worship is necessarily non-sacramental. The celebrant could distribute bread and wine and his doing so might have meaning of some sort. But since no gestural act has count-as significance, the Eucharist would not be a sacrifice of praise and thanksgiving. Neither would the presider's distribution of the bread and the wine have the count-as significance of Christ thereby offering himself to the participants. The congregants could eat the bread and drink the wine, and their doing so could have some sort of meaning; but it would not have the count-as significance of their receiving Christ's offer.

There would be no declaration of pardon and no blessing of the people. The people could *read* words of pardon and *read* words of blessing; upon reading the words they might *feel* pardoned and *feel* blessed. But reading words of blessing and feeling blessed is not the same as God blessing the people by way of the minister or priest pronouncing words of blessing.

In the disembodied worship we are imagining there would be no singing. Or more precisely, there would be no singing that counted as an act of worship—no sung praise to God, no sung thanksgiving, no sung confession. The participants might go through hymns in their minds; we all do that sometimes. But that's a pale imitation of singing aloud together with others.

I have given a short catalogue of the ways in which worship would be diminished if the participants in liturgical enactments did not worship God with their bodies, and if nobody used their bodies to say or do something that counted as God saying or doing something: there would be no communal worship, there would be no sacraments, there would be no pardon or blessing pronounced by God, there would be no singing. I suggest that this is why even those whose attitude toward the body was negative have not, for the most part, absented themselves from participating together with others in liturgical enactments. They too have wanted communal worship; they too have wanted sacramental worship; they too have wanted to sing their praise of God out loud together with others.

There is a passage in Augustine in which he calls attention to a good that ensues from worshipping God with our bodies that is quite different from the goods I have identified.

> Those who pray by using the members of the body, as when they bend the knees, when they extend the hands, or even prostrate themselves upon the ground, or whatever else they do in a visible manner, they do that which indicates that they are suppliants although their invisible will and the intentions of their heart is known to God, for He has no need of such outward signs to indicate that the human mind is in a state of supplication to Him. By doing this a man excites himself more to a proper state for praying and lamenting more humbly and fervently, and, somehow or other, since these movements of the body cannot be made except by a previous movement of the mind, by these same actions of the visible man, the invisible soul which prompted them is strengthened. Then, by reason of this the devotion of one's heart is strengthened, because he has resolved that these prayers be made and has made them.[29]

I think Augustine is right about this. In some mysterious way our worship is "strengthened" when we worship with our bodies.

Given the fact that worshipping God with their bodies enables participants in liturgical enactments to achieve the goods to which I have pointed, and more besides, it would be appropriate for them not to take their bodies for granted but to thank God for bodies with which they can worship God, and for the items and substances of the material world that they employ in the liturgy—water, bread, wine, oil, ashes, smoke, fire, wood, clay, books, tree branches, and so forth.

Liturgically thanking God for our bodies is relatively rare, however. The Orthodox baptismal liturgy is unusual in that it includes a prayer of thanksgiving for our bodies—not, admittedly, for having bodies with which we can worship God, but, nonetheless, for our bodies. The prayer occurs just before The Tonsure—the priest's cutting the hair of the baptized person in the form of a cross.

> O Master, Lord our God. You honored mankind with Your own image. You have fashioned us with a reason-endowed soul and a pleasing body

29. "The Care to be Taken for the Dead" (*De cura pro mortus*), included in Augustine's *Treatises on Marriage and Other Subjects.* Quoted by Taliaferro (2004), 244.

(for the body serves the reason-endowed soul). You have placed the head above and endowed it with the chief portion of the senses, which, nevertheless, do not impede one another. You have covered the head with hair, that it not be injured with changes of the weather, and have fitly joined together all our members, that with them all we may give thanks to You, the Great Creator.[30]

In most Eucharistic prayers God is thanked for the bread and the wine; in some baptismal liturgies God is thanked for the water.[31] I know of no liturgical text which prescribes that the participants are to thank God for the many other items and substances that are employed in the liturgy.

Have negative attitudes toward the body restrained the role of the body in liturgical enactments?

The body and the material world are employed in a far wider variety of ways in the Orthodox liturgy than in any other traditional liturgy. If we compare how they are employed there with how they are employed, for example, in traditional Reformed and Presbyterian liturgies, their employment in the latter is, to understate the difference, restrained. In Reformed and Presbyterian liturgies there is a great deal of singing and speaking, some laying on of hands, the use of water, bread, and wine in the sacraments. But no kissing of icons, no censing, no genuflecting, no spitting, very little crossing of oneself, and so forth.

May it be that this restrained use of the body and of the material world is due to the fact that members of the Reformed and Presbyterian tradition have a negative attitude toward the body and the material world? May it be that the richer and more varied employment of the body and the material world in the Orthodox liturgy is an indication of the fact that Orthodox people have a more positive attitude toward the body and the material world? I noted in the section "Why worship God with our bodies?" that a negative attitude toward the body has not, in general, led those who have held such an attitude to reject participation in liturgical enactments. But may

30. Translation used by St Luke Orthodox Church in America in Palos Heights, IL.
31. Jeffery Rowthorn notes that in the Thanksgiving over the Water in the Episcopal Rite of Holy Baptism, "the water is not itself the gift for which we thank God. Instead it provides the medium through which the saving acts of God are *effected*." It is for these saving acts that God is thanked. Rowthorn (2015), 4.

it be that such an attitude does account for the relatively restrained use of the body in liturgical enactments of the Reformed and Presbyterian tradition?

An adequate discussion of the matter would require a book. But to me it seems clear that the answer to the question is No. If there had been a negative attitude toward the body and the material world among Dutch Reformed people of the seventeenth century it would surely have manifested itself not only in a restrained use of the body in liturgical enactments but also in an aversion to visual art. There was no such aversion. When the liturgy was concluded, and a Dutch Reformed person of that century stepped out of the sanctuary in which there was little to catch the eye other than light so striking as to be symbolic, he found himself immersed in a flood of paintings. Paintings were everywhere.

It was not a negative attitude toward the body and the material world that accounts for the restrained use of the body and the material world in the early Reformed and Presbyterian tradition but a horror of idolatry and superstition. Everything suspected of being an object of idolatry or superstition on the part of laypeople in the Catholicism of the time was eliminated, as were all gestures and movements that could be interpreted as idolatrous or superstitious: statues were taken down, genuflecting was forbidden, and so forth.

An example of the point was the rejection by the Reformers of the adoration of the host. J. A. Jungmann, fine historian of the Catholic liturgy, describes as follows the participation of laypeople in the Eucharist at the end of the middle ages: "Because the faithful no longer wanted to communicate or dared to (the clergy did not encourage frequent reception, to put it mildly), they wanted to see the sacred Host. From gazing at the sacred Species, they hoped for blessing and help in their earthly needs as well as salvation for their souls."[32] Cranmer describes this practice of veneration of the host in sardonic terms: "What made the people to run from their seats to the altar, and from altar to altar, and from sacring (as they called it) to sacring, peeping, tooting and gazing at that thing which they saw? What moved the priests to lift up the sacrament so high over their heads? Or the people to say to the priest 'Hold up! Hold up!'; or one man to say to another 'Stoop down before'; or to say 'This day have I seen my Maker'; and 'I cannot be quiet except I see my Maker once a day'? What was the cause of all these, and that as well the priest and the people so devoutly did knock

---

32. Jungmann (1959), 511.

and kneel at every sight of the sacrament, but that they worshipped that visible thing which they saw with their eyes and took it for very God?"[33]

In this passage Cranmer does not call such adoration of the host "idolatry," but that, of course, is what he meant. In his discussion of the mass of his day Calvin did call the adoration of the host both "superstitious worship" and "idolatry." "Shall we deny that this is superstitious worship when men prostrate themselves before bread to worship Christ there?"[34] "They have forgotten the living God and fashioned a God after their own desire. For what is idolatry if not this: to worship the gifts in place of the Giver himself?"[35]

In the section of this chapter "Assemble, not ascend" I quoted words from a 1566 form for the celebration of the Lord's Supper in the Dutch Reformed Church: "Let us not cling with our hearts unto the external bread and wine but lift them up on high in heaven where Christ Jesus is, our Advocate." In defense of this use of the *sursum corda* in the liturgy Calvin says the following, immediately after the comment quoted above about superstitious worship: "Doubtless the Council of Nicea meant to forestall this evil when it forbade us to fix our humble attention upon the symbols set before us. And for the same reason it was established of old that before consecration the people should be told in a loud voice to lift up their hearts."[36] Clearly it is the horror of superstition and idolatry that is coming to expression here, not a negative attitude toward the material world. Immediately after being enjoined not to cling to the external bread and wine the congregants are offered bread and wine which they then ingest.[37]

Was the fear of idolatry and superstition on the part of the Reformers warranted at the time? Clearly to some extent it was. Whether it was warranted to the extent to which the Reformers took it is a question historians will have to answer.[38] Surely it is not warranted today. But the restraint of the early Reformers became a tradition and lives on.

---

33. Quoted by Dix (1982), 620.   34. *Institutes* 4.17.36. Calvin (1960), 1412.
35. *Institutes* 4.17.36. Calvin (1960), 1413.   36. *Institutes* 4.17.36. Calvin (1960), 1412.
37. Calvin's discussion of images, in *Institutes* 1.11, is pervaded by accusations of idolatry. He says, "when you prostrate yourself in veneration, representing to yourself in an image either a god or a creature, you are already ensnared in some superstition." *Institutes* 1.11.9 (Calvin [1960], 109). This comment by Calvin on veneration of icons seems to me obtuse and imperceptive. See my discussion in Wolterstorff (2015c).
38. Steven Ozment (1975) makes clear that there was in fact a great deal of religious superstition in central Europe at the time of the Reformation.

Schmemann on the significance of enlisting the body and the material world into worship

In Alexander Schmemann's *For the Life of the World*[39] there is a fine passage in which he argues that we human beings are called to receive the natural world as God's blessing of us and are called to bless God in turn for that blessing.

Schmemann first notes the presence among Christians of two conflicting understandings of how they are called to live their lives. The members of one party see themselves called to lead a life that is "a world in itself, existing apart from the secular world and its life. It is the world of 'spirituality.'... Lost and confused in the noise, the rush and the frustrations of 'life,' man easily accepts the invitation to enter into the inner sanctuary of his soul and to discover there another life, to enjoy a 'spiritual banquet' amply supplied with spiritual food. This spiritual food...will help him to restore his peace of mind, to endure the other—the secular—life." The result of this attitude, says Schmemann, is that the secular life, "the life of eating and drinking," is deprived of any "real meaning."[40]

The "activists" are the opposite of the "spiritualists." They hold that "Christianity has simply lost the world. And the world must be recovered. The Christian mission, therefore, is to catch up with the life that has gone astray. The 'eating' and 'drinking' man is taken quite seriously, almost too seriously. He constitutes the virtually exclusive object of Christian action, and we are constantly called to repent for having spent too much time in contemplation and adoration, in silence and liturgy, for having not dealt sufficiently with the social, political, economic, racial and all other issues of real life."[41]

The alternative Schmemann urges is that the world be received as the gift of God and be returned to God in blessing and thanksgiving. "The food that man eats, the world of which he must partake in order to live, is given to him by God, and it is given as *communion with God*." It is not just material stuff; it is God's "gift," God's "blessing" of God's human creatures. "The only *natural* (and not 'supernatural') reaction of man, to whom God gave this

---

39. In my quotations from Schmemann I will alter some of the punctuation and capitalization.
40. Schmemann (1998), 12.   41. Schmemann (1998), 13.

blessed and sanctified world, is to bless God in return, to thank Him."[42] "The unique position of man in the universe is that he alone is to *bless* God for the food and the life he receives from Him. He alone is to respond to God's blessing with his blessing."[43]

Homo sapiens, homo faber. Yes. "But first of all, *homo adorans.* The first, the basic definition of man is that he is *the priest.* He stands in the center of the world and unifies it in his act of blessing God, of both receiving the world from God and offering it to God.... The world was created as the 'matter,' the material of one all-embracing eucharist, and man was created as the priest of this cosmic sacrament."[44]

Schmemann is right: it is "right and proper" that in response to God's blessing us, human beings would bless God for that which enables us to live as personal bodies. When we do that, our bodies and the material world enter into the content of our prayers. But such prayers can be offered silently, individually. What I have tried to illuminate in this chapter is that when one participates in liturgical enactments, one's body and the material world are not just the content of one's prayers but are *enlisted into* one's praying. It is *with* one's body and *with* the material world that one thanks God *for* one's body and *for* the material world.

42. Schmemann (1998), 15.   43. Schmemann (1998), 14–15.
44. Schmemann (1998), 15.

5

What are those without faith doing in liturgical enactments?

It's easy for those who think and write about liturgy to fall into the habit of thinking of liturgical participants as like themselves: attentive, well-educated, devout adult believers, thoroughly inducted into the relevant liturgical practice. It's a mistake. Those present in liturgical enactments include small children, distracted parents, self-preoccupied teenagers, the bored, the angry, the mentally impaired, persons who have seldom if ever attended a worship service, those who don't understand the unfamiliar words, persons preoccupied by the thought of imminent death, skeptics. Each of these participates in their own distinct way. It would be folly to try to find an analysis of what they are doing that fits all.

Among those present in many liturgical enactments are persons who lack Christian faith. Lacking Christian faith comes, of course, in degrees. For our purposes here, let's say their lack of faith takes the form of not having faith in God and Jesus Christ and not having faith that the claims made in the Apostle's Creed are true. Their lack of faith may lead them to refrain from performing some or all of the prescribed verbal or gestural actions that have count-as significance; alternatively, they may perform those actions in spite of their lack of faith.

My interest in this chapter is especially in the participation of those who perform some of the prescribed verbal, gestural, or auditory actions in spite of their lack of faith. What are such people doing when they participate in this way, and why would they want to participate? My reason for singling out the participation of such people for analysis is that I find it exceptionally difficult to understand, in depth, what those who participate in this way are doing—more difficult than to understand, for example, what those are doing who daydream because they are bored. An ancillary benefit is that some important features of liturgical activity and enactments will come to light that, up to this point, we have not taken note of.

A point made in Chapter 4 must be kept in mind. Most if not all of the verbal, gestural, and auditory acts prescribed by liturgical scripts are conditional: stand if able, sing if able, say if able, and so forth. When the written text for some liturgy says, "All stand," this is to be understood as meaning, "Stand if able." Someone who does not stand because she cannot stand but who nonetheless, in her own way, performs the prescribed counted-as act, has done what is prescribed. Her participation, like that of those who stand, is at that point fully compliant.

Reasons for participating

In his essay, "Liturgical Philosophy," Andrew Chignell makes the following observation about the variety of reasons people have for participating in liturgical enactments:

> Participants in a religious liturgy play a role and follow a script, ... one of the motivations for which is a desire to understand *what it is like* to be a member of the relevant faith community—i.e., to understand what it is like to assert those sorts of things and make those sorts of collective movements and gestures. A participant in the liturgy need not believe the doctrines at all or even think that she believes them; indeed, she might even self-consciously believe their negation. Likewise, she may be unsure as to whether she wants to be a part of the group, and she may be playing the role in order to gain better discernment. Or she may already have decided ... that she wants to be a part of the religious community, and thus be participating in the liturgies ... in an effort not just to get the what-it-is-like knowledge, but to move via "insincerity upwards" into genuine belief.[1]

Chignell is right, of course. Though almost all the verbal, gestural, and auditory actions prescribed by a liturgical script are prescribed for the performance thereby of certain acts of worship, those same actions can be performed, and often are performed, for other reasons than to worship. One might perform them to try out worship for the sorts of exploratory reasons Chignell mentions.[2] Or one might perform them because one has been

---

1. Chignell (n.d.), 7–8.
2. When the prospective leaders of some liturgical enactment practice in advance what they will be doing, this is similar to, but also significantly different from, trying it out. I have been told by

attacked by doubt and finds oneself no longer capable of worshipping God but doesn't want to exclude oneself from the community; one wants to hang on. Who knows, eventually one's doubts may dissipate and one's capacity for worship return.

I judge that the two reasons just mentioned—trying it out and hanging on—are the most common reasons for participating in liturgical enactments other than to worship; but there are others as well. One might participate to give the impression of worshipping. One might participate to show solidarity with the worshippers. Or one might participate because one is coerced. Since I judge that, other than to worship, the most common reasons for participating in liturgical enactments by uttering the words and making the gestures are to try it out or to hang on, it is those that I will refer to in what follows. But the reader should keep in mind that these are just two of many.

The passage quoted from Chignell continues as follows: "Every religious tradition I know of allows for the taking of such a stance by seekers, converts, or initiates, and most concede that such teleological insincerity characterizes many established members of the community as well."[3] The Christian tradition, like other religious traditions, does indeed allow those who lack Christian faith to participate in liturgical enactments for reasons other than to worship—though it must be added that the tradition also includes the periodic emergence of movements protesting participation by such people; the seventeenth- and eighteenth-century "sincerity movement" in England, to be discussed in this chapter, is one of many examples of such movements.

Chignell identifies the mindset of the sort of liturgical participants he has in mind as *not believing the doctrines*. From this I infer that he regards those who do believe the doctrines as paradigmatic participants, other things being equal. Those who do not believe the doctrines are "allowed," but their participation is not paradigmatic.

Shortly I will say something about what Chignell might have in mind with the term "the doctrines"; he himself does not explain. But before we get to that, let me say something about belief. Suppose that by "belief" we mean *belief that* in either of its two forms: belief *that* such-and-such is the case, or belief, about something *that* so-and-so is the case. Call such belief,

those who teach liturgical practice that many students are much more reluctant to practice saying the words and performing the gestures of the sacraments than they are to practice other parts of the liturgy.

3. Chignell (n.d.), 8.

propositional belief. In recent years a number of writers have argued that faith, as commended in Scripture, is not to be identified with propositional belief. Howard Wettstein, in "The Fabric of Faith," argues that the Hebrew Bible almost never uses a word that can be accurately translated into English as "belief." The word often translated as "belief" is *emunah*, meaning "faith." What God asks of God's people is *emunah*, faith. *Emunah*, argues Wettstein, is not cognitive assent but a stance of a certain sort.[4]

In a powerfully argued essay, "Does Faith Entail Belief?" Daniel Howard-Snyder argues that not only is faith not to be identified with propositional belief; it does not entail propositional belief, nor, conversely, does propositional belief entail faith. Faith comes in two forms: faith *in* some person or cause, and faith *that* so-and-so. Howard-Snyder calls the former *objectual* faith and the latter, *propositional* faith.[5] Having faith in my new dentist, as someone who will succeed in diagnosing the cause of my toothache, is neither identical with nor does it entail believing that he will succeed in diagnosing the cause of my toothache. Having faith that the medicine will shrink the cancer is neither identical with nor does it entail believing that the medicine will shrink the cancer. Howard-Snyder defends claims such as these in considerable detail. Faith is trust, not cognitive assent.

In his essay Howard-Snyder addresses the argument of those who appeal to Hebrews 11: 6 in support of the claim that faith in God, as understood in Scripture, entails belief.[6] The passage reads, "Without faith it is impossible to please God, for whoever would approach him must believe that he exists and that he rewards those who seek him." Howard-Snyder observes that whereas the English translation (NRSV) uses two different terms, "faith" and "believe," the original Greek uses two grammatical forms, noun and verb, of the same term: "Without *pisteos* it is impossible to please God, for whoever would approach him must *pisteusai* that he exists and that he rewards those who seek him." A translation that preserved the parallelism in the Greek would read, "Without faith it is impossible to please God, for whoever would approach him must faith that he exists and that he rewards those who seek him."

This, of course, is ungrammatical. Whereas corresponding to our noun "belief" is the verb "to believe," our noun "faith" has no corresponding verb. Nor can we speak of "non-faithers" as we speak of "non-believers."

4. Wettstein (n.d.).   5. Howard-Snyder (2016), 144.   6. Howard-Snyder (2016), 158.

The closest we can come to a fully accurate translation of the Hebrews passage into English would be, "Without faith it is impossible to please God, for whoever would approach him must have faith that he exists and that he rewards those who seek him."[7] The moral to be taken away from this is that almost all English translations of Scripture leave readers with a far more cognitivist understanding of faith in God than do the original Hebrew and Greek.

I inferred from what Chignell said in his essay that he regards *believers* as paradigmatic liturgical participants, other things being equal, of course. But if we attend closely to Scripture in its original languages I think we are led to say that the paradigmatic participants are those who have faith—faith in God and Jesus Christ, and faith that the claims made by the Apostles Creed are true.

For the remainder of our discussion in this chapter we face a choice: shall we ask what *unbelievers* are doing when participating in liturgical enactments, or shall we ask what those who *lack faith* are doing? We could, of course, ask both questions; but that would be cumbersome. Since I hold that the paradigmatic participants are those who have faith, I will ask what those who lack Christian faith are doing when they participate in Christian liturgical enactments.

Chignell described the sort of participants he had in mind as "not believing the doctrines." He doesn't explain what he means by "the doctrines." So let me explain what I think he probably had in mind. Whenever we act, we take certain things for granted. When I put a letter in our mailbox in the morning I take for granted that the mailman will come by later in the day to pick it up—and that the mailbox with my letter in it won't have sunk into the ground before he comes. Many if not most of the things one takes for granted when performing some act are not things one believes, certainly not things one consciously believes at the time—there are far too many of them. When I put a letter in our mailbox for the mailman to pick up I don't consciously believe that the mailbox will not sink into the ground. Do I nonetheless believe it "dispositionally," as some philosophers would say? I doubt that the thought ever crossed my mind before fetching for an example, when writing these words, of *taking something for granted*. Did I nonetheless believe it? I don't know.

What one takes for granted in performing some act is (roughly) that complex of propositions such that, if one believed they were false, one would not perform (or try to perform) the act.[8] What Chignell calls "the doctrines" of some liturgical enactment are then what those who perform the prescribed acts of worship take for granted in performing those acts—about God, about themselves, about human beings more generally, about the world. For example, in thanking God one takes for granted that God exists, that God is the sort of being who can sensibly be thanked, and that God is worthy of being thanked.[9] Let us say that those doctrines are *implicit* in the prescribed liturgical act of thanking God. There is room, of course, for substantial disagreement as to what it is that one takes for granted when performing some prescribed act of worship.

We can now replace the question we set for ourselves with a better one. We asked, what are those who lack Christian faith doing when they participate in Christian liturgical enactments? Let us instead ask, what are those doing who perform some prescribed verbal, gestural, or auditory action but who lack faith that the doctrines implicit in the act of worship prescribed to be performed thereby are true.[10] They say the words "Bless the Lord Oh my soul," but they lack faith that what one takes for granted in blessing God is true.

As Chignell's discussion suggests, the lack of faith can take different forms. It can take the form of firmly believing that the doctrines implicit in some act of worship are false. It can take the form of hoping they are true but not having faith that they are true. Or it can take the form of accepting them as true but not having faith that they are.[11] No doubt we could identify additional attitudes if there were any point in doing so.

---

8. It would not serve our purposes here to refine this formula so that it is not roughly true but strictly true.

9. Howard Wettstein (2014) would disagree that those who thank God are taking these things for granted. Wettstein, a practicing Jew, would say that in praying the prescribed prayers he is addressing God and that it is profoundly right and proper to do so. But he would resist taking the next step of applying the concept of *existence* to God. It's not clear to me whether he would also resist saying about God that God is the sort of being who can sensibly be thanked and who is worthy of being thanked. In general, he is much more comfortable speaking *to* God than *about* God. However, in praying to God he is presumably taking something for granted, reluctant though he is to put that into words. Whatever that is, that would be for him "the doctrines."

10. Strictly speaking, the question to be asked is, what are those doing who perform some pre-scribed verbal, gestural, or auditory action but who lack faith that the doctrines implicit in *what they understand to be* the act of worship prescribed to be performed thereby are true. For the purposes of our discussion here, nothing would be gained by adding the qualifier "what they understand to be."

11. On acceptance, see Alston (1996) and Howard-Snyder (2013).

Chignell's main concern in his essay is to identify what he calls "the liturgical stance" toward the doctrines of liturgical enactments. If it is not required that the participants believe the doctrines, what then is required? Chignell does not settle on an answer to this question. He contents himself with suggesting that philosophers should explore the idea that the liturgical stance toward the doctrines is acceptance. Though participants need not believe the doctrines, they must at least accept them.[12] He does not consider the possibility that *faith* is the stance he is looking for.

I doubt that there is any such thing as "the" liturgical stance toward the doctrines. Not only do liturgical communities differ considerably in the range of stances they allow; it is also typical of Christian liturgical communities to be more tolerant of participation at some points in the liturgy by those who lack faith than at other points—more tolerant of their joining in singing the hymns than of their receiving the Eucharistic elements.

The question that mainly interests me in this chapter is not what forms of non-faith are allowed, though I will have some things to say on that matter toward the end of the chapter, but what it is that those who lack faith are doing when they participate in liturgical enactments by performing the prescribed verbal, gestural, and auditory actions. When they join the other congregants in saying the words, "Thanks be to God," are they thanking God even though they lack faith that the doctrines implicit in that act are true? Or are they just saying the words?

Can those who lack faith thank God?

Before we settle on an answer to these last two questions, let's consider whether both of the alternatives mentioned are possible. Begin with the first. Is it possible to thank God even though one lacks faith that God exists and is the sort of being who can be thanked and who is worthy of being thanked? I think this is possible.

Consider someone who lacks faith that God exists but strongly wishes that God did exist and were the sort of being who can be thanked and who

---

12. There is some inconsistency on this point in Chignell's discussion. In the first passage that I quoted he noted that a participant might "self-consciously believe [the] negation of the doctrines." Though he does not explicitly say so, I infer he thinks that in at least some communities this stance is permitted. But if so, then *acceptance or belief* is not "the" liturgical stance in those communities.

is worthy of being thanked. Suppose he says "Thanks be to God" on the off-chance and in the hope that God does exist and is the sort of being who can be thanked and who is worthy of being thanked. I think that by saying those words this person has in fact thanked God—given that God does exist and is the sort of being who can be thanked and who is worthy of being thanked. Obviously it is not a well-formed instance of thanking God; but it is, I think, an instance of thanking God.

An analogy may help. Suppose a friend of mine has disappeared. He went for a walk one day and never returned; no one has seen him, nor has anyone received a message from him. The police have searched for several months and turned up nothing. I no longer have faith that he is alive.

There is important "unfinished business" between us. I deeply regret something I said to him shortly before his disappearance. I never had a chance to make a face-to-face apology. So I compose a message of apology and send it to his email address on the off-chance and in the hope that he is still alive. Suppose he is still alive and receives my message. Have I apologized to him even though I don't have faith that he is alive? I think I have.

Is it possible for participants in liturgical enactments to just go through the motions?

The other alternative suggested is that those who perform the prescribed verbal or gestural actions but lack faith are just "going through the motions," performing those actions without thereby performing the prescribed acts of worship. Is that possible?

As we saw in Chapter 2, intention does not always determine whether or not one has performed some counted-as action. Raising one's hand at an auction counts as placing a bid no matter what is going through one's mind; one does not get off the hook by saying, even if it's true, "But I didn't intend to bid; I was just stretching my arm." And we all sometimes say what we did not intend to say and do not say what we intended to say. It's on account of certain conventions being in force that when one says, in the course of everyday life, "Thank you," one's saying those words counts as thanking the person whom one is addressing.

Are liturgical enactments different in this regard? Can one suspend the working of linguistic and gestural conventions by just trying out worship? Doesn't saying the words "Thanks be to God" count as thanking God no

matter what one's private state of mind? Doesn't kneeling count as hum-
bling oneself before God no matter what one's intentions?

Consider a prisoner who is falsely accused of having committed some
crime and is coerced by the police into signing a sheet on which are written
words of confession. By signing, the prisoner confesses to the crime. It's a
false confession. He doesn't want to make it; he deeply regrets making it. If
it becomes known that his confession was coerced it will not be admitted
in court and most of us will mitigate our blame of him for what he did,
perhaps to the extent of fully excusing him. Nonetheless, if he signs he does
confess to the crime; if he had not confessed there would be nothing to
regret. If he was mentally competent at the time, then there is no mental
state such that, had he been in that state at the time, his signing the sheet
would not have counted as thereby confessing.

Are liturgical enactments different from these cases, in that the mental
states of the participants—in particular, their intentions—play a role in
determining what they have done? Can their intentions suspend the normal
workings of the conventions of speech and gesture?

Bringing choral groups into the picture will aid in answering the question.
Choral groups typically sing a diverse array of works from the rich heritage
of choral music, with the result that members of such groups often find
themselves singing words that go against their own personal convictions.
Members who do not believe that there will be a Day of Wrath participate
in singing the *Dies Irae* section from settings of the traditional Catholic
Requiem. Jewish members who not believe that Jesus is the lamb of God
participate in singing the *Agnus Dei* section from settings of the traditional
Catholic Mass. Choral groups would find their roster of singers in constant
flux if, for each work, only the true believers sang.

What are those members doing who sing words that do not express their
own personal convictions? Are those who do not believe there will be a Day
of Wrath nonetheless pleading with God to deliver us from the Day of
Wrath when they sing the *Dies Irae*? Are those who do not believe Jesus is
the lamb of God who takes away the sin of the world nonetheless pleading
with Jesus to have mercy on us when they sing the *Agnus Dei*? Surely not.
That may be what the believers are doing; but that's not what they are
doing. They are singing the words, that's all.[13] Choral performances are a

---

13. That said, those who initially just sing the words may eventually find themselves believing.
    A Jewish friend of mine once remarked to me that if he ever converted to Christianity, it
    would probably happen while he was singing Bach's *B minor mass*.

special bounded "zone" in which the normal workings of speech conventions are often suspended.

I suggest that liturgical enactments are like choral performances in this regard; they too are a bounded zone in which the normal workings of the conventions of speech and gesture are often suspended. One can perform the verbal and gestural actions prescribed for some liturgical enactment without thereby performing the prescribed acts of worship. One's performance of those verbal and gestural acts may have no count-as significance whatsoever; one may just be "going through the motions." This is possible because scripted activities are, as I described them in Chapter 1, "bounded" from the ebb and flow of ordinary life.

It's worth noting, by the way, that a performance of a drama is an example of a bounded zone in which the ordinary workings of the conventions of speech and gesture not only *can be* suspended but *are* suspended. When an actor says, "To be or not to be, that is the question," he is not personally declaring that the question is whether to be or not to be. The reason he is not making that declaration is that he is not speaking in his own voice but playing the role of a character who says those words and thereby makes that declaration. On the other hand, it's not possible for him, when playing the role, to just "go through the motions" of saying the words. If he says those words, then perforce he represents the character he is playing as saying those words and thereby making those declarations. Playing a dramatic role is different, in that way, from singing in a choir and from participating in a liturgical enactment. When engaged in these latter activities, one can just "go through the motions."

Our use of language would be undermined if we did not, in most situations, interpret what people say in accord with the extant linguistic conventions. It is not undermined by our making an exception of singing in a choir, participating in liturgical enactments, and playing a role in a dramatic performance. It is not undermined by treating those activities as bounded zones in which the ordinary workings of verbal and gestural conventions can be, and often are, suspended. Once the choir performance is over, once the liturgical enactment is concluded, once the dramatic performance is finished, the ordinary conventions once again apply to the participants; they have stepped out of the bounded zone.[14]

---

14. Of course, it is also possible, in ordinary life, to suspend the working of the conventions. One might, for example, make clear that one is just sounding out the words.

What determines whether one is performing acts of worship or just saying the words and making the gestures?

We have considered two possibilities as to what those who lack faith are doing when they participate in liturgical enactments by performing the prescribed verbal and gestural acts: they may thereby be performing the prescribed acts of worship, or they may just be going through the motions of saying the words and making the gestures. Before we consider which of these two possibilities is actual, let's ask what determines whether the person is performing the prescribed acts of worship or just "going through the motions."

Quite clearly it is the presence or absence of an intention of a certain sort that is determinative. One possibility as to the nature of that intention is this: if one performs some verbal or gestural action with the intention of thereby doing whatever is prescribed to be done thereby, then, whether or not one knows what that is, one has performed that action; otherwise one has not.

I do not find this principle plausible. The sort of intention mentioned is relatively sophisticated. I would guess that few people have ever formed such an intention; certainly children have not. Nonetheless, children can and do worship God.

I suggest that the relevant principle is, rather, this: if a participant performs some prescribed verbal or gestural action with the intention of *not* thereby performing whatever be the act of worship prescribed to be performed thereby, then he has not performed that act of worship; otherwise he has.[15] An intention of that sort in that sort of situation blocks the normal working of the relevant convention.[16]

Suppose this principle is correct. Why is it correct? Why is it the case that intentions, specifically, *negative* intentions, are determinative in liturgical enactments and choral performances in a way that they are typically not

---

15. A qualification is necessary. Someone who performs some prescribed verbal or gestural action without the intention of not performing the act of worship prescribed to be done thereby will not have performed that act of worship if he lacks the mental capacity for doing so because he is a small child or mentally impaired.
16. A possibility in addition to those considered in the text is that by mindlessly saying certain words one might thank God without meaning to.

determinative in ordinary affairs? Why do we treat liturgical enactments and choral performances as bounded zones in this respect?

Partly, I think, because, in ordinary affairs we ourselves for the most part choose words to say what we want to say and gestures to do what we want to do, whereas in liturgical enactments we do not choose the words and the gestures; they are prescribed.[17] That leads us to "cut more slack" for the person who performs those verbal and gestural acts in the context of a bounded liturgical enactment than we would in ordinary life.

But that cannot be the whole of the matter; the words of the prisoner who signs a confession under duress are also prescribed for him. I think the reason we treat confessions differently from participation in liturgical enactments is that usually it's important to know whether someone really was confessing to some crime by saying or signing some words of confession, whereas most of us do not ordinarily regard it as important to know whether someone was performing the prescribed acts of worship by performing the prescribed verbal and gestural acts. As we shall see, the members of the eighteenth-century sincerity movement in England were of a different opinion; they thought it important to know whether someone was really worshipping or just trying it out or hanging on.

I have not yet directly answered the question I posed in this section. When those who lack faith participate in some liturgical enactment by performing the prescribed verbal and gestural actions, are they thereby also performing the acts of worship prescribed to be performed thereby or are they just going through the motions? We have seen that, in principle, each of these modes of participation is possible.

The answer to our question is now obvious: it all depends on the presence or absence of intentions of the sort we have identified. If it is the intention of the participant, when performing the prescribed verbal and gestural acts, that he not thereby perform the prescribed acts of worship, then he has not performed them; otherwise he has.

---

17. I say "for the most part" because the ordinary lives of all of us include mini-scripts. The check-out employees at the grocery store where my wife and I customarily shop invariably ask, "Did you find everything you were looking for?" I feel sure that this is not just a formulaic sentence that they fall into using, like "How are you doing?" They've been taught to use it; it's prescribed by the script for check-out employees. If they did not ask the question, they would be acting incorrectly.

Not many have faith throughout

I took over from Chignell's essay the binary, *participating for the purpose of worshipping* versus *participating for the purpose* of *trying it out or hanging on*. And I adapted from his essay the binary, *those who have faith in the doctrines* versus *those who lack faith in the doctrines*. Up to this point in our discussion these binaries have proved useful. But they conceal what actually takes place in liturgical enactments. Perhaps a few of those who participate in liturgical enactments do so without having faith in any of the doctrines. But probably most of those who are trying out worship or hanging on have faith in some of the doctrines. Conversely, there are probably few participants who are so devout as to have faith in all the doctrines. Let me develop this second point a bit.

In "The Holy Eucharist: Rite One" of the Episcopal Church, the congregants say the following words as part of the prayer of confession: "The remembrance of [our misdoings] is grievous unto us, the burden of them is intolerable."[18] The act of worship to be performed by saying these words is confessing to God that the remembrance of one's misdoings is grievous and their burden intolerable. I would guess that few present-day Episcopalians find the burden of their misdoings intolerable.

In Protestant and Catholic churches it is especially the hymns that pose problems. In Eastern Orthodoxy the hymns to be sung are specified by the liturgical text. Not so in Protestant and Catholic churches; whoever has liturgical authority in the local congregation chooses the hymns to be sung. The words of the hymns are so diverse in theology, imagery, sentiment, and the like that almost all who participate faithfully over a length of time find themselves confronted, on occasion, with thoughts and images that they find unacceptable.

Recently I was confronted with the following words in one of the hymns for the day:

> Within the arms of sovereign love we ever shall remain;
> nor shall the rage of earth or hell make God's sure counsel vain.
> Each one of all the chosen race shall surely heaven attain;
> here they will share abounding grace, and there with Jesus reign.

18. *Book of Common Prayer* (1979), 331.

I interpret these words as alluding to the Augustinian doctrine of predestination. The main support for this doctrine has always been a certain interpretation of what Paul said about justification and election in his letter to the Romans. It is my view that the traditional interpretation of Romans is a misinterpretation.[19] Paul was not teaching predestination, as that has traditionally been understood. I hold that the traditional doctrine has no biblical basis and should be rejected. So what was I to do when confronted with these words in an unfamiliar hymn prescribed for the day? We were into the third line before I realized what was being said. I then refrained from singing the last line. Could I instead have sung the words of the last line without meaning them?

It is to minimize the sort of predicament I experienced that hymn books are regularly revised in accord with changes in the theology and religious sensibility of the community. Recently my own denomination, the Christian Reformed Church in North America, published a new hymnal jointly with the Reformed Church in America.[20] Previous hymnals of the denomination included the well-known nineteenth-century hymns, "Onward Christian soldiers, Marching as to war" and "There is a fountain filled with blood, Drawn from Emanuel's veins." Neither of these hymns is included in the new hymnal.

The Maimonides option

We have discussed two possibilities as to what those are doing who participate in some liturgical enactment by performing the prescribed verbal, gestural, and auditory actions but lack faith in the doctrines. One possibility is that they are doing nothing more than performing those actions. The other possibility is that they are, at certain points, performing the prescribed acts of worship even though they lack faith in the doctrines implicit in those acts. There is another possibility to which I have not thus far called attention: they might be performing acts of worship other than those prescribed. Let me call this "the Maimonides option," since it was the medieval Jewish

---

19. I defend this view and propose an alternative interpretation in chapters 20 and 21 of Wolterstorff (2011a), 243–82.
20. *Lift Up Your Hearts* (2013).

theologian, Moses Maimonides, who strongly recommended this option to his students.

Maimonides addressed his masterpiece, *The Guide of the Perplexed*, to Joseph, possibly a real person, but more likely not. Joseph was a devout young Jew who read Torah and prayed the prayers of his Jewish tradition. But Joseph was also a bright and dedicated student of philosophical theology. This combination of activities, to both of which he was committed, left him deeply perplexed. The understanding of God arrived at in the philosophy classroom was profoundly different from that which appeared to be implicit and explicit in Torah and in the prayers. In the classroom he learned that "the description of God by means of negative terms is the only sound description which contains no element of loose terminology, and implies altogether in no circumstances a lack of perfection in God. [The description of God] by positive terms, on the other hand, imports polytheism and a lack of perfection in God."[21] But Torah and the prayers are full of sentences that ascribe positive terms to God. So Joseph is confused, and sees himself faced by a dilemma.

> Either he follows his reason and rejects those expressions [in Torah and the prophets] as he has been taught to understand them: then he will think that he is rejecting the dogmas of our religion. Or he continues to accept them in the way he has been taught to understand them and refuses to be guided by his reason. He thus brusquely turns his back on his own reason; yet he cannot help but feel that his faith has been gravely impaired. He will continue to hold those fanciful beliefs although they inspire him with uneasiness and disgust, and be continuously sick at heart and utterly bewildered in his mind.[22]

The aim of Maimonides in *The Guide* was to alleviate Joseph's perplexity by showing how the terms ascribed to God in Torah and in the prayers can be interpreted so that what is said of God by using them is consistent with what has been learned in the philosophy classroom. For example: in Torah and in the prayers we find the positive terms "omnipotent," "omniscient," and "possessed of will" applied to God. We should interpret these terms as meaning that God "is neither powerless nor ignorant nor distracted nor disinterested"—all negative concepts.[23]

In short, Maimonides proposed that his students in philosophy of religion develop a distinct idiolect. When terms and sentences from the Torah and the liturgy are uttered with the meaning they have in this alternative

21. Maimonides (1995), 79.   22. Maimonides (1995), 41.   23. Maimonides (1995), 81.

idiolect, rather than with the meaning they have in the idiom authorized by the synagogue, one can in good conscience not only join in saying the words of the prayers but also join in praying.

The Maimonides option is always available to those who lack faith in the doctrines. By employing the Maimonides option they can perform the prescribed verbal and gestural acts and thereby perform their own distinct acts of worship.[24]

The sincerity movement

Lori Branch, in the first chapter of *The Rituals of Spontaneity: Sentiment and Secularism from Free Prayer to Wordsworth*, tells the story of the emergence in the early modern period, especially in England, of a religious mentality that differed sharply from what preceded. The mentality she describes lives on to the present day in some quarters.[25] The chapter is titled, "The Rejection of Liturgy, the Rise of Free Prayer, and Modern Religious Subjectivity." Those who shared this mentality would contest the claim that a legitimate reason for participating in some liturgical enactment is to try it out or to hang on. They insisted that only those who have true faith and who assemble for the purpose of worshipping God should participate in liturgical enactments. Let us consider their case.

The central component in the new mentality was the prizing of religious sincerity, this being understood as expressing in words the religious affections and emotions one feels at the moment. Prayer, wrote John Bunyan, "is a sincere, sensible, affectionate pouring out of the heart or soul to God through Christ."[26] Matthew Henry encouraged his readers to cultivate the "sincere representation of holy affections."[27] Henry Dawbeny, in his treatise

---

24. Was Howard Wettstein, whose liturgical practice I briefly described in footnote 4 of this chapter, practicing the Maimonides alternative? I think not. Wettstein does not regard his understanding of what he is doing when he is praying as rejecting what is prescribed. He does not regard the traditional conservative understanding as prescribed, whereas Maimonides quite clearly did.

25. A good description of some of the ways in which it lives on is to be found in Witvliet (2015). Seligman et al. (2008) contrast sincere action with conventional action, meaning by "sincere" action, action that is expressive of the inner self of the agent. They argue that though both modes of action are present in all societies, in the modern West there are dynamics pressing toward the increase of sincere action and the decrease of conventional action. They refer the reader to Lionel Trilling's *Sincerity and Authenticity* (1972).

26. From Bunyan's *I Will Pray with the Spirit* (1663). Quoted in Branch (2006), 43.

27. From Henry's *A Method for Prayer* (1710); quoted in Branch (2006), 45.

of 1661, *A Sober and Temperate Discourse, Concerning the Interest of Words in Prayer*, made the point more elaborately. We must, he says, follow

> the directions which our *Holy Father* hath given us in his Word for the *acceptable performance* of prayer. God's commandment obligeth us to a performance of [prayer] under such *Circumstances*, as shall neither divert the *intention of our mind*, nor cool the *fervour in our Spirits*, which two things are most essentially necessary to the acceptable performance of our duty in it…and without which our performance is but *lip-labour*, and *lost labour*; yea, no other than a most gross *hypocrisie*, and *mocking* of him *who cannot be mocked*.[28]

In short, we are to prize sincerity because God requires sincerity.

The prizing of sincerity led the members of the movement to oppose set prayers. It might just happen that the words of some set prayer express perfectly one's religious feelings. But that would be rare. Usually when saying a set prayer one finds oneself saying what one does not feel at the time and not saying what one does feel. Thus it was that the proponents of sincerity were opposed not just to the imposition of *The Book of Common Prayer* but to all prescribed words for prayer. The pseudonymous author of *The Common Prayer-Book Unmasked* described *The Book of Common Prayer* as the "very transplantation of the Essence or nature of Prayer, wherein the words are to follow the affections, and not the affections the words, as it doth in the best set forms."[29]

Branch summarizes as follows the line of thought that led members of the sincerity movement to oppose set prayers: "Even more than doctrinal correctness,…the element of true prayer lacking in those who use forms is emotional authenticity and sincerity, to which spontaneous, unwritten, and unpremeditated verbal prayer testifies and to which the formulaic repetition of liturgy is inimical."[30]

Isaac Watts was a paradigmatic example and proponent of the new mentality. He wrote about set prayers:

> 'Tis very apt to make our Spirits cold and flat, formal and indifferent in our Devotion:The frequent Repetition of the same Words doth not always awaken the same Affections in our Hearts which perhaps they were well suited to do when we first heard or made use of them. When we continually tread one constant Road of Sentences or track of Expressions, they become like an old

---

28. Quoted in Branch (2006), 46. Emphasis in the original.
29. From *The Common Prayer-Book Unmasked* (1660); quoted in Branch (2006), 43.
30. Branch (2006), 43.

beaten Path in which we daily travel, and we are ready to walk on without particular Notice of the several parts of the way; so in our daily Repetition of a Form, we neglect due Attention to the full Sense of the Words. But there is something more suited to awaken the attention of the Mind in a conceived Prayer; when a Christian is making his own way toward God according to the present Inclination of his Soul and urgency of his present Wants; ... While we are clothing the Sense of our Hearts in fit Expressions, and as it were digging the matter of our Prayers out of our own Feelings and Experiences, it must needs keep the Heart closer at work.[31]

There was something deeply ironic about Watts objecting to "the frequent repetition of the same words." Watts was one of the great hymn writers of the English tradition.[32] The hymns he composed were first sung by his own congregation in Southampton and then printed and reprinted many times and widely distributed. They became enormously popular. Was not the widespread singing of Watts's hymns "repetition of the same words" on a massive scale?[33]

It was not repetition as such that Watts found objectionable. His basic thought comes to the fore in the last few sentences of the passage quoted. The aim of each Christian should be "making his own way toward God according to the present inclination of his soul and urgency of his present wants" by finding words to express that present inclination and urgency. In short, it was the *prescription of words* for prayer that Watts found objectionable, not repetition as such. It would be a matter of sheer happenstance if prescribed words proved apt for expressing one's "present inclination" and "urgency"; and even if they did prove to be apt, it's likely that frequent repetition would lead one to say them without fully meaning them. Prayers that employ set words will seldom be sincere; that was Watts's basic point.

Of course, it was no less ironic that Isaac Watts, the hymn writer, would object to prescribed words than that he would object to repetition. When singing a hymn, one is singing set words. And it's likely that, when doing so,

---

31. Quoted in Branch (2006), 46–7. Milton's language was more vehement: "To imprison and confine by force, into a Pinfold set of words, those two most unimprisonable things, our Prayer and that Divine Spirit of utterance that moves them, is a tyranny that would have longer hands than those Giants who threatn'd bondage to Heav'n." Quoted in Branch (2006), 46.
32. Many of his compositions were not freely composed hymns but versifications of the psalms.
33. On the matter of repetition, Marilyn Adams writes these wise words: "Adults who regularly put themselves in the pew, who avail themselves of incense and holy water (à la Pascal), expose their unconscious selves and senses to being formed and informed by symbolically loaded liturgy, without or without much conscious faith or goodwill towards God. *Pace* Protestant reformers, such structured repetition is not vain in religion any more than it is in the pedagogy of mathematics and language learning." M. Adams (2006), 298.

one will sometimes find oneself singing words that do not express what one feels at the moment and not singing words that would express what one feels. Was it the view of Watts and others that sincerity is obligatory when saying words but not when singing words? Watts's hymns, for the most part, were not prayers but expressions of praise and thanksgiving. Was that difference thought to be relevant? Was it the view of Watts and others that sincerity is obligatory for petitionary prayer but not for praise and thanksgiving? Not likely.

The accepted role of the minister in leading worship also posed a problem for sincerity. It is especially important that ministers pray with full sincerity, expressing exactly the religious emotions and affections they feel at the moment. But the minister's role is not just to pray his own personal prayer but to lead the people in their praying. The people are to pray with the words that the minister utters. So it turns out that prescription of words for the prayers of the people has not disappeared; rather, the words prescribed for prayers by the people are not words printed in *The Book of Common Prayer* but words uttered by the local minister on the spot.

Henry Dawbeny recognized the problem. This is what he said:

[the minister] needs be no further careful of words in Prayer...than [of] the use of other words, to warm the hearts of those that are to joyn with him, and to boyl them up to a greater degree of *fervency in spirit*.... And indeed, those *phrases* which do this excellent deed, are experimentally found to be such as the inwardly affected heart of the Speaker immediately dictates to his Tongue.... words coming from the heart of the Speaker, find the nearest and readiest way to the heart of the Hearer...as if there were a *Sympathy of devout Souls*, which is indeed from the mighty secret working of the same spirit of Prayer acting in both, and at the same time preparing the Speakers heart and tongue to dictate and speak, and the Hearers souls to hear, sigh, groan, and to give a fiducial assent.

I quoted the pseudonymous author of *The Common Prayer-Book Unmasked* inveighing against the use of the Prayer Book on the ground that whereas words should follow the affections, what happens, at best, when the Prayer Book is used is that affections follow the words. In the passage just quoted, Dawbeny urges the preacher to find words that both express his own "inwardly affected heart" and stir up that same "fervency in spirit" in the people. It's a nice question whether, on a regular basis, the same words can perform this double function. But be that as it may; when things go well in congregational prayer, the words follow the affections for the minister whereas the affections follow the words for the people.

In Branch's summary, quoted in this section, of the line of thought that led members of the sincerity movement to oppose set prayers, she notes that "spontaneous, unwritten, and unpremeditated verbal prayer" was regarded as testifying to the "emotional authenticity and sincerity" of the prayer. There was, indeed, much praise of spontaneity in prayer. The picture that comes to mind, of the person who prays with full sincerity, is that the words well up and pour forth. However, I judge this to be hyperbolic of what the sincerity advocates actually had in mind. What they had in mind, so I suggest, was that to pray sincerely one must oneself choose the words to express one's religious emotions and affections; no one can do that for one. The words need not well up and pour forth spontaneously; one might put considerable forethought into them. But one has to make the choice oneself.

Guidebooks for free prayer began to appear. Reading between the lines, laypeople—and probably ministers as well—found that they were not adept at finding words to express their religious emotions and affections. The guidebooks were intended to help them find words. Isaac Watts published a *Guide to Prayer* (1715) containing "*Directions* how to attain a rich Treasure of Expression in Prayer." "Seek after those ways of Expression that are pathetical," he wrote, "such as denote the Fervency of Affection and carry Life and Spirit with them."[34] Most of the expressions Watts recommended were taken from Scripture.

The most popular and influential of these guides for free prayer was Matthew Henry's *A Method for Prayer, with Scripture Expressions Proper to be Us'd under each Head*, first published in 1710 and often reprinted. This is what he says in one place:

> I would advise that the *Sacred* Dialect be most us'd...that Language that Christian people are most accustom'd to, most affected with, and will most readily agree to.... this is *sound Speech that cannot be condemn'd*. And those that are able to do it may do well to enlarge by way of Descant or Paraphrase upon the Scriptures they make use of; still speaking according to that Rule, and comparing spiritual things with spiritual, that they may illustrate each other.[35]

Henry, in this passage, strikes a significantly different note from that struck by Watts in the passage quoted above. Evidently Henry thought that the free prayers people were offering were not entirely "sound." Were they unsound because the one praying had not managed to find the right words to express

34. Quotations from Branch (2006), 56.
35. Quoted in Branch (2006), 57. Emphasis in the original.

her sound religious emotions and affections, or were they unsound because those feelings were themselves unsound? Henry doesn't say in this passage. But there is another passage in which he clearly has his eye on defects in the feelings themselves, not on defects in the words used to express the feelings. In the introduction to *A Method* he wrote, "It is desirable that our Prayers should be *copious* and *full*. This Storehouse of Materials for Prayer may be of use to put us in remembrance of our several Errands at the Throne of Grace, that none may be quite forgotten."[36] The thought is clearly that when our prayers are not as copious and full as they should be, that's not because we have failed to find copious and full words but because our religious emotions and affections are themselves not copious and full. We have "forgotten" the full range of what we should feel grateful for. Henry aims to "put us in remembrance" of what we have forgotten.

It will be clear by now that, strictly speaking, there was no such thing as a "rejection of liturgy" in the early modern period in England. When the Puritans and the Dissenters assembled for worship they gave a great deal of authority to the local minister to determine the prescriptions for the day. That was not a rejection of liturgical authority but a displacement of liturgical authority from the national church to the local minister. They rejected the use of set texts for the prayers. But they happily used set texts for their singing, repeating those texts over and over. The minister had the authority to choose the words for the congregational prayer. But the *Directory* closely prescribed the content of his prayers. And whether or not the *Directory* was followed, the words that the minister chose for the prayer were thereby prescribed for the congregation. In short, when one looks closely at what members of the late seventeenth- and early eighteenth-century sincerity movement were advocating, one sees that they were not opposed to liturgical prescriptions in general but only to certain sorts of liturgical prescriptions.

The place of sincerity in liturgical enactments

I opened this chapter by observing that most Christian traditions permit the participation in liturgical enactments of those who lack Christian faith; we then explored what such persons are doing when they participate. The members of the sincerity movement would have excluded such people from participation. How should we appraise their line of thought?

36. Quoted in Branch (2006), 57.

A central thesis of my discussion in this volume is that Christian liturgical enactments are for worshipping God—not for placating God, not for appeasing God, not for "centering oneself"—but also not for expressing worshipful feelings. I assume that the act-type of worshipping God is not identical with the act-type of expressing worshipful feelings for God.

Might some members of the sincerity movement have implicitly denied this assumption? Might some have confused worshipping God with expressing worshipful feelings for God? Possibly. But if so, it's easy to see that they would have been mistaken. Here's an analogy. Suppose I want to thank you for a favor you did me. By virtue of various conventions in effect in our society, my writing the appropriate words in a note, signing the note, and posting it to you, counts as my thanking you. It's not necessary that, when writing, signing, and posting the note, I have *feelings* of thankfulness toward you. It would be strange, indeed, if I had had no feelings of thankfulness at the time the favor was done or when I learned about it; but that time may be well in the past and those feelings may have faded away. Conversely, I might address my expression of thankful feelings for you to someone else, in which case I would not have thanked you. From the fact that one can thank someone without expressing thankful feelings for that person and that one can express thankful feelings for someone without thanking that person it follows that thanking someone is not to be identified with expressing thankful feelings for that person. So too for worshipping God and expressing worshipful feelings for God.

Might some members of the sincerity movement have accepted my claim, that the act-type of worshipping God is not to be identified with the act-type of expressing worshipful feelings for God, but denied my central thesis, that Christian liturgical enactments are for worshipping God? Might some have been of the view that Christian liturgical enactments are for expressing worshipful feelings for God—not for thanking God, but for expressing thankful feelings for God, and so forth? Possibly; but not, I think, very likely. This sort of subjectivizing would have been a significant innovation in the Christian tradition. Had they intended that innovation, I think it likely they would have said so clearly and argued for it articulately.

As I interpret them, the members of the sincerity movement were neither contesting my central thesis, that Christian liturgical enactments are for worshipping God, nor contesting the assumption behind that thesis, that worshipping God is not to be identified with expressing worshipful feelings for God. They were instead insisting that worship of God ought always to be sincere, and that a condition of its being sincere is that one have worshipful feelings for God and that one's worship be an expression of those feelings. Let me first consider their claim that sincerity is conditioned on expression of feelings, and then consider their claim that worship ought always to be sincere.

Their claim concerning the sincerity condition for worship was mistaken. Whether or not one's act of thanking God is sincere is determined not by whether or not one has *feelings* of thankfulness to God at the time but by whether or not one is in the state of *being thankful*. The state of *being thankful* to someone is obviously connected with *having feelings of thankfulness* toward them: the state includes the disposition to have the feelings. But the two are not the same: one can be in that state at a certain time without having those feelings at that time. Being in the state of *being thankful* is the sincerity condition for thanking someone, being in the state of *being regretful* is the sincerity condition for telling someone that one regrets what one did to her, and so forth. The sincerity condition for thanking God is not having *feelings of thankfulness* toward God at the time but *being thankful* to God.

What then about the claim that worship of God ought always to be sincere: might the members of the sincerity movement have been wrong in their assumption that a condition of sincere worship is having and expressing worshipful feelings but right in their insistence that worship ought always to be sincere?

Suppose my suggestion as to what is required for sincerity is correct, that the condition for being sincere in thanking someone is that one *be thankful* for what they have done, and so forth. Then I think it is not true, in general, that sincerity in worship is obligatory. Desirable, indeed; but not obligatory. It appears to me that a child can join in thanking God without being in the state of being thankful to God for what God has done. It appears to me that an adult can do so as well. In the case of an adult it requires a certain mindlessness; but such mindlessness in worship is not unheard of. Neither in the case of the child nor in the case of the mindless adult would their thanking God satisfy the condition for being sincere. Is it then blameworthy? Not so far as I can see.

An important point to be noted here is that from the fact that one's thanking God does not satisfy the sincerity condition for that act it does not follow that what one did is *in*-sincere. It may be neither sincere nor *in*-sincere. To be *in*-sincere in thanking God, one must actually *be non-thankful* toward God; one must regard God as not worthy of thanks. It's not enough not to be in the state of *being thankful*; one must be in the state of *being non-thankful*.

Thanking God *in*-sincerely seems to me not just uncommon but rare. If it does ever happen, I agree with members of the sincerity movement that it is blameworthy. But why would someone who is non-thankful toward God—someone who regards God as not worthy of thanks—nonetheless thank God? Though one can be coerced or intimidated into saying the words, "Thanks be to God," one cannot be coerced or intimidated into thanking God by saying those words.

Once more: those who lack faith

Back to those who lack faith. Is their participation in liturgical enactments lacking in sincerity? Worse yet: is it *in*-sincere?

Suppose they are just voicing the words and making the gestures; then the issue of whether they have acted sincerely does not arise, nor does the issue arise of whether they have acted insincerely. The mere voicing of words and the mere making of gestures are not actions to which the concepts of *sincerity* and *insincerity* apply. Participants who just voice the words or just make gestures are like the Jewish person who participates in a choral performance of one of the settings of the *Agnus Dei* and sings the words, "O lamb of God, that takes away the sin of the world, have mercy on us." She is acting neither sincerely nor insincerely.

As we saw, however, it's possible even for those who lack faith to thank God, to praise God, and so forth. They can do so on the off-chance that God does exist and is worthy of thanks and praise. But if they lack faith that God exists, then presumably they will not be in the state of being thankful to God; so their action of thanking God won't satisfy the sincerity condition for that action. They will also not be in the state of regarding God as meriting no gratitude; so their action of thanking God won't satisfy the *in*-sincerity condition for thanking God. Their action of thanking God is done neither sincerely nor insincerely.

The members of the eighteenth-century sincerity movement would have taken the participation in liturgical enactments of those who lack faith as a paradigm example of insincerity. They were wrong about that. On a close look, their participation proves to be neither sincere nor insincere.

PART
II

Liturgy and Scripture

6

On the liturgical reading and singing of Scripture

Christianity is like many other religions in that its liturgical enactments are not only formed and shaped by its sacred text but explicitly invoke that text. This "invocation," as I shall call it, takes a number of different forms. Our project in this part of our discussion, Part II, is to identify and analyze some of those different forms of invocation.

Let's begin with the most obvious form of invocation, namely, the reading aloud, chanting, singing, and reciting from memory of passages from biblical texts. Already by the middle of the second century it was the practice to read aloud passages from what is now the New Testament. Justin Martyr, writing about liturgical practice in the church of Rome around 150 AD, says about the ordinary Sunday liturgy, "the memoirs of the apostles or the writings of the prophets are read for as long as time allows."[1]

Though reading aloud, chanting, singing, and reciting from memory are distinctly different activities, the points I will be making in this chapter

---

1. *Apologia* I.57. In Deiss (1979), 93.

apply to all of them. So rather than referring ad nauseam to all four of these activities, let me focus on the reading aloud of Scripture in the liturgy. When it proves necessary to refer to all four, I will speak of *vocalizing* Scripture.

Where you and I would read a text silently, it was the practice in the ancient world to read the text aloud—to sound the words out. No big difference between reading it silently and reading it aloud to oneself. What we will learn in this chapter is that between the silent reading of a text and the liturgical vocalizing of the text there are great differences. The silent reading of a text is relatively easy to understand; what is going on in the liturgical vocalizing of passages from Scripture proves surprisingly complicated.

I will first discuss the reading aloud by a lector of narrative passages from Scripture in which the author does not refer to himself; I will then discuss the reading aloud by a lector of biblical passages, other than the psalms, in which the author does refer to himself; I will conclude with a discussion of the vocalizing of the psalms by the people.

The type-token distinction is once again indispensable. Our English term "word" is ambiguous as between a universal that can be multiply instantiated and a particular instantiation of that universal; the former is a *type*, the latter, a *token* of the type. In the preceding paragraph there are three instantiations (inscriptions) of the word "will"—three tokens of the type.[2] In modern languages, most words can be both written down and sounded out; they can have both inscribed tokens and auditory tokens.

The four ways of engaging biblical texts that I mentioned—reading aloud, chanting, singing, and reciting from memory—are alike in that they result in the bringing about of a new token of the text, specifically, an auditory token. They are, in that way, unlike reading a text silently. Reading a text silently does not produce a new token; it is not productive in the way that vocalizing a text is productive.

When liturgical participants vocalize a biblical text, are they doing something more than just producing new tokens of the text? Are they also *saying* something? By performing the *locutionary* act of vocalizing the text are they also performing some *illocutionary* act? Let me state the question I have in mind more precisely. In Chapter 5 we saw that it is possible to perform

---

2. To speak more precisely: in any *copy* of this volume there are three tokens of the word "will" in the preceding paragraph.

the verbal and gestural acts prescribed for some liturgical enactment without performing the acts of worship prescribed to be performed thereby. The participants I have in mind in this chapter are not such participants but, instead, those who are fully compliant with the script. Do they just vocalize the prescribed biblical passages without saying anything thereby? Or do they, by vocalizing, say something, that is, perform some illocutionary act?

To me it seems obvious that they do say something. When fully compliant participants sing some biblical passage, they are not just singing words; they are saying something, performing some illocutionary act. And when the person assigned the role of reader or lector reads aloud some biblical passage she is not just vocalizing the text; she is thereby performing some illocutionary act. That, I say, seems obvious. What is not at all obvious is the sorts of illocutionary acts that the participants are performing. Identifying those will occupy our attention for the remainder of this chapter.

What is a lector doing when reading aloud a narrative passage from Scripture?

In almost all Christian liturgical enactments, a person who has been assigned the role of reader or lector reads aloud one or more passages from Scripture. Often what is read aloud has the form of a narrative. Let's begin there.

What is the lector saying when she reads aloud one of the many narrative passages to be found in Scripture—a passage from one of the gospels, for example? What sort of illocutionary acts is she performing? Some of the biblical narratives include first- and second-person pronouns: I, me, my, mine, we, us, ours, you, yours. The reading of such passages raises special issues of interpretation; I propose setting those issues off to the side for the time being and coming back to them in the section "What is the lector doing when reading biblical passages that contain first- and second-person pronouns?"

When someone narrates something, we can distinguish between the narrating and what's narrated—between the telling and what's told. The narrating or telling is an act; what's narrated or told is a proposition or sequence of propositions, for example, *that once upon a time there was an old woman living by herself deep in a wood*. The terms "story," "narrative," and "narration" are ambiguous as between the act of telling and what's told. To avoid confusion, I will use the term "narration" exclusively for the act of telling, the narrating; and I will reserve the terms "narrative" and "story" for what's told.

One can tell a story as what happened or one can tell a story as fiction. We in the modern world tend to draw a sharp distinction between these two rhetorical moods of story-telling—between these two *narrational stances*. In general, we want our narrators to be clear in their own minds as to which of these stances they are employing and to indicate that stance clearly to us, their readers or auditors. Has the author labeled the story "a novel" or "a short story"? Then she is telling it as fiction. Has she labeled it "history," "biography," "autobiography," or "memoir"? Then she is telling it as what happened.

Members of pre-modern societies would also have made and employed the distinction between telling a story as what happened and telling a story as fiction; they could not have managed ordinary communal life without employing the distinction. It would have been important to know whether someone who was telling a story about seeing the enemy lurking in the forest was telling it as what happened or telling it as fiction. It seems clear, however, that in many situations, members of pre-modern societies had no interest in employing the distinction. The important thing was the story itself, not the rhetorical mood of its telling.

We all accept that our writers of fiction frequently incorporate within their stories narratives of what actually happened somewhere sometime, often without indicating that that is what they are doing; Tolstoy's *War and Peace* is a famous example of the point. Our attitude toward history and biography is different. We are purists. We do not want our historians and biographers to make things up. We allow them to order incidents in their *narration* differently from the order in which they occurred; we allow flashbacks and flashforwards. But we do not want them to order incidents in the *narrative* differently from the order in which they occurred.

The attitude in the ancient world was often quite different. Within the context of telling a story as what happened a writer would embellish episodes beyond his evidence, rearrange sequences, combine distinct episodes into one episode, paraphrase what persons had said, flesh out what they had said, imagine what they were thinking, and so forth, all in order better to achieve the point of telling the story. That point was never simply to narrate what had happened *wie es eigentlich geschehen ist*. The point was rather to illuminate the character of the persons in the narrative, to highlight the significance of the events, to heighten the desired effect of the narration on listeners or readers, and so forth. Let me call this way of narrating what happened, *pre-modern narration*. The gospel writers employed pre-modern narration.[3] Their overall aim, in telling the story of Jesus, was to explain to their readers who was this strange and mysterious person and what was the significance of the things he did and underwent.

Another difference between ancient and present-day narrators is that whereas we demand of our writers of history, biography, etc. that they be sparing of figurative speech—"tell us literally what happened"—ancient writers were not so constrained. Most modern readers of the Old Testament book of *Joshua* assume that the author/editor was telling his story as what happened and was speaking literally in his description of the battles Israel waged under Joshua's leadership. Scholars then go on to ask two questions: is there archeological evidence that the story is approximately true to what actually happened, and why is this story of bloody slaughter included in the canon?

I have argued elsewhere that this way of interpreting the book is mistaken.[4] Though the story is quite clearly told as what happened, not as fiction, the text contains numerous internal indications that it is not to be interpreted literally but as a formulaic, hyperbolic, and metaphorical hagiography of Joshua as military leader. Several times over, for example, we read the formulaic declaration, "All the inhabitants of the city were slain with the edge of the sword." Yet toward the end of the book, and in its companion volume, *Judges*, we learn that some of those cities and their inhabitants survived the conquest. At most what we can infer as to what the writer/editor was claiming is that under Joshua's leadership Israel won some significant skirmishes with Canaanite tribes and cities.

Back to our question. We agreed that when a reader or lector reads a narrative passage from Scripture, she is not just producing new auditory tokens of the text but is also thereby *saying* something, performing certain illocutionary acts. Our question was: what sorts of illocutionary acts is she performing?

I suggest that the lector is re-telling the story, re-narrating the narrative. The biblical author or editor told the story long ago. The lector is now telling that same story again, doing so by vocalizing the words of the original telling or a translation of those words. It's like a child saying to his or her parent, "Tell me (read me) the story of Red Riding Hood again."

3. See Burridge (1992).   4. Wolterstorff (2011c).

That seems obvious: the lector is re-telling the story. What is not at all obvious is the rhetorical mood of her re-telling, its narrational stance. One possibility that comes to mind immediately is that she is not only re-telling the story but is also replicating the narrational stance of the original author or editor, that being what I have called the *pre-modern* narrational stance.

I judge that this suggestion, attractive though it may seem at first glance, is not plausible. To replicate the narrational stance of the biblical author or editor the lector would have to know what that stance was and would have to replicate it intentionally. Relatively few liturgical lectors do know what that stance was; it is no longer familiar to us. Scholars of ancient literature know what it was; most laypeople do not. Knowing what that stance was and replicating it is not a condition for filling the role of lector in a liturgical enactment.

If the lector is not replicating the narrational stance of the biblical author or editor in her re-telling of the story, is she perhaps re-telling the story with one of the narrational stances familiar to us in the modern world, namely, as report or as fiction? Perhaps. But let me suggest another possibility.

When you and I in the modern world tell a story of our own making, we almost always tell it either as report or as fiction. Not so, I think, when we re-tell someone else's story. If it's a pre-modern story, it will often not be clear to us which episodes were originally told as report and which were originally told as something imagined; if it's a story from the modern world that was told as report, we often don't want to commit ourselves on whether the author got everything right. In either case, however, we may want to tell the story: it's a rollicking good story, it illuminates character, it shows reality, whatever. So we tell it without adopting any narrational stance whatsoever; we just present the story. When you or I read aloud a passage from Homer, we narrate it neither as report nor as fiction; we just present the story. We tell the story non-committally.

When the person appointed as lector for some liturgical enactment reads aloud the specified passage from Scripture she is functioning in an official liturgical capacity. In case it is a narrative passage that she reads, what the church asks of her in the capacity of lector is that she simply re-narrate the story—simply re-tell it, present it once again. It is then up to the people and their leaders as to what to do with the re-told story. Is it a parable? Is it history? If it is history, is it accurate history? In which respects is it accurate?

In the story of Jesus' nativity as told in the gospel of Luke we read:

> In that region there were shepherds living in the fields, keeping watch over their flock by night. Then an angel of the Lord stood before them, and the glory of the Lord shone around them, and they were terrified. But the angel said to them, "Do not be afraid, for see—I am bringing you good news of great joy for all the people: to you is born this day in the city of David a Savior, who is the Messiah. This will be a sign for you: you will find a child wrapped in bands of cloth and lying in a manger." And suddenly there was with the angel a multitude of the heavenly host, praising God and saying, "Glory to God in the highest heaven, and on earth peace among those whom he favors."
>
> (Luke 2: 8–14)

Did this really happen, literally speaking? Had there been a sound-recording device present in those Judean hills that night, would it have recorded the sound of that hymn being emitted from somewhere in the sky? Was Luke claiming that this really happened, literally speaking? Or did he intend this bit of narrative to convey symbolically his conviction that the birth of Jesus was of cosmic significance? It's not required of the lector that she have views on how these questions are to be answered. And so it is for many of the other biblical narratives that are read aloud in the liturgy.

I say, "for many of the other biblical narratives." When the presider at the Eucharist rehearses the story of Jesus' last meal with his disciples, it's understood in most liturgical traditions that he or she is presenting it as what really happened, literally speaking. So too when the reader re-tells the story of Jesus' death in the course of the Good Friday liturgy, it's understood in most liturgical traditions that she is telling it as what really happened. At the heart of most liturgical traditions is the conviction that these things really happened, literally speaking. Not so for Luke's narrative of the singing angels.

My analysis of what the lector is doing when she reads aloud some narrative passage of Scripture that contains no first- or second-person pronouns also applies, *mutatis mutandis*, to her reading aloud some non-narrative passage from one of the New Testament epistles that contains no such pronouns. Suppose, for example, that she reads this passage from Paul's letter to the Romans: "There is now no condemnation for those who are in Christ Jesus." What the lector is doing, in her official capacity, is restating what Paul said—re-presenting that proposition. She may also be asserting it, not just re-presenting it but affirming it. But the script does not require of a lector who reads a passage from one of the epistles that she thereby perform whatever be the illocutionary act that the author performed by writing the passage; it does not even require that she know what that act was. Almost all readers and listeners find a good many passages in Paul's letters to be dark sayings. Nonetheless, when the lector reads aloud such a passage, her doing so counts as re-presenting whatever it is that Paul said even if she doesn't know what that was.

What is the lector doing when reading biblical passages that contain first- and second-person pronouns?

After noting that a lector's reading of biblical passages containing first- and second-person pronouns poses special problems of interpretation, I temporarily set such passages aside so that we could first understand what the lector is doing when she reads passages that do not pose those problems. Let us now take up the passages we set aside.[5] The complications that came to light in the section "What is a lector doing when reading aloud a narrative passage from Scripture?" pale by comparison to those we will now encounter.

Let's have some examples. The Gospel of Luke opens with the words: "Since many have undertaken to set down an orderly account of the events that have been fulfilled among us, just as they were handed on to us by those who from the beginning were eye-witnesses and servants of the word, I too decided, after investigating everything carefully from the very first, to write an orderly account for you, most excellent Theophilus, so that you may know the truth concerning the things about which you have been instructed."What then follows is Luke's narrative about Jesus. The Acts of the Apostles, written by the same author, begins: "In the first book, Theophilus, I wrote about all that Jesus did and taught from the beginning until the day when he was taken up to heaven." What then follows is Luke's narrative concerning the doings of the apostles.

How are we to understand what the lector is doing when she reads aloud such passages as these? I assume that in this case, too, she is doing something

---

5. The problems raised by reading aloud a text containing first- and second-person pronouns that was composed by someone other than oneself are also raised by reading aloud a text containing spatial, temporal, or other indexicals that refer to aspects of the situation in which the text was composed. An example would be someone's reciting for an audience the text of Lincoln's Gettysburg Address. The text begins, "Four score and seven years *ago*."

more than just producing a new auditory token of the text. She is saying something. What is she saying? What is the illocutionary act that her utterance of the words counts as? In particular, how are the pronouns "I," "us," and "you" functioning when she reads aloud what Luke wrote?

Or suppose she reads the following words from the opening of Paul's Letter to the Romans: "Paul, a servant of Jesus Christ, called to be an apostle, set apart for the gospel of God....I thank my God through Jesus Christ for all of you, because your faith is proclaimed throughout the world." What is the lector saying when she reads these words? In particular, how are the pronouns "I," "you," and "your" functioning?

Lest the reader get the impression that the problem of interpretation we confront here is peculiar to the liturgical reading of Scripture, let me bring a couple of non-liturgical examples into the picture. Imagine someone reading aloud or reciting from memory Shakespeare's Sonnet 73. The sonnet opens with these lines:

> That time of year thou mayst in me behold
> When yellow leaves, or none, or few, do hang
> Upon those boughs which shake against the cold,
> Bare ruin'd choirs where late the sweet birds sang.

Or imagine someone reading aloud or reciting from memory the lyric poem by Emily Dickinson that begins with the lines:

> I reckon—when I count at all—
> First—Poets—Then the Sun—
> Then Summer—Then the Heaven of God—
> And then—the List is done—
>
> But looking back—the First so seem
> To Comprehend the Whole—
> The Others look a needless Show—
> So I write—Poets—All   (#569)[6]

What is one doing when one reads aloud or recites from memory such lines as these from Shakespeare and Dickinson? In particular, how is the pronoun "me" functioning when one reads aloud or recites Shakespeare's sonnet and how is the pronoun "I" functioning when one reads aloud or recites the Dickinson poem?

A thesis espoused or assumed by a good many contemporary literary theorists is that the author of a lyric poem never speaks in his or her own

---

6. In Dickinson (2003).

voice but instead invites us to imagine someone saying the words of the poem. We are not to understand Dickinson as having declared, by writing her poem, that *she* reckons and writes so-and-so but are instead to understand her as having invited us, her readers, to imagine a person who reckons and writes so-and-so. The person to be imagined is typically called *the implied speaker.*

As a claim about lyric poetry in general, I find this thesis dubious. But let me not argue that point here.[7] Clearly Luke was speaking in his own voice in the passages I quoted, as was Paul in the passage quoted. So for the purposes of our discussion here let us assume that Shakespeare was also speaking in his own voice when he authored the lines quoted and was referring to himself with the pronoun "me," and that Dickinson was likewise speaking in her own voice and referring to herself with the pronoun "I."

Once again, then, our question: what is the lector doing when she reads aloud such biblical passages as the ones quoted? And what is one doing when one reads aloud or recites the passages quoted from Shakespeare and Dickinson? To make things easier for ourselves, let us suppose that the passages I quoted from Luke and Paul are not English translations of the original Greek but are what the authors actually wrote.

When Luke wrote the opening lines of his gospel he referred to himself with the word "I" and to Theophilus with the word "you," and he said, about himself, that he had decided to write an orderly account for Theophilus. Is a lector who reads the words, "I decided to write an orderly account for you, most excellent Theophilus," thereby doing and saying the same thing Luke did? Is she referring to Luke with the word "I" and to Theophilus with the word "you," and is she saying, about Luke, that he had decided to write an orderly account for Theophilus?

Surely not. The pronoun "I" doesn't work that way. It can be used in other ways than to refer to someone. But when it is used to refer to someone, that person is always the one speaking or writing. One can restate what Luke said; one can refer to him and say, about him, what he said about himself, namely, that he had decided to write an orderly account for Theophilus. But one cannot do this by using Luke's own words; one cannot do it by producing a new token of the sentence he wrote. The same point holds, *mutatis mutandis,* for reading aloud or reciting the passage from Paul's letter to the Romans, Shakespeare's sonnet, and the Dickinson poem.

7. I argue the point in Wolterstorff (1980), 163–71.

Given that the word "I," when used to refer, is used to refer to the one speaking or writing, might the lector who reads aloud the Lukan passages be referring to herself with the pronoun "I" and saying, about herself, what Luke said about himself?

The idea is preposterous. The lector, on this interpretation, would be guilty of propounding a stupefying falsehood. It was not she who wrote an orderly account for Theophilus; it was Luke who wrote such an account. It is only slightly less preposterous to interpret the reader of the Dickinson poem as referring to herself with the word "I" and attributing to herself the exalted view of poetry that Dickinson expressed. A person who has a rather low view of poetry can read aloud the Dickinson poem without thereby speaking falsely. It is only slightly less preposterous to interpret the reader of the Shakespeare sonnet as referring to himself with the word "I" and attributing to himself the melancholy mood that Shakespeare expressed.

Let's consider a quite different possibility. Might it be that though the reader of the Dickinson poem is not referring to Dickinson with the pronoun "I" and saying about Dickinson what Dickinson said about herself, Dickinson is nonetheless present on the scene in a certain way? Might it be that the reader or reciter is *playing the role* of Dickinson? Might it likewise be the case that when a lector reads aloud the opening verses of Luke's Gospel she is playing the role of Luke?

Performances of Shakespeare's plays provide us with paradigmatic examples of role-playing. The preface to the text lists the *dramatis personae*, that is, the roles that must be filled by actors for the play to be performed. The *dramatis personae* for many dramas consist entirely of fictional characters; in the case of Shakespeare's historical plays, the *dramatis personae* include persons who once lived. In the case of some dramas, the *dramatis personae* include persons alive at the time the play was written and first performed.

To identify what seems to me the essence of role-playing, compare a novel with a performance of a play based on the novel. The novel and the performance are alike in that both project a certain world for our imagining. The mode of their world-projection is significantly different, however, with the consequence that the worlds projected are also significantly different.[8]

---

8. When I wrote Wolterstorff (1980) I had not noticed this difference.

Suppose that Arthur Miller's *Death of a Salesman* had been based on a novel (as it was not). The author of the novel would have imagined a world containing a salesman named "Willie Loman" who did so-and-so and underwent such-and-such, and would tacitly have invited his readers to do so as well. In the original production of the play, the actor Lee J. Cobb played the role of Willie. In doing so, he would have imagined himself, Lee J. Cobb, to be a salesman named "Willie Loman" who did so-and-so and underwent such-and-such, and his audience would tacitly have been invited to do so as well. In reading the novel, we imagine a salesman named "Willie Loman" doing and saying such-and-such; in watching and listening to a performance of the play we imagine Lee J. Cobb to be a salesman named "Willie Loman" doing and saying such-and-such. The actor, Lee Cobb, is himself a component in the projected world of the dramatic performance. He is not a component in the world projected by the novel, nor is the author—unless, of course, there are words in the text of the novel that refer to the author.

"The Belle of Amherst" is a play written by William Luce whose sole *dramatis persona* is Emily Dickinson. In the original Broadway production, and in some subsequent productions, Julie Harris played the role of Dickinson. Since Dickinson was a real historical person, the role-playing in this case took the form of impersonation. Julie Harris imagined that she was Dickinson and the members of the audience were tacitly invited to do so as well. The text for the play included a number of Dickinson's poems. When Julie Harris spoke those poems in the course of performing the play, she was doing so in the role of Emily Dickinson. She was imagining herself to be Emily Dickinson reading aloud poems that she had written, and the audience was tacitly invited to do so as well.

An ordinary reading or recitation of a Dickinson poem is so different from what Julie Harris was doing when reciting Dickinson poems in the course of performing "The Belle of Amherst" that, in my judgment, it is implausible to interpret the reader as impersonating Dickinson when reading the poem beginning, "I reckon." The reader is not imagining herself to be Emily Dickinson reading one of her poems, nor are the listeners tacitly being invited to do so.

So too, though it's possible for someone to impersonate St Luke and, in the course of doing so, to speak the opening words of Luke's Gospel, it's implausible to think that that is what the lector is doing when she reads aloud those words in the course of some ordinary liturgical enactment. She is not imagining herself to be St Luke writing to Theophilus what Luke did write to Theophilus, nor are the congregants tacitly being invited to imagine that.

When I was growing up in the small village of Edgerton, Minnesota, the annual Memorial Day[9] celebration included a schoolchild reciting Lincoln's Gettysburg Address in public. One year I was that schoolchild. Had I been dressed more or less as Lincoln was dressed when he delivered the address, and had I spoken the words with great gravity, it would have been plausible to think of me as playing the role of Lincoln delivering the address. It would have been plausible for me to imagine that I was Lincoln delivering the address and for the listeners to do so as well. But I was dressed in ordinary street clothes and spoke in a voice that had not yet broken. Implausible to interpret what I was doing as impersonating Lincoln delivering the Gettysburg Address.

What then is someone doing who reads or recites that poem of Emily Dickinson? I suggest that she is tacitly inviting us to imagine Emily Dickinson reciting the poem and saying what Dickinson would have said when reciting it. We are not to imagine that *the reader is* Emily Dickinson reading the poem; we are to imagine *Emily Dickinson* reading the poem. The reader may join the audience in imagining Emily Dickinson reciting the poem; but that seems to me not essential. She may be so focused on reading well that she does no imagining.

So too for the lector who reads the opening of Luke's Gospel. She is tacitly inviting us to imagine Luke writing to Theophilus what he did write to Theophilus and as saying what he did say by writing those words. We are not to imagine that *she*, the lector, *is* Luke addressing Theophilus with those words; we are to imagine *Luke* addressing Theophilus with those words. The lector is not impersonating, she is not role-playing.

In Luke's Gospel, the words that immediately follow those I quoted are these: "In the days of King Herod of Judea, there was a priest named Zechariah, who belonged to the priestly order of Abijah." When the lector reads those words, it's possible to interpret what she is doing as once again tacitly inviting us to imagine Luke writing those words to Theophilus and thereby saying what he did say. But our discussion in the section "What is a lector doing when reading aloud a narrative passage from Scripture?" implies that that interpretation is not required. What she is now doing can

9. Last Monday of May.

be interpreted as re-presenting to the congregants the illocutionary content of what Luke said, doing so by reading aloud the very words that he wrote. The congregants are tacitly invited to grasp that content, to cognize it. By contrast, to understand what the lector is doing when she reads those opening lines containing the pronouns "I" and "you," we have to bring imagination into the picture, not just cognition; and we have to bring into the picture Luke's *act* of writing to Theophilus, not just the illocutionary content of what he wrote.

In concluding this section of our discussion, let me make clear that it is not my contention that the illocutionary content of the opening verses of Luke's Gospel cannot be stated. My contention is that the content cannot be stated by reading aloud Luke's own words. The function of the pronouns "I" and "you" prevents that. To state the illocutionary content one has to paraphrase: "Luke said to Theophilus that he had decided to write an orderly account for him."

When I, Adam

As a transition to our analysis of the liturgical vocalizing of the psalms, let me call attention to the remarkable opening words of the Orthodox liturgy for Vespers on the eve of the Sunday before Lent. The words are sung by the people (choir). They are not from Scripture; so taking note of them here is an interpolation within our discussion of the liturgical vocalizing of Scripture. But some of the points made in the section "What is the lector doing when reading biblical passages that contain first- and second-person pronouns?" can be used to help us understand what is going on.

> The Lord my creator took me as dust from the earth and formed me into a living creature…; He honoured me, setting me as ruler upon earth over all things visible, and making me companion of the angels. But Satan, the deceiver, using the serpent as his instrument, enticed me by food; he parted me from the glory of God and gave me over to the earth and to the lowest depths of death. But Master, in compassion, call me back again.
>
> In my wretchedness I have cast off the robe woven by God, disobeying Thy divine command, O Lord, at the counsel of the enemy; and I am clothed now in fig leaves and in garments of skin. I am condemned to eat the bread of toil in the sweat of my brow, and the earth has been cursed so that it bears thorns and thistles for me. But, Lord, who in the last times wast made flesh of a virgin, call me back again and bring me into paradise.

O precious paradise, unsurpassed in beauty...: may [the maker of all] open unto me the gates which I closed by my transgression and may he count me worthy to partake of the tree of life and of the joy which was mine when I dwelt in thee before.[10]

What are the people doing when they sing these remarkable words? Just a bit later in the same liturgy they sing, "Adam sat before paradise and, lamenting his nakedness, he wept: 'Woe is me! By evil deceit was I persuaded and led astray, and now I am an exile from glory...'"[11] When singing these words they are quoting Adam's imagined lament. The structure of the three opening paragraphs is different; the people are not quoting what Adam is imagined to have said.

What are they doing instead? Ignore, for a moment, the words, "Lord, who in the last times wast made flesh of a virgin." Then the section "What is the lector doing when reading biblical passages that contain first- and second-person pronouns?" suggests two possibilities: by singing these words, either each participant is imagining *Adam* lamenting his fall and pleading for salvation, or each participant is imagining *she* is Adam lamenting his fall and pleading for his salvation. On the latter interpretation, each participant is impersonating Adam. The word "pretending" has misleading connotations in this context; but if we strip off those connotations, each participant, on the latter interpretation, is pretending to be Adam lamenting his fall and pleading for his salvation, the point of such pretending being, surely, that thereby the participant is lamenting her own fall and pleading for her own salvation.

Both interpretations seem to me not only possible but plausible. The rubric for the liturgy, namely, "The Sunday of Forgiveness, on Which We Commemorate the Casting Out of Adam from Paradise," inclines me to the view that the official body that authorized this liturgy intended that the participants would do both things at once: each would imagine *Adam* lamenting his fall, and each would imagine *she* is Adam lamenting his fall, thereby lamenting her own fall. Saying that the liturgy is to "commemorate the casting out of Adam from Paradise" suggests that the enactment of the liturgy is a commemorative imagining of Adam's lament over his fall and of his plea for forgiveness and salvation. Calling it the "Sunday of Forgiveness" suggests that each participant is impersonating Adam lamenting his fall and

10. *Lenten Triodion* (1978), 168–9. I thank Terence Cuneo for calling this passage to my attention.
11. *Lenten Triodion* (1978), 169.

pleading for forgiveness and salvation, thereby lamenting her own fall and pleading for her own forgiveness and salvation.

However, the line, "Lord, who in the last times wast made flesh of a virgin," militates against both of these interpretations. This line cannot belong to Adam's imagined lament; and given that it cannot belong to his lament, we are forced to a different interpretation of the passage as a whole from the two we have considered.

I suggest that each participant is lamenting her sins and pleading for forgiveness *in her own voice*, not Adam's, doing so, however, not by employing her own words but by employing the words of Adam's imagined lament, thereby forcing a highly metaphorical interpretation of many of those words. Like Adam, I was placed as a ruler upon earth. Like Adam, I was enticed by Satan, the deceiver. Like Adam, I am condemned to eat the bread of toil in the sweat of my brow. And so forth.

Before we move on, let me note that *The Lenten Triodion* contains a number of other passages that have exactly the same structure and raise exactly the same issues that the Adam's-lament passages raise. For example, the third Sunday before Lent is titled "The Sunday of the Prodigal Son." Vespers for the preceding evening opens with the people (choir) singing these words:

> I was entrusted with a sinless and living land, but I sowed the ground with sin and reaped with a sickle the ears of slothfulness; in thick sheaves I garnered my actions, but winnowed them not on the threshing floor of repentance. But I beg thee, my God, the pre-eternal husbandman, with the wind of Thy loving-kindness winnow the chaff of my works, and grant to my soul the corn of forgiveness; shut me in thy heavenly storehouse and save me.[12]

Solemn Reproaches of the Cross

Let me postpone for just a bit longer our analysis of the liturgical vocalizing of the psalms by taking note of a remarkable section in the liturgy for Good Friday in the *Book of Common Worship* of the Presbyterian Church (USA). The liturgy contains nine "Solemn Reproaches of the Cross," from which a selection are to be sung or said. To give the reader a sense of what these are

---

12. *Lenten Triodion* (1978), 112.

like, let me quote three of them.[13] In each case, the reproach is preceded by the words, "Holy God, | Holy and mighty, | Holy immortal One, | have mercy on us." Here is one of the solemn reproaches:

> What more could I have done for you
> that I have not done?
> I planted you, my chosen and fairest vineyard,
> I made you the branches of my vine;
> but when I was thirsty, you gave me vinegar to drink
> and pierced with a spear the side of your Savior,
> and you have prepared a cross for your Savior.

Here is another:

> I grafted you into the tree of my chosen Israel,
> and you turned on them with persecution and mass murder.
> I made you joint heirs with them of my covenants
> but you made them scapegoats for your own guilt,
> and you have prepared a cross for your Savior.

And here is a third:

> I came to you as the least of your brothers and sisters;
> I was hungry and you gave me no food,
> I was thirsty and you gave me no drink,
> I was a stranger and you did not welcome me,
> naked and you did not clothe me,
> sick and in prison and you did not visit me,
> and you have prepared a cross for your Savior.

Our discussion in the section "When I, Adam" makes clear what is being done when someone sings or speaks these remarkable words: the singer or speaker is inviting the people to imagine God lamenting.

On praying the psalms

The psalms are poems, many of them prayers addressed to God, others in the form of what can perhaps best be called "proclamation"; many contain

---

13. *The Book of Common Worship* (1993), 285–91. I thank John Witvliet for calling the "Solemn Reproaches" to my attention.

the first-person pronouns "I," "me," "we," and "us."[14] It's possible to read them in the same way one reads Shakespeare's sonnet or Dickinson's lyric poem. But when they are said or sung by the people in an enactment of some liturgy, the people are doing something very different from what one is doing when reading that Shakespeare sonnet or that Dickinson poem. The people are not *imagining the psalmist* praying or proclaiming; nor are they *imagining themselves to be the psalmist* praying or proclaiming. Rather than *imagining*, they are themselves *actually* praying or proclaiming, doing so with the words of the psalm rather than with their own words. Here is what one of the desert fathers, John Cassian, said on the matter:

> He [the congregant] will take into himself all the thoughts of the Psalms and will begin to sing them in such a way that he will utter them with the deepest emotion of his heart, not as if they were the compositions of the Psalmist, but rather as if they were his own utterances and his very own prayer…and will recognize that their words were not only fulfilled formerly by or in the person of the prophet, but are fulfilled and carried out daily in his own case.[15]

To the best of my knowledge it is universally agreed that when the people vocalize a psalm in a liturgical enactment, they are doing what Cassian says they are doing, namely, themselves praying or proclaiming with the words of the psalm. The question that calls for discussion is *what* they are praying or proclaiming when they pray or proclaim the psalm.

Sometimes it's easy to discern what they are saying. When the psalmist sang, "Though I walk through the valley of the shadow of death, I will fear no evil" (23: 1), he was addressing God and, referring to himself with the pronoun "I," saying about himself that even though he walk through the valley of the shadow of death, he will fear no evil. When the people in some liturgical enactment say or sing those same words, they are each addressing God and, referring to themselves with the pronoun "I," saying about themselves that even though they walk through the valley of the shadow of death, they will fear no evil.

In many cases, however, it's not at all easy to know what the people are saying, or should be saying, when vocalizing a psalm. Consider the opening three verses and the closing three verses of the most infamous of all psalms, Psalm 137:

14. Strictly speaking, they contain Hebrew terms that are translated into English as "I," "me," "we," and "us."
15. John Cassian, *Conferences* 10.11.5. In Cassian (1997), 384.

By the rivers of Babylon—
   there we sat down and there we wept
   when we remembered Zion.
On the willows there we hung up our harps.
For there our captors
   asked us for songs,
and our tormentors asked for mirth, saying,
   "Sing us one of the songs of Zion."

Remember, O Lord, against the Edomites
   the day of Jerusalem's fall,
how they said, "Tear it down! Tear it down!
   Down to its foundations!"
O daughter Babylon, you devastator!
   Happy shall they be who pay you back
   what you have done to us!
Happy shall they be who take your little ones
   and dash them against the rock!

What are the people praying when they say or sing these words? The psalmist referred to himself and his fellow captives with the pronoun "we," and
he said, about them, that they sat down by the rivers of Babylon and wept.
Those who pray this psalm today are not referring to the psalmist and his
fellow captives with the pronoun "we"; the pronoun "we" cannot function
that way. They are referring to themselves with the pronoun "we." That
much is obvious. But what are they saying about themselves? They are
not saying about themselves what the psalmist said about himself and his
fellow captives, namely, that they hung their harps on the willows of Babylon.
None of the congregants has ever done that. Nor are they pronouncing blessing on those who will repay Babylon for her violence by taking Babylonian
infants and dashing them against rocks. Babylon is long gone; no one can
wreak vengeance on her.

   When the people pray this psalm, they are engaged in what I call, in
Divine Discourse, "appropriation" of speech.[16] Appropriation of speech comes
in several different forms. One form consists of taking an extant token of
some words that were not inscribed to perform some illocutionary act and
using those word-tokens to perform some illocutionary act of one's own.
In Chapter 2 I gave, as a common example of this form of appropriation,
buying a greeting card in a card shop, signing it, and sending it off to a

16. Wolterstorff (1995), 51–4.

friend. One did not oneself inscribe the words; one appropriated the inscription. Sitting in a rack in the card shop, the inscription had no illocutionary function. By signing the card and sending it off to one's friend, one performs the illocutionary act of greeting one's friend.

A different form of appropriation occurs when one takes the propositional content of an illocutionary act that someone else performed and one affirms that content without restating it. This form of appropriation occurs when someone makes a declaration in a meeting and someone else says, "I agree with that," or when someone makes a motion in a parliamentary session and someone else says, "I second the motion." Without himself restating the propositional content of the declaration or the motion, the second person has appropriated that content from the speech of the first person.

A third form of appropriation occurs when one takes the words that someone used to perform some illocutionary act and performs that same illocutionary act by uttering or inscribing those same words. Someone declares that rain is predicted by uttering the words "Rain is predicted." I then repeat what he said, both his utterance and his declaration, by uttering the words, "Rain is predicted." Call this form of appropriation, *repetition-appropriation*. The praying of some of the psalms, and of passages in some, is repetition-appropriation of the psalm. An example would be praying by voicing the opening lines of Psalm 106:

> Praise the Lord!
> O give thanks for the Lord, for the Lord is good;
> for the Lord's steadfast love endures forever.

Yet another form of appropriation occurs when one takes a text that was used to perform one or more illocutionary acts and uses that text to perform one's own distinct illocutionary acts. Let me call such appropriation, *revisionist*-appropriation. Jorge Borges's story, "Pierre Menard, Author of the *Quixote*," is a fictional account of the revisionist-appropriation of a literary work; the story is quirky, as are most of Borges's stories.[17]

The main character, Pierre Menard, is an obscure early twentieth-century writer who undertook to write a novel whose text was identical, word for word, with the text of Cervantes's *Don Quixote*. He did not undertake to copy the text of Cervantes's work; that's easy, anybody can do that. He undertook to write a new novel whose text was, word for word, the same as Cervantes's text.

17. Reprinted in Borges (1998).

"It is unnecessary," says the narrator in Borges's story, "to add that his aim was never to produce a mechanical transcription of the original; he did not propose to copy it. His admirable ambition was to produce pages which would coincide—word for word and line for line—with those of Miguel Cervantes," and to do so by continuing to "be Pierre Menard and to arrive at *Don Quixote* through the experiences of Pierre Menard."[18] The narrator observes, "To compose *Don Quixote* at the beginning of the seventeenth century was a reasonable, necessary and perhaps inevitable undertaking; at the beginning of the twentieth century it is almost impossible. It is not in vain that three hundred years have passed, charged with the most complex happenings—among them, to mention only one, that same *Don Quixote*."[19]

The narrator of Borges's story nicely describes the difference between one of the passages from the *Don Quixote* of Cervantes and the same passage from the *Don Quixote* of Pierre Menard:

> The text of Cervantes and that of Menard are verbally identical, but the second is almost infinitely richer. (More ambiguous, his detractors will say; but ambiguity is a richness.) It is a revelation to compare the *Don Quixote* of Menard with that of Cervantes. The latter, for instance, wrote: "...truth, whose mother is history, who is the rival of time, depository of deeds, witness of the past, example and lesson to the present, and warning to the future." Written in the seventeenth century, written by the "ingenious layman" Cervantes, this enumeration is a mere rhetorical eulogy of history. Menard, on the other hand, writes: "...truth, whose mother is history, who is the rival of time, depository of deeds, witness of the past, example and lesson to the present, and warning to the future." History, *mother* of truth; the idea is astounding. Menard, a contemporary of William James, does not define history as an investigation of reality, but as its origin. Historical truth, for him, is not what took place; it is what we think took place. The final clauses—*example and lesson to the present, and warning to the future*—are shamelessly pragmatic.[20]

Very often the form of appropriation that takes place when the psalms are prayed by the congregants is revisionist-appropriation rather than repetition-appropriation. However, it is a distinctly different form of revisionist-interpretation from that which Pierre Menard practiced. Menard paid no attention to the story Cervantes had told by inscribing the text of *Don Quixote*; all he cared about was the words of the text. Call such appropriation,

---

18. Borges (1998), 91.   19. Borges (1998), 91.   20. Borges (1998), 94.

free revisionist-appropriation. Revisionist-appropriation of the psalms by the people for their own prayers is not free but *bound*. The illocutionary content of the prayers of the people is derived from the illocutionary content of the psalmist's prayer; it's an adaptation of the content, a function of it.

Consider again the words quoted from Psalm 23: "though I walk through the valley of the shadow of death, I shall fear no evil." When the psalmist wrote those words, he was referring to himself with the pronoun "I" and was saying, about himself, that he would fear no evil even though he walked through the valley of the shadow of death. When a person prays using those words she is not referring to the psalmist with the pronoun "I" and repeating what he said. She is referring to herself and saying, about herself, that she will fear no evil even though she walks through the valley of the shadow of death. The content of her prayer is not a repetition of the psalmist's prayer, but neither does it ignore the content of the psalmist's prayer in the way that Pierre Menard ignored the content of Cervantes's novel. It's a function of that content.

What typically forces bound revisionist-appropriation of a psalm rather than repetition-appropriation is not just that the reference of "I" has shifted but the fact that, whereas the psalmist was speaking literally in offering his prayer, we cannot take ourselves to be speaking literally when using his words for our prayer. The psalmist spoke now and then of shields and bucklers; few of us have ever handled shields and bucklers. When we pray by voicing a psalm containing those words, they function for us as metaphors.

Every psalm that calls for bound revisionist-appropriation rather than repetition-appropriation is susceptible to a range of appropriations; the psalmist's prayer can be used to pray a number of somewhat different prayers, and can be used to pray the same prayer with a number of somewhat different intentions. I very much like what the editors of *Psalms for All Seasons* say in this regard. Let me quote what they say in its entirety.

We might speak, pray, or sing a psalm in one or more of the following modes:

• As an expression of our own experience: "*Given our despair over the persecution we face, let us sing Psalm 22 together—as our own prayer, testimony, and vow.*"

• As a text which we do not yet experience fully, but which we are growing into: "*Let us sing Psalm 116 as a way of stretching ourselves toward the kind of thanksgiving and dedication to God we desire to exhibit as God's covenant people.*"

• As a way of praying in solidarity with those whose experience is quite different from our own: "*Let us sing Psalm 22 in solidarity with all those who are facing persecution today.*"

• As a way of entering into or responding to a particular biblical narrative: "*Let us sing Psalm 22 as a way of entering into the drama of Jesus' passion,*" or "*Let us sing Psalm 38 in order to sense the despair experienced by the prophet Jeremiah.*"

• As a way of contemplating wrestling with a given text without committing to a particular way of understanding our relation to it: "*As we read Psalm 41 together, consider whether this text describes our experience of betrayal, or if it might be prayed by others who have been betrayed by us.*"

• As a way of distancing ourselves from the text, in light of our wrestling with another part of scripture: "*We read Psalm 109 not only to sense the anger and frustration that the ancient people experienced, but also to mark the stunning contrast with Jesus' response to those who crucified him.*"[21]

Among these various ways of praying the psalms, I judge that it would be especially fascinating to explore praying a lament psalm "in solidarity with all those who are facing persecution today."What is one doing when one prays in this way? Is one imagining the people facing persecution to be praying the psalm? Perhaps. But I think it's more plausible to understand oneself as praying *on their behalf.* I will have to resist the temptation to explore this possibility.[22]

Bound revisionist-appropriation of a psalm requires training and theological sensitivity if one is to pray or proclaim what one's liturgical script or tradition prescribes to be prayed or proclaimed by voicing the words of the psalm. Many liturgical participants lack that training and sensitivity. If asked to state in their own words what they are praying or proclaiming, they would stumble. Their praying or proclaiming of the psalm is one more example of a phenomenon we discussed in Chapter 2, namely, that of performing some illocutionary act without having a clear idea of what that act is.

Suppose a congregant realizes that she has only a vague idea of what she is to be praying or proclaiming when bound revisionist-appropriation of some psalm is called for. Where might she look for assistance?[23] One place to look would be to commentaries on the psalms by writers whose aim is

21. *Psalms for all Seasons* (2012), iii–iv.

22. *Lift Up Your Hearts* offers a prayer that can be spoken before or after singing Psalm 7 in solidarity with those who experience injustice: "Almighty and loving God, | We pray these ancient words | in solidarity with those in our world | who suffer from injustice. | Encourage us in our ministry | of prayer on their behalf, | and strengthen them with courage and patience." *Lift Up Your Hearts* (2013), 643.

23. About the "Responsorial Psalm," which occurs in the contemporary Catholic liturgy after the Old Testament reading, the "General Introduction" in *The Sunday Missal* (2011) says this: "We should become acquainted with the way the Church re-interprets the Psalms and gives them a Christian meaning. Often the refrain indicates how we should adapt a particular psalm in its liturgical setting on Sunday" (5).

not just to excavate the historical background of the psalms but to assist contemporary Christians in praying and proclaiming the psalms. Another place to look would be to sermons on the psalms. A third place to look would be to so-called versifications of the psalms: revisions of the psalms into verses that are to be sung as strophes (stanzas). Beginning with Luther, Protestants especially have produced a great many versifications of psalms; the Genevan Psalter was the first complete versification.

A versification of a psalm is not, of course, to be identified with the psalm itself; it's a composition that is more or less closely *based on* the psalm. When the people sing the versification, they are not singing the psalm. Almost always, however, the versification will incorporate a bound revisionist-interpretation of the psalm. Many psalters could be mined for examples. Let me give a few from a psalter that I happen to be familiar with, the *Psalter Hymnal*.

The opening verse of Psalm 138 reads thus:

> I give you thanks, O Lord, with my whole heart;
> before the gods I sing your praise.

No contemporary Christian believes there are gods. Here is how one of the versifications in the *Psalter Hymnal* handles the opening lines:

> With grateful heart my thanks I bring,
> Before the great Thy praise I sing.[24]

Psalm 104: 5–6 alludes to ancient cosmology:

> You set the earth on its foundations,
>   so that it shall never be shaken.
> You cover it with the deep as with a garment,
>   the waters stood above the mountains.

Nobody today accepts this cosmology. Here is how one of the versifications in the *Psalter Hymnal* treats the lines:

> The earth He has founded her station to keep,
>   And wrapped as a vesture about her the deep.   (#206)

Psalm 95: 8 reads,

> Do not harden your hearts, as at Meribah,
>   as on that day at Massah in the wilderness,

---

24. *Psalter Hymnal* (1959), #286.

> when your ancestors tested me,
>   and put me to the proof, though they had seen my work.

The *Psalter Hymnal* contains four versifications of Psalm 95; all of them delete the reference to Meribah and Massah. One of them (#285) makes no use of v. 8. Here is what the others make of the verse, starting with the versification that remains closest to the psalm:

> Oh, harden not your hearts, like those who wandered
>   The desert forty years to Jordan's strand.   (#186)
>
> Take heed and harden not your heart
>   As did your fathers, nor depart
> From God to follow in their ways.   (#183)[25]
>
> While He proffers peace and pardon
>   Let us hear his voice today,
> Lest, if we our hearts should harden,
>   We should perish in the way.   (#184)

Sometimes it appears that the versifier has found the language of the psalm too strong and has, accordingly, toned it down. The opening verse of Psalm 12 reads:

> Help, O Lord, for there is no longer anyone who is godly;
>   the faithful have disappeared from humankind.

The versification in the *Psalter Hymnal* is this:

> Help, Lord, for those who love thee fail,
>   Thy faithful ones fall from the ranks.   (#17)

Psalm 38 opens with these vivid words:

> O Lord, do not rebuke me in your anger,
>   or discipline me in your wrath.
> For your arrows have sunk into me,
>   and your hand has come down on me.
>
> There is no soundness in my flesh
>   because of your indignation;
> there is no health in my bones because of my sin.   (vv. 1–3)[26]

---

25. The versification leaves unclear who "your fathers" refers to.
26. V. 5 of the Psalm reads, "My wounds grow foul and fester"; v. 7 reads, "For my loins are filled with burning."

One of the versifications in the *Psalter Hymnal* removes all references to the body, the result being a versification that is anodyne by comparison to the psalm:

> In thy wrath and hot displeasure,
>   Chasten not thy servant Lord;
> Let thy mercy, without measure,
>   Help and peace to me afford.
>
> Heavy is my tribulation,
>   Sore my punishment has been;
> Broken by thine indignation,
>   I am troubled by my sin.   (#66)[27]

And how is the psalm with which we began, Psalm 137, versified? The *Psalter Hymnal* contains just one versification of the psalm. The reference in the opening verses of the psalm to the streams of Babylon is preserved in the versification, with the result that the congregants are left to make their own appropriation:

> By Babel's streams we sat and wept,
>   For memory still to Zion clung;
> The winds alone our harp-strings swept,
>   That on the drooping willows hung.   (#285)

The psalm's closing verses about vengeance are versified thus:

> Remember, Lord, the dreadful day
>   Of Zion's cruel overthrow;
> How happy he who shall repay
>   The bitter hatred of her foe.

There is no reference or allusion to the dashing of Babylonian infants against the rocks.

A more recent psalter, *Psalms for all Seasons*, includes the following versification of the psalm:

> God of memory, I remember how our captors wanted song.
> I will not forget the willows where our silent harps were hung.
>
> God of memory, I remember burning, broken city wall,
> I will not forget the city, cherish Zion over all.

---

27. An alternative versification does preserve some of the bodily references "In every limb lurks foul disease, | Loathsome my flesh in every part" (#67).

> God of memory, I remember children tumbling, not in play.
> I will not forget the longing to strike back.   (#137E)[28]

I mentioned that bound revisionist-appropriation of the psalms by the people requires training and theological sensitivity if it is to be done properly. A passing comment a Melkite priest from Galilee once made to me opened my eyes to the fact that, even if one has received the necessary training and possesses the requisite theological sensitivity, one may still not be able to pray certain of the psalms. The social or political situation in which one finds oneself may make it impossible to bring off the revisionist-appropriation required. The priest remarked to me that many of the psalms were no longer used in his church. Surprised, I asked him why. "Because," he said, "when we come across the word 'Jerusalem' in a psalm we cannot help but think of the Jerusalem down the road."

---

28. The words are by Richard Leach.

7

Liturgical repetition and reenactment

It is often said by liturgical scholars that a celebration of the Eucharist or Lord's Supper is a reenactment of Jesus' last meal with his twelve disciples before his arrest and execution.[1] Some scholars go farther and suggest that the performance of a Christian liturgy as a whole is a reenactment of episodes of biblical narrative. This position was espoused, for example, by Sigmund Mowinckel in his book, *Religion and Cult*. Mowinckel's interpretation of the liturgies of Judaism and Christianity was an application to those liturgies of his general concept of cult. "In the cultic festival, it is the past which is reenacted and the future which is created."[2] J.-J. von Allmen was of the same view. In *Worship: Its Theology and Practice*, he says of the Christian cult that when it is enacted, "the past is reenacted and made present."[3] The past he has in mind is the central events of the biblical narrative. In particular, the anamnesis of the Lord's Supper "is a re-enactment of the event which the celebration commemorates."[4]

In his essay, "Liturgical Immersion,"[5] Terence Cuneo rejects the attempt of these liturgical scholars to fit under the single concept of reenactment all the ways in which performances of Christian liturgies invoke episodes of the biblical narratives. He argues—correctly, in my view—that there is no one concept that covers all the cases; we should acknowledge and honor the diversity. He does hold, however, that the concept of reenactment fits a good many of the cases; he takes for granted that the Eucharist is a reenactment.

---

1. This chapter is a substantial revision of my essay, "Liturgical Repetition and Reenactment," in W. Curtis Holtzen and Matthew Nelson Hill, eds, *In Spirit and in Truth: Philosophical Reflections on Liturgy and Worship* (Claremont, CA: Claremont School of Theology Press, 2016), 7–36.
2. Mowinckel (1981), 109.   3. Von Allmen (1965), 34.
4. Von Allmen (1969), 24.   5. Cuneo (2016a).

In this chapter I will swim against the current and argue that there is little by way of reenactment of episodes in the biblical narratives in present-day Christian liturgies; in particular, celebrations of the Eucharist are not reenactments. Performances of Christian liturgies do incorporate a good many repetitions of episodes in the biblical narratives. A celebration of the Eucharist is obviously some sort of repetition, some sort of *doing again*, of what St Paul and the writers of the synoptic Gospels report Jesus as having said and done at his last meal. But a repetition is not a reenactment. As we shall see, a reenactment of X is a depiction of X; a repetition of X is not a depiction. Reenactments are representational; repetitions are not.

I will develop and defend these claims by first taking note of some of the ways in which biblical narrations and episodes in biblical narratives are repeated in Christian liturgical enactments. I will then move on to reenactments, first analyzing the nature of reenactments in general, and then using that analysis to argue that present-day performances of Christian liturgies, though pervaded by repetitions of the sorts just mentioned, contain very little by way of reenactments of episodes in the biblical narratives, and that, in particular, celebrations of the Eucharist are not such reenactments. I will conclude by considering whether liturgical performances can be understood as performances of a drama.

The distinction between *recurrences* and *repetitions*, and between those and *reenactments*, will figure prominently in my discussion; let me explain how I will be using the terms. Recall the distinction between act-types and act-tokens that we introduced in Chapter 1; now we will need the counterpart distinction between event-types and event-tokens. A token of an act- or event-type is an *instantiation* of the type. Most act- and event-types can be multiply instantiated; they can *recur*. I will call an instantiation of an act- or event-type that takes place after its first instantiation, a *recurrence* of that act- or event-type. And I will say, of someone who produces a recurrence of some act- or event-type, that he has *repeated* that type. It is act- and event-types that are repeated, not act- and event-tokens. Act- and event-tokens cannot recur;[6] and since they cannot recur, one cannot repeat them. They can be imitated, as we shall see; but they cannot be repeated.

As for reenactment, it is act- and event-tokens that are reenacted. Therein lies the ontological divide between repetition and reenactment. It is act- and event-types that are repeated; it is act- and event-tokens that are reenacted.

6. Not all philosophers would accept the claim that act- and event-tokens cannot recur.

For some readers, these abstractly formulated distinctions will be dark sayings. I trust that as we employ them in our analysis the darkness will dissipate.

Intentional repetition

Every act-token that one performs is a token (instantiation) of a multiplicity of act-types. Neil Armstrong's setting foot on the moon was a token of the act-type of stepping out of a vehicle, a token of the act-type of setting foot on solid ground, and so forth, on and on. Most of the act-types that one is instantiating, when performing some act-token, never cross one's mind. They couldn't; there are vastly too many of them. When kneeling in some liturgical enactment, one might instantiate the act-type of *kneeling at ten o'clock* without giving it a thought. And if one has not given it a thought, then obviously one has not formed and acted on the intention to produce an instantiation of that act-type.

I make the point for the purpose of drawing a contrast. Liturgical scripts prescribe the instantiation of certain act-types. Those who follow such a script, knowing what it prescribes, form and act on the intention to instantiate those act-types. They have in mind the act-type, *praising God*, and they form and enact the intention to produce a token of that type. They have in mind the act-type, *interceding with God*, and they form and enact the intention to produce a token of that act-type. And so forth. Such actions are *intentional instantiations* of the act-types. One's action is an intentional instantiation of some act-type if one has that act-type in mind and forms and enacts the intention to produce an instantiation (token) thereof.

When a participant in some liturgical enactment intentionally instantiates some act-type prescribed by the script, her action is ordinarily a *repetition* of that act-type; ordinarily that act-type has been instantiated many times before. The act-type *praising God* has been instantiated billions of times. Most of the participants will be aware of the fact that by intentionally producing tokens of the prescribed act-types they are repeating those act-types. They will be aware of the fact that they are carrying on a liturgical tradition.

Probably some are not only aware that by instantiating the act-types specified by the script they are *as a matter of fact* repeating those act-types; probably some have it *as their intention* to repeat those act-types. They intend to produce additional tokens, additional recurrences, of the act-types. Sometimes it will not be clear which of these two sorts of intentions is being enacted: *intending to instantiate* the act-type in question, versus *intending to repeat* that act-type, that is, intending to instantiate it *again*. Nonetheless, intending to instantiate some act-type is not the same as intending to instantiate that act-type *again*—not even if one realizes that one will in fact be doing so again. Intending to confess one's sins is not the same as intending to confess one's sins *again*.

It's a subtle point; so a non-liturgical example may prove helpful. When the conductor at a rehearsal of some musical work stops the rehearsal, says to the players, "Let's play those last ten bars again," and the orchestra does what the conductor asks, then he and the orchestra *intend to repeat* playing those ten bars of music. Previously their intention was just to play the work, including the ten bars; if it's a standard work, they will have done so in the realization that their performance of the work is a repetition. Their intention now is to play the ten bars *again*, to produce a *recurrence* of those ten bars.

Now for a new point. Suppose the conductor does not just say, "Let's play those last ten bars again." Suppose he adds, "and let's play them a bit faster this time." And suppose the orchestra tries to do what the conductor asks for, namely, play the last ten bars again and a bit faster. Then they don't just intend to repeat the last ten bars. Now it is *with their eye on the token they just produced* that they intend to repeat the last ten bars. Let me call such repetition, *token-guided* repetition. The idea of token-guided repetition will figure prominently in our analysis of liturgical repetitions.

Token-guided repetition of some act-type occurs when, with that act-type in mind, and with an already-performed token of that act-type also in mind, one is in some way guided in one's repetition of that act-type by that token. It's not the act-token that one intends to repeat; that's impossible. It's the act-type that one intends to repeat, being guided in one's repetition by that previously performed token. For ordinary intentional repetition of some act-type to occur, one need only have that act-type in mind. For token-guided repetition to occur, one must have two things in mind: a particular act-type, and a particular token of that act-type.

As we shall see, one might have any one of a number of different reasons for wanting to be guided, in one's instantiation of some act-type, by some previous token of that act-type. A common reason for doing so is that one wants to imitate or emulate the act-token in question; another common reason is that one wants to produce a better token. Our example of the orchestra playing the ten bars again was implicitly an illustration of this latter sort of reason; they want to produce a better token of playing the ten bars than the token they just did produce by playing them a bit faster.

Liturgical repetitions of biblical narrations

With these distinctions in hand, let us look at some of the different kinds of repetitions that occur in Christian liturgical enactments. In almost all such enactments, a good deal of intentional repetition occurs by way of the introduction, in one way or another, of biblical narratives. I will focus on such repetitions.

When a story is told, one can distinguish between the *telling* of the story, on the one hand, and *what's told and can be extrapolated from what's told*, on the other hand.[7] I will use the term "narration" for the act of telling, and the term "narrative" for what's told and can be extrapolated therefrom.

When a lector reads aloud a passage from Scripture, she intentionally repeats the act of producing tokens of the words of the text—in this case, auditory rather than inscribed tokens. An implication of our discussion in Chapter 6 is that, when the passage read is a narrative and the narrative contains no first- or second-person pronouns, something more takes place as well: the reader intentionally repeats the telling of that narrative. She re-narrates the story. A good deal of the intentional repetition that occurs in Christian liturgical enactments is such repetition: the lector repeats the narration of some part of the biblical narrative by reading aloud a narrative passage from Scripture.

Liturgical acts of intentionally repeating the telling of some part of the biblical narrative are not confined to the reading of Scripture; intentional re-telling also occurs when there is a *rehearsal* of some episode in a biblical narrative. What I mean by a "rehearsal" of some episode is a narrating of the

---

7. By "extrapolating from what's told" I mean inferring from what's told what else was the case. If we are told that someone walked a mile, we can infer that it took him at least six minutes to do so. In Part Three of Wolterstorff (1980) I develop an account of how extrapolation works.

episode couched wholly or in part in the speaker's own words or arrange-
ment of words, rather than in the very words of Scripture, or couched in the
words of whoever it was that composed the liturgical text.

Many sermons and homilies contain rehearsals of this sort: the preacher
tells a biblical story in his or her own words. But rather than illustrating the
point by quoting some rehearsals of that sort, let me illustrate the point by
noting that a component of all mainline Eucharistic liturgies is a rehearsal
of what Jesus is reported in the New Testament as having said and done at
his last meal with his disciples. Though the texts of these rehearsals draw
on the four biblical accounts of the episode, few of them simply repeat
the words of any one of those accounts. Almost all of them are new compositions, differing in their details from one liturgy to another. When the
priest or minister reads this part of the liturgical text, he or she is thereby
re-telling, re-narrating, rehearsing, the episode. He or she is repeating the
act-type, already instantiated by Paul and the authors of the three synoptic
Gospels, of narrating what Jesus said and did at his last supper—intentionally
repeating that act-type.

To the best of my knowledge, the Eucharistic texts currently in use
for the rehearsal by the celebrant of what was said and done at Jesus' last
supper do not go beyond what St Paul and the three synoptic Gospel writers
report as having been said and done. Each of the texts makes a selection
from the various reports and combines that selection into a unified account;
they do not extrapolate. They are restrained in that respect. By contrast,
the presentation of episodes in the biblical narratives that one finds in the
Orthodox *Lenten Triodion* are often astonishingly unrestrained. Adam's
imagined lament, discussed in Chapter 6, is an example of the point. Though
we can be confident that Adam did lament his fall, Scripture contains no
record of his lament.

Let's have another example of the point. In the liturgy for Vespers on
Holy Friday the people (choir) sing these words:

Joseph [of Arimathea] with Nicodemus took you down from the tree ...; and
looking upon you dead, stripped, and without burial, in his grief and tender
compassion he lamented, saying, "Woe is me, my sweetest Jesus! When but
a little while ago the sun saw you hanging on the cross, it wrapped itself in
darkness: the earth quaked with fear and the veil of the temple was rent in twain.
And now I see you for my sake submitting of your own will to death. How
shall I bury you, my God? How shall I wrap you in a winding sheet? How shall

I touch your most pure body with my hands? What song at your departure shall I sing to you, O compassionate saviour?"[8]

A bit later the people (choir) sing these words:

The pure Virgin Mother wept as she took him on her knees; her tears flowed down upon him, and with bitter cries of grief she kissed him. "My son, my lord and God, you were the only hope of your handmaiden, my life and the light of my eyes; and now, alas, I have lost you, my sweet and most beloved child....I see you, my beloved child, stripped, broken, anointed for burial, a corpse....In my hands I hold you as a corpse, O loving lord, who has brought the dead to life; grievously is my heart wounded and I long to die with you....I reflect, O master, how never again shall I hear your voice; never again shall your handmaiden see the beauty of your face as in the past; for you, my son, have sunk down before my eyes....Release me from my agony, and take me with you, O my son and God....Leave me not to live alone."[9]

These passages are extraordinary, extraordinary in the intensity of the emotions expressed, extraordinary also in the degree to which they flesh out what happened at Jesus' crucifixion beyond what the biblical narrations report and beyond what can be extrapolated therefrom. Matthew and Mark report Mary as present at the crucifixion; and Matthew and Luke report Joseph of Arimathea as taking the body of Jesus down from the cross, wrapping it in a clean linen cloth, and laying it in a new tomb. They report Mary as present when this occurred. We can confidently extrapolate that Joseph and Mary both lamented the death of the one they so deeply loved. But the words of their lament in the Orthodox liturgy are entirely imagined. The restraint, of not going beyond what Scripture reports and what can be extrapolated therefrom, has been cast off and we have entered the domain, as it were, of fictional realism. The poets of the Eastern church have enjoyed far greater liturgical freedom and recognition than the poets of the post-medieval Western church.

8. *Lenten Triodion* (1978), 615–16. In my quotations from *The Lenten Triodion* I have modernized the grammar and the capitalization.
9. *Lenten Triodion* (1978), 618–20. In "Liturgical Immersion," Terence Cuneo says about these two hymns that "The liturgical script...invites the participants to take up something like Joseph of Arimathea's and Mary's first-person perspectives on Jesus' death and burial." Cuneo (2016b), 68. This is true. But it should be noted that the participants do so not by speaking in the voice of Joseph and of Mary but by speaking in their own voice and saying what Joseph and Mary are imagined to have said. In the text I am using, the words attributed to Joseph and to Mary are in quotation marks—correctly so.

When the Orthodox liturgy for Vespers on Holy Friday is enacted and the people (choir) sing these words, are they rehearsing part of the biblical narrative? Are they re-narrating part of what happened? I think not. When preachers, in their sermons and homilies, present to the congregation episodes in the biblical narratives, they often go beyond rehearsing in their own words what is explicitly narrated and can be extrapolated therefrom to imagine what might have happened. Their presentation is a blend of rehearsal and imagination. The laments of Joseph and Mary in the Orthodox liturgy—and of Adam—leave rehearsal behind and go all the way toward imagination.

Liturgical repetition of episodes in the biblical narratives

We have been discussing the repetition, in enactments of Christian liturgies, of biblical narrations, these repetitions taking the form of reading aloud or reciting the words of those narrations, or of rehearsing in our own words episodes from the narratives. Let us move on to liturgical repetitions of *episodes* from the narratives. Recall my use of the terms "narration" and "narrative." Given the telling of a story, the narration is the act of telling the story; the narrative is what's told plus what can be extrapolated therefrom.

Christian liturgical enactments are replete with repetitions of episodes in the biblical narratives. The people pray, just as persons in the narratives prayed; the people praise God, just as persons in the narratives praised God. The interesting question is not whether there are repetitions of episodes in the biblical narratives but whether, in present-day Christian liturgical enactments, there is much by way of *token-guided* repetitions of episodes in the biblical narratives.

Celebrations of the Lord's Supper are token-guided repetitions of Jesus' last supper with his disciples, and Palm Sunday processions are token-guided repetitions of Jesus' reception by the people when he made his final entry into Jerusalem. I will have something to say about both of these when I discuss liturgical reenactments of episodes in the biblical narratives. Let me here call attention to the foot washings included in many Maundy Thursday liturgies.

In the Gospel of John, Jesus is reported as washing the feet of his disciples as they assembled for what would prove to be his last meal. At the conclusion of this foot washing he explains what he has done:

> Do you know what I have done to you? You call me Teacher and Lord—and you are right, for that is what I am. So if I, your Lord and Teacher, have washed your feet, you also ought to wash one another's feet. For I have set you an example, that you also should do as I have done to you.   (13: 12–15)

In many liturgies for Maundy Thursday this passage is read aloud and the minister or priest then washes the feet of a few members of the congregation; sometimes they, in turn, wash the feet of others. Clearly this is a token-guided repetition of what Jesus did, the point of the repetition being to emulate what he did. That the point is emulation is particularly clear in the Orthodox liturgy for matins on Maundy Thursday when the people (choir) sing:

> Let us remain at the Master's side, that we may see how he washes the feet of the disciples and wipes them with a towel; and let us do as we have seen, subjecting ourselves to each other and washing one another's feet.[10]

While we are on the topic of emulation of biblical episodes, it's worth noting that Christian liturgical enactments rather often include *injunctions* to the congregants to emulate episodes in the biblical narrative, both within the liturgy and outside. Justin Martyr, describing the liturgical practice of the church in Rome around 150 CE writes, "When the lector has finished, the president addresses us and exhorts us to imitate the splendid things we have heard."[11]

The Lenten Triodion is replete with injunctions to emulate, often issued by the people to themselves. Here is an example from matins for the Sunday of the Publican and Pharisee (fourth Sunday before Lent):

> Let us make haste to follow the Pharisee in his virtues and to emulate the Publican in his humility....In our prayer, let us fall down before God, with tears and fervent cries of sorrow, emulating the Publican in the humility which lifted him on high; and let us sing in faith: O God of our fathers, blessed art thou.[12]

And sometimes the people, when enacting one of the liturgies in *The Lenten Triodion, declare that they are* emulating some biblical figure rather than

---

10. *Lenten Triodion* (1978), 552.   11. *Apologia* I.67. Deiss (1979), 93.
12. *Lenten Triodion* (1978), 105, 107.

enjoining themselves (or being enjoined) to do so. Here is an extraordinary example from the Great Compline for Wednesday in the first week of Lent:

> Like the thief I cry to thee, "Remember me"; like Peter I weep bitterly; like the publican I call out, "Forgive me, Saviour"; like the harlot I shed tears. Accept my lamentation, as once thou hast accepted the entreaties of the woman of Canaan....
>
> Like the woman of Canaan I cry to thee, "Have mercy on me, son of David." Like the woman with an issue of blood, I touch the hem of thy garment. I weep as Martha and Mary wept for Lazarus.[13]

Though injunctions to the people to emulate some episode in the biblical narrative, and declarations by the people that they are emulating some episode in the biblical narrative, occur more frequently in *The Lenten Triodion* than in any other liturgical text, they are by no means absent from the liturgical enactments of other traditions. The place to look is not primarily to the fixed liturgical texts but to the hymns appointed to be sung. A vivid example is the evangelical hymn, "Dare to Be a Daniel," composed by Philip P. Bliss in 1873. The first stanza and the refrain go as follows:

> Standing by a purpose true,
> Heeding God's command,
> Honor them, the faithful few!
> All hail to Daniel's band!
>
> *Refrain*
> Dare to be a Daniel,
> Dare to stand alone!
> Dare to have a purpose firm!
> Dare to make it known!

Do present-day Christian liturgies include other token-guided repetitions of episodes in biblical narratives, in addition to the ones mentioned, namely, celebrations of the Lord's Supper, Palm Sunday processions, Maundy Thursday foot washings, and certain of the Orthodox prayers? Might baptisms, for example, be such repetitions?

The New Testament reports a number of baptisms, the most prominent of them being the baptism of Jesus by John the Baptist (Matthew 3: 13–17; Mark 1: 9–11; Luke 3: 21–2). Liturgical baptisms are, obviously, intentional repetitions of the act-type *baptism*. But are they token-guided repetitions? If they are, the token guiding the repetition is presumably John's baptism of Jesus. When the church repeats the act-type *baptizing*, does it have its eye on

13. *Lenten Triodion* (1978), 245.

John's baptism of Jesus, and is it in some way guided by that token of the type in what it does? Does it perhaps aim at emulating John's baptism of Jesus?

I think not. In the Orthodox liturgy for Maundy Thursday the foot washing is introduced by the people singing, "Let us do what we have seen [Jesus] do." I know of no present-day baptismal rite in which the celebrant introduces the baptism by saying some such thing as, "Let us do what John did when he baptized Jesus." The rites contain no suggestion that the baptism about to take place is to be understood as done in imitation of John's baptism of Jesus.[14]

Some baptismal rites do make some reference to John's baptism of Jesus; but that's not enough, by itself, to give to the baptism about to take place the structure of an imitation of John's baptism of Jesus. In Paul's teaching on the significance of baptism he does not refer to John's baptism of Christ. What he says is, all "who have been baptized into Christ Jesus were baptized into his death" so that, "just as Christ was raised from the dead by the glory of the Father, so we too might walk in newness of life" (Romans 6: 3–4; cf. Colossians 2: 12).

Might the people's praying of the Lord's Prayer be a token-guided repetition? Obviously it is an intentional repetition of the praying of the Lord's Prayer. But is it a token-guided repetition? Again, I think not. Typically the liturgical leader bids the recitation of the prayer with such words as these: "As our Lord taught us to pray, let us pray." Had Jesus' teaching of the prayer taken the form of actually praying the prayer, then the people's praying of the prayer would be a repetition guided by that token of praying the prayer. They would be imitating or emulating what Jesus did. But we are not told that Jesus actually prayed the prayer; we are only told that he taught it. The liturgical leader does not bid the praying of the prayer with the words, "Let us pray as Jesus prayed."

So far as I can see, present-day Christian liturgies, with the exception of the Orthodox, incorporate relatively few token-guided repetitions of episodes in the biblical narratives. From histories of liturgy one learns that things were different in the middle ages in the West; the liturgies of those days were

14. What I say in the text holds for present-day baptismal liturgies. In his essay "Historicism Revisited," Robert Taft SJ remarks, "Gabriele Winkler has demonstrated that the earliest Semitic stratum of the Syrian and Armenian initiation rites was modeled not on the eschatological death-resurrection motif of Rom. 6, but on the messianic anointing of Jesus at his baptism in the Jordan, which was ritually re-enacted in the baptismal rites." Taft (1984), 23.

crowded with token-guided repetitions of biblical episodes, often incorporated into reenactments of those episodes.

Reenactments

More could be said about liturgical repetitions. But let's move on to liturgical reenactments, first considering the nature of reenactments in general, and then considering whether present-day enactments of Christian liturgies incorporate reenactments of episodes in the biblical narratives.

Perhaps some readers would call everything that I have called a repetition, a "reenactment." I doubt that that is a correct use of the term. But I won't argue the point. Suppose that it is a correct use of the term. Then the thing to say would be that the term "reenactment" has two significantly different meanings. It means what I call *a repetition* and it also means what I call a *reenactment*. These are not the same. What we repeat are act- and event-types; what we reenact are act- and event-tokens. A reenactment of some act- or event-token may incorporate intentional repetitions; most of them do. But a reenactment is not, as such, a repetition of an act- or event-type. It's a *depiction* of an act- or event-token. Reenactments are representational.

Imagine a reenactment of some historical episode. The American Civil War effectively ended on April 9, 1865, when General Robert E. Lee, head of the Confederate army, surrendered to General Ulysses S. Grant, head of the Union army, in the courthouse located in the tiny Virginia village of Appomattox. The courthouse is still standing and is now part of a National Historical Park.

A historian who writes about the end of the Civil War offers to his readers a narrative of Lee's surrender. As we saw earlier, that same narrative can be re-narrated by reading aloud the historian's narration, by reciting it from memory, or by rehearsing in one's own words what happened. But verbal narration is not the only way in which a narrative of Lee's surrender can be presented. It can also be presented by the performance of a live reenactment of the surrender.

As preparation for such a reenactment one person would be assigned to play the role of Lee and another would be assigned to play the role of Grant. The person assigned to play the role of Lee would be dressed more or less as Lee was dressed, and the person assigned to play the role of Grant would be dressed more or less as Grant was dressed. A number of men would be assigned to play the role of Union soldiers and would be dressed as Union soldiers were dressed at the time; others would be assigned to play the role of Confederate soldiers and would be dressed as Confederate soldiers were dressed. Those playing the role of Union soldiers would be carrying real or fake guns.

When the time came for the reenactment to begin, the persons playing the role of Lee and Grant would arrive at the courthouse on horseback. By acting in the roles assigned them by the script, and by employing various entities as props—guns, horses, a desk, etc.—they would be presenting to viewers and listeners a reenactment of what happened in Appomattox on April 9, 1865.

What I have been calling a "reenactment" of Lee's surrender is a depiction of the surrender. To reenact is not to repeat but to depict. A repetition of Lee's surrender would be another surrender; it would be another instantiation of the act-type, *surrendering one's army to one's opponent*. In a reenactment of the surrender, no surrender takes place. The person playing the role of Lee depicts Lee surrendering; but to depict Lee surrendering is not to surrender. And since the actor does not actually surrender, there is no surrender that imitates Lee's surrender, and hence none that emulates Lee's surrender. Of course, some of the things the actor does are imitating-repetitions of what Lee did; getting off a horse and walking up the steps of the courthouse repeats-by-imitating what Lee did. But most of the repetitions-by-imitation of what Lee did are in the service of depicting what he did.

My imaginary example has been that of a live reenactment. Reenactments of historical events can also take the form of film reenactments. On November 4, 1979, Iranian activists stormed the US embassy in Teheran. Six of the staff escaped and hid in the home of the Canadian ambassador; the others, more than fifty, were taken hostage. Tony Mendez, a US Central Intelligence Agency specialist, eventually succeeded in getting the six out of the country in a derring-do escapade. He described the escape in his book, *The Master of Disguise*. The film *Argo*, directed by Ben Affleck, is a film reenactment of the escape, depending heavily on the book for its information.

Are celebrations of the Eucharist live reenactments?

As I mentioned at the beginning of this chapter, celebrations of the Eucharist are often said to be reenactments of Jesus' last meal with his disciples. Is that true? St Paul and the writers of the synoptic Gospels composed verbal narrations of what happened at that last meal. Is a celebration of the Eucharist an alternative way of presenting the same episode, namely, by means of a live reenactment?

One can imagine a reenactment of Jesus' last meal. One person would play the role of Jesus. That is, in fact, how one of the Greek Church Fathers, Theodore of Mopsuestia, described the role of the presider at the Eucharist in one of his catechetical homilies: "The duty of the High Priest of the New Covenant [i.e. Christ] is to offer this sacrifice which revealed the nature of the New Covenant. We ought to believe that the bishop who is now at the altar is playing the part of this high priest."[15] There would be other people playing the role of the disciples. In the paradigmatic case there would be twelve of these; but circumstances might call for fewer—or more. And there would be bread and wine on a table. At a certain point the person playing the role of Jesus would pick up the bread and say some such words as these: "This is my body, which is given for you. Do this as a memorial of me." He would then offer the bread to the people playing the role of the disciples, and they would eat the bread. The person playing the role of Jesus would then take a cup of wine and say some such words as these: "This is my blood of the new covenant, which is shed for you and for many for the forgiveness of sins. Whenever you drink it, do this as a memorial of me." He would then pass the cup to those playing the role of the disciples, and they would drink the wine.

Celebrations of the Eucharist are not even remotely like this. Typically there are more than twelve people present, in addition to the priest or minister. So which, of all those present, are playing the roles of the disciples? No designation has been made—not in any Eucharistic celebration that I have ever participated in. And if, implicitly or explicitly, some participants have been designated to play the role of disciples, what role in the reenactment is being played by those who are not so designated? The role of onlooker? But they too eat the bread and drink the wine. And we can be confident that there were no onlookers at Jesus' last supper.

Someone determined to interpret the Eucharist as a reenactment might argue, I suppose, that all the participants, with the exception of the priest or minister, have implicitly been designated to play the role of a disciple. That brings us to what seems to me the decisive consideration against the reenactment interpretation. The words that the priest or minister speaks are

15. Quoted by Meyendorff (1984), 29.

not right for someone playing the role of Jesus. In no Eucharistic liturgy that I know of does the priest or minister, when offering the bread to the people, repeat Jesus' words, "Take, eat, this is my body which is given for you." He or she quotes those words in the course of rehearsing, before the distribution, what took place at Jesus' last meal, not when he or she is offering the bread to the people. Here is the relevant section of the rehearsal in one of the Episcopal texts for the liturgy:

> On the night he [Jesus] was handed over to suffering and death, our Lord Jesus Christ took bread; and when he had given thanks to you, he broke it, and gave it to his disciples, and said, "Take, eat. This is my Body, which is given for you. Do this for the remembrance of me."[16]

What the Episcopal priest says to the people, when he invites them to take and eat the bread and drink the wine, is not those words, which are the words he would say if he were playing the role of Christ, but these: "The gifts of God for the people of God. Take them in remembrance that Christ died for you, and feed on him in your hearts by faith, with thanksgiving." These are not words that someone playing the role of Christ would say. Here, and throughout, the priest or minister is speaking in his own voice. What Protestants call "The Lord's Supper" is not a reenactment of the last supper.[17]

We reach the same conclusion, that a celebration of the Eucharist is not a reenactment of Jesus' last supper, when we take account of the theology of the Eucharist. There are many theologies of the Eucharist. For the purposes at hand I have no choice but to take one particular Eucharistic theology and analyze it with our question in mind, of whether the Eucharist is a live reenactment. Because John Calvin's theology of the Eucharist is the one I am most familiar with, and the one I favor, let me choose it.

It was Calvin's view that, by way of the priest or minister offering the consecrated bread and wine to the congregants, Christ is offering himself to them—offering to dwell within them to sanctify them. The priest's or minister's act of offering the consecrated bread and wine to the people counts as Christ offering himself to them. And a person's act of taking and

---

16. *Book of Common Prayer* (1979), 362. If the celebrant, after repeating these words of Jesus, then breaks the bread, his saying those words and breaking the bread can perhaps be regarded as a reenactment of what Jesus did, with the celebrant filling the role of Jesus; so too for the celebrant's saying the counterpart words over the wine and then pouring the wine.

17. Among the mystery plays that emerged in Europe in the late middle ages were plays in which the last supper clearly was being reenacted. See McCall (2007), 27.

eating the bread and drinking the wine counts as his or her acceptance of Christ's offer.

If this is one's theology of the Eucharist, one will reject the suggestion that a celebration of the Eucharist is a reenactment of what transpired at Jesus last meal. On Calvin's interpretation, the Eucharist, at the point of the offering, taking, and consuming of the bread and wine, is not backward-looking but present-oriented. The acts performed by the presider and the congregants are not acts of role-playing that depict what happened 2,000 years ago; rather, the presider's act of offering the bread and wine counts as Christ here and now offering himself. Christ repeats what he did at his last supper: he offers himself. And the people's act of taking and consuming the bread and wine counts as their here and now accepting Christ's offer. No role-playing is involved.

Rather than being a reenactment of what took place at Christ's last meal, a celebration of the Eucharist is (in part) a complex, layered, token-guided repetition thereof.

Are there liturgical reenactments?

In medieval times, liturgical enactments commonly included components that were clearly live reenactments of episodes in the biblical narrative.[18] This was particularly true on the high holy days. On Easter, for example, the episode of the women arriving at the empty tomb was reenacted.[19] Eventually these "tropes"—as they are commonly called by scholars—fell out of the liturgy and, after considerable elaboration, gained new life in the late middle ages as independent mystery plays.

In present-day liturgical enactments there are, so far as I can see, only a few reenactments of episodes in the biblical narratives. Enactments of Christian liturgies do pervasively invoke episodes from the biblical narratives. The congregants sing about such episodes, at some points they imitate such episodes, readers narrate such episodes, preachers interpret and apply such episodes. But not often do the participants reenact such episodes.

18. This is one aspect of what Robert Taft (1984) calls the "historicizing" trend in liturgy. What he has in mind is the tendency, at first especially on Good Friday and Easter, to make the liturgy a sequence of reenactments and celebrations of episodes in the biblical narrative. He describes it as the "fragmentation of the unitary paschal feast into a sequence of celebrations that follow the déroulement of the historical events of the passion" (25). He thinks the historicizing trend in medieval liturgy had its roots "in the historicizing piety of the type called 'Franciscan'" (25).
19. See McCall (2007), 10.

Perhaps the most obvious example of a liturgical reenactment is what occurs in many liturgical enactments on Palm Sunday. All three synoptic Gospels report that, as Jesus approached Jerusalem for what would prove to be the last time, a large crowd turned out to greet him. They spread their cloaks on the road, waved branches cut from trees, and shouted:

> Hosanna to the Son of David!
> Blessed is the one who comes in the name of the Lord!
> Hosanna in the highest heaven![20]

In many liturgical enactments on Palm Sunday the people enter the church waving palm branches and singing an adaptation and expansion of what the crowd shouted on that day long ago when Jesus entered Jerusalem for the last time. In doing so, they are reenacting the crowd's reception of Jesus on that fateful day. My guess—I don't know—is that in medieval times the Palm Sunday reenactment would have been fleshed out by having someone representing Jesus come riding on a donkey and by having the people throw their garments on the ground while shouting "Hosanna."

I did not use the term "reenactment" when I analyzed, in Chapter 6, the imagined lament of Adam in the Vespers and matins of the Orthodox liturgy for the last Sunday before Lent. But on one interpretation of what takes place, that is what the people are doing when they voice the lament: they are reenacting Adam's (imagined) lament. They are not just imagining Adam's lament; they are *depicting* his lament by voicing it. They are *playing the role* of Adam and *reenacting his lament*. They are acting representationally. In so doing, they are lamenting their own fall into wretchedness, thereby also emulating his lament. By reenacting Adam's lament they are emulating his lament.

Many people, myself included, do not believe that the name "Adam" in the book of Genesis refers to a historical figure. What this example shows is that we can reenact not only the doings of historical persons but also the doings of characters in some narrative. I will forgo articulating the ontology of such reenactments!

Even more striking than the reenactment of Adam's lament in the Orthodox liturgy is the reenactment of Christ's entombment that takes place when the Orthodox liturgy for Vespers on Holy Friday is performed. What the Orthodox call an *epitaphion* is a depiction, usually on cloth, of Christ after

---

20. This is Matthew's report (21:9) of what the crowd shouted. Mark's report (11:9–10) and Luke's (19:38) are both slightly different.

he had been removed from the cross and was lying supine, his body ready for burial. At a certain point in an enactment of the Orthodox liturgy for Vespers on Holy Friday the people (choir) sing, "Noble Joseph, taking down thy most pure body from the tree, wrapped it in clean linen with sweet spices, and he laid it in a new tomb."[21] While this is being sung the priest takes the local church's epitaphion from where it has been hanging, wraps it in a white cloth, and leads a procession that culminates with his laying the epitaphion on a table decorated with flowers set up in the center of the church. By laying the epitaphion on the table the priest reenacts the entombment of Christ. The people sing about the entombment; the priest reenacts the entombment.

The epitaphion is so unlike a corpse, and the table so unlike a tomb, that some readers will be inclined to employ the general term "symbolize" and describe the priest's action as symbolizing the entombment rather than reenacting it. Sometimes the table has a canopy over it; that makes it more like a tomb. And sometimes the epitaphion is laid on a bier or catafalque; either of those is more reminiscent of a tomb than is a table. Neither of them is very much like a tomb, however; and the epitaphion is not very much like a corpse.

Be that as it may, I think the ceremony is nonetheless best interpreted as a reenactment of Christ's entombment. The priest plays the role of Joseph, the epitaphion functions as a prop standing in for Christ, and the table functions as a prop standing in for a tomb. The priest's action of wrapping the epitaphion in a white cloth reenacts (depicts) Joseph wrapping Christ's body in a linen cloth; and the priest's action of laying the wrapped epitaphion on the table reenacts (depicts) Joseph laying Christ's shrouded body in a tomb. It doesn't matter that the epitaphion doesn't look much like a corpse; it stands for the dead Christ, and that's enough. And it doesn't matter that the table doesn't look much like a tomb; it's enough that it stand for the tomb. In general, it is not a condition of something functioning as a prop in a reenactment that it look a good deal like what it stands for. What stands for a star in a Christmas pageant never looks much like a star.

In his little treatise, *On the Divine Liturgy*, St Germanus of Constantinople (seventh century) offers a highly symbolic interpretation of the liturgy: one is left with the impression that almost everything the participants do and almost everything they touch symbolizes something or other. Here is a small sample:

21. *Lenten Triodion* (1978), 616.

"The entrance of the Gospel [from the sanctuary into the church] signifies the coming of the Son of God and his entrance into this world."[22] "The ascent of the bishop to the throne and his blessing the people signifies that the Son of God, having completed the economy of salvation, raised his hands and blessed his holy disciples."[23] "The eiliton[24] signifies the winding sheet in which the body of Christ was wrapped when it was taken down from the cross and placed in a tomb."[25] "The discos[26] represents the hands of Joseph and Nicodemus, who buried Christ."[27] And so forth, on and on.[28]

What mainly impresses a present-day reader of St Germanus is his extra-ordinarily fertile and fanciful imagination. But the question our discussion suggests is whether, on Germanus' interpretation, the liturgy is full of brief reenactments. Given Germanus' symbolic interpretation of the liturgical act of bringing the Gospel from the sanctuary into the church, is that act a reenactment of the coming of Christ into the world? Given his symbolic interpretation of the liturgical act of the bishop blessing the people, is that act a reenactment of Christ's blessing of his disciples? And so forth.

Given Germanus' symbolic interpretations, I think these are indeed reenactments of episodes in the biblical narrative. The liturgy, on his inter-pretation, is full of mini-reenactments. The question, of course, is whether his symbolic interpretations are defensible. When I remarked that Christian liturgical reenactments contain very few reenactments of biblical episodes, I was assuming that his interpretations are not defensible.

What's the point?

We do not exaggerate if we describe enactments of Christian liturgies as saturated with biblical narrations and narratives. Over and over, in multiple ways, the narrations and narratives are invoked and introduced. Our focus in this chapter has been on repetitions and reenactments: repetitions of biblical narrations, repetitions of biblical episodes, especially token-guided

---

22. Germanus of Constantinople (1984), 73.   23. Germanus (1984), 77.
24. A large cloth that was placed on the altar near the beginning of the Eucharist.
25. Germanus (1984), 84–5.   26. The plate holding the Eucharistic bread.
27. Germanus (1984), 87.
28. McCall (2007), 10ff., briefly traces the origins and history of the symbolic interpretation of the liturgy.

repetitions, and reenactments of biblical episodes. The obvious question our discussion raises is, what's the point of these repetitions and reenactments?

In his essay, "Liturgical Immersion," Terence Cuneo suggests that the point is that by participating in the liturgy, the people are immersed in the narratives.[29] He explains what he means by "immersion" by describing, in some detail, the experience of being immersed or absorbed in the narrative of some work of history, biography, autobiography, or fiction. Liturgical immersion is like that, he says. The aim of the repetitions and reenactments is that the participants be immersed in the biblical narratives, absorbed in them.

Certainly it's true that one of the functions of liturgical re-narrations of biblical narratives, of token-guided repetitions of biblical episodes, and of reenactments, is that the congregants are thereby immersed in those narratives.[30] The same is true of the often-vivid elaborations of biblical narratives that occur in Orthodox, Catholic, and Protestant hymnody: the aim is that the participants be immersed in those narratives. But often the intended function goes beyond immersion. When there is a washing of feet on Maundy Thursday, not only are the congregants immersed in the biblical narrative concerning that episode. The one washing the feet is *emulating* what Jesus did, and the people are participating vicariously in that emulation. So too, the intended function of Eucharistic repetitions goes well beyond immersion in the narrative.

So far as I can see, there is no general answer to the question, why the repetitions of biblical narrations and the repetitions and reenactments of episodes in the biblical narrative. We can describe the rationale or intended function of particular repetitions and reenactments. But to the disappointment of the theorist, there is no single rationale or intended function that covers all the cases. The church mines Scripture for its art, for its music, for its poetry, for its ethics, for its imagery, for its wisdom, for its faith, for its hope, for its love—and for its liturgy. Why does it do this? Count the reasons!

---

29. Cuneo (2016a).
30. It has not always been so. Robert Taft observes that in the Alexandrines of the third century there was "a decided attenuation of the importance of Salvation History as history. The salvific *event* becomes a *type*, a symbol of an interior, spiritual reality." He quotes Origin: "the perfect Christian,…who considers that 'Christ our Passover was sacrificed for us'…never ceases to keep the paschal feast. For pascha means 'passover', and he is ever striving in all his thoughts, words, and deeds to pass over from the things of this life to God, and is hastening toward His city." Taft (1984), 19.

Is a liturgical enactment a performance of a drama?

Rather often it is said that liturgical enactments are performances of a drama. Let us conclude our discussion of liturgical repetitions and reenactments by assessing this claim. The most articulate development of the idea that I know of is by the philosopher Gordon Graham in his essay, "Liturgy as Drama." A liturgical enactment, says Graham, is "a dramatic enactment of the Gospel in which all present participate in a variety of roles."[31] "Together the faithful enact the cosmic drama of the world's salvation."[32] Let's consider the case Graham makes for this interpretation.

Before he turns to liturgy, Graham makes two observations about performances of works of drama in general. First, for a performance of a dramatic work to be a good performance, the actors and actresses

> have to fuse their own persons with that of the imagined character whose part they play so that the distinction between performer and performed is imperceptible. One way of expressing this is to say that, for the duration of the performance, the actor must *be* the character. Of course, there is a plain sense in which the character is not a real person, and the actor is....
>
> The sense in which the actress is the character is this. The animating spirit in a theatrical performance is the whole being of the actress.... Without the person of the actress, the character remains simply a name and some lines in a script. On the other hand, the character is not of the actress's invention, but the playwright's.[33]

Second, in a performance of a dramatic work "the eternal comes into being in time (Kierkegaard)."

> Lear (the character) is an imaginary creation that requires a real actor for its realization. Any realization of the part has temporal duration. We can put a date and place on the performance. Yet "Lear" the character is timeless. No date (or place) can be assigned to his existence. In this sense, the timeless and the temporal are united....Now this, I want to say, is precisely the model that is needed for liturgical action. Any celebration of communion can be dated. But communion itself is timeless. Participation thus means that the action of the communicants, like the performance of the actor, is both in time *and* timeless.[34]

---

31. Graham (2007), 77.   32. Graham (2007), 79.
33. Graham (2007), 76.   34. Graham (2007), 79.

Here, then, is part of Graham's analysis of liturgical enactments as dramatic performances. After some preparatory actions "the first main act of the drama is ready to begin—the Liturgy of the Word." "An ordinary member of 'the people' emerges from the crowd, as the Hebrew prophets did, to declare to the assembled company the Word of God as it is found in the Old Testament. In response, the people, like the people of Israel, together sing (or say) one of the ancient Psalms...characteristic of Israel's worship. Then, a second prophet emerges from the crowd, this time a prophet of the 'new' Israel, and there is a reading from the Epistles." Then, after the gradual hymn is sung, "the Gospel is carried in procession from the altar to the people, signifying that the words of Jesus come down from God, and thus are not simply those of a human prophet, however visionary."[35]

Shortly "the second act of the drama begins—the Liturgy of the Sacrament." Ordinary bread and wine, symbolizing "the basic foods required to sustain physical life," are placed on the table. "With the gifts on the altar, the celebrant leads the people in lifting up their hearts in praise." Soon there follows "the prayer of Consecration by means of which God transforms the ordinary gifts of bread and wine to the extraordinary gift of the sacrament. In some places, a bell rings to signify that in a special, mystical way, God himself has entered the Sanctuary, and waits for his people."[36]

What comes through in Graham's description is that an enactment of a traditional liturgy, if it is anywhere near adequate, has a strong dramatic quality. But is it a performance of a drama? By no means is everything that has a strong dramatic quality a performance of a drama. Are the worshippers performing "the cosmic drama of the world's salvation"?

We saw in Chapter 6 that one plausible interpretation of what is going on in the Adam's lament passages of the Orthodox liturgy is that the congregants are "pretending" to be Adam lamenting. Presumably these "pretendings" are examples of what Graham has in mind by "fusion." We also saw that a plausible interpretation of what is going on when a lector reads the opening works of Luke's Gospel is that the listeners are being invited to imagine that the reader is St Luke speaking those words. If they do so, perhaps that is another example of what Graham has in mind by "fusion."

But notice the fundamental ontological difference between Shakespeare's character King Lear and St Luke. The character King Lear is indeed outside

35. Graham (2007), 78.
36. Graham (2007), 78. No doubt the reader will be struck, as I was, by the similarity of Graham's description to that of St Germanus.

of time and space; it's an abstract entity. St Luke was very much *in* time and space, a man of flesh and blood. So too, the Old Testament prophets and the New Testament gospel and epistle writers that Graham mentions were men of flesh and blood *in* time and space. When Shakespeare's play *King Lear* is performed, the timeless and the temporal are, as Graham observes, united in a certain way: the timeless character is united with the temporal actor. Nothing of that sort happens when the words of an Old Testament prophet or of a New Testament gospel or epistle writer are read aloud in a liturgical enactment.

What Graham calls the "cosmic drama of the world's salvation" is not a work of drama; it is not comparable to Shakespeare's *King Lear*. It is, rather, a component of world history. Episodes in that component of world history can be reenacted, just as the historical surrender of Lee can be reenacted. What I have argued, however, is that when we look closely at Christian liturgical enactments, we find very few reenactments of biblical episodes. A good many repetitions, including some token-guided repetitions; but very few reenactments.

8

Liturgical commemoration

One of the many ways in which Christian liturgical enactments invoke Scripture is by the participants doing something as a memorial of a person or event in the biblical narrative. In most Eucharistic celebrations the celebrant quotes words that Luke and Paul report Jesus as having spoken at his last supper: "Do this as a memorial [in remembrance, *eis anamnêsin*] of me."[1] Our project in this chapter is, first, to clarify and analyze what it is to perform some liturgical action as a memorial or remembrance, and then to consider which liturgical actions, in addition to the Eucharist, can be understood as memorial actions.[2] Some liturgical scholars go so far as to suggest that liturgical enactments in their entirety can be understood as memorials. J.-J. von Allmen, says, "The cult is firstly an anamnesis [memorial] of the past work of Christ."[3] I think he is right about that.[4]

Biblical usage

The concept that Jesus employed when he said, "Do this as a memorial of me," would have been familiar to Jews of the time from their acquaintance with the Hebrew Bible, if not from ordinary life. In the Hebrew Bible/Old Testament we find Israel frequently being instructed to do or make something as a *zikkaron*. In the Greek Septuagint translation of the Hebrew Bible/Old Testament the Hebrew term *zikkaron* is translated as *anamnesis*.

---

1. Luke 22: 19; 1 Corinthians 11: 24.
2. My line of thought in this chapter represents a substantial revision of what I wrote about liturgical memorials in Wolterstorff (1990).
3. Von Allmen (1965), 34.
4. In Chapter 9 it will become clear, however, that my understanding of an anamnesis is very different from von Allmen's.

This is the term that Luke and Paul used to report what Jesus said. Both the Hebrew and Greek terms are commonly translated into English as "memorial" or "remembrance." Israel's social environment and its practices were to incorporate memorials or remembrances.

Let's have a few examples. As a remembrance of God's deliverance of Israel from slavery in Egypt members of Israel were to keep their fellow Hebrews as slaves for no more than six years, setting them free in the seventh year (Deuteronomy 15: 12–15). As another remembrance of God's deliverance of Israel from Egypt landowners were to render justice to the widows, the orphans, and the aliens by leaving for them what remained after the first gleanings of their crops (Deuteronomy 24: 19–22). As yet another remembrance of God's deliverance of Israel from Egypt members of Israel were to set aside the seventh day of the week as a holy day; everyone was to rest, animals included (Deuteronomy 5: 12–15).[5] And as a remembrance of the night of Israel's deliverance from Egypt members of Israel were to celebrate the Passover yearly (Deuteronomy 16: 1–12; Exodus 12: 14–15; 13: 3–10).

Exodus 28: 15–30 gives instructions for decorating two of the high priest's garments. The ephod was to contain two stones on which were engraved the names of the twelve sons of Israel. These were "stones of remembrance"; the high priest was to bear the names before the Lord "for remembrance." The breast-piece was to contain twelve stones, each engraved with the name of one of the twelve sons of Israel; the high priest was to bear these twelve names "for a continual remembrance before the Lord."

What was the force of these various instructions to do or make something *as a remembrance* or *to remember*? A common assumption by twentieth-century liturgical scholars is that the concept employed by the ancient Hebrews, of doing or making something as a remembrance (*zikkaron*), was peculiar to them, or peculiar, more generally, to the ancient Semitic peoples. One liturgical scholar writes, "The bread over which the thanksgiving is spoken is a *memorial* (anamnesis). This idea of 'memorial' is a Jewish idea and has often been analyzed."[6]

---

5. In the three cases just mentioned it is the verb *zakar* rather than the noun *zikkaron* that is used in the original Hebrew. I assume that there is no difference between Israel releasing her slaves *to remember* her deliverance and Israel releasing her slaves *as a remembrance of* her deliverance. So also, *mutatis mutandis*, for the other cases mentioned.

6. Jourjon (1978), 81.

Given the assumption that the idea of a memorial was an ancient Hebrew idea, scholars have tried to grasp the concept by looking at uses of the term "*zikkaron*" in the Hebrew Bible—thus engaging in the project of biblical word studies so popular during the middle decades of the twentieth century. The most thorough practitioner of this strategy was the liturgical theologian Max Thurian in *The Eucharistic Memorial*.[7] From his analysis of the uses of the term in the Old Testament Thurian concluded that for Israel to do or make something as a memorial of X was for them to do or make that thing so as to remind someone of X. Sometimes it was God who was to be reminded of the memorialized person or event, in which case the context of the memorial action proper, often expressed in words, was that of blessing God for God's covenant fidelity, of which the memorialized person or event was an indication, and of interceding with God for God's continued fidelity.[8] In other instances it was the people who were to be reminded of the memorialized person or event, in which case the context of the memorial action proper was the people thanking God for God's covenant fidelity, manifested in the memorialized person or event, and pledging anew their obedience. Thurian was inclined to think that though some memorials were oriented more toward God and some more toward the people, in each case there were traces of the other orientation as well.[9] He went on to argue that to understand the Eucharist, Christians must recover the concept of a memorial that was employed in the Hebrew Bible/Old Testament.

If this analysis of the Hebrew Bible's concept of a memorial or remembrance (*zikkaron*) is correct, namely, that a memorial is essentially a reminder, and if this is the concept Jesus used at his last supper and that the church should use for understanding the Eucharist (and certain other liturgical actions as well), then the function of memorial actions in the liturgy is not significantly different from that of the congregants listening to someone reading aloud some passage of biblical narrative: thereby memory of the narrative is aided.

I do not doubt that the remembrances (memorials) that we find mentioned in the Hebrew Bible/Old Testament were meant to function as reminders. But I find it implausible that that was the main point, let alone the whole of the matter. The old folk remedy for the forgetfulness of a husband

---

7. Thurian (1960).
8. Von Allmen reports J. Jeremias as also holding that the Eucharist is celebrated "so that God may remember and act." Von Allmen (1969), 280.
9. The Old Testament scholar Brevard Childs agreed with Thurian on this point. Childs (1962), 66–8.

was to tie a piece of string around his finger to remind him to buy bread, pay the butcher, or whatever. The memorials or remembrances mentioned in the Hebrew Bible/Old Testament are clearly more than mere reminders.

A number of twentieth-century biblical and liturgical scholars, after acknowledging this point, have suggested that what is distinctive of a zikkaron or anamnesis is that the event remembered is somehow *made effective* for the celebrants in the present. Brevard Childs wrote, "Recent Old Testament scholarship has been almost unanimous in pointing out that the chief function of [Israel's] cult was to actualize the tradition."[10] Von Allmen agreed: "The anamnesis is therefore much more than a mnemonic ceremony; it is a re-enactment of the event which the celebration commemorates."[11]

I do not find plausible the assumption of Thurian and his colleagues in liturgical and biblical studies that the ancient Hebrews (or Semites) had a concept of a memorial or remembrance that was peculiar to them, and that to understand in what sense the Eucharist is a memorial we must recover that concept. No such conceptual recovery is necessary. The concept is familiar to all of us.

Doing or making something as a memorial

In ordinary life you and I speak of doing something to commemorate some person or event; we likewise speak of doing or making something as a memorial or remembrance of some person or event. (Henceforth I will use the terms "memorial," "commemoration," and "remembrance" interchangeably.) I see no reason to think that there is any significant difference between our concept of a commemoration, a memorial, a remembrance, and the concept of a *zikkaron* employed in the Hebrew Bible/Old Testament and the concept of an *anamnesis* employed in the New Testament (and in the Septuagint). In the section "Memorial actions of the liturgy" of this chapter I will take note of a minor point of difference between our concept and the concept of an *anamnesis*.

---

10. Childs (1962), 75.
11. Von Allmen (1969), 24. Referring specifically to the Lord's Supper von Allmen wrote that the church celebrates the Lord's Supper "so that through this memorial she may renew and deepen her integration into the history of salvation, the crowning moment of which is re-enacted in this very memorial." Von Allmen (1969), 29.

It's true that some of the things said about one or another *zikkaron* in the Old Testament would not be said by us about any of our memorials; about none of our memorials would we say that they are "for a continual remembrance before the Lord." But from the fact that certain of the acts and objects identified as a *zikkaron* in the Hebrew Bible/Old Testament functioned quite differently from how our memorials function it does not follow that their *concept* of a *zikkaron* was different from our concept of a memorial and was peculiar to them.

Not only is the *concept* of a memorial or commemoration familiar to us; the things themselves, memorials and commemorations, are a common part of ordinary life, far from exotic. We do many different sorts of things as memorials or commemorations and make many different sorts of things as memorials or commemorative objects: we strike coins, issue stamps, shoot off fireworks, give speeches, perform plays, plant trees, hold academic conferences, paint portraits, march in processions, perform dances, raise cenotaphs, construct mausoleums, found and name cities. Memorials pervade our lives and pervade the social and physical environments within which we live our lives. Evidently something deep about ourselves is manifested by our repeatedly engaging in memorial activities and by our surrounding ourselves with memorial objects; something of great importance to us would be lost if we ceased doing so. All the evidence points to the conclusion that we and the ancient Hebrews are not unusual in this regard. In many places and at many times human beings have found themselves impelled to make or do something as a memorial. To be human is to commemorate.

Yet there is, so far as I know, only one substantial philosophical discussion of commemoration, that by Edward Casey in *Remembering*. Let's look at what he says.

Casey's theory: commemorating is a distinctive way of remembering

Casey does not refer to the views of biblical and liturgical scholars. Nonetheless, his theory is basically an elaboration of their claim that the essential function of memorials and commemorations is to aid memory. What he adds to that claim is that commemorations do this by being a *distinct way* of remembering.

He packs his theory into a few sentences:

> In acts of commemoration remembering is intensified by taking place *through* the interposed agency of a text (the eulogy, the liturgy proper) and *in* the setting of a social ritual (delivering the eulogy, participating in the service). The remembering is intensified still further by the fact that both ritual and text become efficacious only in the presence of others, *with* whom we commemorate together in a public ceremony. The "through", "in", and "with" that I have underlined suggest that commemoration is a highly mediated affair— that it involves a quite significant component of otherness at every turn.[12]

Of the three dimensions of commemorating that he identifies in this passage, Casey places special emphasis on the dimension of *remembering through*. He says, "I commemorate, in short, by *remembering through* specific commemorative vehicles such as rituals or texts."[13]

Notice that Casey's theory, as stated, applies only to *acts* of commemoration; commemorative or memorial objects do not enter the picture. Perhaps he allowed the term "commemoration" to shape his theory; we do not naturally speak of some object as a commemoration. We do, however, speak of certain objects as commemorative objects, and we speak of both acts and objects as memorials. We both do certain things as memorials and make certain things as memorials. An adequate theory of commemoration must apply not only to commemorative acts but also to commemorative objects. In the course of his discussion Casey does offer examples of commemorative objects; but his theory is framed only for commemorative acts.

What Casey has in mind, when he describes commemorating as "remembering through" texts and rituals, is that commemorations typically include texts and rituals that are *about* the commemorandum by virtue of containing words, objects, or actions that stand for, represent, or refer to the event or person commemorated. Casey describes the rituals enacted when something is commemorated as incorporating "an allusion, however indirect, to a pre-existing event or person," namely, the event or person commemorated.[14]

It is this same function of texts and rituals that Casey has in mind when he describes a commemoration as *embodying* the commemorandum. Mere reminders do not embody the commemorandum; and, when, on the other hand, I recollect something in my mind, "it presents itself to me limpidly, as if through a transparent glass."[15] Commemorations are intermediate between

---

12. Casey (1987), 218.   13. Casey (1987), 218.
14. Casey (1987), 222.   15. Casey (1987), 219.

mere reminders and mental recollections. In commemorations, "I remember the commemorated past through various commemoratively effective media in the present. It is as if this past were presenting itself to me translucently [not transparently] in such media—as if I were viewing the past in them, albeit darkly: as somehow set within their materiality."[16] The commemorandum is *embodied in* the texts and rituals in the sense that the texts and rituals are *about* the commemorandum by virtue of containing words, objects, or actions that stand for, represent, or refer to the commemorandum. We remember the commemorandum "through" the texts and rituals that "embody" it.

Casey is right, of course, in his claim that commemorations often incorporate texts and rituals that are about the person or event commemorated by virtue of containing words, objects, or actions that stand for, represent, or refer to that person or event. But his theory implies that this is not just often or typically the case, but always and necessarily the case. Commemorating is that distinct way of remembering which consists of remembering "through" texts and rituals that "embody" the commemorandum by virtue of containing words, objects, or actions that stand for, represent, or refer to the commemorandum. Is this strong claim true? Does that distinct way of remembering constitute the essence of commemoration?

It does not. On Sunday, March 17, 2002, the Vienna Philharmonic performed a concert in St Patrick's Cathedral in New York that was described, in a review in the *New York Times* of Tuesday, March 19, as a "free program to honor the victims of Sept. 11." The review was headed, "A Somber Memorial from the Vienna Philharmonic." In short, this was a memorial concert commemorating the victims of 9/11. If there was a component of the commemoration that consisted of texts and rituals that were about the persons being commemorated, the review did not mention them. And in any case, the commemoration need not have incorporated such texts or rituals. Words had to be used to explain that the concert was a memorial to the victims of 9/11. But the explanation *about* the concert, that it was a memorial to the victims of 9/11, was not a component *of* the memorial. And just as a commemorative act need not incorporate a text or ritual, so too a commemorative object need not incorporate a text; obviously it will not incorporate a ritual. A commemorative coin may have an image of the emperor and nothing more—no text.

16. Casey (1987), 219.

Might these examples of commemorations that do not incorporate texts or rituals about the commemorandum miss the point Casey really wants to make? Now and then Casey adds a qualifier to his claim that commemorations require texts and rituals: "or any other available *commemorabilia*."[17] Might his point not be that commemorations require texts or rituals containing words, objects, or actions that stand for, represent, or refer to the commemorandum, but rather that they require *something* that functions in that way, be it a text, a ritual, or something else—a pictorial image, for example? Might his point be that whatever entity it is that in some way stands for, represents, or refers to the commemorandum, it is that entity which functions as the translucent (not transparent) medium that "embodies" the commemorandum and "through" which we remember the commemorandum?

Perhaps this is what he had in mind. But even this weaker claim seems to me not true. We can commemorate some person or event without there being anything at all in our commemoration that stands for, refers to, or represents the commemorated person or event. In the Vienna Philharmonic's memorial concert there was nothing, either in their performance of the music or in the music performed, that stood for, referred to, or represented the victims.

Casey's theory: commemorations function to intensify memory

Casey's theory makes two basic claims about the relation between commemorating and remembering. Commemorating is a distinct *way* of remembering; when we commemorate, we remember *through* such mediating factors as texts and rituals and *along with* other persons who are likewise commemorating. And commemorating *intensifies* remembering. His theory holds that these two dimensions of commemorating are connected: commemoration is a distinct way of remembering whose specific function is to enhance the commemorators' memory of the commemorandum. We have considered Casey's claim that commemorating is that distinct way of remembering in which the commemorandum is embodied in the commemoration. Let us move on to his claim that the function of commemorations is to intensify memory.

<hr />

17. Casey (1987), 218.

Suppose that a group of Luther scholars decide to hold a conference on October 31, 2017, in commemoration of Luther's nailing of his ninety-five theses to the door of the Wittenberg church 500 years earlier. Does their commemoration of Luther's fateful act intensify their recollection of that act? I doubt it. Being the Luther scholars that they are, that event is already vividly before their minds. If the commemoration does intensify the memory of some attendees, that seems wholly coincidental.

Do they perhaps attend the memorial conference so that their memory will be positively affected in some other way than intensified? Do they perhaps attend in the expectation that their memory will be *shaped* by the papers read at the conference? Let us say that their memory is *enhanced* if it is positively affected in some way or other. Do they attend the conference so that their memory may be enhanced? And more generally, is the *enhancement* of memory the defining function of commemoration?

I think not. Some commemorations have no significant impact whatsoever on memory, nor is it expected that they will have. Consider again the memorial concert that the Vienna Philharmonic played in St Patrick's Cathedral to commemorate the victims of 9/11. A condition of the concert functioning as a public memorial of those victims was that the public remember what had happened; had amnesia settled over the public, the concert could not have been a public memorial concert. But it's doubtful that the concert functioned to significantly enhance the public's memory of that event and its victims; it's equally doubtful that those who organized the concert expected it to have that effect.

Not only is it the case that some memorials do not function, and were not intended to function, to significantly enhance memory of the person or event memorialized; the example of the Luther conference shows that sometimes we feel impelled to do or make something as a memorial of some person or event even though our memory of that person or event is firm and vivid and there is no prospect whatsoever of its fading in the foreseeable future. The Lincoln Memorial on the Mall in Washington DC, dedicated in 1922, is an example. Every American at the time was familiar with Lincoln from books on American history, biographies of Lincoln, informal conversations, recitations of Lincoln's Gettysburg Address, and the like. There was no prospect whatsoever of Lincoln fading from the memory of the American people. Or if there were some at the time who did fear that the memory of Lincoln was in danger of fading, why would they not have poured their efforts into school educational programs, documentary and quasi-documentary films, Lincoln biographies, and the like? Those would reach many more members of the public than would ever see the memorial. Clearly it was felt that even though Lincoln was well remembered, something was lacking. It was important to have a memorial of Lincoln. Evidently memorials do something that remembering by itself does not do. The memory may be alive and well; we still want a memorial.

Casey's theory, that it is the definitive function of memorials to enhance memory, is standard doctrine. It's the theory concerning the memorials of ancient Israel that Max Thurian developed in *The Eucharistic Memorial*; and, to cite a more recent example, it's the theory James Young employs in *Holocaust Memorials and Meaning*.[18]

Memorials and commemorations as modes of honoring

If commemorating, in essence, is neither that distinct way of remembering that Casey describes as *remembering through* nor something that enhances memory, what, then, is the essence of commemorating? Or to bring memorial objects into the picture along with memorial acts: what is it to do, make, or commission something as a memorial? What was the Vienna Philharmonic doing when it performed its concert *as a memorial* of the victims of 9/11?

The clue to what the Philharmonic was doing is to be found in the description of the concert: "a free program to honor the victims of Sept. 11." The Philharmonic was performing the concert *to honor* the victims, performing the concert *in honor of* the victims. To do, make, or commission something as a memorial or commemoration of some person or event from the past is thereby to *honor* that person or event. The doing, making, or commissioning of the thing in question *counts as* honoring that person or event. Memorials do often enhance memory. But the example of the memorial concert performed to commemorate the victims of 9/11, and the example of the conference held to commemorate Luther's nailing of his ninety-five theses to the door of the church, show that that's not essential; something can be a memorial or commemoration of some person or event without, in any significant way, enhancing anybody's memory of that person or event.

18. Young (1993).

Memorials are essentially a way of honoring. There are, of course, other ways of honoring some person or event than by doing or making something as a memorial of that person or event; one can pay honor to the king by bowing before him. Doing, making, or commissioning something as a memorial is just one species of the genus: paying honor to.[19]

Admittedly, honoring is not always what is most prominent in memorials and commemorations. The Byzantines for generations commemorated the fall of Constantinople; the dominant mood of their commemorations was lament. But in their lament over the fall of the great city, were they not also honoring the city that had fallen? Groups commemorate wounds inflicted upon them so as to keep outrage alive and spur the struggle for justice; but in so doing, are they not also honoring those who fell and the cause for which they gave their lives?

Enhancement of memory is something that happens to one. It only happens if one actively listens, watches, or reads; but the enhancement as such is a causal effect of one's attention, not something one does. By contrast, honoring someone by commemorating them is something one does, not something that happens to one. *By* performing the commemorative actions one performs that other distinct act of honoring the person; one's performance of the commemorative actions *counts as* one's performing the act of honoring the person. To this it should be added that, in some situations, attentive listening to someone counts as honoring that person; conversely, inattention sometimes counts as dishonoring.

What brings it about that certain actions count as commemorating some person or event from the past? Schoolchildren can plant a tree on the school grounds without thereby honoring anyone. So what accounts for the fact that their planting a tree counts as their honoring their deceased classmate, Michael? What accounts for the fact that they plant the tree *as a memorial of* Michael?

Often one act counts as another because a certain convention is in force; it's because the conventions of the English language are in force that my uttering the sentence "It's snowing again" counts as my asserting that it's snowing again. In the case of memorials and commemorations, the situation is often that the actions performed count as commemorating a certain person or event because someone with authority on the matter has *declared* that they will so count. The officers of the Vienna Philharmonic declared that

---

19. In Wolterstorff (2015a), 123–51, I give an extensive analysis of the nature of commemorative honoring. I refer those readers who want such an analysis to those pages.

the performance would be in honor of the victims of 9/11; thereupon, when the orchestra performed the concert, their doing so counted as their honoring those victims. That's why it was a memorial concert.

There is always some fittingness, or perceived fittingness, between the memorial action or object, on the one hand, and the action of honoring that particular person or event, on the other hand. What we do or make to commemorate some person or event is not a matter of arbitrary decision on our part; given the desire to commemorate some person or event, we can rationally choose between ways of doing so that are fitting and ways that are not fitting. Given the desideratum that Israel commemorate its deliverance from slavery in Egypt, there was an obvious fittingness in the members of Israel freeing their slaves every seventh year; going out every seventh year to capture and enslave members of surrounding nations would not do. Given the desire of the schoolchildren to commemorate their deceased classmate, planting a tree is eminently fitting; throwing stones at the classroom windows is not an option.

Doing, making, or commissioning something as a memorial presupposes a narrative that brings to light why the person or event is thought worthy of honoring. Presupposed by the commissioning and preservation of the Lincoln Memorial on the Mall in Washington DC was, and is, a narrative of the history of the American people which makes evident Lincoln's significance for the American people.

A consequence of the fact that commemorations presuppose a narrative that brings to light the honor-worthiness of the commemorated person or event is that what is commemorated is never *simply* commemorated but is always commemorated *as so-and-so*; the persons commemorated by the Vienna Philharmonic's concert were commemorated *as victims of the 9/11 attack*. Sometimes it is generally understood what the commemorandum is commemorated *as* and no attempt is made to put it into words. Often, however, it is made explicit—in publicity for the commemoration, in programs handed out to those who attend, in speeches introducing the commemoration: "We are assembled here to commemorate Abraham Lincoln as the great emancipator." Perhaps it was such declarations that Casey had his eye on when he said that in commemorations we *remember through* texts and rituals. However, the function of these declarations is not that we remember the commemorandum through them but that we commemorate it *as so-and-so*.

Differing background narratives concerning the same person or event will often lead to some people commemorating the person or event *as* so-and-so and others commemorating the person or event *as such-and-such*. If what is said and done in the commemoration is non-committal on these differing interpretations, or if it commits to one of them but the two are complementary rather than conflictual, the two parties can commemorate together. If not, they have no choice but to part ways.

Just as the same person or event can often be commemorated for two quite different modes of honor-worthiness, so too the commemorative acts themselves can often be interpreted in different ways.[20] If what is said and done commits the participants to one of these interpretations and the differing interpretations are conflictual rather than complementary, the parties once again have no choice but to part ways. The divisions among Christians over the Eucharist are paradigmatic examples of this last point. Different traditions attribute different significance to the celebrant's actions of blessing and distributing the bread and wine and to the people's eating the bread and drinking the wine.

Memorial actions in the liturgy

Christians find it important in their liturgical enactments to go beyond *being reminded* of biblical persons and events to *actively honoring* certain of them. They want not just to be reminded but to honor. Liturgical commemorative honoring occurs most obviously in celebrations of the Eucharist. When Jesus said to his disciples, "Do this in remembrance [as a memorial, *eis anamnēsin*] of me," what the words meant in that context was that the disciples were to eat the bread and drink the wine in remembrance of Jesus. When the celebrant at the Eucharist repeats those words in the course of rehearsing what transpired at Jesus' last meal with his disciples, they carry the implication that the liturgical actions that follow are done as a memorial of Jesus.

Sometimes this implication is made explicit. In a Eucharistic prayer attributed to Serapion of Thmuis (fourth-century Egypt) the celebrant, after rehearsing what transpired at Jesus' last supper says, "For this reason we too, celebrating the memorial of his death, have offered this bread."[21] It is

---

20. This point is made repeatedly in Humphrey and Laidlaw (1994).
21. Deiss (1979), 195. Another example from the ancient church is a line from *The Third Anaphora of St. Peter*. The priest says, "We offer to you, God our Father, Lord of all, an offering and a commemoration and a memorial." A bit later the people say, "We make the memorial, Lord, of your death." Jasper and Cuming (1987), 46, 48.

likewise made explicit in the Eucharistic Prayer II of Rite One of the Episcopal Church. After rehearsing what Jesus did and said at his last supper, the celebrant says:

> Wherefore, O Lord and heavenly Father, we thy people do celebrate and make, with these thy holy gifts which we now offer unto thee, the memorial thy Son hath commanded us to make; having in remembrance his blessed passion and precious death, his mighty resurrection and glorious ascension....[22]

And it is made explicit in several of the Eucharistic prayers in the contemporary Catholic liturgy. In one of them the celebrant says:

> Therefore, O Lord,...we celebrate the memorial of the blessed Passion, the Resurrection from the dead, and the glorious Ascension into heaven of Christ, your Son, our Lord.[23]

In the section of this chapter, "Doing or making something as a memorial," I mentioned that there is a minor point of difference between our concept of a memorial or remembrance and the concept of an *anamnesis* as employed in the New Testament. Jesus was still alive when he said to his disciples that they were to eat the bread and drink the wine as an *anamnesis* of him; Paul believed that Jesus was resurrected and alive when he instructed the Corinthians to eat the bread and drink the wine as an *anamnesis* of Jesus. We would not say we were doing something as a memorial or in remembrance of someone if we believed the person was still alive. We would say instead that we were doing it in honor of the person.

A noteworthy feature of the three declarations just quoted is that the focus of the memorial has been shifted from the person Jesus in the last supper to the long ago events of his passion, death, resurrection, and ascension in the Eucharist. Why this shift of focus? Is this because those who composed these liturgical texts were uneasy with saying that they were celebrating the Eucharist as a memorial of Jesus, whom they believed was alive? I do not know the answer to this question.

In addition to the Eucharist, I know of just one liturgical act that is explicitly called a "memorial." In the contemporary Catholic Easter Vigil, the ceremony of sprinkling the congregants with water is described as "a memorial of the Baptism we have received."[24] But something can fit the concept of a commemorative honoring without being explicitly called a

---

22. *Book of Common Prayer* (1979), 342.   23. *Sunday Missal* (2011), 27.
24. *Sunday Missal* (2011), 415.

memorial. The singing of certain hymns quite clearly fits the concept. An example is the well-known hymn by the nineteenth-century English evangelical, John Bowring (1825), whose opening lines are these:

> In the cross of Christ I glory,
> Towering o'er the wrecks of time;
> All the light of sacred story
> Gathers round its head sublime.

Those who sing this hymn do not just recall the cross; they commemoratively honor it. The hymn is a memorial hymn.

A good many hymns resemble Bowring's in being hymns of praise; but because they make no mention of persons or events in the biblical narrative, they are not memorial hymns. The Sanctus composed by Reginald Heber (1827) and familiar to many Protestants is an example. Here is the first stanza:

> Holy, Holy, Holy, Lord God Almighty!
> Early in the morning our song shall rise to Thee;
> Holy, Holy, Holy, Merciful and mighty!
> God in Three Persons, blessed Trinity.

Neither in this stanza nor in the other three is there any mention of persons and events in the biblical narrative. This is not a memorial hymn.

Liturgical enactments as memorials

On the high holy days of the church year the entire liturgical enactment is a commemoration, a memorial, a remembrance, an *anamnesis*. The enactment of the liturgy on Christmas is a commemoration of Christ's birth; the enactment of the liturgy on Holy (Good) Friday is a commemoration of Christ's entombment; the enactment of the liturgy on Easter is a commemoration of Christ's resurrection; the enactment of the liturgy on Pentecost is a commemoration of the coming of the Holy Spirit.

In Orthodoxy and Catholicism, a good many liturgical enactments are also memorials of some saint. Let one example suffice. In the Orthodox Church, Vespers on Friday in the first week of Lent are in commemoration of "the holy and great martyr Theodore the Recruit." Theodore was a Roman soldier in the first decade of the fourth century, stationed along the Black Sea. When his commanding officer ordered him to offer sacrifice to

idols he refused and instead confessed his faith in Christ in a loud voice. He
was sentenced to death by burning. About fifty years later, when the emperor,
Julian the Apostate, ordered the military officer in charge of Constantinople
to sprinkle all the food in the marketplaces with blood that had been offered
to idols, Theodore appeared in a dream to Archbishop Eudoxius, revealed to
him the emperor's order, and instructed him to warn all Christians to buy
no food in the marketplaces.

In the Vespers in commemoration of St Theodore the people (choir) sing:

> Using as his tool the Apostate Emperor, the enemy devised a cruel plot: with
> food polluted by unclean sacrifices he sought to defile the people of God....
> But thou hast defeated his design by a more skillful plan: appearing in a dream
> to the Archbishop, thou hast revealed to him the evil plot. Therefore we offer
> thee a sacrifice of thanksgiving, honouring thee as our protector and keeping
> the yearly memorial of what then was done.[25]

A bit later the people (choir) sing, "Bless this grain and fruit,... for they have
been offered by thy servants to thy glory, in honour and memory of the holy
and great martyr Theodore the Recruit, and for those who have fallen asleep
in the Orthodox faith."[26] Later they sing, "O glorious martyr,... we honour
thy holy and venerated memory."[27] And a bit later: "Let us rejoice on this
radiant festival of the divine martyr; and let us all who love to keep the feasts
make glad in faith, as we honour the joyful celebration of his death."[28]

Is every liturgical enactment a memorial?

This brings us to von Allmen's claim, cited at the beginning of this chapter,
"The cult is firstly an anamnesis of the past work of Christ." By the term
"the cult" von Allmen means Christian liturgical enactments; he is thinking
primarily of the regular Sunday enactments. His claim is that every such
enactment is "an anamnesis of the past work of Christ." Not just enactments
on the high holy days and on those Sundays when some saint is honored,
but every such enactment. Is this true?

I think it is. Near the beginning of this chapter I listed some of the things
that the ancient Israelites were instructed to do as memorials, among them,
that they were to rest on the seventh day of the week as a memorial or

25. *Lenten Triodion* (1978), 274–5.   26. *Lenten Triodion* (1978), 281.
27. *Lenten Triodion* (1978), 298.   28. *Lenten Triodion* (1978), 295.

remembrance of God's deliverance of Israel from slavery in Egypt.[29] Among the many indicators of the fact that Christianity emerged from Judaism is the fact that the church preserved the Jewish seven-day cycle. It preserved it while revising it, however. Early in the history of the church it became the practice to gather together on the first day of the week rather than the seventh. The reason for the change is clear: Jesus arose on the first day of the week. In *The Apostolic Constitutions* (*c.*380 CE) we read, "On the day of the resurrection of the Lord, which we call 'the Lord's Day,' you must always gather to give thanks to God and to bless him for all the benefits he has heaped upon us through Christ, by rescuing us from the bonds of ignorance and error."[30]

Wholly apart from what Christians do within their liturgical enactments, the very act of assembling on the first day of the week to enact their liturgy is a commemoration of the resurrection of the one whom they call "Lord." Sunday "is the commemoration of the Resurrection of Christ."[31] The New Testament writers view the significance of Christ's resurrection from a number of different angles, among them that to which *The Apostolic Constitution* alludes: Christ has rescued us from bondage. Jews rest on the seventh day as a memorial of God's deliverance of Israel from bondage in Egypt. Christians assemble on the first day as a commemoration of Christ's deliverance of creation from the bondage of ignorance, error, and evil.

29. In the Ten Commandments as they are found in Exodus, rest on the seventh day is given a different, albeit compatible, significance. Israel is to rest on the seventh day as a memorial of God's resting on the seventh day after six days of creation (Exodus 20: 8–11). Though the word for "remembrance" is not used in the Exodus passage, *doing as a memorial* was clearly the idea.
30. Deiss (1979), 215–16.
31. Daniélou (1956), 243. In Daniélou (1956), 242–86, there is an extended discussion of the emergence of Sunday as the day of worship for Christians and of the elaborate symbolism attached to the day.

9

The liturgical present tense

One of the most striking and baffling ways in which items of biblical narrative are invoked in Christian liturgical enactments is the use of what I shall call *the liturgical present tense*.[1] A vivid example is a sentence from one of John Chrysostom's Easter sermons: "The day before yesterday the Lord was hanging on the cross; today he is risen."[2]

The use of the liturgical present tense is especially prominent in the liturgies enacted and in the hymns sung on Christmas, Good Friday, and Easter. Let's have a few examples.

The first verse of Charles Wesley's Christmas hymn, "Hark, the Herald Angels Sing," goes like this:

> Hark, the herald angels sing,
> "Glory to the new-born king.
> Peace on earth and mercy mild,
> God and sinners reconciled."
> Joyful all ye nations rise,
> Join the triumph of the skies,
> with the angelic hosts proclaim,
> "Christ is born in Bethlehem."
> Hark, the herald angels sing,
> "Glory to the new-born king."

Here is the first verse of a Christmas hymn by Paul Gerhardt, in English translation:

> All my heart this night rejoices
> as I hear, far and near,
> sweetest angel voices:

---

1. This chapter is a revision of Wolterstorff (2016a).
2. Quoted in Taft (1984), 16.

> "Christ is born," their choirs are singing,
> 'til the air everywhere
> now with joy is ringing.

The first verse of a hymn for Holy/Good Friday by Bernard of Clairvaux goes as follows, in English translation:

> O sacred head, now wounded,
> With grief and shame weighed down,
> Now scornfully surrounded,
> With thorns thine only crown.
> O sacred head, what glory,
> What bliss till now was thine!
> Yet, though despised and gory,
> I joy to call thee mine.

The first verse of an Easter hymn by Charles Wesley goes like this:

> Christ the Lord is risen today, Alleluia!
> Sons of men and angels say; Alleluia.
> Raise your joys and triumphs high; Alleluia.
> Sing, ye heavens, and earth reply. Alleluia!

It's likely that the old Latin hymn, *Surrexit Christus Hodie*, was ringing in Wesley's ears when he composed those lines. Its first verse, in English translation, is this:

> Jesus Christ is risen today, Alleluia!
> Our triumphant holy day, Alleluia!
> Who did once, upon the cross, Alleluia!
> Suffer to redeem our loss. Alleluia!

It is characteristic of hymns in the liturgical present tense to insert such indexicals as "now," "today," "this night," "this day," "this happy morn," as if to make doubly sure that we do not miss the point.

Alexander Schmemann is one of the few writers who explicitly take note of the liturgical present tense. He writes, "In the commemoration of the events of Christ's life, the Church very often, if not always, transposes past into present. Thus, on Christmas Day we sing: '*Today* the Virgin gives birth...'; on Good Friday: '*Today* He stands before Pilate...'; on Palm Sunday: '*Today* He comes to Jerusalem...'."[3]

---

3. Schmemann (1969), 80.

What is the point? How are we to understand the use of the liturgical present tense? If the use of the present tense in these hymns is to be taken literally, then those who sang the Christmas hymns on Christmas Day 2015 were declaring that Christ was born earlier that very day, and those who sang the Easter hymns on Easter 2016 were declaring that Christ arose earlier that day. If that is what they were declaring, did they also believe it? Did they believe that Christ was born on Christmas Day 2015 and did they believe that he arose on Easter 2016?

Those who sing these hymns believe that Christ was born, died, and rose well in the past. They are reminded of this when Scripture is read. They declare they believe this when they recite the Apostles' or Nicene Creed. They use the past tense: "He *was* conceived by the Holy Spirit, born of the Virgin Mary." "He *came* down from heaven and *was* incarnate by the Holy Spirit of the Virgin Mary." So if they also believe that Christ was born on Christmas Day 2015, then they believe that an event in the distant past became present on that day—that it happened again, that it was reactualized. What could possibly bring about something so extraordinary as that?

Before I address the question of how the liturgical present tense should be understood, let's take a look at the Orthodox liturgy for Vespers on Holy Friday; here we find a density in the use of the tense that goes beyond anything we find in the hymns commonly sung in Catholic or Protestant churches. To forestall ambiguity in references, let us suppose that we are discussing the enactment of the liturgy that took place on Holy Friday 2016.

Early in the liturgy the choir sings, "Today the most pure virgin saw thee hanging on the cross . . . ; and with a mother's love she wept and bitterly her heart was wounded. She groaned in anguish from the depth of her soul, and in her grief she struck her face and tore her hair."[4] Here the crucifixion is sung about as if it had happened earlier that day. Just a bit later, the crucifixion and the events immediately preceding it are sung about as happening simultaneously with the enactment of the liturgy. "Today the Master of Creation stands before Pilate; today the maker of all things is given up to the cross, and of his own will he is led as a lamb to the slaughter. He who sent manna in the wilderness is transfixed with nails; his side is pierced, and a sponge with vinegar touches his lips. The deliverer of the world is struck on the face, and the creator of all is mocked by his own servants."[5] The tense then switches abruptly to the past tense: "He prayed to his father, saying: 'Forgive

4. *Lenten Triodion* (1978), 612.   5. *Lenten Triodion* (1978), 612.

them this sin.'"[6] Then, shortly, back to the present tense: "A dread and marvelous mystery we see come to pass this day. He whom none may touch is seized; he who looses Adam from the curse is bound. He who tries the hearts and inner thoughts of man is unjustly brought to trial."[7] Then, a bit later, back to the past tense: "Down from the tree Joseph of Arimathaea took thee dead, who art the life of all, and he wrapped thee, O Christ, in a linen cloth with spices. Moved in his heart by love, he kissed thy most pure body with his lips."[8]

This, to say the least, is extraordinary—extraordinary in the employment of paradox, extraordinary also in the use of the present tense. And extraordinary in the seamless weaving back and forth between the present and the past tense; such weaving back and forth is not typical of the Good Friday hymns sung in Catholic and Protestant churches. Any theory as to the significance of the use of the present tense in liturgical contexts will have to enable us to explain why the Orthodox liturgy would weave back and forth between the present tense and the past. We can safely assume that it is not because the Orthodox are careless or insecure in their use of tenses!

The passages just quoted are followed by passages in which words in the present tense are put into the mouths of Joseph of Arimathaea and of Mary, mother of Jesus. The passages are extraordinary in the intensity of the emotions expressed.

Joseph with Nicodemus took thee down from the tree...; and looking upon thee dead, stripped, and without burial, in his grief and tender compassion he lamented, saying, "Woe is me, my sweetest Jesus! When but a little while ago the sun saw thee hanging on the cross, it wrapped itself in darkness: the earth quaked with fear and the veil of the temple was rent in twain. And now I see thee for my sake submitting of thine own will to death. How shall I bury thee, my God? How shall I wrap thee in a winding sheet? How shall I touch thy most pure body with my hands? What song at thy departure shall I sing to thee, O compassionate saviour?"[9]

The pure virgin mother wept as she took him on her knees; her tears flowed down upon him, and with bitter cries of grief she kissed him. "My son, my lord and God, thou wast the only hope of thine handmaiden, my life and the light of mine eyes; and now, alas, I have lost thee, my sweet and most beloved child.... I see thee, my beloved child, stripped, broken, anointed for burial, a corpse.... In my hands I hold thee as a corpse, O loving lord, who has

6. *Lenten Triodion* (1978), 612.   7. *Lenten Triodion* (1978), 613.
8. *Lenten Triodion* (1978), 614.   9. *Lenten Triodion* (1978), 615–16.

brought the dead to life; grievously is my heart wounded and I long to die with thee. . . . I reflect, O master, how never again shall I hear thy voice; never again shall thy handmaiden see the beauty of thy face as in the past; for thou, my son, hast sunk down before mine eyes. . . . Release me from my agony, and take me with thee, O my son and God. . . . Leave me not to live alone."[10]

Though the present tense is prominent in these passages, its uses here are not examples of what I have in mind by "the liturgical present tense." Its uses here occur within what are presented as quotations of what was said long ago, these quotations being introduced by words in the past tense.

The reactualization interpretation

A view frequently espoused by liturgical scholars in the twentieth century is that, by enacting the liturgy on certain days of the church year, some of the central events narrated in Scripture are reactualized. Christ's birth was reactualized on Christmas Day 2016, as it has been on every other Christmas Day; his resurrection was reactualized on Easter 2017, as it has been on every other Easter day. Let me call this the *reactualization interpretation* of the liturgy. I am not aware of any defender of the reactualization interpretation who explicitly presents his view as an explanation of the liturgical present tense; but I assume that, in part at least, they all see themselves as articulating the understanding implicit in the liturgy and its accompanying hymnody when these employ the liturgical present tense. So let's begin our inquiry by getting a grip on this interpretation and then assessing its tenability.

Let's be clear on what the reactualization interpreters are claiming. Recall the distinction drawn in Chapter 7 between *event-types* and *event-tokens*. Event-types are universals; event-tokens are particular instances of event-types. Reactualization theorists are not just claiming that the event-type, *Christ being born*, is re-instantiated every Christmas day. That claim, taken literally, is remarkable. They are claiming something even more remarkable, namely, that the *event-token* that was Christ's birth is reactualized every Christmas day, made present again. They are claiming that, by enacting the liturgy, we reactualize certain event-tokens from the past.[11] As with

---

10. *Lenten Triodion* (1978), 618–20.
11. Cf. Crichton (1978), 14: "By the liturgical mystery we are *actualizing* the past event, making it present so that the saving power of Christ can be made available to the worshipper in the here and now."

remarkable claims in general, one wants to be doubly sure that we are not misinterpreting the words of those who seem to be making the claim. So rather than just stating the view in my own words, let me allow a few proponents of the view to state it in their own words.

The most influential exponent of the reactualization interpretation was probably the Catholic liturgical theologian, Dom Odo Casel; he called it the "mystery" conception of the liturgy. His mystery conception of the Christian liturgy was suggested to him by his prior study of archaic rituals. His interpretation of how archaic peoples understood their rituals was this: "for the ancients... the play is a sacred thing. Men carry out its action in a way all can see; but the real actors are the gods who dwell at the feast. They are the ones through whom men fulfill the actions which they do. For this reason what the play represents is made real in the deepest fashion."[12] All indications in Casel's text are that he is stating literally what he understands archaic peoples to have believed.

Casel holds that the relation between events in the biblical narratives and enactments of the Christian liturgy is to be understood along similar lines. Here are a few passages in which he presents his interpretation. His description of certain events in the biblical narratives as "primaeval" is no doubt meant to suggest a similarity between the biblical narratives and archaic myths.

> When the church on Septuagesima Sunday begins her reading of the book of Genesis, she brings the primaeval fact to life: creation, the Fall and all the rest.... With the reading of the Scripture we return to the first age; we place ourselves into the primaeval act which is made present.[13]
>
> Still more strongly do we perceive the power of the primaeval saving act made present, in the Eucharist; by the transformation and the consumption of the bread and wine man is filled with the power of Christ. He returns to that primaeval force with which God gave life to the world in the death and resurrection of Christ. Man's action in the rite is made one with God's action.[14]
>
> In the view of some theologians Christ placed the grace which he had earned by his sacrifice in the sacraments; when the sacrament is performed those who perform it receive the grace it contains. The sacrament is the cause of grace. In the mystery conception it is the primaeval saving act which is made present.... The myth is lived out in worship; the rite is living myth.[15]

12. Casel (1962), 159.   13. Casel (1962), 124.
14. Casel (1962), 125.   15. Casel (1962), 124–5.

Worship is the means which brings back the Origin; in it the new Beginning is made present for Christians. What he experiences in his worship is not only an after-effect of the saving act; the saving act itself takes on presence.[16]

The mystery is no mere recalling of Christ and his saving deed; it is a memorial in worship. The church does what the Lord did, and thereby makes his act present.[17]

Five times over Casel speaks of some primeval saving act as "made present" when the liturgy is enacted. In one passage he speaks of a primeval saving act as "taking on presence." There are no indications in the text that Casel intends his talk about *making present* and *taking on presence* to be understood figuratively.

Whereas Casel moved from a study of archaic rituals to liturgical theology, the Reformed liturgical scholar, J.-J. von Allmen, confined his writing to liturgical theology. In *Worship: Its Theology and Practice* he says that liturgy *recapitulates* the biblical narratives and, more generally, recapitulates the history of salvation. His explanation of what he means by saying that the liturgy "recapitulates" the history of salvation is that it "sums up and confirms ever afresh the process of saving history which has reached its culminating point in the intervention of Christ in human history."[18] But then, in the course of developing this summing-up idea, he employs the language of reactualization rather than the language of recapitulation. He describes an enactment of the liturgy as an anamnesis, a memorial. And he explains as follows what he understands an anamnesis to be: "It is a restoration of the past so that it becomes present."[19] It is "a real actualization of the past in the present."[20] "The past is reenacted and becomes present."[21] I judge that von Allmen's use of the language of reactualization was the more significant for having been almost inadvertent; this way of thinking and speaking about the liturgy was in the air at the time.

Mircea Eliade was an anthropologist of religion, not a liturgical scholar. On occasion, however, he turned his attention to the Christian liturgy; and when he did he, like Casel, interpreted what he saw through the lens of his interpretation of archaic rituals.

Eliade emphasized that archaic persons did not regard their myths as mere stories; the myths relate what really happened. "Myth tells how, through the deeds of Supernatural Beings, a reality came into existence, be it the whole of reality, the Cosmos, or only a fragment of reality—an island,

16. Casel (1962), 128.   17. Casel (1962), 141.   18. Von Allmen (1965), 33.
19. Von Allmen (1965), 34.   20. Von Allmen (1965), 34.   21. Von Allmen (1965), 34.

a species of plant, a particular kind of human behavior, an institution."[22] Though archaic persons regarded their myths as narrating what really happened, they thought of those events as occurring in another time, in mythic time rather than historical time. To that time, our time bears no relation; the events that occur in mythic time bear no temporal relations to events that occur in historical time. The thought of trying to find out *when*, with respect to historical events, the events in mythic time occurred, would have made no sense to archaic persons.

Eliade's central thesis concerning the understanding by archaic persons of their rituals is that they regarded themselves, when performing the rituals, as entering into the mythic time of origins. They regarded themselves as doing the things narrated in the myth and doing them in mythic primordial time.

> The participants in the festival become contemporaries of the mythical event. In other words, they emerge from their historical time—that is, from the time constituted by the sum total of profane personal and intrapersonal events— and recover primordial time, which is always the same, which belongs to eternity. Religious man periodically finds his way into mythical and sacred time, re-enters the *time of origin*, the time that "floweth not" because it does not participate in profane temporal duration, because it is composed of an *eternal present*, which is indefinitely recoverable.[23]

In ritual, the events narrated in the myths are reactualized.[24] All indications in Eliade's text point to the conclusion that he is stating literally what he understands archaic peoples to have believed about their rituals. On his interpretation, they had what is for us an extraordinary view of time.

---

22. Eliade (1963), 5.
23. Eliade (1959), 88. Cf. Eliade (1963), 19: "What is involved is not a commemoration of mythical events but a reiteration of them. The protagonists of the myth are made present, one becomes their contemporary. This also implies that one is no longer living in chronological time, but in the primordial Time, the time when the event *first took place*."
24. Cf. Eliade (1959), 105–6: "The religious festival is the reactualization of a primordial event, of a sacred history in which the actors are the gods or semidivine beings. But sacred history is recounted in the myths. Hence, the participants in the festival become contemporaries of the gods and the semidivine beings. They live in the primordial time that is sanctified by the presence and activities of the gods. The sacred calendar periodically regenerates time, because it makes it coincide with the *time of origin*, the strong, pure time. The religious experience of the festival—that is, participation in the sacred—enables man periodically to live in the presence of the gods.... In so far as he imitates his gods, religious man lives in the *time of origin*, the time of the myths. In other words, he emerges from profane duration to recover an unmoving time, eternity."

The view that Eliade attributes to archaic persons concerning the relation between myth and reality could not possibly be true. On one interpretation of the view, a human being, when participating in the ritual, becomes a participant in what took place in the mythic time of origins. For that to happen, that human being has to be, for a time, one of the *personae* of the myth. But in the myths there are no human beings, only gods. "The actors in myths are supernatural beings."[25] On another interpretation, a human being, when participating in the ritual, loses his identity as a human being for a time and becomes one of the gods in that mythic time of origins. But we who are human beings cannot lose our identity as human beings; it's essential to us.[26]

The fact that the view could not possibly be true is not a reason for concluding that archaic peoples did not hold it. It is, however, a reason for requiring strong evidence that they did hold it. Is Eliade perhaps interpreting too literally what archaic people said about their rituals and what they said when performing them? I get the sense, when reading Eliade, that he allows them no figures of speech. Since I am not a scholar of archaic religions, I can do no more than register my doubts.

After discussing the archaic understanding of mythic time, Eliade observes that "interest in the 'irreversible' and the 'new' in history is a recent discovery in the life of humanity." "Archaic humanity...defended itself, to the utmost of its powers, against all the novelty and irreversibility which history entails."[27] In the rituals of the archaic person we see his "refusal to grant value to memory and hence to the unusual events (i.e., events without an archetypal model) that in fact constitute history. In the last analysis, what we discover in all these rites and all these attitudes is the will to devalue time."[28]

Eliade argues that the discovery of the new and irreversible in history is to be credited to the interpretation and valorization of history as theophany that we find in ancient Israel. In Judaism, he says, "Yahweh no longer manifests himself in cosmic time (like the gods of other religions) but in a *historical time*, which is irreversible. Each new manifestation of Yahweh in history is no longer reducible to an earlier manifestation....Hence the historical event acquires a new dimension; it becomes a theophany."[29]

25. Eliade (1963), 6.
26. In Wolterstorff (1990), 125–6, I take note of some additional impossibilities and puzzles.
27. Eliade (1974), 48.   28. Eliade (1974), 85–6.   29. Eliade (1959), 110–11.

When Eliade looks at the Christian liturgy he thinks he sees some of the same phenomena that he identified in archaic rituals; he interprets the presence of those phenomena in the Christian liturgy as *remnants* from archaic times. Narratives are recited; the participants leave behind "profane" time and enter the "sacred" time of the narrated events; the narrated events are reactualized; etc. The "Christian liturgical year," says Eliade, "is based upon a periodic and real repetition of the Nativity, Passion, death, and Resurrection of Jesus, with all that this mystical drama implies for a Christian; that is, personal and cosmic regeneration through reactualization *in concreto* of the birth, death, and resurrection of the Savior."[30]

There is a big difference, however: "when a Christian of our day participates in liturgical time, he recovers the *illud tempus* in which Christ lived, suffered, and rose again." So far, similarity to archaic rituals. But the *illud tempus* "is no longer a mythical time, it is the time when Pontius Pilate governed Judaea."[31] That time is historical time.

Instead of speaking of events from the past as being "made present," as Casel does, Eliade speaks of them as being reactualized; he says that there is a "real repetition" of those events. (Von Allmen says both that they become present and that they are reactualized.) The ideas are slightly different: *made present* versus *made actual again*. But if an event from the past is made present, then it is reactualized, and if it is reactualized, then it is made present. So the two views are equivalent. There is no indication in the text that Eliade intends his talk of "making present" to be understood figuratively.

Eliade does appear to part ways from Casel when he speaks of the participants in the Christian liturgy as leaving behind profane time and entering sacred time; Casel does not speak of leaving behind one time and entering another. But surely Eliade's use of the metaphors of leaving and entering has to be judged as misleading; he himself emphasizes that Christians regard the time of the events they hold sacred as historical time. His thought is not that participants in the liturgy see themselves as entering some non-historical time in which the events they hold sacred occurred; his thought is that certain sacred events that occurred in the historical past are regarded as becoming actual again.

I mentioned that the reactualization interpretation was common among liturgical scholars in the twentieth century. It lives on into the twenty-first century. In the Introduction to her translation of six "festal orations" by

---

30. Eliade (1974), 130.   31. Eliade (1959), 111.

Gregory of Nazianzus the church historian and liturgical scholar, Nonna Verna Harrison, quotes three passages from Gregory's sermons that she interprets as expressing the reactualization view; from her comments it is clear that that is her own view. Here are the three passages from Gregory:

> Christ is born; give glory; Christ is from the heavens, go to meet him; Christ is on earth; be lifted up. "Sing to the Lord, all the earth," and, to say both together, "Let the heavens be glad and let the earth rejoice," for the heavenly one is now earthly.
>
> Christ is illumined, let us flash like lightning with him. Christ is baptized, let us go down with him [into the water], that we may also come up again.
>
> Today salvation has come to the world, to things visible and to things invisible. Christ is risen from the dead; rise with him. Christ has returned to himself; return. Christ is freed from the tomb; be freed from the bonds of sin. The gates of hades are opened and death is destroyed.[32]

Harrison interprets Gregory as thinking of the enactment of the liturgy as an anamnesis. Her interpretation of anamnesis is essentially the same as von Allmen's: "Anamnesis means re-presentation of God's saving works so that the worshipers can participate in these events as present realities.... [I]t is important to note that the saving *events* are made present in their liturgical celebration, not only the persons who once participated in those events and are now glorified in heaven. Since God's saving actions transcend the limitations of temporal sequence, the historical events in which God has acted can be present now and in the future."[33] This is the language of the reactualization interpretation: "The saving events are made present," "the historical events in which God has acted [are] present now."[34]

Be it noted, however, that whereas Gregory does use the liturgical present tense, he does not use the telltale language of the reactualization

---

32. The passages from Gregory are quoted in Harrison (2008), 25.
33. Harrison (2008), 24–6.
34. Laurence Hull Stookey (1996) is among the few writers who take explicit notice of the liturgical present tense. He holds that the use of the tense presupposes a "theology of anamnesis"; apart from that theology, its use is "nonsense" (32). He takes for granted the view common among biblical and liturgical scholars that the concept of anamnesis was peculiar to the ancient Hebrews. In anamnesis, "the past becomes present by an active kind of remembrance.... It is not that the events we refer to in the present are happening again as we sing and pray. Rather it is that events that occurred only once nevertheless become contemporaneous with us because the Risen One holds all time in unity.... Because past and present are not sealed boxes, completed action enters into our time with the force of reality experienced by us" (29–32). Stookey does not elaborate these ideas; he does not explain what it is for Christ to "hold all time in unity."

interpretation; he does not speak of events from the past as becoming present, as being reactualized. Harrison is over-interpreting the passages from Gregory, interpreting them in the light of the twentieth-century reactualization theory concerning the relation between biblical narrative and Christian liturgy.

Eliade interprets archaic persons as believing in a certain sort of time travel: participants in the ritual exit historical time, enter the mythic time of origins, and then, a bit later, exit mythic time and reenter historical time. Neither he nor anyone else who embraced the reactualization interpretation of the Christian liturgy attributed to Christians the counterpart belief that, when participating in the liturgy, one travels back in time to when Christ lived. It is noteworthy, for example, that Eliade does not say that participants in the Christian liturgy *enter* the *illud tempus* in which Christ lived, suffered, and rose again; he says they *recover* the *illud tempus*. The idea is not that participants in the liturgy travel back to the time when those events occurred; the idea is that those events become actual again, become present. It is not we who travel about within time; it is event-tokens that travel about within time, from past to present. The very same event-token that happened in the past is happening again now, in the present—apparently while continuing to be an event-token that happened in the past, though on this point the writers I have read are not clear.

Is reactualization possible?

Is this possible? Is it possible for an event-token that was actual in the past—began, lasted for a while, and ended—to become actual again in the present? Is it possible for it to become actual again next week, yet again the following week, etc.? I think not. An event-*type* can occur again; the event-type, eating the bread of the Eucharist, has recurred billions of times. But the event-*token* of my eating the bread of the Eucharist which happened last Sunday can never happen again; it cannot become actual again, cannot become present again.

I concede that it is not self-evident that my claim, that event-tokens cannot happen again, is true; a defense is called for. The defense would be complex; fortunately, for our present purposes it's not necessary. No need to make the general claim that *no* event-token that occurred in the past *can* become actual again; all that is required is to note that the event-tokens which the reactualization theory claims to become actual again when Christian liturgies are enacted do not in fact become actual again.[35]

What would it take for the event-token of Christ's birth to be reactualized? That event-token had certain essential properties and relations, among them that of Mary standing to Christ in the relation of delivering him as an infant from her womb. So for Christ's birth to be reactualized, the original actor, Mary, and the original "patient," the infant Christ, would once again have to show up in space-time and Mary's giving birth to that infant would have to happen again. The reactualization theory of the liturgy implies that each enactment of the liturgy on Christmas Day brings that about. Since there have been millions and millions of such enactments, the theory implies that it has been brought about millions of times.

It can confidently be asserted that nothing has ever brought about the reappearance of Mary and the infant Jesus and the happening again of her giving birth to him. Enactments of the Christmas liturgy have not brought this about, nor has anything else brought it about. The reactualization theory of what happens when the Christian liturgy is enacted does not fit the facts. We have to look elsewhere for an interpretation of the significance of the liturgical present tense.

Harrison says of God's saving actions that they "transcend the limitations of historical sequence" so that "the historical events in which God *has* acted can be present *now* and [again] in the *future*."[36] She gives no reason for holding that this remarkable view is true. Charity requires that one give serious consideration to the possibility that she and all the other writers who have used the language of reactualization were not speaking literally. But I discern no clue in the writers I have discussed that they were not speaking literally. They do not say, for example, that when we participate in the liturgy we speak *as if* certain events from the past are happening presently. They say that events from the past *become* present.

On speaking as-if

Just now I used the phrase "speak as if." I suggest that when those who participate in an enactment of a Christian liturgy use the liturgical present

35. The point that follows was suggested to me by Trenton Merricks.
36. Emphasis added.

tense, they are speaking *as if* certain event-tokens from the distant past are happening now and that, in so doing, they are employing a distinct rhetorical trope. They know full well that the events they are singing and speaking about happened in the past. Nonetheless, they sing and speak about them *as if* they were happening now. Evidently Christians find it important, at least on the high holy days, to sing and speak about certain events in the distant past as if they were happening now.

We saw that, in an enactment of the Orthodox liturgy for Vespers on Holy Friday, events in the distant past are at a certain point spoken about as if they had happened earlier on that Holy Friday, before the liturgy was enacted, rather than as if they were happening at the time of the enactment. In such cases, the past tense is used. Obviously the issues raised by this use of the past tense on a certain day, to speak or sing about events in the distant past as if they had happened earlier that day, are the same as those raised by the use of the present tense to speak or sing about events in the distant past. It would be cumbersome, however, always to keep both of these uses in play. So I will speak only of the use of the present tense to speak or sing about events in the distant past, while urging the reader to keep in mind that everything I say by way of interpreting such speech and song applies also to the use of the past tense to speak or sing about events in the distant past as if they had happened earlier that day.

I said that when we use the liturgical present tense, we are employing a distinct rhetorical trope. It's not metaphor, it's not simile, it's not personification, it's not synecdoche. It's a *sui generis* trope. Though, as we shall see, its use is common, encompassing much more than just the liturgical present, I am not aware that the rhetorical tradition has ever singled it out, identified it, and given it a name. So let me give it a name. Let me call it *the as-if trope*.

Before I set out to elucidate this trope, I should explain why I reject the answer to our question as to the significance of the liturgical present tense that probably some readers regard as the obvious answer, namely, that the liturgical present tense is a particular use of what grammarians call "the historical present." The historical present is the use, in English and a number of other languages, of the present tense as an alternative to the past tense when describing events that happened in the past. Those of us who write about thinkers from the past regularly use the historical present. I did so when stating the views of the reactualization theorists.

What seems to me a decisive reason for not interpreting the liturgical present tense as a particular case of the historical present is the use, in hymns cast in the present tense, of such temporal indexicals as "now," "today," "this night," "this day," "this happy morn," and so forth. These indexicals are used to refer to the day on which the hymn is sung, not to that day in the distant past when the event that is sung about took place. The first line of Charles Wesley's Easter hymn, "Christ the Lord is risen today," is a good example of the point. Christ is declared to have arisen earlier on whatever be the day on which the hymn is sung.[37] Not all hymns that employ the liturgical present tense include such temporal indexicals as those I have mentioned; Wesley's Christmas hymn, "Hark, the herald angels sing," does not. But I submit that such indexicals can always be inserted without any change of sense. "Hark, the herald angels now sing . . ."[38]

The use of the as-if trope pervades ordinary life. We all employ it, and we all know how to identify and interpret it. So far as I am aware, the use of the trope to speak about an event from the distant past as if it were happening now is not common outside enactments of the liturgy. But other uses of the trope are common. So let's reflect for a while on the trope as such, with the aim of discerning how it works and why we use it. Then, in the expectation that what we have learned about the as-if trope in general will illuminate special uses of it, let us look at the liturgical present tense.

We use the as-if trope both when speaking *to* someone or something and when talking *about* someone or something. Let me begin with an example of the former. A dog, so it is said, is a boy's best friend. Boys sometimes talk to their dogs as if the dog were their best personal friend. The language they use is a selection from the language they would use when talking to their best personal friend: personal best-friend language. The boy doesn't believe that his dog is a person; he knows full well that it is not. Nonetheless, he uses personal best-friend language in talking to the dog. Just listening to him talk, one would infer that he was talking to a personal friend—a friend who, for some reason, makes no verbal response.

Why does the boy talk to his dog as if the dog were his personal friend, all the while being fully aware that the dog is not a person at all? Well, the language that we use in talking to personal friends has a distinct *resonance*, as I shall call it. That is to say, it is associated in one's mind with distinct feelings,

---

37. By itself, the first line of the hymn might be interpreted to mean that Christ today retains the status of *being risen*. But when the opening line is interpreted in the context of the hymn as a whole it becomes clear that that is not what it means; it means that the event of Christ's resurrection took place earlier today.

38. And of course the angels have to be singing when we are singing if we are to hearken to them.

thoughts, and images. When the boy talks to his dog as if the dog were a personal friend, he projects a good deal of that resonance onto the dog.

That he does so is not arbitrary. He will already have an *attitudinal take* on his dog: certain feelings about his dog, certain thoughts, certain images. His attitudinal take on his dog coincides with, or comes close to coinciding with, the resonance of a good deal of personal friendship language. So it feels right to him to talk this way. Speaking this way *gives voice to* his attitudinal take on his dog. At the same time it *reinforces* those feelings, those thoughts, those images about his dog.

The boy might be able to state in literal language some of the attitudinal take on his dog that he gives voice to when he talks to the dog as if the dog were a personal friend. But the literal description will never be the equivalent. The as-if trope is open-ended in the same way that metaphors are open-ended. By virtue of their open-endedness, both metaphors and instances of the as-if trope have an evocative power that literal speech lacks.

Everything I have said about using the as-if trope when talking *to* someone or something applies as well to using it when speaking *about* someone or something. Let me introduce an example of the point that will, at the same time, make another important point about the use of the as-if trope. My example of the boy and his dog may give the impression that the employment of the as-if trope is interesting, quaint, amusing, and the like, but that it carries no moral freight. To the contrary: it often carries profound moral freight. Often it is used to demean certain of one's fellow human beings. The trope is often employed as an instrument of injustice.

Slavery as depicted in Harriet Beecher Stowe's novel *Uncle Tom's Cabin* was substantially true to slavery as it existed in the American South in the mid-nineteenth century. Stowe depicts slave owners as often talking about male slaves as if they were work animals. Owners discussed the physical strength of their slaves, their endurance, their health, their age, whether or not they were of a compliant nature, how much food they required, etc. At least some of those who talked this way knew that their slaves were human beings, not mere work animals. Nonetheless they talked about them as if they were work animals; they used work-animal language in talking about them. If one did not know that they were talking about human beings, one would infer from their speech that they were talking about work animals. Their talking about them as if they were work animals was part and parcel of their treating them like work animals: they put them on the block for sale, inspected their teeth and muscles before purchasing them, etc.

Augustine St Clare, one of the slave owners in Stowe's novel, describes as follows what it was like to buy a slave: "buying a man up, like a horse,— looking at his teeth, cracking his joints, and trying his paces, and then paying down for him."[39] Upon St Clare's death, his wife put Tom up for sale. The narrator describes as follows the scene in the slave warehouse in New Orleans where Tom and others were auctioned: "Various spectators, intending to purchase, or not intending, as the case might be, gathered around the group, handling, examining, and commenting on their various points and faces with the same freedom that a set of jockeys discuss the merits of a horse."[40] Shortly before the auction was to begin Simon Legree arrived on the scene; his attention was drawn to Tom: "He seized Tom by the jaw, and pulled open his mouth to inspect his teeth; made him strip up his sleeve, to show his muscle; turned him round, made him jump and spring, to show his paces."[41]

The language we use when talking about work animals has a certain resonance; in speaking of their male slaves as if they were work animals the slave-owners projected a good deal of that resonance onto their slaves. Their doing so was not arbitrary; they already had an attitudinal take on these human beings that coincided with the resonance of a good deal of work-animal language. So it felt right to them to talk this way; talking about them in this way gave voice to their attitudinal take on these creatures: their feelings, their thoughts, their images. At the same time it reinforced those feelings, thoughts, and images. And one person's speaking about them as if they were work animals encouraged others to do so as well, thus encouraging others to feel and think about them, and to image them, in accord with the resonance of work-animal language.

Apparently some slave owners believed that African-Americans really were non-human animals; they believed that these creatures lacked what is necessary for being a human being. So of course they talked about them as if they were animals. In so speaking, were they using what I have identified as the *as-if trope*?

They were not. When speaking about some entity that is not ø as if it were ø, a condition of its being the *sui generis* as-if trope that one is using is not believing that it is ø. If one is under the misapprehension that it is ø and one speaks about it accordingly, one is speaking literally; one is not using the as-if trope. The slave owners who believed that their slaves were not human

39. Stowe (2005), 195.   40. Stowe (2005), 282.   41. Stowe (2005), 283.

beings but mere animals and spoke accordingly were speaking literally. They were speaking as if they were mere animals when in fact they were human beings; but they were not using what I have identified as the as-if trope.

Either way, whether those who spoke about these human beings as if they were work animals were or were not using the as-if trope, they wronged them deeply. They profoundly demeaned them. Such speech has to be counted among the deep injustices of slavery.

Is the use of the as-if trope a species of pretending? Not in general. It's not clear to me whether or not the boy who uses the language of personal friendship when speaking to his dog is thereby pretending that his dog is a personal friend of his; perhaps he is. But it seems clear that those slave owners who used the as-if trope of work-animal language in speaking about their slaves were not, in so doing, pretending that their slaves were mere animals. Nor, I think, were they imagining that they were mere work animals. Though the use of the as-if trope is closely related to pretending and imagining something to be what one knows it is not, it is not, in general, a species of either of those.[42]

It's important that we not confuse using the as-if trope to speak about something that is not ø as if it were ø, with saying about some event which is not ø *that it is as if it were ø.* An example of the latter is this: "It was as if all the air had been sucked out of the room." If one used this sentence to describe the atmosphere in some room, one would be using a simile rather than the as-if trope. The sentence is the equivalent of, "It was like all the air being sucked out of the room."

I have claimed that the as-if trope is a *sui generis* form of non-literal speech, not to be identified with either simile or metaphor. My sense is that it is often much more powerful than either simile or metaphor. It is extremely demeaning for one person to say to another, "You are nothing but an animal." My sense is that it is even more demeaning for one person to talk about another as if he were nothing but a work animal.

42. Michael Bergmann has called my attention to the fact that imagining something to be what one knows it is not is rather common in certain forms of therapy and in certain forms of meditative practice. Therapists sometimes invite clients to relive a traumatic experience, to imagine it as happening now, perhaps with some loving figure present who was not in fact present. Those spiritual directors who employ the strategies of Ignatian spirituality invite their directees to imagine themselves as present at, say, the crucifixion. (Recall the first line of the spiritual, "Were you there when they crucified my Lord?") Others invite the directee to imagine Christ as bodily present in the room and speaking to them now.

Interpreting the liturgical present tense

With these general reflections on the as-if trope in hand, let us turn to the liturgical present tense. Those who participate in the Christian liturgy on Christmas Day know full well that Christ was born roughly 2,000 years ago. And, apart from some liturgical theologians, few believe that that event-token is being reactualized on that Christmas Day and made present again. Nonetheless they sing, "Christ is born in Bethlehem." Not *was* born, but *is* born. What they are doing, so I suggest, is employing the as-if trope. They are singing about Christ's birth as if it were happening at the time of their singing or earlier on that particular Christmas Day.

Those who participate in the Christian liturgy on Easter likewise employ the liturgical present tense. They sing, "Christ the Lord is risen today." They know full well that Christ's resurrection took place thousands of years ago. Nonetheless they sing about his resurrection as if it were happening at the time of their singing or earlier on that particular Easter day. They are employing the as-if trope.

The resonance of the language that we typically use when talking about something that is happening now or that happened earlier today is very different from the resonance of the language that we use when talking about something that happened in the distant past. "Hark, the herald angels sing," present tense, has a very different resonance from "The herald angels sang," past tense. "Christ the Lord is risen today," present tense, has a very different resonance from "Christ the Lord arose," past tense. When Christians celebrate Christ's birth on Christmas Day, they find that the resonance of the present tense fits their attitudinal take on Christ's birth far better than does the resonance of the past tense. So, too, when they celebrate Christ's resurrection on Easter they find that the resonance of the present tense fits their attitudinal take on Christ's resurrection far better than does the resonance of the past tense. Of course, their having that attitudinal take on those events is due, in part, to their often having sung about those long-ago events with hymns in the present tense.

Is it possible to put into words some of the resonance of present-tense language as opposed to past-tense language? Perhaps. Start with past-tense language. When we use past-tense language to speak about events that occurred 2,000 years ago, spatial images of length are evoked: the events are *long* past, *far* in the past, *long* ago. They are distant from us. The opposite is true when we use present-tense language to talk about events that are happening now or that happened earlier today: there is no distance, no gap.[43]

When we talk about events in the distant past as if they were happening now, we project onto them this resonance of present-tense language. One might say that thereby we make them *present to us now.* We do not make them present again; we make them *present to us now.* My guess is that it was this phenomenon that led liturgical theologians to develop their theory of reactualization.[44]

Christians feel intuitively that the right language for hymning Christ's birth and resurrection is not language whose resonance is that of distance but language whose resonance is that of immediacy. Christ's birth and resurrection are as immediately relevant to us as they were to those who were living at the time. The language of distance that we use for speaking of what happened long ago is literally accurate but theologically and emotionally all wrong. The language we need is the language we use for speaking of what is presently happening.[45]

The Eastern Orthodox liturgical scholar, Alexander Schmemann, makes a closely similar point in the following passage.

> To be sure, the Virgin does not give birth today, no one "factually" stands before Pilate, and as facts these events belong to the past. But *today* we can remember these facts and the Church is primarily the gift and the power of that remembrance which transforms facts of the past into eternally meaningful *events.*
>
> Liturgical celebration is thus a re-entrance of the Church into the event, and this means not merely its "idea," but its joy or sadness, its living and concrete

43. This removal in imagination of the temporal gap can also take place in the opposite direction. Witness the opening line of the nineteenth-century hymn, "Were you there when they crucified my Lord?"

44. Cf. Childs (1962), 85: "Actualization is the process by which a past event is contemporized for a generation removed in time and space from the original event. When later Israel responded to the continuing imperative of her tradition through her memory, that moment in historical time likewise became an Exodus experience. Not in the sense that later Israel again crossed the Red Sea. This was an irreversible, once-for-all event. Rather, Israel entered the same redemptive reality of the Exodus generation. Later Israel, removed in time and space from the original event, yet still in time and space, found in her tradition a means of transforming her history into redemptive history. Because the quality of time was the same, the barrier of chronological separation was overcome."

45. Recall the passage from Ludolph of Saxony's *Life of Christ* that I quoted in Chapter 4. "With the affections of the heart make present to yourself, in a loving and delectable way, everything the Lord Jesus said and did, just as present as if you were hearing it with your ears and seeing it with your eyes.... And even when it is related in the past tense, you should consider it all as if it were occurring today." (The passage is quoted in von Balthasar [1982], 377–8.) "*As if* you were hearing it," says Ludolph, and "*as if* it were occurring today." It would be interesting to know whether it was common for those who recommended this type of spiritual exercise to use as-if language in this way when giving instructions.

reality. . . . We were not there in Bethany at the grave [of Lazarus] with the crying sisters. From the Gospel we only know *about* it. But it is in the Church's celebration today that an historical fact becomes an event for us, for me, a power in my life, a memory, a joy.[46]

In conclusion

The examples of the use of the liturgical present tense that I gave at the beginning of this chapter were all taken from hymns and liturgies used on the high holy days of Christmas, Holy Friday, and Easter and from sermons preached on those days. To the best of my knowledge, all Christian uses of the liturgical present tense occur in hymns and liturgies used on those days and in sermons preached on those days. The passages from Gregory of Nazianzus quoted in this chapter, in which he employed the liturgical present tense, came from "festal orations" by Gregory, that is, from sermons Gregory preached on one or another of the church's high holy days.

A good many contemporary Eucharistic liturgies include the acclamation, spoken by the people, "Christ has died, Christ is risen, Christ will come again." And a good many include the words, spoken by the celebrant just before he or she distributes the bread and wine, "Christ our Passover is sacrificed for us." The verbs "is risen" and "is sacrificed" are in the present tense. The question is whether the tense is the *liturgical* present tense.

I think it is not but that it is, instead, the *continuous* present tense. Both verbs refer to Christ's present status: Christ has the status of *being* risen and the status of *being* sacrificed. A test for whether some use of the present tense is an example of the liturgical present tense is whether, without changing the sense, one can insert the indexicals "today" or "this morning." I judge that these two sentences fail that test. The congregants are not declaring that Christ arose that morning; the celebrant is not declaring that Christ is sacrificed today.

My discussion of the significance of the liturgical present tense has been limited to its significance in Christian liturgical enactments. A full discussion of the topic would look at the liturgies of other religions as well, especially those of Judaism. Unfortunately, that is beyond my competence.

---

46. Schmemann (1969), 82–3. I thank Terence Cuneo for calling this passage to my attention.

PART III

God in the liturgy

10
God's liturgical activity

When Christians participate in liturgical enactments so as thereby to worship God, they do so in the expectation and with the prayer that God will participate along with them in enacting the liturgy. Or to speak more cautiously, many of them participate in that expectation and with that prayer.[1] That makes their worship distinctly different from worshipful adoration of The Good Itself by Platonists and from worshipful adoration of The One by Neoplatonists. Neither The Good Itself of the Platonists nor The One of the Neoplatonists is capable of agency.

On this occasion I will not undertake to defend the view that God is a liturgical agent. Rather, assuming that God is a liturgical agent, I will explore the various forms that God's agency takes in liturgical enactments. It is the view of many Christians, myself included, that among the things God does as a liturgical agent is speak to the congregants. Some writers talk as if

---

1. Those who share with Paul Tillich the view that God is the impersonal ground of being would not participate in that way. If they say the prescribed words, they will follow the "Maimonides strategy" (Chapter 5) of giving those words different meanings from their authorized meanings.

that's the only thing God does; they identify God's liturgical activity with proclamation. I regard that as a serious mistake. Since God's speaking proves a good deal more difficult to understand than the other modes of God's liturgical activity, I will spend the bulk of my time discussing it. But to reinforce the point that it is not the only mode of God's liturgical activity I will discuss some other modes first.

God enables and accepts our worship, God sends the Spirit

In Chapter 3 I noted that it is typical of liturgical scripts to prescribe not only the acts the congregants are to perform but also, for some of those acts, *how* they are to be performed: reverently, worthily, in peace, with one accord, and so forth. What must now be noted is that it is also typical of liturgical scripts to prescribe that the congregants pray to God that God will enable them to perform the prescribed acts of worship as they should be performed. They are to pray that God will enable them to worship worthily. The prayer is self-reflexive: it is itself among the acts of worship that the congregants pray God to enable them to perform worthily.

Let's have a few examples. Near the beginning of Holy Communion: Setting One of the Evangelical Lutheran Church the minister says, "Almighty God,... cleanse the thoughts of our hearts by the inspiration of your Holy Spirit, that we may perfectly love you, and worthily magnify your holy name, through Christ our Lord."[2] In the Orthodox liturgy of St John Chrysostom the priest says, before the reading of the Gospel, "O Lord and lover of mankind: make the imperishable light of thy divine knowledge to shine in our hearts; and open the eyes of our understanding that we may apprehend the preaching of thy Gospel."[3] In the contemporary Catholic liturgy the priest says to the reader of the Gospel, "May the Lord be in your heart and on your lips, that you may proclaim his Gospel worthily and well."[4] And in the liturgy that Calvin instituted in Geneva the Eucharistic prayer begins with the words, "As our Lord Jesus has not only offered his body and blood once on the cross for the remission of our sins, but also

---

2. *Evangelical Lutheran Worship* (2007), 95. The same words are said by the priest near the beginning of The Holy Eucharist: Rite One, of the Episcopal Church.
3. *The Orthodox Liturgy* (1982), 48.   4. *Sunday Missal* (2011), 17.

desires to impart them to us as our nourishment unto everlasting life, grant us this grace: that we may receive at his hands such a great benefit and gift with true sincerity of heart and with ardent zeal. In steadfast faith may we receive his body and blood, yea Christ himself entire."[5] When God answers these prayers, God acts liturgically to enable the participants to worship God worthily.

It is also typical of liturgical scripts to prescribe that the congregants pray that God will accept their acts of worship. This, of course, is the force of the familiar prayer-responses by the people, "Lord, have mercy" and "Lord, hear our prayer." But let's have a few additional examples. The Eucharistic prayer I of the Episcopal Church includes the sentence, "We earnestly desire thy fatherly goodness to accept this our sacrifice of praise and thanksgiving."[6] In the Prayer of the Trisagion in the Orthodox liturgy the priest says, "Accept, O master, from the mouths of us sinners the thrice-holy hymn."[7] And in the contemporary Catholic liturgy the priest says, just before the bread and wine are distributed, "Be pleased to look upon these offerings with a serene and kindly countenance, and to accept them, as once you were pleased to accept the gifts of your servant Abel the just, the sacrifice of Abraham our father in faith, and the offering of your high priest Melchizedek."[8] When God answers these prayers, God performs the liturgical act of accepting the worship of the participants.

Third, all traditional liturgical scripts prescribe that the celebrant of the Eucharist pray that God will send the Holy Spirit to sanctify the Eucharistic elements and those who receive them. In Eucharistic Prayer A of the Episcopal Church the celebrant says, "Sanctify [these gifts] by your Holy Spirit to be for your people the body and blood of your Son, the holy food and drink of new and unending life in him. Sanctify us also that we may faithfully receive this holy sacrament."[9] In Holy Communion: Setting One of the Evangelical Lutheran Church the minister says, "We ask you mercifully to accept our praise and thanksgiving and with your Word and Holy Spirit to bless us, your servants, and these your own gifts of bread and wine."[10] The priest in the Orthodox liturgy says, "We pray, we beseech and implore thee: send down thy Holy Spirit upon us and upon these gifts

5. Thompson (1962), 202.   6. Book of Common Prayer (1979), 335.
7. The Orthodox Liturgy (1982), 44.   8. Sunday Missal (2011), 27.
9. Book of Common Worship (1993), 363.   10. Evangelical Lutheran Worship (2007), 109.

here set forth."[11] And in one of the options for the Eucharistic prayer in the contemporary Catholic liturgy the priest says, "Make holy, therefore, these gifts, we pray, by sending down your Spirit upon them like the dewfall, so that they may become for us the body and blood of our Lord Jesus Christ."[12] God's answer to these prayers consists of the Holy Spirit performing the liturgical act of sanctifying the Eucharistic elements and those who receive them.

In traditional liturgies it is common, though not universal, for a so-called Prayer of Illumination to precede the reading of Scripture. This too has traditionally been understood as a prayer for the activity of the Spirit. Here is an example from Calvin:

> Almighty and gracious Father, since our whole salvation standeth in our knowledge of thy Holy Word, strengthen us now by thy Holy Spirit that our hearts may be set free from all worldly thoughts and attachments of the flesh, so that we may hear and receive that same Word, and, recognizing thy gracious will for us, may love and serve thee with earnest delight, praising and glorifying thee in Jesus Christ our Lord.[13]

And here are two options for "The Prayer of Illumination" from *The Worship Book* of the Presbyterian Church:

> Prepare our hearts, O Lord, to accept your word. Silence in us any voice but your own, that, hearing, we may also obey your will, through Christ our Lord.
> O God, tell us what we need to hear, and show us what we ought to do to obey your Son, Jesus Christ.[14]

God listens

It's easy to overlook the act on God's part that the participants are taking for granted when they pray that God will enable them to worship God worthily, when they pray that God will accept their worship, and when the minister or priest prays that God will send the Spirit to enable right listening to Scripture and sermon and to sanctify the Eucharistic elements

---

11. *The Orthodox Liturgy* (1982), 75.
12. *Sunday Missal* (2011), 31. Von Allmen (1965), 28–32, discusses the theological significance of this invocation of the Spirit—the so-called *epiklesis.*
13. Bard Thompson (1962), 209.   14. *The Worship Book* (1975), 28.

and those who receive them. They are taking for granted that God will perform the act of listening to their prayers.

Christian liturgical enactments are pervaded by address to God. When the participants address God, they take for granted that God listens. This is even true when the congregants respond to certain of the prayers with the words, "Hear our prayer, O Lord." They are not asking God to listen. Taking for granted that God is listening, they ask God to "hear" their prayer, that is, to respond favorably.[15] In *The God We Worship* I devoted three chapters to the topic of God as listener. Rather than repeating here what I said there, I refer the reader to those chapters.

Of the various modes of God's liturgical activity that I have thus far identified, God's action in the Eucharist has received the great bulk of attention by philosophers and theologians. On the other end of the attention-spectrum is God's act of listening; God's listening has received almost no attention. In concluding my discussion in *The God We Worship* I asked why that is. Why have philosophers and theologians, including liturgical theologians, paid almost no attention to God as listener? The only suggestion I had to offer was that it is because of the grip on them of the traditional conception of God as pure act, unconditioned in any way, immutable. On the face of it, God so understood cannot listen. I left the matter there, however; I did not delve into the issue. In Chapter 12 of this present volume I do: if God is pure act, unconditioned in any way, immutable, can God listen?

God greets, absolves, and blesses

Now we enter territory where it's much less clear what is taking place in traditional liturgical enactments. The contemporary Catholic liturgy begins with an entrance chant followed by "The Greeting" spoken by the priest. The first of three options for this opening greeting is, "The grace of our Lord Jesus Christ, and the love of God, and the communion of the Holy Spirit, be with you." The same words begin the Anaphora in the Orthodox liturgy.[16]

---

15. What I say in the text is not true for those participants who lack Christian faith but nonetheless perform the prescribed verbal and gestural actions. Some of them, rather than taking for granted that God will listen, pray in the hope that God will listen, or on the off-chance that God might listen.

16. The words are taken from 2 Corinthians 13: 13.

In the Episcopal liturgy, one of the options for the absolution of sin, following confession, is these words, spoken by the priest: "Almighty God, have mercy on you, forgive you all your sins, through our Lord Jesus Christ."

Just before the dismissal in the Orthodox liturgy the priest says, "The blessing of the Lord be upon you, by his divine grace and loving-kindness, always, now, and forever: world without end." A closing blessing that has traditionally been used in Reformed and Presbyterian churches is the so-called Aaronic blessing: "The Lord bless you and keep you; the Lord make his face to shine upon you, and be gracious to you; the Lord lift up his countenance upon you, and give you peace."[17] One of the options for concluding the Episcopal liturgy are the words, spoken by the priest, "The blessing of God almighty, the Father, the Son, and the Holy Spirit, be upon you and remain with you forever."

"The grace of our Lord be with you." "Almighty God, forgive you all your sins." "The blessing of the Lord be upon you." "The Lord bless you." What is the presider doing when he or she says these words? In *Worship: Its Theology and Practice*, J.-J. von Allmen groups together the opening greeting, the absolution, and the closing blessing, as what he calls the "clerical" proclamation of the word of God, and he argues that these are not to be understood as prayers. Clearly he is right about that; the grammar is wrong for a prayer. The second-person pronoun "you" refers to the congregants, not to God. And the gesture that the presider typically makes when speaking these words likewise resists this interpretation. The presider performs the biblical benediction gesture of raising his or her hands and extending them toward the people. The presider is addressing the people, not God.

Von Allmen notes that in some contemporary liturgies the traditional words of greeting and blessing addressed to the people have been altered into a prayer addressed to God. This, he says, is an act of cowardice on the part of the priest or minister. Though defended as an act of humility, the clerical proclamation "is devalued and diminished if the ministers have not the courage to make it in the second person plural."[18]

What is the presider doing when he or she addresses the congregants with the traditional words of greeting, absolution, and blessing? The answer hangs on the force of the verb "be" in the sentences, "The grace of our Lord be with you" and "The blessing of our Lord be upon you." Clearly these

---

17. Numbers 6: 24–6.   18. Von Allmen (1965), 142.

sentences are not in the declarative mood; the presider is not declaring that the blessing of the Lord is upon the congregants. Are they perhaps in the optative mood?

In old-fashioned English the words "Oh would that" begin a sentence in the optative mood: "Oh would that it weren't so cold." In current English we typically begin a sentence in the optative mood with "may": "May the rain hold off until the picnic is over." The closing blessing in the contemporary Catholic liturgy uses "may" rather than "be": "May almighty God bless you" rather than "The blessing of almighty God be upon you." So, too, the absolution uses "may": "May almighty God have mercy on us, forgive us our sins and bring us to everlasting life." Are these sentences in the optative mood? Is the contemporary Catholic liturgy making explicit what is implicit in all the formulations I quoted, namely, that these should all be understood as optatives?

What is one saying or doing when one uses the optative mood? I'm not sure. Suppose I say, "May the rain hold off until the picnic is over." My saying that is not identical with declaring that I wish the rain would hold off. It is, however, related to my wishing that the rain would hold off; if I did not have that wish, my saying that would be insincere and misleading. So is it perhaps an *expression* of that wish—not a *declaration* that I have that wish, but an *expression* of my wish? I think it is. But is it also more than that? Is it more than just the expression of a wish. I'm not sure.

In any case, Von Allmen vigorously rejects the interpretation of the greeting, the absolution, and the blessing as the expression of a wish on the part of the minister or priest. "Those ministers who transform the proclamation into a wish ... are ... sabotaging the liturgy, depriving the faithful of part of the grace which God wills to give them."[19] That seems right. The presider is not expressing his wish that God bless the congregants. But if the presider is not doing that, what then is he or she doing?

Referring to the opening greeting, the absolution, and the closing blessing, von Allmen says,

It is the creative and efficacious Word of God which is then uttered and that is why those moments of the service when this Word resounds are especially fraught with spiritual power. The blessing is a word charged with power, in which God Himself or a man representing Him transmits to persons, living beings or things, salvation, welfare, and the joy of living, and this same power

19. Von Allmen (1965), 142.

is operative in the greeting and the absolution. In the absolution, it operates as a power delivering us from the chains of sin, in the greeting as a power which sends forth upon us the divine grace.[20]

What is von Allmen's thought here? What does he think is the relation between the utterance by the presider of words of blessing and God's blessing the congregants? The word he uses is "transmits": by uttering the words of blessing, the presider *transmits* God's blessing to the congregants. Presumably "transmits," as used here, means the same as "bestows." But surely the priest or minister is not bestowing God's blessing on the congregants; only God can do that!

Let me offer a suggestion as to what von Allmen might have been trying to get at. (In the section "God speaking" I will offer an alternative suggestion.) Suppose that I am head of the Olympics committee and that, by virtue of occupying that position, I have the privilege of opening the 2016 Olympic games. At the appointed time I say, "Let the games begin," whereupon the games begin. I am not myself a participant in any of the games; I don't myself begin jumping, running, swimming, or anything else of the sort. My role is to bring about their beginning by saying, "Let the games begin," whereupon the contests are to begin. One might say that I *invoke* the beginning of the games.[21]

I do not have it in my power to invoke the holding off of rain. The reason I don't say, "*Let* the rain hold off until the picnic is over" is that my saying those words would not bring about the rain holding off. That's why I say, "*May* the rain hold off" (or, "Oh would that the rain would hold off").

The saying of the creed by the participants in liturgical enactments is often prefaced by the presider saying some such words as, "Let us together say what we all believe," whereupon the people say the creed together. The presider's saying those words invokes the saying of the creed by the congregants; it sets in play their saying of the creed.

I suggest that it may have been this phenomenon of *invoking* that von Allmen was getting at. When the presider speaks the words of greeting and blessing, he invokes God's blessing; when he speaks the words of absolution, he invokes God's forgiveness. He cannot bestow God's blessing and God's forgiveness; that's for God to do. But neither is he merely praying or wishing

---

20. Von Allmen (1965), 142.
21. Among the definitions of "invoke" given by the Merriam-Webster's Collegiate Dictionary (Eleventh Edition) are these: "to call forth by incantation," "to put into effect or operation."

for God's blessing and forgiveness. By speaking the words of blessing and absolution the presider invokes God's blessing and forgiveness; he, as it were, sets God's blessing and forgiveness in play.[22] Call this interpretation of the greeting, the absolution, and the blessing the *invocative* account of those liturgical acts. We must have the courage to believe, says von Allmen, that God "has chosen ministers to bring into effect the process of salvation."[23]

Return, now, to the words of absolution and blessing in the contemporary Catholic liturgy. The words of absolution are, "May almighty God have mercy on us, forgive us our sins and bring us to everlasting life." The words of the closing blessing are, "May almighty God bless you, the Father, and the Son, and the Holy Spirit." I asked whether these sentences are in the optative mood. In my brief discussion of the optative mood I said that in using the optative mood one expresses something that one wishes for. Perhaps one does more than that; but one does at least that.

When the Catholic priest pronounces the words of the closing blessing he is not expressing the wish that almighty God will bless the people. It's possible that, sad to say, he doesn't even have that wish. What he is doing, so I suggest, is invoking God's blessing of the people. Consider, once again, my example of being the official who opens the Olympic games with the words, "Let the games begin." I might equally well have said, "May the games begin." "May" would then have the same invocative force as "Let." The minister invokes God's blessing by saying, "May almighty God bless you"; so too he invokes God's blessing by saying, "The blessing of almighty God be upon you."

God speaking

What remains to consider is God speaking by way of what is done in liturgical enactments. In this volume I have made considerable use of the concept of one act counting as another; it's impossible to understand what we do when participating in liturgical enactments without employing this concept. Up to this point in our discussion the examples I have given, of doing something that counts as doing something else, have all been examples

22. In the Reformed and Presbyterian tradition, the rubric for the opening greeting was often "The Invocation."
23. Von Allmen (1965), 142.

of the same person performing the counting-as act and the counted-as act. In ordinary affairs it often happens, however, that the agent of the two acts is not identical; what one person does counts as another person doing something. A lawyer signs documents on behalf of his client, a guardian signs papers on behalf of her ward, an ambassador speaks on behalf of his head of state, and so forth.

In *Divine Discourse* I discussed at some length this phenomenon of double agency, as I called it; and I went on to argue that it is possible for a human being to be one of the agents in double-agency activity and for God to be the other agent: a human being's doing something can count as God's doing something. In particular, it's possible for a human being's saying something to count as God's performing some act of discourse, that is, some illocutionary act. Rather than rehearsing that argument here, let me assume that the conclusion is correct.

I distinguished two ways in which God might perform some act of discourse by way of what some human being says. God might *deputize* some human being to speak on God's behalf; that's how prophecy in the Hebrew Bible/Old Testament was sometimes understood. Or God might *appropriate* a locutionary act (and perhaps an illocutionary act) of some human being and thereby perform an act of discourse. These are both to be distinguished from *transmitting* to others what God has said to one. Near the beginning of the Book of Jeremiah we read, "Now the word of the Lord came to me saying, 'Before I formed you in the womb...I appointed you a prophet to the nations'." When Jeremiah wrote those words, he transmitted to his readers what God had said to him.

In many liturgies, the prescribed response to the reading of Scripture is, "This is the Word of the Lord," sometimes said by the congregants, sometimes by the reader, in which case the congregants typically respond, "Thanks be to God."[24] How is this declaration to be interpreted? What is the referent of the pronoun "this"? The declaration carries the clear implication that what the people hear, if they listen, is the Word of the Lord. But what do they hear? In the Sunday morning liturgy suggested by the Presbyterian *Worship Book* the Scripture reader says, after announcing the passage that he or she will read, "Listen for the word of God!"[25] What, exactly, are the people to listen for?

24. It is noteworthy that this locution is not to be found in the Orthodox liturgy. What is said before and after the readings is instead "Wisdom."
25. *The Worship Book* (1975), 28.

In *The God We Worship* I offered two possible interpretations of the declaration. Suppose that Scripture conveys to us what God said to certain people in ancient times. Then one way of interpreting the declaration is that the pronoun "this" refers to the content of what God said in ancient times. That is the word of the Lord that is presented to the congregants by the reading of Scripture.

Those who interpret the declaration this way will naturally want to go on to distinguish those things God said in ancient times that are in some way relevant to us and those that are not. In the first chapter of the book of the prophet Amos we read, "Thus says the Lord: 'For three transgressions of Damascus, and for four, I will not revoke the punishment, because they have threshed Gilead with threshing sledges of iron'." What God said to ancient Damascus by way of these words of the prophet Amos is not relevant to us. No doubt certain extrapolations from what God said to ancient Damascus are relevant to us; but not the very thing itself.

I do not find this interpretation of the declaration "This is the word of God" attractive. On this interpretation, God is doing nothing when Scripture is read. In this chapter we have explored the ways in which God's present action is taken for granted in Christian liturgical enactments and the ways in which God's present action is petitioned and invoked. Strange, then, if God is to be understood as sitting back when Scripture is read.

In the section "God enables and accepts our worship, God sends the Spirit" I quoted two prayers for illumination from the Presbyterian *Worship Book*:

> Prepare our hearts, O Lord, to accept your word. Silence in us any voice but your own; that, hearing, we may also obey your will; through Jesus Christ our Lord.
>
> O God, tell us what we need to hear, and show us what we ought to do to obey your Son, Jesus Christ.

These prayers fit very poorly, to say the least, with interpreting the reading of Scripture as simply transmitting to the listeners the content of what God said in ancient times.

An alternative interpretation of the declaration, "This is the word of the Lord," goes as follows. Suppose that, by way of the reading aloud of Scripture, God speaks anew, here and now, to the congregants. Then the natural interpretation of the pronoun "this" in the declaration is that it refers to the particular content of what God said anew just before the declaration was uttered.

St Anthony (*c.*251–356) inherited a great deal of wealth. In his *Life of Anthony*, Athanasius reports the episode that led Anthony to dispose of his wealth:

> He went into the church,...and just then it happened that the Gospel was being read, and he heard the Lord saying to the rich man, *If you would be perfect, go sell what you have and give to the poor, and and you shall have treasure in heaven* [Matt. 19: 21]. It was as if by God's design he held the saints in his recollection, and as if the passage were read on his account. Immediately Antony went out from the Lord's house and gave to the townspeople the possession he had from his forebears.[26]

On Athanasius' narration, it appears that Anthony was convinced that, by the reading aloud of the passage from the Gospel of Matthew, God then and there spoke to him telling him to give all his possessions to the poor. Had Anthony declared, "This is the Word of the Lord," the reference of the pronoun "this" would have been what God had just said to him.

Most people do not normally have an Anthony-type experience upon hearing Scripture read aloud; probably most people have never had such an experience. However, someone who has never had such an experience might be convinced for theological reasons that God speaks anew, by way of the reading aloud of Scripture, to the people listening. Anyone who held this view would naturally want to learn how to listen for what it is that God says here and now by way of the reading aloud of Scripture.

I find this interpretation of the declaration more attractive than the first interpretation we considered. What gives me pause, however, is that Christian practice seems to militate against it. If it were thought that this is how the declaration should be understood, one would expect the church to pour a great deal of energy into teaching its members how to listen for the presently spoken word of God. I do not find the church doing that. Or is it perhaps assumed that the sermon does that for the congregants?

I do find this a plausible way of understanding the greeting, the absolution, and the blessing, however. In the section "God greets, absolves, and blesses" I offered what I called the *invocative* account of what takes places in these liturgical acts: the minister invokes God's greeting, God's absolution, and God's blessing. An equally plausible account seems to me to be that the minister's saying the words of greeting, absolution, and blessing *counts as*

26. Athanasius (2006), 6.

God greeting, absolving, and blessing the people. God performs those illocutionary acts *by way of* the minister performing those locutionary acts.

Continuant illocutions

Rather than pursuing further the two ways mentioned of interpreting the declaration, "This is the word of the Lord," let me explore a third way. One frequently hears preachers say things like, "What Paul is saying here in this passage from his letter to the Romans is so-and-so," or, "What Paul's letter to the Romans is saying here is so-and-so." In both cases it is the present tense that is employed, this in spite of the fact that the letter was written long ago.

One interpretation to consider of the use of the present tense in these locutions is that it is what grammarians call *the historical present*. We employ the historical present when we use the present tense to refer to some event in the past, as when a historian, describing the Battle of the Somme in World War I, writes, "The battle is about to begin." On this interpretation of the locutions, the preacher is employing the historical present to refer to the long ago event of Paul saying so-and-so.

Another interpretation to consider of the use of the present tense in these locutions is that it is an example of what I called, in Chapter 9, the *as-if trope*. On this interpretation the preacher speaks, about the long ago event of Paul's saying so-and-so, as if Paul were saying it now.

I want now to explore a way of interpreting these locutions that does not treat them as a way of talking about a past event. To do so, I must introduce a dimension of discourse that I have thus far said nothing about. It's a dimension of discourse that speech-act theory was not designed to deal with and that had not previously occurred to me. After exploring this dimension of discourse I will then employ what we have learned to suggest an interpretation of the declaration "This is the word of the Lord" that is distinctly different from all of those mentioned above.

Speech-act theory applies most directly to spoken speech: I perform the locutionary act of uttering words with a certain meaning in mind and thereby I perform some illocutionary act. The two acts coincide temporally; they begin at the same time and end at the same time. The model is easily adapted to writing: I perform the locutionary act of writing words with a certain meaning in mind and thereby I perform some illocutionary act. In this case, too, the two acts coincide temporally.

An important difference between speaking and writing is that the written words, unlike the spoken words, typically endure beyond the conclusion of the act of writing; they are, as it were, a trace of the locutionary act of writing the words. Recorded speech is like written words in this respect; the recording is a trace of the locutionary act of uttering the words, enduring beyond the conclusion of the locutionary act.

Let me now introduce and explore the phenomenon of what I shall call *continuant* illocutions, in contrast to *occurrent* illocutionary acts, the latter being those that are over when the locutionary act that generates them is over.

Imagine a public building set back a bit from the street and sidewalk with a well-kept swath of grass in front and with a sign posted near the sidewalk on which are written the words, "Keep off the grass." We can describe what is going on here thus: the sign is warning the public to keep off the grass. The tense of the verb "is warning" is the continuous present. One might say that the sign has the "continuant illocutionary power" of warning the public to keep off the grass.

It has that power by virtue of some authorized person (or body) in the Parks Department having decided that the public should be warned to keep off the grass and having instructed employees of the department to erect the appropriate signs. That person authorized the erection of the sign. But I think it would not be correct to say that that person warned the public to keep off the grass, nor would it be correct to say that he or she *is warning* the public to keep off the grass. It's the sign that is warning the public, rather than that person; and the warning is ongoing, continuant. Signs not only have causal powers but continuant illocutionary powers. Warnings are, of course, not the only thing signs do. Signs advise, inform, indicate turns in the road, and the like.

To someone like myself who has long thought about discourse within the framework of speech-act theory, the idea of artifacts such as signs having continuant illocutionary powers initially seems bizarre, something to be explained away. But useful though speech-act theory is, we should not allow it to become a strait-jacket that forces us to deny or reduce dimensions of discourse that the theory was never designed to account for.

It's worth noting, in this connection, that someone who has always thought of agency in terms of causal agency will initially find speech-act theory itself bizarre, since at the heart of the theory is the assumption that not all agency is causal. By performing some locutionary act, I bring about some illocutionary act. But my locutionary act does not cause my illocutionary act; it *counts as* my illocutionary act.

I propose that we accept that signs and other artifacts do have continuant illocutionary powers. They do not have the power to perform *occurrent* illocutionary acts; only persons have that power. And it's not in "the nature of things" that signs possess continuant illocutionary powers; they possess such powers on account of fitting into the fabric of human action in a certain way. And they can lose those powers. That same sign with the words "Keep off the grass," if removed from its position in front of the public building and tossed onto a dump heap or put up for sale in an antique store, no longer has the continuant illocutionary power of warning the public to keep off the grass. It has lost that power.

With this idea of a continuant illocution in hand, let us now turn to a quite different sort of example. As I have noted, it's not uncommon for preachers, when commenting, say, on a passage from one of St Paul's letters, to remark, "What Paul is saying to us here is so-and-so." In these cases, too, the idea of a continuant illocution is being employed; but now the illocution is attributed to a person rather than to a sign or some other sort of artifact. Let's try to gain some insight into what is going on in such cases, starting with an example or two from ordinary life.

Imagine a young woman who is deeply alienated from her father. Suppose he says to her, face-to-face, "I continue to have no regrets." If a friend asks her, sometime later, what her father said to her, her natural response would be, "He told me that he continued to have no regrets." Her reference is to the occurrent illocutionary act that her father performed; that act is over, hence the past tense.

Now suppose that her father, instead of speaking face-to-face with her, sends her a letter with the same message. A few days after he posts it she receives and reads it. A friend asks her what her father says in the letter. Her natural response would be, "He is telling me that he continues to have no regrets." The tense is the continuous present. Her father's telling her that he has no regrets is a continuant illocution, not an occurrent illocutionary act that was over sometime in the past. If we are willing to attribute continuant illocutionary powers to signs and letters, I see no reason why we should not be willing to attribute them to persons as well.

Spoken words vanish with the conclusion of the speaking; written words endure. The endurance of the written words is necessary for the ongoing existence of the father's continuant illocution. The father's act of inscribing the words is over, but the words he wrote endure. They are a trace of the locutionary act that he performed. But they are not only a trace of that perishing occurrent act. By virtue of their endurance, they sustain the father's continuant illocution of telling her that he continues to have no regrets; the words effect the continuance of that illocution. If the letter is destroyed without any copies having been made, then the continuant illocution ceases; her father is then no longer telling her that he continues to have no regrets. The invention of writing introduced a fundamentally new phenomenon into human affairs: continuant illocutions attributable to persons and/or texts.

Had the father spoken into a recording device rather than writing a letter, and had he sent the recording to the daughter, then the sort of things I have said about the letter would be true of the recording. The daughter could say, when listening to the recording, "He's telling me that he continues to have no regrets." The endurance of the recording would effect the continuance of her father's telling her that he continues to have no regrets. If the recording is destroyed without any copies having been made, the continuant illocution ceases.

Let's vary the example once more. Suppose the father asks a friend to tell his daughter that he continues to have no regrets; and suppose the friend does this. The friend might say, "Your father asked me to tell you that he continues to have no regrets." But he might also say, "Your father says that he continues to have no regrets." In this latter case, the friend's speech plays essentially the same role as the recording in our previous example: it orally presents to the daughter the father's continuant illocution. Let me simplify matters by treating it as a recording.

The enduring existence of a copy of the father's letter or of a recording of his speech is a condition of the continuance of the father's telling his daughter that he continues to have no regrets. Is the survival of the father likewise a condition? Suppose the father dies between the time he pens the letter and the time his daughter reads it, and suppose she knows this. In that situation, how would she report the content of the letter? She might use the past tense and say, "He said that he continued to have no regrets." But she might also use the continuous present tense and say, "He's saying here that he continued to have no regrets." I think the best way to interpret the fact that she might give either of these two responses is that, in the former case, it is her father's occurrent illocutionary act that she has in mind whereas, in the latter case, it is his continuant illocution that she has in mind. It appears not to be a condition of the endurance of a continuant illocution of a person that the person remain alive.

Here's another example of the point. Suppose that, at the end of her novel, a writer attaches a "Note to the Reader." And suppose that you and I read what she wrote a hundred years after she wrote it. One of us might say to the other, using the past tense, "She said in her Note to the Reader that so-and-so." But if we keep in mind that the note is addressed to her readers in general and that we are among those readers, hence among those to whom she addressed her note, then I think one would more naturally say, using the continuous present tense, "She is saying to her readers that so-and-so." The continuant illocution survives the death of the author.

I introduced my discussion of continuant illocutions by remarking that preachers not infrequently say such things as "What Paul is saying here in this passage from his letter to the Romans is so-and-so" or "What Paul's letter to the Romans is saying here is so-and-so." The conclusion to which we have been led is that a plausible interpretation of this use of the continuous present tense is that the preacher is doing what we all do on many occasions, namely, referring to continuant illocutions, attributing the illocution in the first case to Paul and in the second case to Paul's letter.

Back to the acclamation

We were considering the force of the acclamation, "This is the word of the Lord," pronounced in response to the reading aloud of Scripture in liturgical enactments. I asked what the pronoun "this" in the acclamation refers to. I suggested two possibilities. On the assumption that God spoke in ancient times and that the reading of Scripture conveys to the listeners some of what God said then, one possibility is that the pronoun refers to the content of what God said in ancient times that was conveyed to the listeners by the reading aloud of Scripture. Alternatively, on the assumption that God speaks anew by way of the present reading of Scripture, the pronoun refers to the content of what God said just now by way of the reading aloud of Scripture.

A third possibility is now obvious. Suppose that, in addition to illocutionary acts that God performed in ancient times that are now long over, and in addition to illocutionary acts that God performs on the occasion of the reading aloud of Scripture, there is God's continuant discourse, that is, God's continuant illocutions; and suppose that the reading aloud of Scripture presents to the listeners some of God's continuant discourse. Then the pronoun "this" in the acclamation "This is the word of the Lord" can be understood as referring to the continuant discourse of God that the reading presented.

I suggest that Christians do often think of Scripture as presenting to its readers and listeners God's continuant discourse. Let me cite just two pieces of evidence for this claim, one from a theologian and one from liturgy. Heinrich Bullinger, a prominent figure in the first generation of the Swiss Reformation, composed the Second Helvetic Confession. The second sentence of the Confession reads, "God himself spoke to the fathers, prophets, and apostles, and still speaks to us through the Holy Scriptures."[27] The locution "still speaks to us" is naturally interpreted as a reference to God's continuant discourse.

In the *Book of Common Prayer* there is "An Exhortation" that may be used "either during the Liturgy or at other times." The exhortation concludes with two versions of the Decalogue, one in King James English, the other in contemporary English. The former begins with the priest saying,

> God spake these words and said: I am the Lord thy God who brought thee out of Egypt, out of the house of bondage. Thou shalt have none other gods before me.

To this the people respond:

> Lord, have mercy upon us, and incline our hearts to keep this law.[28]

The priest then reads the second commandment, to which the people make the same response. And so forth, for all ten commandments.

The prescribed response of the people indicates that it is God's continuant discourse that the reader is understood as presenting to them. God continues to say what God said to ancient Israel: you are to have no other gods before me.

The contemporary version dispenses with the past tense reference to God's speaking to ancient Israel. The priest says,

> Hear the commandments of God to his people: I am the Lord your God who brought you out of bondage. You shall have no other gods but me.

The people respond:

> Amen. Lord have mercy.[29]

---

27. *Second Helvetic Confession* (online).   28. *Book of Common Prayer* (1979), 316.
29. *Book of Common Prayer* (1979), 350.

The sermon

We come, finally, to the sermon. It has long been held by a good many Christians that the sermon, in some way, presents the word of God to the listeners. Let me offer just three pieces of evidence. *The Apostolic Tradition* is an anonymous writing from (probably) the late second century CE. It contains a considerable number of liturgical texts and a good many comments about the liturgical practices of the time. Among the comments is this: "If...there is an instruction on the word of God, everyone should go to it gladly. He will reflect in his heart that he is listening to God speak through the mouth of the one giving the instruction."[30] The third paragraph of the Second Helvetic Confession, to which I referred just above, reads, "The preaching of the Word of God is the Word of God (*Praedicatio verbi Dei est verbum Dei*). Wherefore when this Word of God is now preached in the church by preachers lawfully called, we believe that the very Word of God is proclaimed, and received by the faithful.... The Word itself which is preached is to be regarded, not the minister that preaches; for even if he be evil and a sinner, nevertheless the Word of God remains still true and good."[31] And in my copy of the contemporary Catholic liturgy, the following explanation is given of how the homily is to be understood: "God's word is spoken again in the Homily. The Holy Spirit speaking through the lips of the preacher explains and applies today's biblical readings to the needs of this particular congregation."[32]

Though these three passages come from different times and traditions in the church's history, what they say about the function of the sermon or homily is remarkably similar: in some way, the sermon or homily presents the word of God to the listeners. The question is, in *what* way?

In *The God We Worship* I considered just two ways of understanding the relation of the word of God to the preaching of the sermon. One possibility is that the preaching of the sermon transmits to the congregants what God once said. The other possibility is that, by way of the preaching of the sermon, God speaks anew to the listeners then and there. This latter was clearly John Calvin's view. In the *Institutes* he wrote, God "uses the ministry of men to

---

30. Deiss (1979), 150–1. Deiss attributes *The Apostolic Tradition* to Hippolytus; that attribution has now been discredited.
31. *Second Helvetic Confession* (online).   32. *Sunday Missal* (2011), 17.

declare openly his will to us by mouth, as a sort of delegated work, not by transferring to them his right and honor, but only that through their mouths he may do his own work."[33] In his commentary on Isaiah 11: 4 he said, of faithful ministers, that "Christ acts by them in such a manner that he wishes their mouth to be reckoned as his mouth, and their lips as his lips; that is, when they speak from his mouth, and faithfully declare his word."[34] And in his commentary on 2 Corinthians 5: 18 he wrote that when a minister proclaims the gospel "he is to be listened to just as an ambassador of God [*Dei legatus*]."[35] The Reformed liturgical theologian J.-J. von Allmen shared Calvin's view. He calls preaching the "prophetic" proclamation of the word of God,[36] and says, "in the hands of God, the sermon is a basic means by which there takes place a direct prophetic intervention in the life of the faithful and of the Church, with the object of consoling, setting to rights, reforming, questioning."[37]

On Calvin's interpretation and von Allmen's, the implicit preface to the sermon or homily is, "Thus saith the Lord," whereupon God speaks anew then and there to the listeners by way of what the preacher says. Our discussion in this chapter suggests a third possibility. Perhaps the basic function of the sermon is to convey to the listeners, in its own distinct way, the continuant discourse of God that the reading aloud of Scripture already conveyed to them and to make clear how that continuant discourse applies to their lives. It's often not clear just what is the continuant discourse of God that some scriptural passage presents. The basic function of the sermon is to present that continuant discourse in such a way that the listeners "get it." On this interpretation, the implicit preface to the sermon is, "What God is saying in this passage is...," whereupon the preacher makes clear to the listeners what is the continuant discourse of God presented in the passage read and how that discourse applies to them.

The issue merits a long and detailed theological discussion. My guess as to the conclusion at which such a discussion would arrive is that the basic function of the sermon or homily is the third of the three functions identified, but that it also sometimes performs the second function. It did in St Anthony's case.

33. *Institutes* IV.3.1. Calvin (1960), 1053.
34. Calvin (1948a), 381.   35. Calvin (1948b), 236.
36. Von Allmen (1965), 142.   37. Von Allmen (1965), 143.

The terrain beyond

We have by no means canvassed all the ways in which God is active in the liturgy. Different Christian traditions have different views as to what it is that the Spirit brings about in the Eucharist. It was John Calvin's view that the Spirit brings it about that Christ offers himself to the participants by way of the celebrant offering them the bread and wine, and that the participants accept that offer by eating the bread and drinking the wine. Calvin writes, "Our Lord gives us in the Supper what he signifies by it, and we thus really receive the body and blood of Jesus."[38] This then is another way in which God is active in the liturgy: Christ offers himself in the Eucharist. Calvin is by no means unique in holding this view.

A traditional view of baptism is that God acts by way of the immersion of the baptismal candidate in water or the sprinkling of him or her with water. Many would testify that God acts by way of the music of the liturgy. And the Orthodox would insist that God acts by way of engagement by participants with the icons. We have done no more than introduce the topic of God as liturgical agent.

---

38. Calvin (1954), 163. I discuss Calvin's view of the Eucharist in some detail in Wolterstorff (2015b), 146–62, and in Wolterstorff (2013a), 97–113.

Does God know what we say
to God?

Pervasive in Christian liturgical enactments are acts of addressing God: thanking God, praising God, interceding with God, and so forth. Some Christians share with Paul Tillich the view that God is the non-personal Ground of Being and that, accordingly, God is not the sort of entity that can know what we say to God—or, indeed, know anything else. On their view, addressing God is like a gardener looking at the small oak he has just planted and saying, "May you flourish and provide shade for many generations." Most Christians are of the contrary view, that God does have knowledge and that, in particular, God knows what they say to God when they address God.

As most readers of this volume will know, there is a long and powerful theologico-philosophical tradition which holds that God is *a se*, that is, not conditioned in any way by anything that is not God. In the literature on the topic of aseity one finds, in addition to the formulation of aseity that I have just now given, weaker formulations.[1] Call aseity as I have just now defined it, *strong aseity*. Strong aseity has enjoyed a far more prominent position in the tradition than any weaker form. When I speak of aseity in what follows, it will always be strong aseity that I have in mind.

My project in this chapter is to show that if God is strongly *a se*, then God cannot know what we say to God. If my argument is sound, then those who participate in liturgical enactments face a choice: if they are convinced that God knows what we say to God, they must give up the doctrine of God's aseity; if they are convinced that God is *a se*, they must give up the belief that God knows what we say to God. If they choose the latter option, they can either refrain from performing the verbal actions prescribed for

---

1. For a presentation of some of the weaker understandings of aseity see Grant (2016).

addressing God or they can interpret, along Tillichian lines, what they are doing when they address God.

No one has ever drawn out more brilliantly and systematically the implications of strong aseity for our understanding of God than Thomas Aquinas. And, unlike Tillich, Aquinas insisted that God does have knowledge, including knowledge of things other than God. So, rather than striking out on my own, I will conduct my argument by looking closely at Aquinas's attempt to account for God's knowledge of things other than God within the framework of his commitment to God's strong aseity.[2]

Ways of knowing illocutionary acts

A few preliminary distinctions are in order. In their discussions of knowledge philosophers in the contemporary analytic tradition have focused most of their attention on *propositional* knowledge. Such knowledge comes in two forms: knowledge that so-and-so is the case, and knowledge, *about* something, that it is such-and-such. What is now commonly called *objectual* knowledge, knowledge of some person, animal, thing, or substance, has received much less attention. Aquinas's discussion of knowledge in general, and of God's knowledge in particular, is focused exclusively on objectual knowledge. In the course of discussing God's knowledge Aquinas takes note of knowledge of what he calls "enunciables" (*ST* Ia.14.14). I understand an enunciable to be an assertively uttered sentence. But his discussion of knowledge of enunciables is no more than a parenthesis in his discussion of God's objectual knowledge.

Bertrand Russell distinguished between two forms of objectual knowledge. What he called *knowledge by acquaintance* consists of being aware of some entity: seeing the tree, hearing the sound, feeling the prick of the pin, and so forth.[3] What he called *knowledge by description* consists of having some entity in mind under some singular concept which applies to that entity alone: having in mind an item of furniture under the singular concept, *the*

---

2. The translations I will be using are *Summa theologica* (1947) and *Summa contra Gentiles* (1975). I will incorporate references into the text.

3. At the time he drew the distinction between two forms of objectual knowledge, Russell seems to have thought that one has acquaintance with (awareness of) only one's own states of mind. When I speak of *awareness* and *acquaintance*, I intend to leave it open as to which sorts of entities one can be aware of or acquainted with.

couch in the next room, having in mind something someone said under the singular concept, *the assertion you just made*, and so forth.

It seems intuitively obvious that, in general, knowledge of something by awareness is superior to knowledge of something by description.[4] Knowledge of something by awareness puts one in direct epistemic contact with the thing known; one directly receives reality's input. Knowledge of something by description does not do that. Further, knowledge by awareness is basic; if we had no awareness of anything, we would have no objectual knowledge at all.

The distinction between locutionary and illuctionary acts, employed throughout our discussion, will once again be indispensable. The term "what was said" is ambiguous as between these two sorts of acts. Sometimes the ambiguity doesn't matter; in our discussion in this chapter it often will matter. When it does I can, of course, use either the term "locutionary act" or the term "illocutionary act." But the constant repetition of those terms would prove tedious. So now and then I will use the term "utterance" instead of "locutionary act" and "act of discourse" instead of "illocutionary act."

Listening to what someone is saying is a way of gaining cognizance. It's a way of gaining cognizance, in the first place, of the locutionary act the person performed. By listening, I become aware of the person's utterance; I acquire knowledge by acquaintance of it. Listening to what someone is saying is typically also a way of gaining cognizance of the illocutionary act the person performed. The cognizance in this case is more complex than in the case of the locutionary act.

We do not have direct awareness of the illocutionary acts performed by our fellows. Those acts are imperceptible. We do not hear them or see them, nor do we have any other sort of direct acquaintance with them. We infer their existence. If we are listening to a person speak, we infer the existence of the person's illocutionary act on the basis of our awareness of their locutionary act.

Here is what seems to me a plausible account of how it goes. I have auditory awareness of your locutionary act. On the basis of my awareness of that act, and my knowledge of the relevant conventions in force, I infer that you are thereby performing an illocutionary act. If that inference is correct, I now have cognizance of your illocutionary act under the singular concept,

---

4. Of course, a specific case of knowledge by awareness might be inferior to a specific case of knowledge by description. An awareness obscured by static is inferior to a highly detailed and precise description.

the illocutionary act you just now performed. Or perhaps I infer, more specifically, that you are performing an illocutionary act of asserting something. If that inference is correct, then I now have cognizance of your illocutionary act under the singular concept, *the assertion you just now made.* Or perhaps I infer, yet more specifically, that you are asserting that it has been unusually cold this past month; if that inference is correct, then I now have cognizance of your illocutionary act under the singular concept, *the assertion you just now made that it has been unusually cold this past month.* Cognizance of a person's illocutionary act, when gained by listening to the person speak, is knowledge by description that is *grounded in* knowledge by acquaintance of the locutionary act performed, along with propositional knowledge of the relevant conventions in force.

There are, of course, other ways of gaining knowledge of the acts of discourse performed by one's fellow human beings than by listening to their utterances. Among the most important of those other ways is reading what the person wrote, if she did write, or listening to a recording of her speech, if it was recorded. Gaining cognizance of someone's act of discourse by reading what she wrote or by listening to a recording of her speech resembles gaining cognizance by listening to her utterance in that it too is knowledge by description of her act of discourse based on inference from knowledge by acquaintance plus propositional knowledge of the relevant conventions. The object of the acquaintance is significantly different, however. Rather than hearing her utterance when and where it occurs, I read or hear an enduring trace of the locutionary act that she performed.

God has no auditory apparatus—no ears, no auditory nerves. So whatever knowledge God has of our locutionary acts is not gained by listening, literally speaking. From this it follows that whatever cognizance God has of the acts of discourse we address to God, that cognizance is also not gained by means of listening, literally speaking.

But suppose that God, unlike us, has direct acquaintance with our illocutionary acts. Whereas we have direct perceptual acquaintance with the locutionary acts of our fellows but no direct acquaintance with their illocutionary acts, God would have direct acquaintance with our illocutionary acts but no perceptual acquaintance with our locutionary acts. On the principle that knowledge by acquaintance or awareness is, in general, a superior form of knowledge to knowledge of that same thing under a singular concept, God's cognizance of our acts of discourse would be superior to our cognizance of the acts of discourse of our fellows.

Aquinas's account of God's knowledge

Let us now turn to Aquinas's account of God's knowledge.[5] Once we have in hand his general account of God's knowledge, it will be obvious how the account applies to the special case of God's cognizance of our acts of addressing God.

The over-arching consideration shaping Aquinas's account of God's knowledge is that the account has to be consistent with God's (strong) aseity. Aquinas argues that God's aseity implies that God is simple, immutable, impassible, pure act, and more besides. So the account has to be consistent with those doctrines as well.

It will greatly aid our understanding of Aquinas's account of God's knowledge if we preface it with a brief presentation of his account of human perceptual knowledge. Aquinas declares, "All knowledge takes place through a certain assimilation" (SCG I.63.2). Specifically, "Everything understood is apprehended by some likeness [of the thing] within him who understands it" (ST Ia.55.2. obj. 1). "Intelligent beings are distinguished from non-intelligent beings in that the latter possess only their own form; whereas the intelligent being is naturally adapted to have also the form of some other thing; for the idea of the thing known is in the knower" (ST Ia.14.1. resp.).

In the case of human perceptual knowledge this "assimilation" of the intellect to the thing known goes as follows. Suppose I see a table. When that happens, the table affects me in such a way as to cause in me what Aquinas calls a "sensory image" of the table, a "phantasm," a "sensible species." This image of the table, though "free from matter" (ST Ia.14.1. resp.) and indispensable to cognition, is not yet cognition of the table. Cognition of the table requires that I see it *as* something that it is—see it as a table, see it as a piece of furniture, whatever. Suppose I see it as a table. For that to happen, I must have the form *table* in mind and, on the basis of the sensory phantasm that the object caused in me, see the object as having that form.

> Every cognition is in accordance with some form, which is the source of
> cognition in the cognizer. But this sort of form can be considered in two ways.
> In one way, in keeping with the being that it has in the cognizer; in another
> way, in keeping with the relation it bears to the thing whose likeness it is.

5. Though, as we shall see, I have a fundamental disagreement with Eleonore Stump's interpretation of Aquinas's account of God's knowledge (Stump, 2003), nonetheless I have benefited very much from her discussion.

Considered in the first relationship, it makes the cognizer actually cognizant. Considered in the second relationship, however, it determines the cognition to some determinate cognizable thing.[6]

Aquinas's point can be made by using our term "concept." To see the object before me as a table I must have the concept *table* in mind and, on the basis of the sensory phantasm, apply the concept to the object. Assume that to possess the concept *table* is to grasp the property of *being a table*. Then, if the thing I see is in fact a table, what I grasp mentally is the very same entity that the thing possesses, namely, the property of *being a table*. What I am calling "the property" of *being a table* is among the things that Aquinas calls a "form." When we cognize some object, the form "of the thing known is in the knower" (*ST* Ia.14.1. resp.).

Aquinas emphasizes that when my cognition takes the form of perceiving a table as a table, the object of my cognition is neither the sensory image (phantasm) caused by the table nor the form table, but the table itself. The image and the form are *that by which* I cognize the table. Using the term "intelligible species" for "form" he says, "The intelligible species is to the intellect what the sensible image is to the sense. But the sensible image is not what is perceived, but rather that by which sense perceives. Therefore the intelligible species is not what is actually understood, but that by which the intellect understands" (*ST* Ia.85.3. resp.). The thing cognized is the table, not the sensory image of the table and not the concept *table*.

We can now turn to Aquinas's account of God's knowledge. Given that God has no sensory equipment, and given that, on Aquinas's account, God is *a se*, God's knowledge is, of necessity, radically different from human knowledge. Of course, what Aquinas calls "God's knowledge" must not prove to be so different from human knowledge as to make it misleading to call it "knowledge."

The first step in Aquinas's account of God's knowledge is his account of God's self-knowledge. God knows himself. Indeed, "primarily and essentially God knows only himself" (*ScG* I.48). God knows himself through himself. The argument for that claim goes as follows. In our case, the reason "we actually feel or know a thing is because our intellect or sense is actually informed by the sensible or intelligible species.... It follows that sense or intellect is distinct from the sensible or intelligible object, since both [sense and intellect] are in potentiality." But "God has nothing in him of potentiality

6. Quoted in Stump (2003), 183.

but is pure act." It follows that God's "intellect and its object are altogether the same; so that He neither is without the intelligible species, as is the case with our intellect when it understands potentially; nor does the intelligible species differ from the substance of the divine intellect, as it differs in our intellect when it understands actually; but the intelligible species itself is the divine intellect itself, and thus God understands Himself through Himself" (*ST* Ia.14.2. resp.).

Aquinas moves on to argue vigorously for the thesis that God not only knows himself but knows other things as well. In knowing himself, God knows them. "From the fact that God understands himself primarily and essentially we must posit that he knows in himself things other than himself" (*ScG* I.49.1).

> In order to know how God knows things other than himself, we must consider that a thing is known in two ways: in itself, and in another. A thing is known in itself when it is known by the proper species adequate to the knowable object, as when the eye sees a man through the image of a man. A thing is seen in another through the image of that which contains it, as when...a man is seen in a mirror by the image in the mirror.   (*ST* Ia.14.5. resp.)

"God's essence contains the similitudes of [all] things other than himself." So whereas God "sees himself through himself, he sees other things not in themselves but in himself" (*ST* Ia.14.5. resp.).

Aquinas is at pains to insist that God's knowledge of things other than God is "proper" knowledge. He notes that some writers have said, "God knows things other than himself only in general, that is, only as beings" (*ST* Ia.14.6. resp.). This claim is mistaken, says Aquinas. Such knowledge would not be proper knowledge. "To have a proper knowledge of things is to know them not only in general, but as they are distinct from each other" (*ST* Ia.14.6. resp.). To lack proper knowledge of a thing, "to know a thing in general and not in particular, is to have an imperfect knowledge of it" (*ST* Ia.14.6. resp.). God's knowledge cannot be imperfect. "We must therefore hold that God knows things other than himself with a proper knowledge; not only in so far as being is common to them, but in so far as one is distinguished from the other" (*ST* Ia.14.6. resp.). God knows "singular things in their singularity" (*ST* Ia.14.11. resp.).

To understand how it can be that, in knowing himself, God knows all things other than God in their singularity, Aquinas proposes that we think of God's knowledge of things other than God on the model of an artisan's knowledge: "The knowledge of God is to all creatures what the knowledge of the artificer is to things made by his art" (*ST* Ia.14.8. resp.). An artisan has in mind a paradigm or exemplar of the thing he will create; his cognizance of that paradigm or exemplar is "the cause of the things made by his art" (*ST* Ia.14.8. resp.). Obviously it is not a sufficient cause; the artisan must also decide to produce an example of the exemplar. If he does produce an example of the exemplar, he can then cognize that thing as *what he brought about as an example of the exemplar.*

Think of God's knowledge of things other than God along the same lines. God's essence is the paradigm or exemplar for everything that exists that is other than God. (For our purposes here, we need not get into Aquinas's attempt to explain how God's simple essence could be the paradigm for each thing other than God.) Thus in knowing God's essence, God knows the paradigm for each individual thing other than God. God's essence constitutes the paradigms or exemplars not only for all actual entities but also for all possible entities (*ST* Ia.14.9. resp.). Actual entities are those whose paradigms or exemplars God wills to be exemplified. Thus "the knowledge of God joined with his will is the cause of things" (*ST* Ia.14.9. ad. obj. 3). Of course, God not only knows the paradigms but also knows which of those paradigms God has willed to be exemplified. So it would not be a mistake to say, "the knowledge of God is the cause of things" (*ST* Ia.14.8. resp.). God's knowledge is "the cause of things in so far as his will is joined to it. Hence the knowledge of God as the cause of things is usually called the *knowledge of approbation*" (*ST* Ia.14.8. resp.). "God knows all things through a cause; for, by knowing himself, who is the cause of other things, he knows other things as his effects" (*ScG* I.66.6).

Here is a summary in his own words of Aquinas's line of thought:

> Whoever has a knowledge of matter and of what designates matter, and also of form individuated in matter, must have a knowledge of the singular. But the knowledge of God extends to matter and to individuating accidents and forms. For, since his understanding is his essence, he must understand all things that in any way are in his essence. Now, within his essence, as within the first source, there are virtually present all things that in any way have being, since he is the first and universal principle of being. Matter and accidents are not absent from among those things, since matter is a being in potency and an accident is a being in another. Therefore, the knowledge of singulars is not lacking to God. (*ScG* I.65.3)

Let me illuminate how Aquinas was thinking of God's knowledge of things other than God by elaborating, a bit, the model of an artisan that he was using. Imagine an artisan with a detailed design-plan in mind for a table. Imagine, further, that this artisan has the godlike power, and knows he has, of bringing about the existence of an example of that design-plan just by willing that there be an example, and that he also has the power of determining the location of the example just by willing it: he can will it to be located in his workshop, where he can see it, or hundreds of miles away.

Call the design-plan *D-P.* Suppose the artisan does in fact bring a table into existence by willing that there be an example of *D-P* 500 miles away and wills no additional examples of *D-P.* He is directly aware, obviously, of the design-plan *D-P;* he is also directly aware of his act of willing. Let us suppose that he conceptualizes that act of willing as *his act of willing into existence one and only one example of D-P.* Aquinas's idea is that, in possessing these two items of self-knowledge, knowledge of his design-plan and knowledge of his act of willing, the artisan cognizes the table.

I judge that Aquinas was mistaken in his claim that by virtue of having knowledge of his design-plan and of his act of will, the artisan has knowledge of the table. The model of an artisan fails him. Before I explain why it fails him, let me introduce into the discussion Eleonore Stump's very different interpretation of Aquinas's understanding of God's knowledge. If her interpretation is correct, the failure of the artisan model is beside the point.

Stump's alternative interpretation of Aquinas on God's knowledge

Stump interprets Aquinas's account of God's knowledge of things other than God as an incomplete account of God's knowing such things by acquaintance—or as she calls it, by "epistemic contact." Commenting that "Aquinas himself finds it acceptable to attribute a 'perceptual paradigm of knowledge,' analogously understood, to God,"[7] she claims that, on Aquinas's account, God's knowledge of things other than God is structurally analogous to our perceptual knowledge in that it "involves at least three elements: (a*) God's being in epistemic contact with everything he cognizes, (b*) God's possessing a concept or intelligible form of

7. Stump (2003), 185.

what he cognizes, and (c★) God's applying that concept or form to what he is in epistemic contact with."[8]

Stump then observes that "most of Aquinas's explicit discussion of God's knowledge is an explanation of (b★), an attempt to say how God has the form requisite for cognition of things other than himself."[9] Stump indicates that she finds it regrettable that Aquinas says little about (a★), God's epistemic contact with things other than God; but she regards that as an incompleteness in the account, nothing more. She says, "So far as I can see, Aquinas provides no further help in analyzing God's epistemic contact than to hold that God applies his ideas to what he cognizes and that God atemporally 'sees' things other than himself. In this respect, then, Aquinas' account is incomplete."[10]

Aquinas does not just say less about (a★) and (c★) than about (b★). He says nothing about "(a★) God's being in epistemic contact with everything he cognizes," and hence also nothing about "(c★) God's applying [a] concept or form to what he is in epistemic contact with."

Had Aquinas been thinking of God's knowledge of things other than God on the model of our perceptual knowledge of things, then the absence of any discussion on his part of God's epistemic contact with things would be not only regrettable but surprising. But Aquinas makes unmistakably clear that he is not using the model of a perceiver. He is using the model of an artisan producing an example of a paradigm or exemplar that the artisan has in mind. I quoted a passage from the *Summa Theologica* in which Aquinas explicitly declares that it is the model of an artisan that he is working with. He makes the same point in the *Summa contra Gentiles*: "The knowledge of the divine intellect is to other things as the knowledge of an artisan to artifacts" (*ScG* I.66.3).

As evidence for her interpretation, Stump points to the fact that every now and then Aquinas speaks of God's "vision" of things, God's "gaze" at things, and so forth. So let's look at some of those passages. In *ST* Ia.14.9, Aquinas addresses the question "whether God has knowledge of things that are not." He begins his answer as follows:

God knows all things whatsoever that in any way are. Now it is possible that things that are not absolutely, should be in a certain sense. For things absolutely are which are actual; whereas things which are not actual, are in the power

---

8. Stump (2003), 184.   9. Stump (2003), 184.   10. Stump (2003), 187.

either of God himself or of a creature, whether in active power, or passive; whether in power of thought or of imagination, or of any other manner of meaning whatsoever. Whatever therefore can be made, or thought, or said by the creature, as also whatever he himself can do, all are known to God, although they are not actual. And in so far it can be said that he has knowledge even of things that are not.

A bit later in the same article Aquinas remarks that God is said to know actual things "with the knowledge of vision" and to know merely possible things with "the knowledge of simple intelligence."[11] He explains: "this is so called because the things we see around us have distinct being outside the seer."

I submit that this passage offers no evidence for interpreting Aquinas as holding that God has direct epistemic contact with things other than God. The only work the term "vision" does in the passage is to distinguish God's knowledge of actual things from God's knowledge of merely possible things. The last sentence quoted suggests that the reason the term "vision" is appropriate is that, just as things we see have distinct being outside the perceiver, so also actual things, as opposed to mere possibilities, have distinct being outside of God.

After distinguishing between the possibilities that God actualizes and those that God does not actualize, Aquinas remarks, in the same article,

> A certain difference is to be noted in the consideration of those things that are not actual. For though some of them may not be in act now, still they were, or they will be; and God is said to know all these with the knowledge of vision: for since God's act of understanding, which is his being, is measured by eternity; and since eternity is without succession, comprehending all time, the present glance of God extends over all time, and to all things which exist in any time, as to objects present to him. (*ST* Ia.14.9)

The question Aquinas is implicitly considering here is whether God's knowledge of past and future things is the knowledge of "simple intelligence," in contrast to God's knowledge of present things which, as we have seen, is the knowledge of "vision." His answer is that God's knowledge of anything that ever exists is the knowledge of vision, the reason being that God's knowledge of what is past or future does not differ from God's knowledge of what is present. "All things that are in time are present to God

---

11. The same distinction is drawn and the same terminology is employed in *ScG* I.66.8.

from eternity, not only because he has the types of things present within him, as some say; but because his glance is carried from eternity over all things as they are in their presentiality" (*ST* Ia.14.13. resp.; cf. *ST* Ia.14.9. resp.). God's knowledge of successive events is an all-at-once knowledge rather than a successive knowledge.

I submit that these passages also offer no evidence for interpreting Aquinas as holding that God has direct epistemic contact with things other than God. Here, too, the only work being done by the terms "vision" and "glance" is to distinguish God's knowledge of actual things from God's knowledge of mere possibilities.

As has been noted, Aquinas insists that God has a "proper" knowledge of all things (*ScG* I.50.1), his argument being that if God did not have a proper knowledge of all things, God's knowledge would be imperfect. The question comes to mind, might Aquinas mean by "proper knowledge," knowledge that has epistemic contact as a component? From the passages I quoted in the section "Aquinas's account of God's knowledge" it's clear that that is not what he meant. Proper knowledge is knowledge of "singular things in their singularity." Here is another passage in which he makes the same point: "God knows whatever is found in reality. But this is to have a proper and complete knowledge of a thing, namely, to know all that there is in the thing, both what is common and what is proper. Therefore, God has a proper knowledge of things, in so far as they are distinct from one another" (*ScG* I.50.3).

In short, I know of no text in Aquinas that supports Stump's interpretation of Aquinas's account of God's knowledge. To the contrary; Aquinas's explicit statement, that the model to be used for understanding God's knowledge of things other than God is the knowledge an artisan has of what he makes, is decisive evidence against her interpretation.

Why Aquinas could not have ascribed to God knowledge by acquaintance with things other than God

I have argued that there is no textual basis for interpreting Aquinas as holding that God has direct epistemic contact with things other than God. Let me now take the next step of arguing that there is a very good systematic reason why Aquinas did not hold such a view; it would have been inconsistent with his commitment to God's strong aseity.

Suppose that God had direct epistemic contact with Julius Caesar. Then among God's properties would be, *being in direct epistemic contact with Julius Caesar.* If Caesar never existed, neither God nor anyone else could have that property. So God's having the property of being in direct epistemic contact with Julius Caesar depends on the existence of Julius Caesar. Caesar is not identical with God. Though the paradigm in accord with which God created Caesar is, on Aquinas's account, identical with God, Caesar himself is not identical with God. So if among God's properties there were the property of *being in direct epistemic contact with Caesar,* God would be, in that respect, conditioned on something other than God, namely, the existence of Julius Caesar. And that is incompatible with God's strong aseity.

There is another way in which God's being in direct epistemic contact with Julius Caesar would be incompatible with God's aseity. When an artisan sets about implementing a design-plan that he has for a table, he acts upon the world. When he is finished and looks at the table he has made, his orientation is the opposite: he opens himself up to the world, receives information from the world. At the core of all perception is what Kant called "receptivity." Perception is not, indeed, purely receptive. Though Aquinas and Kant were starkly different in their thinking, both taught that, in perception, receptivity has to be combined with what Kant called "spontaneity." We have to apply concepts to what is given us. But there has to be a core of receptivity.

So it is with all awareness. Aquinas writes, "the reason why we actually feel or know a thing is because our intellect or sense is actually informed by the sensible or intelligible species" (*ST* Ia.14.2. resp.). "The intellect is perfected by the intelligible object, *i.e.*, is assimilated to it" (*ST* Ia.14.2. ad. 2). For God to know something other than God by the assimilation of God's intellect to that thing would be starkly inconsistent with God's aseity.

Epistemic contact with things other than God would also be inconsistent with God's simplicity. "The operations of the intellect," says Aquinas, "are distinguished according to their objects. If, then, God understood himself and something other than himself as the principal object, he will have several intellectual operations. Therefore, either his essence will be divided into several parts, or he will have an intellectual operation that is not his substance. Both of these positions have been proved to be impossible" (*ScG* I.48.4).

Stump recognizes that the attribution to God of epistemic contact with things other than God poses a "problem" for Aquinas. She locates the problem in God's impassibility rather than in God's aseity (as I noted in the section "Aquinas's account of God's knowledge," Aquinas regarded impassibility as implied by aseity). Stump writes, "Any process which could count as seeing of contingents must also involve reception. And since receiving is a kind of undergoing it seems that God's 'seeing' of creatures must be incompatible with his impassibility."[12] By calling this a "problem" for Aquinas and letting it go at that, Stump is no doubt indicating that she regards it as possible, in principle, to harmonize God's having direct epistemic contact with things other than God with God's impassibility.

In her Aquinas Lecture of 2016, Stump undertakes to show in detail that the God of Aquinas's philosophical theology is fully compatible with the God of the Bible. I judge that, in good measure, she is successful. Though she does not directly take up the issue of God's knowledge, in the course of her discussion she makes two points that might appear to bear on the topic.

She argues that deciding to be responsive to something is not to be identified with being acted upon by that thing. The example she uses to make the point is this: if, in writing a book, she decides "to use the story of Jonah *because* of what the writer of the book of Jonah wrote," she is "responsive to that writer and that writer's narrative" but the writer "is not acting on" her. "That writer is dead."[13] The application of the point to God is that God wills to be *responsive to* what transpires in the world but is not *acted upon* by what transpires in the world.

Stump is certainly right in her claim that deciding to be responsive to something is not to be identified with being acted upon by that thing. But the point is irrelevant to Aquinas's account of God's knowledge. Aquinas's thought is not that God's knowledge of something other than God is a case of God's deciding to be responsive to that thing. His thought is that in knowing himself, God knows that thing.

Immediately after making the point that deciding to be responsive is not to be equated with passivity, Stump says,

On Aquinas's view, even a human intellect need not be acted upon when it knows something.... For Aquinas, the human intellect is always active when it knows. That is, in the process of cognition the human intellect acts on the

12. Stump (2003), 186.   13. Stump (2016), 94–5.

phantasms derived from sensory input to abstract the intelligible species enabling intellect cognition; the phantasms do *not* act on the intellect.[14]

It's true that, on Aquinas's view, in acquiring perceptual knowledge of a tree one's *intellect* is not acted upon by the phantasm of the tree. The tree does, however, act on one's sensory apparatus, producing the phantasm on which the intellect acts. Human perceptual knowledge is a blend of passivity and activity.

I assume Stump's reason for making the point about the role of the intellect in human perceptual knowledge immediately after making the distinction between responsiveness and passivity is that, since God has no sensory apparatus, God is actively responsive in knowing things other than God, not passive. But Aquinas's account of God's knowledge of things other than God is not that God is actively responsive to those things; his account is that God knows those things in knowing himself.

I see no way in which God's having epistemic contact with things other than God can be harmonized with the doctrines of aseity and impassibility. Given his commitment to those doctrines, Aquinas could not have developed an account of God's knowledge on the model of human perceptual knowledge. Given aseity, God can have direct epistemic contact only with himself. And that was Aquinas's view.

A distinction commonly made by philosophers is that between the *intrinsic* and the *extrinsic* properties of things. An intrinsic property of something is a property such that, had the thing lacked that property, that would constitute a real change or difference in the thing; properties that are not intrinsic are extrinsic. To the best of my knowledge, no one has succeeded in giving an illuminating account of "real" change or difference; we have to make do with examples. An example of one of my intrinsic properties is the property of *being a philosopher*. Had I not been a philosopher, that would constitute a real difference in me. An example of one of my extrinsic properties is the property of *being referred to yesterday by my neighbor John*. Had John not referred to me, that would not have constituted any real difference in me.

If having direct epistemic contact with Julius Caesar were an extrinsic property of God, having that property would not be incompatible with God's aseity. God would be no more dependent on Julius Caesar's existence by virtue of having that property than God is dependent on my existence

---

14. Stump (2016), 95.

by virtue of having the property of being referred to by me. It's obvious, however, that having direct epistemic contact with something is an intrinsic property of a person, whether that person be God or a human being. If the person had lacked that property, that would constitute a real difference.[15]

Why the model of the artisan fails Aquinas

We come, at last, to the question of the tenability of the theory that, on my interpretation, Aquinas did develop, namely, his artisan model for God's knowledge of things other than God. I hold that the model fails him. To see why it fails him, consider once again our imagined artisan with the godlike causal power of willing into existence an example of his design-plan for a table, a power that he knows he has. The artisan has direct awareness of his design-plan. In order to keep it distinct from the other design-plans he has in mind, he names it "D-P." He also has direct awareness of the act of will on his part that consists of willing into existence one and only example of D-P. The artisan, in possessing these two items of self-knowledge, namely, direct awareness of his design-plan and of his act of will, does not yet have objectual knowledge of the table, for the simple reason that the pair whose members are his design-plan and his act of will is not identical with the table.

On Aquinas's view of the matter, we are to think of God's knowledge of, say, a cat, on the analogy of an artisan's knowledge of a table that he made. God has direct awareness of God's paradigm for that cat, call it PC, and direct awareness of having willed an example of that paradigm. Aquinas assumes that for God to have these two items of direct awareness is for God to know the cat. That is mistaken, for the simple reason that the pair whose members are the paradigm PC and God's act of willing is not identical with the cat.

Earlier we saw that Aquinas had systematic reasons for holding that God does not have epistemic contact (knowledge by acquaintance) with things

---

15. Brower (2009) argues that God's knowledge of things other than God is extrinsic to God. His treatment of the topic is extremely brief. The sort of knowledge he attributes to God is clearly not, however, epistemic contact; it is, indeed, very similar to the sort of knowledge Aquinas attributes to God. Brower says, "strictly speaking, what God depends on for his knowledge that human beings exist is not anything distinct from himself (namely, human beings themselves), but only his own free acts of will or choice" (121).

other than God; such knowledge would be incompatible with God's aseity, with God's impassibility, and with God's simplicity. Now we have seen that Aquinas fails in his attempt to show that in knowing himself, God knows things other than himself. That leaves one possibility: might it be that God has knowledge by description of things other than himself?

The artisan's knowledge by acquaintance of his design–plan *D-P* and of his act of willing into existence an example of *D-P*, coupled with his propositional knowledge that his causal powers are godlike, enables him to cognize the table under the singular concept, *being the table he brought about by willing that there be one and only one example of D-P.* That would be knowledge by description of the table. Could God similarly cognize the cat under the singular concept, *what was brought about by willing into existence an example of PC*?

As we saw, knowledge by description is a mode of knowledge inferior to knowledge by acquaintance. For Aquinas, that was a reason for refusing to attribute knowledge by description to God. Given Aquinas's criterion for the non-identity of acts of knowledge, knowledge by description of things other than God would also be incompatible with God's simplicity. The criterion was this: if acts of knowledge *X* and *Y* have different objects, then the acts are not identical (*ScG* I.48.4).

To summarize: God's having epistemic contact (knowledge by acquaintance) with things other than God would be incompatible with God's aseity, with God's impassibility, and with God's simplicity. And if we agree with Aquinas, as I think we should, that aseity implies simplicity, and if we also agree with him, as I think we should, on his criterion for the non-identity of acts of knowledge, then God's having knowledge by description of things other than God would be incompatible with God's simplicity, and hence with God's aseity. I see no way in which God's having knowledge of things other than God can be harmonized with the doctrine of God's aseity.

The upshot

We are faced with a choice. All scripts for traditional liturgical enactments prescribe that the participants address God at various points. If one believes that God knows what we say when we address God, one has to give up the traditional doctrine of strong aseity. If one holds to the traditional doctrine of God's aseity, one has to give up the belief that God knows what we say

when we address God. And not only does one have to give up the belief
that God knows what we say to God; one has to give up the belief that God
knows things other than God in general. The doctrine of divine aseity
implies that God knows nothing other than Godself. As for myself, I choose
the former option; I give up the doctrine of strong aseity. In choosing this
option I assume, of course, that the arguments philosophers and theologians
have offered in favor of strong aseity are not compelling. Here is not the
place to explain why I do not find them compelling.

Has the person who rejects strong aseity stepped onto a slippery slope
leading to a radical version of process theology, according to which God is
through and through conditioned by what is other than God? Not at all.
One can agree that God has epistemic contact with things other than God,
and that God is thereby conditioned in a certain way by things other than
God, while insisting that there are many fundamental ways in which God is
unconditioned. God's existence is not conditional on things other than
God, God's activity as creator is not conditional on things other than God,
and so forth. The theological project that beckons is to formulate a doctrine
of aseity that articulates the fundamental ways in which God is not conditioned while taking due account of the various ways in which God is conditioned by things other than God. My guess is that if we succeed in
formulating such a fine-grained doctrine of aseity, we will see that all the
ways in which God is conditioned by things other than God are ways in
which God has allowed Godself to be conditioned. But in the absence of
such a formulation, that's only a guess.

Aquinas on prayer

In *Summa Theologica* II–II.83, Aquinas addresses the topic of prayer. In my
discussion thus far I have paid no attention to what he says there. Readers
who know their Aquinas may find that surprising. If the topic is what
Aquinas has to say on whether God can know what we say to God, why not
start with what Aquinas says about prayer? My reason for not starting there
is that, in what he says about prayer, Aquinas does not address our topic. In
concluding this chapter, let's look briefly at what he does say about prayer.

He writes, "It belongs to prayer to be heard" (83.1. obj. 1). "The Lord is
said to hear the desire of the poor" (83.1. ad. 1). "It is useless to pray to one
who is ignorant of the prayer" (83.4. obj. 2). Contrary to what these words,

taken out of context, might suggest, Aquinas's topic is not the topic we have been addressing, namely, whether God has cognizance of what we say to God. Aquinas assumes that God does have such cognizance. His topic is rather the point of praying to God.

He considers the view that it makes no sense to pray to God. He imagines an objector saying, "By prayer we bend the mind of the person to whom we pray, so that he may do what is asked of him. But God's will is unchangeable and inflexible" (83.2. obj. 2). Aquinas agrees that God's will is unchangeable, but he rejects the conclusion that prayer is pointless. "Our motive in praying is not that we may change the divine disposition" (83.2. ad. 2). We have "so to account for the utility of prayer as ... not to imply changeableness on the part of the divine disposition" (83.2. resp.).

Why, then, do we pray if not to "change the divine disposition"? One reason is that God has ordained that God will bestow certain goods on us upon our asking God to do so. Our asking God to bestow those goods on us doesn't *cause* God to do so; it doesn't bend God's will. Rather, God has ordained from eternity that God will bestow them on us upon our asking. "God bestows many things on us out of his liberality, even without our asking for them." But God also "wishes to bestow certain things on us at our asking" (83.2. ad. 3).[16] God does this for our improvement, "so that we may acquire confidence in having recourse to God, and that we may recognize in him the author of our goods" (83.2. ad. 3).

In sum, we do not pray to God in order "that we may bend him" (83.9. ad. 5); we pray because God has ordained from eternity that God will bestow certain benefits on us upon our praying for those benefits and because prayer enhances our spiritual lives.

But isn't an advance in our spiritual lives to be attributed to the increased indwelling of the Spirit within us, and doesn't that represent a change in God? It does not. "That a divine person may newly exist in anyone, or be possessed by anyone in time, does not come from change of the divine person, but from change in the creature" (*ST* Ia.43.2. ad. 2).

---

16. Cf. 83.2.resp.: "Men do certain actions not that thereby they may change the divine disposition, but that by those actions they may achieve certain effects according to the order of the divine disposition. ... And so is it with regard to prayer. For we pray, not that we may change the divine disposition, but that we may impetrate [def: "obtain by request or entreaty"] that which God has disposed to be fulfilled by our prayers, in other words, that by asking, men may deserve to receive what almighty God from eternity has disposed to give."

PART
IV

Liturgy, love, and justice

12

Liturgical love

Those who write about the relation between liturgy and the moral life usually focus on the formative effects of liturgical enactments on the participants.[1] If liturgical assemblies are in fact formative of the participants' moral life, that is because of what is done in those assemblies. It is, in good measure, by manifesting love that liturgical assemblies are formative of love. So let us continue our analysis of the performative dimension of liturgical enactments by exploring the ways in which Christian liturgical assemblies can be manifestations of love.

Some preparation is required for us to address our topic. We must distinguish two forms of love that Jesus enjoined, and we must take note of a dimension of the moral life that is commonly overlooked. Let's begin with the first of these.

---

1. This is a common theme in essays of Stanley Hauerwas. See Hauerwas (2001), 37–284. See also Smith (2013). The current chapter is a revision and expansion of my essay, "Liturgical Love," which appeared in *Studies in Christian Ethics* (March 30, 2017).

Two forms of agapic love

In all three synoptic Gospels Jesus is reported as stating, in response to a question by a hostile interrogator, what have come to be known as "the two love commands." Luke's report of the incident differs from the reports of Matthew and Mark in that the question posed by the interrogator is different and in that Jesus tells the Parable of the Good Samaritan in response to a follow-up question by his interrogator. The two commands themselves, how-ever, are essentially the same in all three reports. Here is Matthew's formulation: "You shall love the Lord your God with all your heart, and with all your soul, and with all your mind. This is the greatest and first commandment. And a second is like it: You shall love your neighbor as yourself" (Matthew 22: 37–9). The first of these two commands is a quotation of Deuteronomy 6: 5, the second is a quotation of Leviticus 19: 18. In both instances, the Greek verb translated into English as "love" is *agapaô*. In order to mark the difference between the form of agape that Jesus refers to in the second command and the other form that I will shortly be calling attention to, let me follow what has become common practice and call this first form of agape, *neighbor love*.

Entire books have been written concerning the force of what Jesus was saying with the command to love one's neighbor as oneself.[2] Here I must confine myself to two points of interpretation that will prove important for the discussion that follows.

First, it's important to take note of what we learn about the scope of neighbor love when we bring into the picture Jesus' Parable of the Good Samaritan and some of the things he said in the Sermon on the Mount. In *Justice in Love* I wrote the following about what we learn from the Parable of the Good Samaritan concerning the scope of the love that is commanded: "I take Jesus to be enjoining us to be alert to the obligations placed upon us by the needs of whomever we happen on, and to pay no attention to the fact, if it be a fact, that the needy person belongs to a group that is a disdained or disdaining out-group with respect to oneself."[3] In his essay, "Love and Liturgy," Terence Cuneo agrees that this is "a central message" of the parable; but he goes on to suggest that when we also bring into the picture the Sermon on the Mount, we are led to conclude that this is not the whole of what Jesus had in mind.[4]

2. See, for example, Outka (1972).   3. Wolterstorff (2011b), 131.
4. Cuneo (2016b), 20–36.

In Matthew's report of the Sermon on the Mount Jesus says, "You have heard that it was said, 'You shall love your neighbor and hate your enemy.' But I say to you, Love your enemies and pray for those who persecute you" (5: 33–4). In the background here is Jesus' opposition to what I call the *reciprocity code*, a norm for behavior that was evidently common at the time. The reciprocity code said that one is to answer favors with favors and harm with harm. I interpret Jesus' response to the positive side of the reciprocity code as shrugging acceptance: "Yes, by and large it's a good thing to answer favors with favors. But it's no big deal; Gentiles do that. And in any case, don't be rigid about it; do not, for example, limit your dinner invitations to those who can return the favor." To the negative side of the reciprocity code Jesus was unremittingly opposed. Luke's report of what Jesus said is essentially the same as Matthew's: "Love your enemies, do good to those who hate you, bless those who curse you, pray for those who abuse you" (Luke 6: 27). Paul picks up this opposition to the negative side of the reciprocity code in his letter to the church in Rome when he says, "Bless those who persecute you; bless and do not curse them.... Do not repay anyone evil for evil, but take thought for what is noble in the sight of all.... If your enemies are hungry, feed them; if they are thirsty, give them something to drink" (12: 14–20).[5]

Cuneo asks whether Jesus' injunction to love one's enemies and to bless and pray for one's persecutors does not suggest something more concerning the scope of neighbor love than that we be open to the needs of those we happen on, which is what I suggested in *Justice in Love*. He says,

> In the Sermon on the Mount, when Jesus says that we should pray for our enemies, part of what he seems to be driving at is that we are not only to be open to recognizing those obligations that come our way but also to take actions designed to re-orient ourselves to those who belong to various out-groups. We are not simply to be open to the needs of others. We are also *to open ourselves up* to the needs of others and the various sorts of obligations we may have toward them.
>
> If this is correct, Jesus's teaching is that to fulfill the second love command-ment, we are not simply to react with an open heart to the needs and obligations we find but also to, some significant degree, direct our attention and energy to the needs of (and obligations to) those who belong to out-groups, making them the subject of our concern.[6]

5. I discuss Jesus' attitude to the reciprocity code in Wolterstorff (2011a), 120–9.
6. Cuneo (2016b), 24–5.

I think Cuneo is right about this. He describes the second love command, so understood, as enjoining an *ethic of outwardness* in contrast to an *ethic of proximity.*

In *Justice in Love* I also spent a good deal of time discussing another point of interpretation of the second love command that will prove important for our purposes in this chapter. Let us understand justice in the traditional way, as rendering to a person what is due him or her, what they have a right to.[7] Let us also understand benevolence in the traditional way, as seeking to enhance the well-being of another person without regard to whether or not justice requires it; if one treats someone as one does because justice requires it, one is not acting out of benevolence. It is commonly held that by agape in the second love command Jesus meant *benevolence*, so understood.[8]

In *Justice in Love* I argued that when one looks at the context in which the second love command occurs in Leviticus one has to conclude that this interpretation of agape in the second love command is mistaken. The context consists of Moses giving a long list of quite specific injunctions as to how Israel is to conduct its life. Among those injunctions are some that explicitly or implicitly instruct the members of Israel to treat each other justly. Neighbor love has to be understood in such a way that doing justice is an example of neighbor love rather than incompatible with it.

Agapic neighbor love does, of course, include seeking to enhance the well-being of the person who is the recipient of one's love; it's like benevolence in that respect. But it includes something more as well; it includes seeing to it that she is treated justly, that she is rendered what is due her—that she is treated in a way that befits her worth.[9] Those who interpret agape as benevolence have their eye only on the first of these two components. Cases of paternalistic and demeaning benevolence show that the first does not automatically carry the second along with it; the paternalist seeks to enhance the well-being of the recipient of his largesse while riding rough-shod over what is required for treating her justly.

In *Justice in Love* I suggested that our English term "care about" catches what the term agape means, so interpreted, in the second love command. When I care about someone, I both seek to enhance her well-being and I see to it that she is treated justly. And whereas benevolence can be extended only to others, one can care about oneself.

---

7. The classic formula comes from the third-century Roman jurist Ulpian: *suum ius cuique tribuere.*
8. For a comprehensive analysis of the modern literature on agape see Outka (1972).
9. I develop at length this understanding of justice in Wolterstorff (2008), 241–310.

Let us now turn to the second form of agapic love that Jesus enjoined. The Gospel of John reports Jesus as saying, in his farewell address to his disciples, "I give you a new commandment, that you love one another. Just as I have loved you, you also should love one another. By this everyone will know that you are my disciples, if you have love for one another" (13: 34–5). "No one has greater love than this, to lay down one's life for one's friends. You are my friends if you do what I command you" (15: 13–14).

In these passages, too, the Greek verb translated into English as "love" is *agapaô*. To the best of my knowledge there is no standard term for the form of agape that Jesus is here enjoining on his disciples—other, of course, than just "love." Let me pick up on the fact that Jesus twice uses the term "friends" and call it *friendship love*. I do so with some reluctance, since what Jesus is enjoining is no ordinary love among friends but a love that imitates the love of Jesus for his disciples: "as I have loved you, you also should love one another." I will sometimes use the clunky term "Christ-like friendship love" as a way of encouraging the reader to keep this in mind.[10]

The new love command is for followers of Jesus—for those who were followers then and, by extrapolation, for those who would follow him down through the ages. It is not a universal ethic. By contrast, the command to practice neighbor love is a universal ethic. Though the command was contained in the Torah given to Israel, it's an ethic for everyone. No one is to engage in payback, no one is to answer harm with harm; everyone is to answer harm with good. I agree with the way in which the universality of the command is most often argued. The reason one is to love one's neighbor as oneself is not the sheer fact that Jesus commanded us to do so. Love for the neighbor is called for by the fact that each and every neighbor, along with all other human beings, bears the image of God.[11]

The scope of the recipients of the love enjoined by the two commands is also different. The recipients of one's friendship love are those who are

10. When I wrote *Justice in Love* I overlooked friendship love and spoke only of neighbor love. It was when writing this chapter that it became clear to me that recognizing that there are these two distinct modes of agape is indispensable for understanding the relation between liturgy and love.

11. Perry (1998), 16ff., reviews some of the literature in which this line of argument is worked out. The following consideration is also worth mentioning. In Romans 12: 19 Paul quotes Deuteronomy 32: 35, "Vengeance is mine, I will repay, says the Lord." If vengeance, payback, is God's prerogative, then obviously it is not just forbidden to Jews and Christians but to human beings generally. Retribution understood as payback is to be eliminated from human society.

fellow followers of Jesus. The recipients of one's neighbor love are all those who are one's neighbor.

A third difference is that one is to love one's neighbor even if that love is not reciprocated, even if the neighbor is an enemy who seeks one's harm rather than one's good. Neighbor love need not be reciprocated; often it is not. Friendship love, by contrast, is intrinsically mutual. In friendship, each party is both agent and recipient of love; someone can be my friend only if I am his friend.[12]

Neighbor love and Christ-like friendship love differ not only in these structural ways but often in content as well, as we will see when we look at Christ-like friendship love in some detail. As I have noted, and as the term "Christ-like" suggests, Christ-like friendship love models itself on the love Jesus had for his disciples; neighbor love need not. For example, Christ-like friendship love includes empathy with the recipient of one's love. Neighbor love need not; often it does not.

Before moving on we should briefly consider what Jesus meant when he called the command that he issued to his disciples in the course of his farewell address a "new" commandment. Was he suggesting that this command superseded the command to love one's neighbor as oneself? Was he suggesting that that command was "old" and outdated?

He was not. Nowhere in his lengthy farewell address does Jesus say or suggest that the command to love one's neighbor as oneself is "old." The clue to what he had in mind by "new" is contained in a passage that comes later in the same discourse: "I did not say these things to you from the beginning, because I was with you" (16: 5). The implicit contrast is not between this command and the command from the Torah; the implicit contrast is between this command and what Jesus had said to his disciples previously. He had not previously given this command. Throughout his farewell discourse Jesus is giving instructions to his disciples on how to live as his disciples after his departure. In the course of giving these instructions he says things he had not previously said, or things he had not said in quite the same way. The new commandment is the most fundamental and comprehensive of the instructions he is now giving to his disciples for their life together after his departure.

---

12. A more extensive treatment of friendship love than is called for here would consider what is to be said about those cases in which mutuality is no longer possible—when, for example, someone has fallen into a coma.

Though neighbor love and friendship love are different in the ways I have highlighted, the followers of Jesus are to exercise both. They are to love their neighbor as themselves and they are to be united in bonds of Christ-like friendship love with those who are joined with them in following Christ. In Romans 12: 9–21, Paul weaves back and forth between speaking of neighbor love and of friendship love, thereby indicating that he was calling his readers to exercise both forms of agape.

An overlooked dimension of the moral life

Let us now turn to an often-overlooked dimension of the moral life that will prove important for our discussion. A good way to introduce what I have to say on the matter is to quote some passages from Robert Adams's fine book, *Finite and Infinite Goods*.

Adams observes that a good many modern theories of ethics construe the task of ethics as "guidance for *action*."[13] That, he argues, is to construe the task too narrowly. Ethics "is not only about how to act well, but more broadly about how to *live* well." He then goes on to make the following observation:

> Helplessness is a large part of life. Human life both begins and ends in help-lessness. Between infancy and death, moreover, we may find ourselves in the grip of a disease or a dictatorship to which we may be able to adapt but which we cannot conquer. Even if our individual situation is more fortunate, we will find ourselves relatively helpless spectators of most of the events in the world about which we should care somewhat, and many of those about which we should care most, if we are good people. Dealing well with our helplessness is therefore an important part of living well. An ethical theory that has nothing to say about this abandons us in what is literally the hour of our greatest need.
>
>   A central part of living well is being for the good and against evils. We face the question, how we can be for and against evils and goods that we are relatively powerless to accomplish or prevent.[14]

Adams suggests in this passage that one way in which we can be against evils that we are relatively powerless to do anything about is to acquire and employ strategies for adapting or coping. Strategies for coping were prominent in the writings of the ancient Stoics, as they were, for example, in the

---

13. Adams (1999), 224; emphasis in original.   14. Adams (1999), 224.

writings of John Calvin; they are not prominent in the writings of modern
and contemporary ethicists.

Though Adams mentions adapting as a way of being against evils that
we are relatively powerless to do anything about, he spends more time discussing what he calls the "symbolic expression" of our moral commitments.
Here is some of what he says:

> Acts of martyrdom represent a particularly important possibility of living well
> for people who find themselves in situations of comparative helplessness—
> oppressed peoples, persecuted minorities, and inmates of concentration camps,
> for example. For the same reason sickbeds are rightly surrounded by acts of
> mainly symbolic value. . . . When our friends are ill, most of us are not able to
> do much about their health. But we can still be *for* them, and that is important
> to all of us. Sending cards and flowers are ways of being for a sick person
> symbolically. They may also have the good consequence of cheering up the
> patient; but that will be because he is glad that his friends are for him. The
> symbolic value of the deed is primary in such a case.[15]

Let me describe the terrain here differently from how Adams describes it.
Sending a card and flowers to a sick friend is not just symbolic of one's care;
it's a way of putting one's care into practice. Cards and flowers do not, of
course, function like medicine. Nonetheless, receiving a card and flowers from
a caring friend enhances one's well-being; it's a good in one's life. Sending a
card and flowers to a friend is a way of exercising one's care for them.

Now consider, by way of contrast, expressing one's care about the sick
person by telling a mutual friend how concerned one is. In this case, one is
expressing one's love but not putting it into practice, not exercising it. One is
not enhancing the well-being of one's friend.[16] Though Adams doesn't mention this sort of case, it's clearly an example of what he would call a "symbolic
expression" of love. I don't much like calling it "symbolic." But no more fitting
term comes to mind; so I too will call it "symbolic." It's a symbolic expression
of love rather than an exercise of love. Of course, an exercise of love is also an
expression of love. But as I will be using the term "symbolic," an exercise of
love is not a *symbolic* expression of love, not even if it employs symbols.
What I call a "symbolic expression" of love is a *merely* symbolic expression.
When I need a term that covers both the exercise or practice of love and
the symbolic expression of love, I will use the term "manifestation."

15. Adams (1999), 224.
16. If the sick friend gets news of what one said, *getting news of what one said* might enhance his
    well-being.

This contrast, between a symbolic expression of love and an exercise of love, will prove important for our discussion. For our purposes it makes no difference whether one's exercise of love does or does not employ symbols such as cards and flowers. If one interacts with someone in such a way that one enhances their well-being and pays them due honor, then one has exercised love as care.

Liturgical enactments as manifestations of Christ-like friendship love

We are now prepared to address our topic, namely, liturgical enactments as sites for the manifestation of agapic love in its two forms of neighbor love and friendship love. Before we do so, however, let me briefly call attention to a form of love for one's fellow participants that is to be exercised in the assemblies but which is not readily classified either as friendship love or as neighbor love. Participating on a regular basis in the liturgical enactments of a community requires that one tolerate a good many things that one doesn't like: some of the hymns that are sung, the casual way some people dress, the fact that God is regularly referred to as "he," the minister's telling jokes in his sermons, and so forth, on and on. Tolerating what one doesn't like is a form of love.[17] When prayers are offered for the peace and unity of the congregation, this is part of what is prayed for.

To keep our discussion within limits, I will only be talking about what Catholics call "the Sunday Mass" and what Protestants typically call "the Sunday worship service," not about liturgical enactments in all their forms. This means that I will not be talking about the Catholic Rite of Reconciliation, or as it was formerly called, the Rite of Penance. A discussion devoted to the topic of liturgy and reconciliation would attend not only to the Sunday liturgy but also to the Rite of Reconciliation. And let me make clear that my topic is liturgical enactments as sites for the exercise of love of one's fellow human beings. Every worship service is intrinsically an exercise by the participants of their love of God. That is not my topic here.[18]

One way in which both neighbor love and friendship love are exercised within liturgical enactments is by the collection of funds as support for

17. I thank John Witvliet for calling this form of liturgical love to my attention.
18. I have discussed this dimension of liturgy in Wolterstorff (2015b), 21–40.

various social causes and as alms for impoverished members of the church. This way of putting love into practice is so obvious that I will say nothing more about it.[19]

Let's begin with friendship love. As we saw in Chapter 3, liturgical scripts often prescribe not only what is to be done but how the participants are to be related to each other when they perform the actions prescribed: "Let us say with one accord." Some of the prescriptions as to how the participants are to be related to each other find their way into the written text for the liturgy, as in the sentence just quoted; most are embedded in liturgical practice and remain implicit.

An implicit if not explicit component of all scripts for Christian liturgical enactments, provided those scripts are appropriately shaped by the New Testament, is that the participants are to be related to each other in bonds of Christ-like friendship love. To the church in Rome Paul writes, "love one another with mutual affection" (Romans 12: 10). "Live in harmony with one another, in accordance with Jesus Christ, so that together you may with one voice glorify the God and Father of our Lord Jesus Christ" (15: 5–6). The author of First John says to his readers, "This is the message you have heard from the beginning, that we should love one another" (1 John 3: 11). Insofar as those who participate in Christian liturgical enactments are not related to each other in bonds of friendship love, they are not following the New Testament prescriptions for participation. Christ-like friendship love is to prevail in the assemblies.

Christians do not assume that it lies entirely within their own power to be united in bonds of friendship love; they must be empowered by the Spirit. Hence it is that liturgies often incorporate prayers that God create and sustain such love among the participants. Here is an example of a brief prayer of this sort that comes from the Egyptian monastery of Balyzeh in the sixth century:

> May God give us charity and brotherly love
> in the bond of peace.[20]

To say that an important component of what is prescribed for Christian liturgical enactments is that Christ-like friendship love is to prevail among

19. If the "collection" were our main topic, it would be important to take note of the fact that the way in which these funds are distributed is often unjust. The distribution of alms, for example, is often oppressively paternalistic; not infrequently it is demeaning.
20. In Deiss (1979), 244.

the participants is to speak in very general terms. Let's be more specific. What are the components of such love? What are the salient features of the harmony of which Paul spoke in the passage I quoted from his letter to the Romans? We are not left to our own devices in answering this question about the nature of friendship love; the epistolary literature of the New Testament offers some clear indications. Let me call attention to four of them.

Christ-like friendship love in the assemblies includes reconciliation

When one member has something against another, or when two have a quarrel with each other, Christ-like friendship love takes the form of reconciliation. In the Sermon on the Mount, as recorded in the Gospel of Matthew, Jesus says,

> You have heard that it was said to those of ancient times, "You shall not murder"; and "whoever murders shall be liable to judgment." But I say to you that if you are angry with a brother or sister, you will be liable to judgment; and if you insult a brother or sister, you will be liable to the council; and if you say, "You fool," you will be liable to the hell of fire. (5: 21–2)

Jesus then applies this general proscription against anger to the liturgical assemblies:

> So when you are offering your gift at the altar, if you remember that your brother or sister has something against you, leave your gift there before the altar and go; first be reconciled to your brother or sister, and then come and offer your gift. (5: 23–4)

This teaching of Jesus, that the mutual love that is to prevail in the assemblies requires that when one member has something against another, they are first to be reconciled, is repeated in the early Christian document *Didache* (*The Teaching*), dated by most scholars to the late first or early second century.

> On the Lord's day,... come together, break bread and hold Eucharist, after confessing your transgressions that your offering may be pure; but let none who has a quarrel with his fellow join in your meeting until they be reconciled, that your sacrifice be not defiled.[21]

21. *Didache* xiv (1953), 331.

How is the reconciliation required for acceptable participation in a liturgical enactment to be achieved? By the combination of repentance and forgiveness. In the Gospel of Luke Jesus is reported as saying to his disciples, "If another disciple sins, you must rebuke the offender; and if there is repentance, you must forgive. And if the same person sins against you seven times a day, and turns back to you seven times and says, 'I repent,' you must forgive" (17: 3–4). One imagines the disciples discussing with each other this saying of Jesus and finding it incredible that Jesus could really have meant seven times. So in Matthew's narration Peter says to Jesus, "Lord, if another member of the church sins against me, how often should I forgive? As many as seven times?" Jesus' reply is hyperbolic: "Not seven times, but, I tell you, seventy-seven times" (18: 21–2). That is to say, as many times as the wrongdoer repents.

Both Jesus and *Didache* suggest that the reconciliation that is to prevail in the assemblies is to be brought about in advance. A question that naturally comes to mind is whether there is also opportunity within liturgical enactments for alienated participants to become reconciled by the combination of repentance and forgiveness. Congregations do, on occasion, hold services of reconciliation in which there is an explicit expression of repentance for wrongdoing and an explicit expression of forgiveness.[22] But *Didache* clearly has the regular Sunday liturgy in view. Is there opportunity in regular Sunday liturgies for reconciliation to take place?

The obvious place to look is to the prayer of confession and to the absolution that follows upon the confession. Do these offer opportunity for reconciliation? I think not. The sins the people confess are, of course, not just sins of failing to love God with all their being and their neighbors as themselves but also sins of failing to love each other in Christ-like fashion. But in no traditional liturgy (that I know of) do the people actually say that they have sinned against each other. In some liturgies they address their confession to their fellow worshippers as well as to God. For example, in the contemporary Catholic liturgy they say:

22. In the Orthodox Church, the last Sunday before Lent is called "The Sunday of Forgiveness." At the end of Vespers on that Sunday there follows "the ceremony of mutual forgiveness." The people prostrate themselves before the priest and say, "Forgive me, a sinner." The priest then does the same to each of them. After this ceremony is finished, "the faithful may also ask forgiveness of one another." *Lenten Triodion* (1978), 183.

> I confess to almighty God
> and to you, my brothers and sisters,
> that I have greatly sinned.[23]

But confessing *to* one's brothers and sisters that one has sinned falls short of confessing to them that one has sinned *against them*. And in any case, the confession remains general. The people do not name sins they have committed against each other; and so, of course, do not declare that they repent of those sins and ask forgiveness of the person they sinned against. Further, the forgiveness pronounced in the absolution is not forgiveness by their fellow worshippers but forgiveness by God.[24]

Most liturgies incorporate a recitation by the people of the Lord's Prayer. As one of their petitions the people say, "Forgive us our sins/ trespasses as we forgive those who sin/trespass against us." The people here declare that they forgive those who sinned against them. If they have already made known to those who sinned against them that they forgive, that may well have resulted in reconciliation. If in the future they make known to those who sinned against them that they forgive, that may result in reconciliation in the future. But praying this prayer is not itself an act of reconciliation.

If reconciliation does occur within the enactment of traditional liturgies, it occurs implicitly rather than explicitly. On this point, what Cyril of Jerusalem (314–87) taught his catechumens about the significance of the kiss of peace is suggestive:

> The deacon then says in a loud voice: "Welcome one another and embrace one another!"
> Do not think of this kiss as being like the kiss people exchange in the public squares when they meet friends. No, this kiss is not of that kind. It unites souls, it requires that we forget all grudges.
> This kiss thus signifies the union of souls with one another, and the forgetfulness of all wrongs done us.

---

23. *Sunday Missal* (2011), 12. The prayer of confession in the Eucharistic liturgy of the Taizé community resembles the prayer of confession in the contemporary Catholic liturgy. It opens with the words, "I confess to God Almighty in the communion of the saints of heaven and of the earth, and to you my brethren, that I have sinned exceedingly in thought, word, and deed." *Eucharistic Liturgy of Taize* (1962), 30.

24. The contemporary Catholic Mass liturgy contains two Eucharistic Prayers for Reconciliation; both are prayers for reconciliation between the people and God. *Sunday Missal* (2011), 43–51.

Cyril then quotes the passage from Matthew about being reconciled before one brings one's offering, and concludes:"This kiss, then, is an act of reconciliation. That is why it is holy, as blessed Paul proclaims it to be when he says, 'Greet one another with a holy kiss'" (1 Corinthians 16: 20).[25]

Cyril's instruction to his catechumens is that they are to be reconciled with each other by forgetting the grudges they hold and the wrongs done to them. That is not what Jesus taught; Jesus taught that reconciliation is to be achieved not by forgetting but by the combination of repentance and forgiveness. But let that pass. Cyril first says that the kiss "signifies the union of souls with each other." That's a common interpretation of the kiss: the kiss is a sign of reconciliation, a symbolic expression of reconciliation. What Cyril says next is striking and not at all common: the kiss is "an act of reconciliation." Not a *sign* of reconciliation but an *act* of reconciliation.

I submit that, sometimes at least, this is right. Two of the congregants are alienated from each other; one has wronged the other. The wrongdoer repents of what he has done. Now the time arrives in the liturgy for the participants to pass the peace to each other. The wrongdoer and the one he has wronged happen to be seated near each other. The wrongdoer offers the peace to the one he has wronged; she interprets this as an expression of repentance, so she accepts and returns the peace. Thereby repentance and forgiveness have been exchanged; this is an act of reconciliation. If all goes well, the reconciliation implicit in this passing of the peace will subsequently be made explicit.

Suppose, however, that though the wrongdoer knows the other person believes that he has wronged her, he insists that he has done nothing wrong. Then for him to offer the peace to her is to act hypocritically. It is, of course, sincere passing of the peace that Cyril had in mind when he said that passing of the peace is an act of reconciliation.

Before we move on let me briefly summarize what we have learned in this section. One dimension of the Christ-like friendship love that is to prevail in the assemblies is the presence of reconciliation. In case one member has wronged another, they are to reconciled by the combination of repentance and forgiveness. Jesus, and the early Christian document, *Didache*, declare that alienated members of the community are to be reconciled before they join together in the assembly. A question that naturally suggests itself is whether there is also opportunity within the regular Sunday liturgy

---

25. *The Catecheses of Cyril of Jerusalem* in Deiss (1979), 284.

for reconciliation. What we have learned, somewhat surprisingly perhaps, is that the only opportunity for reconciliation within the regular Sunday liturgy is the opportunity implicit in the passing of the peace.

Christ-like friendship love in the assemblies includes empathetic grieving and rejoicing

A second dimension of the Christ-like friendship love that is to prevail in the assemblies is mutual empathetic concern, grieving, and rejoicing. In his letter to the church in Rome Paul says, "rejoice with those who rejoice, weep with those who weep" (12: 15). He makes the same point in his first letter to the church in Corinth: "If one member suffers, all suffer together with it; if one member is honored, all rejoice together with it" (12: 25–6). Participants in liturgical assemblies are to be united in a solidarity of mutual empathy. Instead of being envious and resentful of those who experience good fortune, one is to rejoice along with them; instead of being hard-hearted or indifferent to those who have suffered ill-fortune, one is to grieve along with them.

When extending neighbor love to someone, one might or might not feel empathy with the recipient of one's love; one can seek to advance some-one's well-being and see to it that he is rendered what is due him without grieving with his grieving and rejoicing with his rejoicing. And even if one does feel empathy, he might well not reciprocate. In Christ-like love, there is a solidarity of mutual empathy.

All traditional liturgies provide opportunity for giving voice to the solidarity of empathetic concern, grieving, and rejoicing. It is especially in the prayers of thanksgiving that the members give voice to their solidar-ity of empathetic rejoicing; often the names are mentioned of those who have recovered from illness, of those who have found work, of those who have safely returned from travel, of those who have married, of those to whom a child has been born. It is especially in the prayers of intercession that the members give voice to their solidarity of empathetic concern and grieving; often the names are mentioned of the sick in the congregation, the dying, the unemployed, those who will be traveling long distances. In the offering of alms the members go beyond giving voice to their solidar-ity of empathetic concern and grieving to giving tangible expression to that solidarity.

Christ-like friendship love in the assemblies includes the rejection of all natural and social categories of exclusion in the assemblies

The Christ-like friendship love that is to prevail in the assemblies includes the rejection of all natural and social categories of exclusion. In his letters to the Romans, to the Galatians, and to the Ephesians, Paul declares that in Christ, God has offered justification to Gentiles and Jews alike. Thereby God has made these two groups "into one and has broken down the dividing wall, that is, the hostility between" them, to the end that God "might create in himself one new humanity in place of the two, thus making peace, and might reconcile both groups to God in one body through the cross, thus putting to death that hostility" (Ephesians 2: 14–16). "In Christ Jesus, neither circumcision nor uncircumcision counts for anything; the only thing that counts is faith working through love" (Galatians 5: 6).

The apostle Peter drew the same conclusion from the visionary trance that befell him one day as he was traveling to Joppa.

> He saw the heaven opened and something like a large sheet coming down, being lowered to the ground by its four corners. In it were all kinds of four-footed creatures and reptiles and birds of the air. Then he heard a voice saying, "Get up, Peter; kill and eat." But Peter said, "By no means, Lord; for I have never eaten anything that is profane or unclean." The voice said to him a second time, "What God has made clean, you must not call profane." This happened three times, and the thing was suddenly taken up to heaven.
>
> (Acts 10: 11–16)

Peter's interpretation of his vision was that he had to give up his traditional Jewish exclusivism. "God shows no partiality, but in every nation anyone who fears him and does justice is acceptable to him" (10: 34–5).

In his letter to the Galatians Paul makes clear that it is not just the exclusionary Jew/Gentile dichotomy that is to be rejected. There is also "no longer slave or free, there is no longer male and female; for all ... are one in Jesus Christ" (3: 28). The three dichotomies Paul mentions were prominent in the ancient Mediterranean world: Jew/Greek, slave/free, male/female. Each was regularly used to include some and exclude others. But these three are no more than a small sample of the inclusionary and exclusionary dichotomies that societies employ. All are to be irrelevant for participation in the liturgy. Poor and rich, servants and masters, black and white, handicapped and able, gay and straight: all are to be welcomed. You don't have to be rich to participate, you don't have to be powerful, you don't have to be white, you don't have to be male. But neither do you have to be poor, powerless, black, or female. When Christ-like friendship love is present in the assemblies, no one is excluded on the basis of his or her membership or non-membership in some natural or social group. "Welcome one another," says Paul, "just as Christ has welcomed you" (Romans 15: 7).

Liturgical assemblies regularly fall short of fully conforming to the prescription that all exclusionary dichotomies are to be rejected; many, perhaps most, are defective in this respect. A dramatic example of the point is the following. The Reformed Church in the Cape colony (South Africa) originated as a mission of the Dutch Reformed Church and was originally under the supervision of the classis of Amsterdam. Amsterdam insisted that the whites worship together with their African converts. Tensions arose over this racial integration; and when the church in the Cape colony was freed from Dutch control in 1824, sustained attempts were initiated to segregate Africans and whites in the worship services, and then, later, to segregate Africans and whites into separate congregations. In 1857 the campaign for congregational segregation succeeded. The church adopted a resolution stating that, while it recognized the call and demands of the gospel, congregations had to be racially segregated in order to accommodate "the weakness of some." "Some" was a euphemism for all those who opposed racially integrated worship.

Christ-like friendship love in the assemblies includes no partiality

The Christ-like friendship love that is to prevail in the assemblies is thicker yet. A liturgical assembly that is radically inclusive in membership and whose participants are united in empathetic solidarity might still favor some members over others: wealthy over poor, educated over non-educated, free over slaves, men over women, whites over people of color, and so forth. While including women along with men as members they might, for example, exclude them from leadership positions. The New Testament epistles teach that within the liturgical assemblies there is to be no favoritism, no partiality, no deference. Nobody is to be favored over another because of the natural or social class to which he or she belongs. Friendship love is radically egalitarian.

In his first letter to the Corinthians Paul writes that he has heard that there are "divisions" and "factions" within the Corinthian church. He has heard that "when the time comes to eat [the Lord's Supper], each of you goes ahead with your own supper, and one goes hungry and another becomes drunk." When you do this, Paul says, "do you [not] show contempt for the church of God and humiliate those who have nothing?" (11: 21–2). To the church in Rome he writes, "love one another with mutual affection; outdo one another in showing honor.... Live in harmony with one another; do not be haughty, but associate with the lowly" (Romans 12: 10–16). Do not "despise your brother or sister" (14: 10).

It is in the letter of James that this theme of no-partiality is sounded most forcefully. Let me quote the entire passage.

> My brothers and sisters, do you with your acts of favoritism really believe in our glorious Lord Jesus Christ? For if a person with gold rings and in fine clothes comes into your assembly, and if a poor person in dirty clothes also comes in, and if you take notice of the one wearing the fine clothes and say, "Have a seat here, please," while to the one who is poor you say, "Stand there," or, "Sit at my feet," have you not made distinctions among yourselves and become judges with evil thoughts? Listen, my beloved brothers and sisters. Has not God chosen the poor in the world to be rich in faith and to be heirs of the kingdom that he has promised to those who love him? But you have dishonored the poor.... [I]f you show partiality, you commit sin and are convicted by the law.   (2: 2–8)[26]

When Christ-like love prevails in the assemblies there is no favoritism, no partiality. Each is the equal of each; each is honored by each. "Honor everyone," wrote the author of First Peter; "love the family of believers" (1 Peter 2: 17). Men are to honor women and women are to honor men;

---

26. In *The Didascalia of the Apostles*, dating from the third century, there is a truly baffling set of prescriptions concerning seating arrangements in the assemblies. "Young people are to sit apart, if there is room; if not, they are to remain standing. Those who are older are to sit apart. Children are to stay on one side, or else their parents are to take them with them, and they are to remain standing. Again: girls too are to be seated apart; if there is no room, they are to remain standing behind the women. Married women who are still young and have children are to remain standing apart. Older women and widows are to remain seated apart. The deacon is to watch and see that each person who enters goes to his own place and does not seat himself anywhere else."

But then we read: "If a poor man or woman comes, whether they are from your own parish or another, especially if they are advanced in years, and there should be no room for them, then make a place for them, O bishop, with all your heart, even if you yourself have to sit on the ground. You must not make any distinction between persons, if you wish your ministry to be pleasing to God." Deiss (1979), 175–6.

masters are to honor their slaves and slaves are to honor their masters; the wealthy are to honor the poor and the poor are to honor the wealthy; the mayor is to honor the garbage collector and the garbage collector is to honor the mayor.

The injunction to show no partiality was then, and remains now, truly extraordinary. Nothing like it was to be found in the ancient world. Both Jewish and Gentile societies were hierarchical. Honor was to be paid to those above one in the social scale; paying deference to one's social superiors was obligatory. The injunction to each to honor everyone would have been heard as a recipe for social anarchy.

The injunction that in the assemblies no one was to be favored or honored over another because of the natural or social class to which he or she belonged was not taken by the New Testament writers as implying that there was to be no recognition in the assemblies of different gifts of the Spirit. Paul is explicit on the point. In his first letter to the Corinthians he says that the Spirit has bestowed on members of the church gifts of many sorts. To one is given "the utterance of wisdom," to another "gifts of healing," to another "prophecy," to another "various kinds of tongues," and so forth. This diversity of gifts is to be acknowledged and honored; for "the body does not consist of one member but of many" (12: 4–14; cf. Romans 12: 4–8).

Christ-like friendship love symbolized and enjoined in the Lord's Supper

The passage I quoted from the letter of James calls attention to the fact that seating arrangements are among the ways in which Christ-like friendship love is to be put into practice in the assemblies; the passage I quoted from Paul's letter to the Corinthians calls attention to the fact that it is also to be put into practice in how the Lord's Supper is conducted. This last point reminds me of a passage in Calvin's discussion of the Lord's Supper in which he says that the Lord's Supper, by representing or symbolizing the concord of friendship love, is an exhortation to such concord.

> The Lord also intended the Supper to be a kind of exhortation for us, which can more forcefully than any other means quicken and inspire us both to purity and holiness of life, and to love, peace, and concord. For the Lord so communicates his body to us that he is made completely one with us, and we

with him. Now, since he has only one body, of which he makes us all partakers, it is necessary that all of us also be made one body by such participation. The bread shown in the Sacrament represents this unity. And it is made of many grains so mixed together that one cannot be distinguished one from another, so it is fitting that in the same way we should be joined and bound together by such great agreement of minds that no sort of disagreement or division may intrude.[27]

Calvin employs the trope of one bread from many grains to call attention to one of the ways in which friendship love is symbolically expressed in the liturgy. The bread from many grains *represents* (symbolizes) the unity of such love. And given that that unity is often not fully present among the members of the assembly, this symbolizing of unity functions simultaneously as an *exhortation* to the unity of Christ-like friendship love. It would be interesting to explore these ideas, of liturgical acts and objects *symbolizing* and *exhorting* to Christ-like friendship love. But that will have to await another occasion.

Neighbor love in the assemblies

It's time to turn our attention to liturgical assemblies as sites for the manifestation of neighbor love. Recall that neighbor love is to be extended to everyone who is one's neighbor, not just to those with whom one is joined in following Christ, and that it is to be extended to the neighbor whether or not the neighbor reciprocates, even if the neighbor is an enemy. Also recall the point we took from Cuneo, that neighbor love requires not just that we "react with an open heart to the needs" of those we happen on but that we "direct our attention and energy to the needs of (and obligations to) those who belong to out-groups, making them the subject of our concern."

How can neighbor love be manifested in a liturgical assembly? It can, of course, be exercised by making a contribution to the offering, assuming that at least some of the offering is designated for those who are not church members. But apart from that, doesn't one have to exit the assembly to show

---

27. *Institutes* IV.xvii.38. Calvin (1960), 1414–15. The trope that Calvin uses here, of one bread from many grains, goes back to *Didache*. "Just as the bread broken was first scattered on the hills then was gathered and became one, so let your Church be gathered from the ends of the earth into your kingdom." Deiss (1979), 75.

love for those neighbors who do not happen to be fellow members of the assembly? How can one fulfill the second love command in church? I mentioned earlier that, in Luke's Gospel, Jesus tells the Parable of the Good Samaritan in reply to the querulous lawyer who, after Jesus had enunciated the second love command, asks, "And who is my neighbor?" In the parable, a Samaritan comes across a man who has been mugged and left half dead in a ditch; he puts the wounded man on his pack animal and takes him to the nearest inn where he can be cared for. Jesus clearly intended this as a paradigmatic example of neighbor love. There are no pack animals in church.

True. But recall a point made in this chapter when we were discussing a passage from Robert Adams: one can manifest one's moral commitments by giving voice to those commitments. It is especially by participating in the intercessory prayers that one gives voice to one's love for the neighbor. Consider this sentence from the Orthodox liturgy of St Basil:

> Remember, O God, them that stand trial, that are in prisons, that live in exile; and all that are in affliction and tribulation. Likewise, O God, all them that have need of thy great and tender mercy; them that love us and them that care not for us.[28]

And consider this sentence from Form I of the prayers of the people in the Episcopal liturgy:

> For the poor and the oppressed, for the unemployed and the destitute, for prisoners and captives, and for all who remember and care for them, let us pray to the Lord.[29]

In participating in such prayers, one is manifesting one's love for one's neighbors by giving voice to that love. One is declaring that one is *for* one's neighbors. One is standing in solidarity with them.[30]

Is giving voice in the prayers to love of the neighbor a symbolic expression of neighbor love or an exercise of neighbor love? Christians have traditionally believed that God answers prayer. Those who dissent from the tradition on this point will interpret giving voice to love for the neighbor as the symbolic expression of neighbor love; those who believe that God answers prayer will interpret giving voice to love for the neighbor as not just the symbolic

---

28. *Orthodox Liturgy* (1982), 133.
29. *Book of Common Prayer* (1979), 384.
30. Terence Cuneo, in his essays "Love and Liturgy" and "Protesting Evil," discusses standing in solidarity with the neighbor by participating in the intercessory prayers of the liturgy. Cuneo (2016b), 20–36 and 37–51.

expression of such love but also as an exercise of such love. They are putting their love for the neighbor into practice by praying to God for the neighbor in the confidence that God answers prayer.

To this they are compelled to add that the shalom of God's kingdom for which they pray is mysteriously slow in coming. They pray for those in slavery, believing this to be one way of putting into practice their love for the enslaved; yet millions remain enslaved. They pray for the destitute, believing this to be one way of putting into practice their love for the impoverished; yet millions remain impoverished. They pray for the unemployed, believing this to be one way of putting into practice their love for those without work; yet millions remain without work.

Correcting an impression

I have discussed, in succession, the manifestation of friendship love in the assemblies and the manifestation of neighbor love. That may have led the reader to think of these as independent of each other, existing side by side in liturgical assemblies. That would be a mistake. They are joined together, united.

This is most obvious in the case of the intercessory prayers; almost always these include both prayers for members of the church and prayers for the neighbor. And whereas one might have expected, in advance, that these would move from prayers for members of the church to prayers for the neighbor, often that proves not to be the case. For example, in Form V of the Prayers of the People in *The Book of Common Prayer* the congregants pray "For all who fear God and believe in you, Lord Christ, that our divisions may cease, and that all may be one as you and the Father are one." After a few more prayers for the church and its members they pray "For the peace of the world, that a spirit of respect and forbearance may grow among nations and peoples." Then, after a few more prayers for society in general they pray "For this congregation... that we may show forth your glory." Immediately after that they pray "For our enemies and those who wish us harm." Immediately after that they pray "For ourselves, for the forgiveness of our sins."[31] The movement is cyclical rather than linear.

But there is a more fundamental way in which friendship love and neighbor love are joined together in liturgical enactments. The most fundamental

---

31. *Book of Common Prayer* (1979), 390–1.

liturgical prescription, usually implicit rather than explicit, is that everything is to be done in the context of the participants being united in bonds of mutual Christ-like friendship love. This includes everything that is done by way of the practice or symbolic expression of neighbor love. The participants do not exercise mutual friendship love *and then also* exercise or symbolically express neighbor love. Their manifestation of friendship love is the all-embracing context within which they exercise or symbolically express neighbor love.

Formation

Up to this point in my discussion in this chapter I have focused on the ways in which liturgical enactments are sites for the manifestation of friendship love and neighbor love. As we now bring our discussion to a conclusion let me briefly call attention to three ways in which participation in liturgical enactments can be formative of one's love of the neighbor.

Recall that in his essay "Love and Liturgy" Terence Cuneo describes neighbor love as an "ethic of outwardness." Such an ethic, he notes, is difficult to practice.

> Our collective situation is that we are naturally drawn to our own needs, the needs of our loved ones, and those who belong to the various communities of which we are a part.... It is only with difficulty... that our attention is drawn from the cares, obligations, and goods that occupy our attention outward toward those who belong to out-groups, whether they be the ritually unclean, strangers, enemies, or oppressors. And... when our attention is drawn outward... it can be difficult to do what Jesus commands, such as blessing those who curse us and praying for those who persecute us.[32]

Assume that the prayers of the people prescribed for some liturgical enactment do in fact include prayers for the neighbor and not just prayers for the church and its members, and assume that several different types of neighbor are mentioned, including various forgotten groups and various out-groups. Then to participate in the prayers is to find oneself praying for those one seldom thinks about, even for those one prefers not to think about: slaves and prisoners, those who hate us, those who govern us. The Episcopalian who thoroughly dislikes the president finds himself praying

32. Cuneo (2016b), 28.

"For those in positions of public trust, especially our President Barack, that they may serve justice, and promote the dignity and freedom of every person."[33]

Some of the prayers of the ancient church that have been preserved for us are exceptional in the scope of the neighbor love that is voiced. Here, are a few lines from the prayers of the people attributed to Serapion, bishop of the Egyptian city of Thmuis (fourth century):

> We pray for all magistrates.... We pray to you, God of mercies, for free men and for slaves, for men and women, for the poor and the rich.... We pray to you for travelers.... We pray to you for the afflicted, the captives, and the poor.... We pray to you for the sick.[34]

To participate in intercessions such as these is to be reminded of the scope of the neighbor love to which one is called. The reminder occurs not by way of some preachment but by way of finding oneself actually giving voice to such love. By voicing love for the despised, the hostile, and the easily overlooked, one is reminded that one's neighbor love is to include the despised, the hostile, and the easily overlooked.

Second, suppose that the liturgical assembly in which one participates does in fact exhibit friendship love in its inclusiveness. Suppose it includes ex-prisoners, recovering alcoholics, unemployed, mentally impaired, para-plegics, refugees, people of color, gays, lesbians, and more besides. Then the friendship love one experiences in the assembly will almost inevitably expand the scope of one's neighbor love. It's more difficult to treat ex-prisoners as members of an out-group that one shuns and whose needs one ignores if one finds oneself worshipping with ex-prisoners and united with them in bonds of Christ-like friendship love. When the assemblies are inclusive, friendship love exercised in the assemblies schools the participants in neighbor love. This, then, is another way in which these two forms of love are joined.

Third, the component of liturgical enactments that most people will have thought of first of all when reflecting on liturgical participation as formative of neighbor love is the reading of Scripture and the preaching of a sermon or homily. Depending, of course, on the content of the Scripture reading and of the sermon or homily, this is one of the most important ways—overall, perhaps *the* most important way—in which Christians are schooled in love for the neighbor, as it is also one of the most important ways in which they are schooled in friendship love.

33. *Book of Common Prayer* (1979), 390.   34. Deiss (1979), 187–8.

13

Justice and injustice in Christian liturgies

The linkages between Christian liturgical enactments on the one hand, and justice and injustice on the other, are multiple. The connection most often discussed is the potential of liturgical enactments for the formation of just persons: if the liturgical assembly itself manifests justice, and if God's love of justice is clearly presented in readings, sermons, and hymns, then the participants are formed into acting justly outside the assembly as well as within.

Another connection, one that I have myself explored in some of my writings, is a pervasive theme in the prophetic literature of the Old Testament/Hebrew Bible: a condition of liturgical enactments being acceptable to God is that the participants be committed to acting justly in their daily lives.[1]

About these two linkages between liturgical enactments and justice in our daily lives I have nothing more to say than what I and others have already said. So in this chapter I propose exploring the *presence within* Christian liturgical enactments of justice and injustice. I will briefly identify and discuss a few ways in which justice is, or can be, present, and I will then explore in some detail one of the ways in which injustice is present.

I cannot assume a shared understanding of justice; so let me preface my discussion with a very brief explanation of how I understand justice. Justice comes in two fundamentally different forms. One form consists of the just treatment of someone for having wronged someone, for having treated someone unjustly; it consists of just reprimand, just punishment, just reparations, etc. The other form consists of all the other ways of treating someone justly: merchants treating clients justly in how they price their goods, teachers

---

1. See my essay, "Justice as a Condition of Authentic Liturgy," in Wolterstorff (2011a), 39–58.

treating students justly in how they answer their questions, etc. I call the former of these *second-order* or *corrective* justice, and the latter *first-order* justice.[2] Second-order or corrective justice becomes relevant when there has been a breakdown in first-order justice, when someone has wronged someone. If there were no such thing as first-order justice, or if there were but there were no breakdowns in it, there would be no occasion for corrective or second-order justice. First-order justice is basic.[3]

Many people, when they hear the word "justice," think immediately of second-order or corrective justice; they think of meting out punishment. In the discussion that follows it is instead the presence of first-order justice and injustice in Christian liturgical enactments that we will be looking at.

In the Western tradition there are basically two ways of understanding the nature of justice. One of them comes from Aristotle. Taking for granted that justice pertains to the distribution of benefits and burdens, Aristotle's thesis was that a distribution of benefits and burdens is *just* if it is equitable. He discussed in some detail what makes for an equitable distribution; and he argued that his thesis holds not only for first-order justice but also for corrective or second-order justice. Punishment is just if the "harm" imposed on the wrongdoer is roughly equal to the "harm" that the wrongdoer imposed on his victim.

The other traditional way of understanding the nature of justice comes from the late Roman jurist Ulpian. Justice, said Ulpian, consists of rendering to each what is his or her *jus*—that is, what is his or her *right* or *due*. Justice consists of rendering to each what is theirs by right, what they have a right to, what is due them. I favor Ulpian's understanding of justice for reasons I have developed in some detail elsewhere and will refrain from repeating here.[4] Treating someone justly consists, on my view, of treating them as they have a right to be treated. Justice is grounded in rights.

2. In previous writings of mine I used the term "primary justice" for this form of justice. I think the term "first-order justice" is better.
3. What I call "first-order justice" has traditionally been called "distributive justice" and what I call "corrective or second-order justice" has traditionally been called "retributive justice." I avoid the term "distributive" because I do not think that all instances of first-order injustice are instances of maldistribution of benefits and burdens; it seems to me grotesque to say that what is wrong about rape is that benefits and burdens are distributed inequitably. I avoid the term "retributive" because I interpret Jesus and Paul as teaching that we are not to engage in retribution. Retribution is getting even, paying back, evening things up. Jesus and Paul say we are not to pay back evil with evil but are instead to answer evil (harm) with good. Punishment is not to be understood, or undertaken, as retribution. See my discussion in Wolterstorff (2011b), 191–206, and Wolterstorff (2013b), 193–9.
4. See Wolterstorff (2008).

The obvious question raised by this way of thinking of justice is, what accounts for someone having a right to being treated a certain way? There are many ways of being treated that one does not have a right to. What brings it about that, of the many ways in which Malchus can treat Matilda, she has a right to being treated in some of those ways and not others? I think the answer to this question is to be found in two facts about Matilda: the fact that she has worth, worth of many different sorts—the worth she has intrinsically as a human being, the worth she has on account of her accomplishments, etc.—and the fact that she can be treated in ways that do or do not befit her worth. Matilda has a right to be treated by Malchus as befits her worth. Rights, so understood, are correlative with duties: if Matilda has the right to be treated by Malchus in a certain way, then Malchus has the duty to treat her that way, and conversely.

Ways in which justice is present in Christian liturgical enactments

With this all-too-brief explanation of justice in hand, let us take note of a few of the ways in which justice is present in Christian liturgical enactments. In The Holy Eucharist: Rite One of the Episcopal Church, The Great Thanksgiving begins with the words, spoken by the celebrant,

> It is very meet, right, and our bounden duty, that we should at all times, and in all places, give thanks unto thee, O Lord, holy Father, almighty, everlasting God.[5]

When the celebrant says these words, the first-person plural "we" refers, quite obviously, not just to the participants in that particular enactment, and not just to Christians more broadly, but to human beings in general: "It is very meet, right, and our bounden duty *as human beings* that we should at all times..."

The idea that it is our duty as human beings to give thanks to God goes back into the ancient church, occurring often in the Eucharistic prayers collected by Lucien Deiss in *The Springtime of the Liturgy* and in those collected by Jasper and Cuming in *Prayers of the Eucharist: Early and Reformed*. Often the English translation in these volumes of the original words are

---

5. *Book of Common Prayer* (1979), 333.

those of the Episcopal liturgy: "bounden duty," or just "duty." In four of the prayers collected by Deiss the English translation is "right and just."[6] In more than fifteen of the prayers in Jasper and Cuming the English translation is "fitting and right" (this is their translation of the words that Deiss translates as "right and just"). Sometimes the word "truly" is added for emphasis: "it is truly fitting and right."[7] In some liturgies the declaration is repeated, some-times with the very same words, "fitting and right, fitting and right,"[8] some-times with synonyms, "fitting and right, just and right."[9] The Egyptian anaphora of St Basil (fourth century) is particularly emphatic: "it is fitting and right, fitting and right, truly it is fitting and right."[10]

It is, of course, good and desirable that we human beings give thanks to God. But that is not what these liturgies are declaring. They are declaring that it is our *duty* to thank God, that it is *right* for us to do so, that it is not just a good thing to do but *fitting*.[11]

Now suppose my claim is correct, that duties and rights are correlative: if X has a duty to treat Y in a certain way, then Y has a right to be treated that way by X, and conversely. Then in declaring that it is our duty to thank God, these liturgies are implying that God has a right to our thanksgiving. In thanking God we are rendering justice to God.

To the best of my knowledge, liturgies have traditionally used the lan-guage of "bounden duty," "fitting and right," "right and just," and so forth, only at the beginning of the Great Prayer of Thanksgiving (the "anaphora," as it is called in the East). But if asked, those who used these liturgies would surely have said that it is also our bounden duty to praise God, to intercede with God, to confess our sins to God, to listen for God's speech—in short, to acknowledge liturgically who God is and what God has done. And that implies, given the thesis of rights and duties as correlatives, that those who perform the prescribed acts of worship are rendering justice to God throughout the enactment, not just in the Eucharist. In the very nature of the case, acknowledging God liturgically is doing justice. Liturgical enactments

6. See Deiss (1979), 130, 193, 225, and 285.
7. See pp. 59, 90, 104, 116 in Jasper and Cuming (1987).
8. Jasper and Cuming (1987), 152–3.
9. Jasper and Cuming (1987), 148, 156.
10. Jasper and Cuming (1987), 70.
11. The Great Prayer of Thanksgiving in The Holy Eucharist: Rite Two of the Episcopal Church drops the reference to duty: "It is right, and a good and joyful thing, always and everywhere to give thanks to you, Father Almighty, Creator of heaven and earth" (*Book of Common Prayer* (1979), 361). The term "right" alludes to duty; if something is the right thing to do, then one ought to do it. But the allusion is weak; and most people will miss it.

are corporate acts of doing justice to God. "Ascribe to the Lord the glory due his name," said the psalmist (96: 8). Among the things for which it is our bounden duty to thank and praise God is God's love of justice.

Our discussion of liturgical love in Chapter 12 suggests a second way in which justice can be present in a liturgical enactment—and a way in which injustice can be present instead. In his first letter to the church in Corinth Paul says he has heard that when they assemble, the well-to-do eat and drink their fill while the poor are left hungry. One infers that the assemblies in Corinth included some sort of potluck and that the well-to-do arrived and began eating and drinking before the slaves and servants got off work. Paul uses striking language in criticizing the behavior of the well-to-do. We can be confident that he regarded them as failing in love for their fellow believers; but that is not what he says. He says, "you show contempt for the church of God and humiliate those who have nothing" (1 Corinthians 11: 22).

The writer of the New Testament Letter of James uses similar language to condemn the favoritism displayed by the seating arrangements in the assemblies of those whom he was addressing: rich people were given seats of honor while the poor were made either to stand or to sit on the floor. God, says the writer, has "chosen the poor in the world to be rich in faith and to be heirs of the kingdom that he has promised.... But you have dishonored the poor" (James 2: 5–6). We can be confident that the writer regarded those who organized or tolerated such seating arrangements as failing in love for the poor. But that is not what he says. He says, you have "dishonored" the poor.

Suppose my suggestion is correct, that treating someone justly consists of treating him or her as they have a right to be treated. Suppose I am also right in suggesting that to treat a person as they have a right to be treated is to treat them as befits their worth. Then Paul and James are both pointing to injustice in the assemblies. Humiliating someone is a patent case of not treating that person as befits her worth, and hence of treating her unjustly. Dishonoring someone is likewise a patent case of not treating that person as befits her worth, and hence of treating her unjustly. By virtue of how the participants in liturgical enactments treat each other, justice and injustice are present in those enactments. The assemblies are to be paradigms of justice. Often they are not; sometimes they fall appallingly short. The point could be developed at length, with many examples in addition to those described by Paul and by the writer of the Letter of James.

Our discussion in Chapter 12 suggests yet another way in which justice can be present in a liturgical enactment: justice can be present in the form of prayers for justice and for the undoing of injustice. The prayers for justice that one finds in traditional liturgies are almost always generic; no injustices are mentioned. On June 16, 1985, a prayer service was held in South Africa in which the prayers for justice were anything but generic; prayers were offered for the end of unjust rule in South Africa. The service, held in a church in Hazendal, Athlone, near Cape Town, was called by the South African Council of Churches in a declaration titled, "A Theological Rationale and a Call to Prayer for the End to Unjust Rule."[12] Both the call to prayer and the subsequent prayer service were the subject of enormous controversy, much of it very angry.

The injustice at the heart of the biblical story

In the remainder of this chapter I will discuss, in some detail, one of the ways in which injustice is present in Christian liturgical enactments. The first sentence of the opening chapter of James Cone's book, *The Cross and the Lynching Tree*, is this: "The paradox of a crucified savior lies at the heart of the Christian story."[13] The point that Cone develops in the chapter is that the death that lies at the heart of the Christian story was a death by lynching.[14] Lynchings are appalling episodes of injustice. At the heart of the Christian story is the paradox of a savior who was the victim of appalling injustice. Jesus had declared, at the beginning of his public ministry, that he was divinely appointed to proclaim that justice for the oppressed was on the way (Luke 4: 18–19). Now he himself was felled by a perversion of justice.[15]

Death by crucifixion was a slow and excruciatingly painful method of execution.[16] It was also shameful. In the Roman empire of the time it was reserved for those whom the officials regarded as despicable; rebellious slaves were commonly executed by crucifixion. "You are scum" was the message.

---

12. The episode is discussed by the contributors to Boesak and Villa-Vicencio (1986). The volume includes the sermon preached at the service by Allan Boesak.
13. Cone (2011), 1.
14. "The crucifixion was clearly a first-century lynching." Cone (2011), 30.
15. The story told by the Gospel writers includes other appalling episodes of injustice: the massacre of the innocents, the beheading of John the Baptist, the stoning of Stephen.
16. The extreme pain of death by crucifixion is well described in Rutledge (2015), 93–6.

Crucifixion "sent an unmistakable signal, 'Not fit to live; not even human' (*damnatio ad bestias*, as the Romans put it—condemned to the death of a beast)."[17] Crucifixion was an assault on human dignity.

All three synoptic Gospels report that, in the case of Jesus' death, mockery was added to the humiliation inherent in crucifixion. Matthew's report is the most explicit. In the governor's headquarters, just before Jesus was led out to be crucified, the attendant soldiers

> stripped him and put a scarlet robe on him, and after twisting some thorns into a crown, they put it on his head. They put a reed in his right hand and knelt before him and mocked him, saying, "Hail, King of the Jews!" They spat on him, and took the reed and struck him on the head. After mocking him, they stripped him of the robe and put his own clothes on him. Then they led him away to crucify him.   (Matthew 27: 28–31)

This report by Matthew makes it sound as if the mockery was the main thing, as if the crucifixion simply finished off the humiliation of mockery by the soldiers.

The mockery was continued by onlookers to the crucifixion:

> Those who passed by derided him, shaking their heads and saying, "You who would destroy the temple and build it in three days, save yourself! If you are the Son of God, come down from the cross." In the same way the chief priests also, along with the scribes and elders, were mocking him, saying, "He saved others; he cannot save himself. He is the King of Israel; let him come down from the cross now, and we will believe in him."...The bandits who were crucified with him also taunted him in the same way.   (27: 39–44).

Behind some of the mockery was hatred. Never has that hatred been more powerfully expressed in visual art than it was by Hieronymus Bosch in his great painting, "Christ Carrying the Cross."[18]

In Judaism, the message of crucifixion was different from its message in the empire, not "You are scum" but "You are cursed," cursed by God and cursed by God's people: "Cursed is everyone who hangs on a tree," wrote Paul, quoting Deuteronomy.[19]

---

17. Rutledge (2015), 89.
18. The painting hangs in the Museum of Fine Arts in Ghent, Belgium.
19. Galatians 3: 13; Deuteronomy 21: 23. Jürgen Moltmann writes, "In Israelite understanding, someone executed in this way was rejected by his people, cursed amongst the people of God by the God of the law, and excluded from the covenant of life....Anyone who, condemned by the law as a blasphemer, suffers such a death is accursed and excluded from the circle of the living and from the fellowship of God." Quoted in Rutledge (2015), 76–7.

The episode of Jesus falling victim to the appalling injustice of lynching by crucifixion is, of course, part of a larger narrative. Christians confess that this same Jesus who died by lynching was raised from the dead. Had he not been raised, he would not have been worshipped as savior. Stories about his baffling sayings, his mysterious doings, and his painful and humiliating death might have been handed on; but it was his resurrection that led to his being worshipped as savior. Absent those, there would have been no Christian church, and hence no Christian liturgy. It was the resurrection of the one who had been lynched that gave birth to Christian liturgy.

Jesus' crucifixion in mainline liturgies

When Paul instructed the Corinthian Christians to enact a memorial celebration of Jesus, one might have expected him to say that they were to do so by incorporating a rehearsal or representation of Jesus' resurrection. But not so. They were to enact a memorial whose centerpiece was a rehearsal and imitation of what Jesus did at his last supper, thereby "presenting the Lord's death until he comes."[20] They were to recall his words, "This is my body, *broken*; this is my blood, *shed*." In short, whenever the Eucharist is celebrated in a way that is faithful to Paul's instructions, the participants are once again confronted with the episode of lynching by crucifixion that Cone rightly describes as lying at the heart of the Christian story.[21]

When one has a clear picture in mind of Jesus' manner of death and then reads mainline present-day Eucharistic liturgies and the earlier ones collected by Deiss in *Springtime of the Liturgy* and by Jasper and Cuming in *Prayers of the Eucharist: Early and Reformed*, one is struck by how veiled is the presentation of Christ's death in most of these liturgies. Some do not even mention his suffering. In the Great Prayer of Thanksgiving of the Episcopal Church the priest says, "we now offer unto thee [God the Father] the memorial thy Son hath commanded us to make; having in remembrance his blessed passion and precious death, his mighty resurrection and glorious ascension."[22]

20. 1 Corinthians 11: 26. The usual translation of the Greek verb *katangellō* is "proclaim" rather than "present."
21. Marilyn Adams writes, the Eucharist "puts horrors front and center. By Christ's own command, its explicit purpose is 'to show forth the Lord's death until He comes'." M. Adams (2006), 282.
22. *Book of Common Prayer* (1979), 335.

Not only is there no mention of Jesus' suffering; the terms "blessed passion," "precious death," "mighty resurrection," and "glorious ascension" tend to put all thought of suffering out of mind.[23] In the anaphora of the Orthodox liturgy there is also no mention of Jesus' suffering; the only allusion to his mode of death occurs when the priest says, "the night he was handed over— or rather surrendered himself for the life of the world."[24]

Though many Eucharistic liturgies do include a reference to Jesus' suffering, albeit usually very brief and unemphatic, seldom is there a clear indication that Jesus was the victim of injustice. The contemporary Catholic liturgy is exceptional in this regard. Early in Eucharistic Prayer No. 1 the priest says, "On the day before he was to suffer."[25] A bit later he says, "We offer to your glorious majesty from the gifts that you have given us this pure victim, this holy victim, this spotless victim."[26] Behind this use of the term "victim" there is an elaborate and controversial liturgical theology. But whatever one thinks of that theology, the suggestion that Jesus was a victim of injustice is unmistakable.

The suggestion pales, however, before what we find in a few of the ancient liturgies. In one of the anaphoras contained in *The Apostolic Constitutions* (late fourth century) the presider says,

> Having brought his entire work to completion, he was betrayed by the man who was corroded by wickedness, and delivered into the hands of the impious by the treachery of priests and high priests unworthy of the name, and of a corrupted people. He suffered painfully at their hands, endured every kind of ignominy in accordance with your plan, and was handed over to Pilate, the governor.
> He, the Judge, was judged.
> He, the Savior, was condemned.[27]

I noted that most Eucharistic texts give only a very veiled presentation of Christ's death; seldom are participants confronted with the gruesomeness

23. In one of the six alternatives for the Great Prayer of Thanksgiving the priest says, "On the night he was handed over to suffering and death." *Book of Common Prayer* (1979), 362.
24. *Orthodox Liturgy* (1974), 47. The idea that Jesus surrendered himself goes back into some of the ancient liturgies. For example, the anaphora included in what has come to be known as *The Apostolic Tradition* (c.200) includes the line, "When he [Jesus] was about to surrender himself to voluntary suffering." Deiss (1979), 130. Jesus did not "surrender himself"; he was arrested. It's true that he did not resist arrest; but not resisting arrest by the police is not the same as turning oneself in to the police. And his suffering was not "voluntary." It's true that he did not try to elude his torturers; but he did not volunteer for suffering.
25. *Sunday Missal* (2011), 26.   26. *Sunday Missal* (2011), 27.   27. Deiss (1979), 233.

of it, the shame, the accursedness, the injustice.[28] But as I have repeatedly emphasized in the course of our discussion, printed liturgical texts always fall short of indicating the full extent of what takes place in liturgical enactments. Usually hymns are sung while the people receive the Eucharistic elements; and it's likely that, on occasion, some of those offer a less veiled presentation of Jesus' lynching by crucifixion than does the liturgical text.

Whatever the case throughout the church year, once a year, on Holy/Good Friday, liturgical participants are almost always confronted with an unveiled presentation of Jesus' lynching by crucifixion, whether in the liturgical text, in the hymns sung, or in the sermon preached. The Orthodox liturgy for Holy Friday describes the crucifixion in vivid language: he received "blows to his face," he was "transfixed with nails," his side was "pierced with a spear," he was "crucified unjustly," "unjust judges dipped their pens in ink," "they incurred the guilt of murder."[29]

Here are the opening lines of some familiar Holy/Good Friday hymns:

> Go to dark Gethsemane, all who feel the tempter's power;
> your Redeemer's conflict see, watch with him one bitter hour.

> To mock your reign, O dearest Lord, they made a crown of thorns.
> Were you there when they crucified my Lord?
> O sacred head, now wounded, with grief and shame weighed down.

> Alas! And did my Savior bleed,
> and did my Sovereign die?[30]

And here are a few lines from a powerful Holy Week sermon preached by Melito of Sardis (second century):

> O Israel, why have you committed this unheard-of crime? You have dishonored him who honored you.... In order to immolate the Lord as evening came, you prepared for him sharp nails and false witnesses and ropes and whips and

28. In the Eucharistic liturgy that was first printed in the Dutch psalter issued by Peter Dathenus in 1566 and used for many centuries in the Dutch Reformed Church, the exhortation that preceded the Eucharistic prayer included these lines: "He was bound that we might be loosed from our sins,... He suffered innumerable reproaches that we might never be confounded;... He was innocently condemned to death that we might be acquitted at the judgment seat of God,... He suffered His blessed body to be nailed to the cross that He might fasten to it the bond written in ordinances that was against us,... and has humbled Himself unto the very deepest reproach and anguish of hell, in body and soul, on the tree of the cross." *Psalter Hymnal* (1959), 93. What comes through more clearly here than the suffering, humiliation, and injustice of Jesus' crucifixion is the theological interpretation given to those.
29. *Lenten Triodion* (1978), 587, 589, 587, 599, 599, 586.
30. These are among the sixteen Good Friday hymns included in *Lift Up Your Hearts* (2013), #161–#177.

vinegar and gall and sword and pain, as for a bandit who had shed blood. You scourged his body, you set upon his head a crown of thorns, you bound his kindly hands that had shaped you from the dust, you gave a drink of gall to the noble mouth that had fed you with life, and you put your Savior to death during the great feast.[31]

African-American liturgies

James Cone is an African-American theologian born in 1938 in Arkansas. In *The Cross and the Lynching Tree* he describes his early church experience.

> During my childhood, I heard a lot about the cross.... We sang about "Calvary," and asked, "Were you there?", "down at the cross," "when they crucified my Lord." "Oh! Sometimes it causes me to tremble, tremble, tremble."... There were more songs, sermons, prayers, and testimonies about the cross than any other theme. The cross was the foundation on which their faith was laid.[32]

Cone's personal experience was typical of African-American Christianity in general. "Black Christians," he writes, "sang more songs and preached more sermons about the cross than any other aspect of Jesus' ministry."[33] The cross of which they sang and spoke was not prettified.

> Though wonderful and beautiful, Jesus' cross was also painful and tragic. Songs and sermons about the "blood" were stark reminders of the agony of Jesus' crucifixion—the symbol of the physical and mental suffering he endured as "dey whupped him up de hill" and "crowned him wid a thorny crown." Blacks told the story of Jesus' Passion, as if they were at Golgotha suffering with him. "Were you there when dey crucified my Lord?" "Dey nailed him to de cross"; "dey pierced him in de side"; and "de blood came twinklin' down."[34]

When blacks celebrated "'Holy Communion,' [they] raised their voices to acknowledge 'a fountain filled with blood,' 'drawn from Immanuel's veins'; 'blood,' they believed, 'will never lose its power,' because 'there is power in the blood,' and 'nothing but the blood'."[35]

---

31. Deiss (1979), 106–7. It should be noted that not only does Melito make no mention of the role of the Roman authorities in the crime; the mockery he attributes to Israel was attributed by the writer of the Gospel of Matthew to the Roman soldiers. Melito structures his rehearsal of the events in such a way that it is an accusation of Israel.
32. Cone (2011), 21.   33. Cone (2011), 25.
34. Cone (2011), 73–4.   35. Cone (2011), 74.

Poor little Jesus boy, made him be born in a manger.
World treated him so mean,
Treats me mean too....

Dey whipped Him up an' dey whipped Him down,
Dey whipped dat man all ovah town.
Look-a how they done muh Lawd.

I was there when they nailed him to the cross.
Oh! How it makes me sadder, sadder,
When I think how they nailed him to the cross.

I was there when they took him down...
Oh! How it makes my spirit tremble,
When I recalls how they took him down.[36]

Why was Jesus' crucifixion so prominent in African-American singing and preaching, and why was its agony, humiliation, and injustice so sharply in view? Cone's explanation is that it was because the daily experience of black people led them to *identify* with Jesus in his suffering, humiliation, and victimization. They "identified with Jesus' rejection in Jerusalem, his agony in the Garden of Gethsemane, and his suffering on the cross of Calvary. Like Jesus, who prayed to his Father to 'let this cup pass from me' (Matthew 26: 39), blacks also prayed to God to take away the bitter cups of slavery, segregation, and lynching. Just as Jesus cried from the cross, 'My God, my God, why hast thou forsaken me?' many lynched victims made similar outbursts of despair to God before they took their last breath, hoping for divine intervention that did not come."[37]

"Blacks told the story of Jesus' Passion, as if they were at Golgotha suffering with him."[38] Ministers "preached sermons about Jesus' crucifixion, as if they were telling the story of black people's tragedy and triumph in America. The symbol of the cross spoke to the lives of blacks because the likeness between the cross and the lynching tree created an eerie feeling of mystery and the supernatural. Like Jesus, blacks knew torture and abandonment."[39] "Black ministers preached about Jesus' death more than any other theme because they saw in Jesus' suffering and persecution a parallel to their own encounter with slavery, segregation, and the lynching tree."[40]

"No matter what songs they sang," writes Cone, "they infused them with their own experience of suffering and transformed what they received into

36. Cone (2011), 22.   37. Cone (2011), 123–4.   38. Cone (2011), 73–4.
39. Cone (2011), 75.   40. Cone (2011), 75.

their own. 'Jesus Keep Me near the Cross,' 'Must Jesus Bear the Cross Alone?' and other white Protestant evangelical hymns did not sound or feel the same when blacks and whites sang them."[41]

An additional note must immediately be added. Those who identified with Jesus in his lynching by crucifixion never lost sight of the fact that this same Jesus had been raised from the dead and conquered injustice and death. His claim, that he had been divinely anointed to proclaim that justice for the oppressed was imminent, had been vindicated in the most astonishing way. That gave black people hope that they too would somehow be "raised up."

> That God could "make a way out of no way" in Jesus' cross was . . . profoundly real in the souls of black folk. Enslaved blacks who first heard the gospel message seized on the power of the cross. Christ crucified manifested God's loving and liberating presence *in* the contradictions of black life—that transcendent presence in the lives of black Christians that empowered them to believe that *ultimately* in God's eschatological future, they would not be defeated by the "troubles of this world," no matter how great and painful their suffering.[42]

"The dialectic of sorrow and joy, despair and hope was central in the black experience."[43]

> My burden's so heavy, I can't hardly see,
> Seems like everybody down on me.
> An' that's all right, I don't worry, oh, there will be a better day,
> The sun's gonna shine on my backdoor some day.[44]

Implicit in the liturgical enactments of black people that Cone describes was liberation Christology: by his crucifixion and resurrection Christ is changing the social order, liberating human beings from the grip of oppression and injustice. Implicit in the liturgical enactments of most North American white people is atonement Christology: by his crucifixion and resurrection Christ has atoned for our personal sins. Experience shapes Christology. The lyrics of the enormously popular hymn, "Amazing Grace," were composed by John Newton, converted slave trader. The grace of which Newton wrote was the grace "That saved a wretch like me," not the grace that saves from oppression. Grace for wrongdoers, not for victims.

---

41. Cone (2011), 22–3.   42. Cone (2011), 2.
43. Cone (2011), 13.   44. Black spiritual, quoted in Cone (1991), 14.

But though the resurrection was never out of mind, it was the cross and not the empty tomb that was central in African-American singing and preaching. "The resurrected Lord was the crucified Lord."[45] For it was in the cross of Jesus that black people heard a "message of justice in the midst of powerlessness, suffering, and death."[46] The African-American theologian, Shawn Copeland, explains the African-American spirituals thus: "If the makers of the spirituals gloried in singing of the cross of Jesus, it was not because they were masochistic and enjoyed suffering. Rather, the enslaved Africans sang because they saw on the rugged wooden planks One who had endured what was their daily portion. The cross was treasured because it enthroned the One who went all the way with them and for them. The enslaved Africans sang because they saw the results of the cross—triumph over the principalities and powers of death, triumph over evil in this world."[47]

A parenthetical note: the Gospel of Matthew reports that the Roman soldiers compelled "a man from Cyrene named Simon" to carry Jesus' cross (27: 32). A traditional view in the African-American community was that Simon was black; he was commonly called "Black Simon." That led African-Americans to identify with Simon as well as with Jesus. In a sermon Martin Luther King Jr preached in 1959 he said,

> I think one day God will remember that it was a black man that helped His son in the darkest and most desperate moment of his life.... It was a black man who picked up that cross for him and who took that cross on up to Calvary. God will remember this. And in all our struggles for peace and security, freedom and human dignity, one day God will remember that it was a black man who aided his only-begotten son in the darkest hour of his life.[48]

The African-American poet James Weldon Johnson wrote:

> Up Golgotha's rugged road
> I see my Jesus go.
> I see him sink beneath the load,
> I see my drooping Jesus sink.
> And then they laid hold on Simon,
> Black Simon, yes, black Simon;
> They put the cross on Simon,
> And Simon bore the cross.[49]

45. Cone (2011), 151.   46. Cone (2011), 156.   47. Quoted in Cone (2011), 150-1.
48. Quoted by Cone (2011), 82.   49. Cone (2011), 47.

Identification

Cone's explanation, of why a sharp focus on the horror of Jesus' crucifixion has been so prominent in African-American liturgical enactments, is that the experience of black people led them to identify with Jesus in his suffering and humiliation as a victim of injustice. There are white people around the world who also identify with Jesus in that way, some in our own society; one thinks immediately of certain prisoners. But most white people in our society do not identify with Jesus in that way; I include myself. To this should be added, however, that one who does not identify with Jesus in his humiliation as a victim of injustice might nonetheless identify with him in his suffering. Some cancer patients, for example, might identify with Jesus in that way.

Identification is mysterious; I don't understand it very well. But let me say a few things about it. In Chapter 4 I quoted a passage from Ludolph of Saxony's *Life of Christ* in which he urged his readers to imagine, as vividly as possible, events in the life of Jesus. "Make present to yourself how he spoke and went about with his disciples and with sinners, how he speaks and preaches, how he walks and rests, sleeps and watches, eats and performs miracles."

Many of the African-American songs about the cross represent extraordinary feats of the sort of visual and auditory imagination that Ludolph urges.

> Jesus, my darling Jesus,
> Groaning as the blood came spurting from his wound.
> Oh, look how they done my Jesus.
> O see my Jesus hangin' high!
> He look so pale an' bleed so free.[50]

And another:

> Oh, dey whupped him up de hill, up de hill, up de hill,
> Oh, dey whupped him up de hill, an' he never said a mumbalin' word....
>
> Oh, dey crowned him wid a thorny crown, thorny crown, crown o' thorns,
> Oh, dey crowned him wid a thorny crown, an' he never said a mumbalin' word....
>
> Well, dey nailed him to de cross, to de cross, to de cross,
> Well, dey nailed him to de cross, an' he never said a mumbalin' word....
>
> Well, dey pierced him in de side, in de side, in de side,
> Well, they pieced him in de side, an' he never said a mumbalin' word....

50. Cone (2011), 74.

Well, de blood came twinklin' down, twinklin' down, twinklin' down,
Well, de blood came twinklin' down, an' he never said a mumbalin' word,
Well, de blood came twinklin' down, an' he never said a mumbalin' word,
Den he hung his head an' he died.[51]

Often the temporal distance between the singer and the crucifixion is collapsed in African-American songs. The singer imagines that she was there: "I was there when they nailed him to the cross"; "I was there when they took him down." Or she employs the liturgical present tense and imagines that the crucifixion is happening now.

But one can do what Ludolph urged, namely, vividly imagine the crucifixion, without identifying with Jesus in what he underwent. Though identification requires imagination, there's more to identifying with Jesus in his suffering than vividly imagining his suffering. One can vividly imagine the suffering of someone with whom one does not identify. Those who sing the Holy/Good Friday hymns whose first lines I quoted may, when singing, quite vividly imagine Jesus' suffering; but most of them do not identify with Jesus in his suffering.

One never just identifies with someone; one identifies with someone *in some respect*. We are considering those who identify with Jesus in respect to his suffering, humiliation, and victimization. Black persons who identify with Jesus in these respects believe that there is a deep similarity between what was done to Jesus and what has been done to them. They believe that just as Jesus was whipped, they have been whipped, and just as they have been whipped, Jesus was whipped. The belief of black people, that Jesus and they are alike in this respect, is a condition of their identification with Jesus as one who was whipped.

But there is more to identification than this sort of belief-that. What also enters into the identification of black people with Jesus, in respect to Jesus' experience of being whipped, is that they know first-hand *what it's like* to be whipped. They know what it is like because they have had the experience of being whipped or of watching others being whipped. They have experiential acquaintance with what it is like to be whipped—knowledge by acquaintance. "I can identify with Jesus," the black person says; "because I know what it's like to be whipped."[52] Those who have neither been

51. Cone (1991), 47–8.
52. Cone quotes the black historian, Lerone Bennett, as saying that black people knew "at the deepest level... what it was like to be crucified." Cone (2011), 22.

whipped nor seen someone being whipped don't know what it's like to be whipped. Experiential acquaintance with *what it's like* is an indispensable component of identification.

This still falls short of actually *identifying* with Jesus in his experience of being whipped. It's a condition of actually identifying, but not yet the thing itself. What is the thing itself? I'm not sure. But it appears to me that two additional things must be present. To identify with Jesus in his experience of being whipped one must not only *believe that* Jesus' experience and one's own experience are similar; one must actively *see or regard* the experience of Jesus as like one's own experience and *see or regard* one's own experience *as like Jesus' experience*. The general phenomenon of which this is an example is that of seeing or regarding something as so-and-so: seeing the tilt of someone's hat as a sign of arrogance, for example. Not just *believing that* it is a sign of arrogance but *seeing it as* a sign of arrogance. In the absence of *seeing or regarding* Jesus' experience as like one's own and *seeing or regarding* one's own experience as like Jesus', there is no identification.

What must also be present, so it appears to me, is emotional bonding in the form of empathy. Identifying with Jesus in his experience of being whipped requires that one empathize with Jesus in this respect. From their songs, it's clear that African-Americans did that.

I have made the point that one can vividly imagine the crucifixion as Ludolph urges his readers to do without identifying with Jesus in his suffering. Let me close this section by noting that vividly imagining the crucifixion may lead one to empathize with Jesus in his suffering even though one does not, strictly speaking, identify with him. I am thinking here of what the pilgrim Egeria reports about the liturgical enactments she encountered in Jerusalem. She reports that in the regular Sunday liturgy the bishop would take "the Gospel book" and read "the account of the Lord's resurrection." As he begins to read, "the whole assembly groans and laments at all the Lord underwent for us, and the way they weep would move even the hardest heart to tears."[53] A bit later she describes the Good Friday liturgy, held on the site reputed to be Gethsemane: "When everyone arrives at Gethsemane, they have an appropriate prayer, a hymn, and then a reading from the Gospel about the Lord's arrest. By the time it has been read everyone is groaning

---

53. § 24.10. Ruth, Steenwyk, and Witvliet (2010), 49.

and lamenting and weeping so loud that people even across in the city can probably hear it all."[54]

Does it matter?

There are many people in situations of oppression around the world, both Christians and non-Christians, who can identify with Jesus as a tortured, humiliated, and accursed victim of injustice; Cone's description of the experience of African-Americans speaks to the experience of these oppressed people. I, along with most readers of this book, cannot identify with Jesus in that way. Nothing in our experience enables us to do so. The weekly liturgical enactments in which we participate could, nonetheless, "proclaim" Christ's death as the gruesome, ignominious, and accursed perversion of justice that it was. But they do not. They veil it from us. The theologian Jürgen Moltmann writes, "The cross in the church symbolizes the contradiction which comes into the church from the God who was crucified 'outside.'... The symbol of the cross in the church points to the God who was crucified not between two candles on an altar, but between two thieves in the place of the skull, where the outcasts belong, outside the gates of the city."[55] True. But as James Cone remarks, "The cross has been transformed into a harmless, non-offensive ornament that Christians wear around their necks."[56]

Does that matter? Wasn't it a matter of happenstance that Jesus' death was a gruesome, humiliating, and accursed perversion of justice? Isn't the manner of his death irrelevant? Could he not just as well have died in some other way? Isn't the fact that he died *for us* the important thing, not *how* he died? What's wrong with speaking of "his blessed passion and precious death" and letting it go at that?

Cone remarks, "during the course of 2,000 years of Christian history, this symbol of salvation [the cross] has been detached from any reference to the

---

54. §36.3. Ruth, Steenwyk, and Witvliet (2010), 54. Describing the response of the people to the readings at a point later in the Good Friday liturgy Egeria says, "It is impressive to see the way all the people are moved by these readings, and how they mourn, You could hardly believe how every single one of them weeps during the three hours, old and young alike, because of the manner in which the Lord suffered for us." § 37.7. Ruth, Steenwyk, and Witvliet (2010), 56.
55. Moltmann (1974), 40. I thank Cornelius Plantinga for calling this passage to my attention.
56. Cone (2011), xiv.

ongoing suffering and oppression of human beings—those whom Ignacio Ellacuría, the Salvadoran martyr, called 'the crucified people of history'."[57] I noted in the section "African-American liturgies" that the Christology implicit in the liturgical enactments of most North American white people is atonement Christology rather than liberation theology: Jesus came to save sinners, not to liberate the oppressed. Does that matter? One can understand why black churches favored liberation Christology. Does it matter that we favor atonement Christology?

The massive treatise[58] on the crucifixion by Fleming Rutledge, *The Crucifixion: Understanding the Death of Jesus Christ,* can be read as an extended answer to this question. Rutledge identifies and discusses a number of distinct "motifs" in the New Testament and subsequent theology concerning the crucifixion of Jesus, that is, a number of distinct angles or perspectives on the crucifixion, a number of different ways of understanding it. Each of the aspects of Jesus' death that I have highlighted—excruciating, humiliating, accursed, a perversion of justice—is intrinsic to one or more of these motifs.

The motif of the Godlessness of the Cross: in his suffering and humiliation Jesus was abandoned even by God.[59] "My God, my God, why have you forsaken me?" Isaiah foretold the suffering, humiliation, and abandonment:

> He was despised and rejected by others;
>   a man of suffering and acquainted with infirmity;
> and as one from whom others hide their faces
>   he was despised, and we held him of no account....
> He was wounded for our transgressions,
>   crushed for our iniquities,
> upon him was the punishment that made us whole,
>   and by his bruises we are healed.   (Isaiah 53: 3–5)

The motif of Substitution: by being cursed, Jesus delivered us from the curse.[60] Paul wrote, "All who rely on the works of the law are under a curse; for it is written, 'Cursed is everyone who does not observe and obey all the things written in the book of the law.'... Christ redeemed us from the curse of the law by becoming a curse for us—for it is written, 'Cursed is everyone who hangs on a tree'" (Galatians 3: 10–13).

---

57. Cone (2011), xiv.   58. 669+ pages.
59. Rutledge discusses the motif of the Godlessness of the Cross in chapter 2 of Rutledge (2015).
60. Rutledge discusses the motif of Substitution in chapter 11 of Rutledge (2015).

The motif of *Christus Victor*: by suffering gross injustice, but then not remaining dead as the authorities intended and expected, but rising from the dead, Jesus conquered the powers of deceit, oppression, and injustice that have society in their grip and liberated us.[61] Paul wrote, "He disarmed the rulers and authorities and made a public example of them, triumphing over them" (Colossians 2: 15).[62]

When the liturgy veils from participants the gruesome, demeaning, and accursed perversion of justice that Jesus underwent, it veils from them the motif of the Godlessness of the Cross and the motif of Substitution. And when the implicit Christology is only atonement Christology and not also liberation theology it veils from them the motif of *Christus Victor*.

When the horror of Jesus' crucifixion is veiled from liturgical participants and Christ's work as liberator ignored, not only is their perception of the reality of what happened blurred and their theological understanding impaired. The possibility of a certain moral formation is foreclosed. The participant who sees clearly that the one he worships is one whose death was a horrific, ignominious, and accursed perversion of justice will not be dazzled by power and prestige. How could he be? It's not those with power and prestige who resemble the one he worships but those who are demeaned and downtrodden. When he sees one of those, he sees someone who resembles Jesus. He will act accordingly.

In conclusion

In the Preface to this volume I distinguished what I called the "performative" dimension of liturgy from its formative and expressive functions. By the "performative" dimension I mean what the participants do when the liturgical script is followed and the liturgy is enacted. It's what they do that forms them and it's what they do that functions (or does not function) expressively for them. The performative dimension is basic in that way.

61. Rutledge discusses the *Christus Victor* motif in chapter 9 of Rutledge (2015). The term "*Christus Victor*" was introduced by the Swedish bishop Gustav Aulén in his enormously influential book of 1931, *Christus Victor: An Historical Study of the Three Main Types of the Idea of the Atonement*.

62. It was Paul's thought that wrongdoing is not to be attributed solely to the actions of individual human beings but that society and its members are in the grip of strange forces that press us into evildoing. It's those forces that he is referring to with the terms "rulers" and "authorities." In other passages he calls them "principalities," "powers," "thrones," and "dominions." The classic discussion of this aspect of Paul's thought is Berkhof (1962).

Whereas most discussions of liturgy focus on its formative or expressive functions, I have focused almost exclusively on its performative dimension. The concluding section of Chapter 12 was an exception; there I took note of some of the ways in which liturgical enactments school the participants in neighbor love.

This present chapter is also an exception. Though I have not used the word "express," in the latter part of this chapter we have implicitly been exploring one of the ways in which liturgy functions expressively. Typically the expressive function of liturgy is identified with the expression by participants of their religious thoughts and affections.[63] If my analysis of identification is correct, it would be a serious mistake to think of the identification of black people with Jesus in his suffering as consisting of having certain religious thoughts and affections. Better to describe it as what Jesus' suffering *meant for them in their lives*. It was the *life-meaning* for them of Jesus' suffering that they expressed when they sang their spirituals and prayed for deliverance.

The life-meaning for black people of Jesus' suffering is one example of a general phenomenon: persons and episodes in the biblical narrative often have a certain meaning or significance in the lives of liturgical participants. It's not just their religious thoughts and affections but that *life-meaning* that they express when they sing the hymns, pray the prayers, etc.

Not only do persons and episodes in the biblical narratives often have a certain meaning in the lives of liturgical participants; often the liturgical acts themselves do. The liturgical act of confession may have a certain meaning in one's life, the liturgical act of receiving the Eucharistic elements may have a certain meaning in one's life, and so forth. Often these meanings differ significantly from person to person. A Catholic interpretation of the theological significance of receiving the bread and wine of the Eucharist is very different from a Zwinglian interpretation. Typically those different theological interpretations result in the Eucharist having a quite different life-meaning for a Catholic from the life-meaning it has for a Zwinglian.

None of the three categories, performative, formative, and expressive, fits the phenomenon of liturgical acts having life-meaning for participants. Obviously this is not an example of the performative dimension of liturgy. Just as obviously it is not an example of the formative function. But so too it is not an example of the expressive function. The meaning that the liturgical confession of sins has in one's life is not to be identified with *expressing*

---

63. The term "religious affections" is borrowed, of course, from Jonathan Edwards.

that meaning by praying. The *life-meaning* for a person of various liturgical acts is a *sui generis* dimension of liturgical activity.

To repeat: whereas most discussions of liturgy focus either on its formative or expressive function, most of my discussion has focused instead on its performative dimension. Nobody, to the best of my knowledge, has given sustained attention to the life-meaning dimension of liturgical acts. A new and unfamiliar terrain beckons to be explored. For now, we will have to resist the call.

References

Adams, Marilyn. 2006. *Christ and Horrors: The Coherence of Christology*. Cambridge: Cambridge University Press.

Adams, Robert. 1999. *Finite and Infinite Goods*. Oxford: Oxford University Press.

Alston, William P. 1996. "Belief, Acceptance, and Religious Faith." In Jeff Jordan and Daniel Howard-Snyder, eds., *Faith, Freedom, and Rationality*. Lanham, MD: Rowman & Littlefield: 3–28.

Aquinas, Thomas. 1947. *Summa theologica*. Dominican translation. New York: Benzinger Brothers.

Aquinas, Thomas. 1975. *Summa contra Gentiles: Book One: God*. Tr. Anton C. Pegis. Notre Dame, IN: University of Notre Dame Press.

Athanasius. 2006. *The Life of Anthony*. Tr. Robert C. Gregg. San Francisco: HarperSanFrancisco.

Augustine. 1959. *Of True Religion*. Tr. J. H. S. Burleigh. Chicago: Henry Regnery Co.

Bell, Catherine. 1992. *Ritual Theory, Ritual Practice*. Oxford: Oxford University Press.

Bell, Catherine, ed. 2007. *Teaching Ritual*. Oxford: Oxford University Press.

Berkhof, Hendrikus. 1962. *Christ and the Powers*. Scottdale, PA: Herald Press.

Boesak, Allan A., and Villa-Vicencio, Charles, eds. 1986. *When Prayer Makes News*. Philadelphia: Westminister Press.

Book of Common Prayer (of the Episcopal Church). 1979. New York: The Church Hymnal Corporation.

Book of Common Worship (of the Presbyterian Church USA). 1993. Louisville, KY: Westminster John Knox Press.

Borges, Jorge. 1998. *Collected Fictions*. Tr. Andrew Hurley. New York: Penguin Books.

Branch, Lori. 2006. *Rituals of Spontaneity: Sentiment and Secularism from Free Prayer to Wordsworth*. Waco, TX: Baylor University Press.

Bratman, Michael E. 2009. "Shared Agency." In Chrysostomos Mantzavinos, ed., *Philosophy of the Social Sciences*. Cambridge: Cambridge University Press: 41–59.

Brower, Jeffrey. 2009. "Simplicity and Aseity." In Michael Rea and Thomas Flint, eds, *The Oxford Handbook of Philosophical Theology*. Oxford: Oxford University Press: 105–28.

Burridge, Richard A. 1992. *What Are Gospels?* Cambridge: Cambridge University Press.

Calvin, John. 1948a. *Commentary on the Book of the Prophet Isaiah: Vol. I*. Tr. William Pringle. Grand Rapids, MI: William B. Eerdmans Publishing Co.

Calvin, John. 1948b. *Commentary on the Epistles of Paul to the Corinthians: Vol. II.* Grand Rapids, MI: William B. Eerdmans Publishing Co.

Calvin, John. 1954. "Short Treatise on the Lord's Supper." In *Calvin: Theological Treatises.* Tr. J. K. S. Reid. Philadelphia: Westminster Press.

Calvin, John. 1960. *Institutes of the Christian Religion.* Tr. Ford Lewis Battles, ed. John T. McNeill. Philadelphia: Westminster Press.

Casel, Odo. 1962. *The Mystery of Christian Worship.* Westminster, MD: Newman Press.

Casey, Edward. 1987. *Remembering: A Phenomenological Inquiry.* Bloomington, IN: Indiana University Press.

Cassian, John. 1997. *The Conferences.* Tr. Boniface Ramsey. New York: Paulist Press.

Chignell, Andrew. n.d. "Liturgical Philosophy." Unpublished manuscript: 1–24.

Childs, Brevard. 1962. *Memory and Tradition in Israel.* London: SCM Press.

Cone, James. 1991. *The Spirituals and the Blues.* Maryknoll, NY: Orbis Books.

Cone, James. 2011. *The Cross and the Lynching Tree.* Maryknoll, NY: Orbis Books.

Crichton, J. D. 1978. "A Theology of Worship." In Cheslyn Jones, Geoffrey Wainwright, and Edward Yarnold, eds., *The Study of Liturgy.* New York: Oxford University Press.

Cuneo, Terence. 2016a. "Liturgical Immersion." In Terence Cuneo, *Ritualized Faith: Essays on the Philosophy of Liturgy.* Oxford: Oxford University Press: 66–87.

Cuneo, Terence. 2016b. *Ritualized Faith: Essays on the Philosophy of Liturgy.* Oxford: Oxford University Press.

Dandelion, Pink. 2005. *The Liturgies of Quakerism.* Burlington, VT: Ashgate Publishing Co.

Daniélou, Jean. 1956. *The Bible and the Liturgy.* Notre Dame, IN: University of Notre Dame Press.

Deiss, Lucien. 1979. *The Springtime of the Liturgy.* Collegeville, MN: The Liturgical Press.

Dickinson, Emily. 2003. *The Collected Poems of Emily Dickinson,* introd. Rachel Wetzsteon. New York: Barnes & Noble.

Didache. 1953. In *The Apostolic Fathers: Vol. I.* Tr. Kirsopp Lake. Cambridge, MA: Harvard University Press.

Dix, Gregory. 1983. *The Shape of the Liturgy.* New York: Seabury Press.

Eliade, Mircea. 1959. *The Sacred and the Profane.* New York: Harcourt Brace Jovanovich.

Eliade, Mircea. 1963. *Myth and Reality.* New York: Harper & Row.

Eliade, Mircea. 1974. *Myth of the Eternal Return.* Princeton: Princeton University Press.

Empson, William. 1957. *Seven Types of Ambiguity.* New York: Meridian Books.

Eucharistic Liturgy of Taize. 1962. Tr. John Arnold. London: The Faith Press.

Evangelical Lutheran Worship. 2007. Minneapolis: Fortress Press.

Ford, David. 1999. *Self and Salvation: Being Transformed.* Cambridge: Cambridge University Press.

Germanus of Constantinople. 1984. *On the Divine Liturgy.* Tr. with introd. and commentary, Paul Meyendorf. Crestwood, NY: St Vladimir's Press.

Graham, Gordon. 2007. "Liturgy as Drama." *Theology Today* 64: 71–9.

Grant, W. Matthews. 2016. "Aseity." In *Routledge Enclyclopedia of Philosophy Online.*

Gregory of Nazianzus, St. 2008. *Festal Orations.* Tr. with introd. and commentary, Nonna Verna Harrison. Crestwood, NY: St Vladimir's Press.

Harbert, Bruce E. 2008. "Liturgies within the Liturgy." In James G. Leachman, ed., *The Liturgical Subject: Subject, Subjectivity, and the Human Person in Contemporary Liturgical Discussion and Critique.* Notre Dame, IN: Notre Dame University Press: 114–31.

Harrison, Nonna Verna. 2008. "Introduction" to *Festal Orations: St. Gregory of Nazianus.* Crestwood, NY: St Vladimir's Seminary Press.

Hauerwas, Stanley. 2001. *The Hauerwas Reader.* Durham, NC: Duke University Press.

Horn, Stacy. 2013. *Imperfect Harmony: Finding Happiness Singing with Others.* Chapel Hill, NC: Algonquin Books of Chapel Hill.

Howard-Snyder, Daniel. 2013. "Propositional Faith: What It Is and What It Is Not." *American Philosophical Quarterly* 50/4: 357–72.

Howard-Snyder, Daniel. 2016. "Does Faith Entail Belief?" *Faith and Philosophy* 33/2 (April): 142–62.

Hughes, Graham. 2003. *Worship As Meaning: A Liturgical Theology for Late Modernity.* Cambridge: Cambridge University Press.

Humphrey, Carolyn, and Laidlaw, James. 1994. *The Archetypal Actions of Ritual.* Oxford: Clarendon Press.

Jasper, R. C. D., and Cuming, G. J. 1987. *Prayers of the Eucharist: Early and Reformed,* third edition. New York: Pueblo Publishing Co.

Jourjon, Maurice. 1978. "Justin." In Willy Rordorf et al., eds., *The Eucharist of the Early Christians.* New York: Pueblo Publishing Co.

Jungmann, J. A. 1959. "Liturgy on the Eve of the Reformation." *Worship* 33: 505–15.

Kelsey, David. 2009. *Eccentric Existence: A Theological Anthropology: Vol. I.* Louisville, KY: Westminster John Knox Press.

The Lenten Triodion. 1978. Tr. from the Greek by Mother Mary and Archimandrite Kallistos Ware. London: Faber and Faber.

Lift Up Your Hearts: Psalms, Hymns, and Spiritual Songs. 2013. Grand Rapids, MI: Faith Alive Christian Resources.

McCall, Richard D. 2007. *Do This: Liturgy as Performance.* Notre Dame, IN: University of Notre Dame Press.

McGowan, Andrew B. 2014. *Ancient Christian Worship: Early Church Practices in Social, Historical, and Theological Perspectives.* Grand Rapids, MI: Baker Academic.

MacIntyre, Alasdair. 1981. *After Virtue.* Notre Dame, IN: University of Notre Dame Press.

Maimonides, Moses. 1995. *The Guide of the Perplexed.* Tr. Chaim Rabin. Indianapolis: Hackett Publishing Co.

Meyendorff, Paul. 1984. "Introduction" to St Germanus of Constantinople, *On the Divine Liturgy.* Tr. Paul Meyendorf. Crestwood, NY: St Vladimir's Seminary Press.

Mitchell, Nathan D. 2006. *Meeting Mystery: Worship, Sacraments.* Maryknoll, NY: Orbis Books.

Moltmann, Jürgen. 1974. *The Crucified God: The Cross of Christ as the Foundation and Criticism of Christian Theology.* New York: Harper & Row.

Mowinckel, Sigmund. 1981. *Religion and Cult.* Tr. John F. X. Sheehan. Milwaukee: Marquette University Press.

O'Donnell, Emma. 2015. *Remembering the Future: The Experience of Time in Jewish and Christian Liturgy.* Collegeville, MN: Liturgical Press.

The Orthodox Liturgy. 1974. Tr. from the Greek by Revd Nicon D. Patrinacos. Garwood, NJ: Graphic Arts Press.

The Orthodox Liturgy. 1982. Tr. from Old Church Slavonic; name of translator not given. Oxford: Oxford University Press.

Outka, Gene. 1972. *Agape: An Ethical Analysis.* New Haven: Yale University Press.

Ozment, Steven. 1975. *Reformation in the Cities: The Appeal of Protestantism to Sixteenth Century Germany and Switzerland.* New Haven: Yale University Press.

Perry, Michael. 1998. *The Idea of Human Rights.* Oxford: Oxford University Press.

Plato. 1945. *The Republic.* Tr. F. M. Cornford. Oxford: Oxford University Press.

Plato, with an English Translation: Lysis, Symposium, Gorgias. 1946. Tr. W. R. M. Lamb. Cambridge, MA: Harvard University Press.

Psalms for All Seasons. 2012. Ed. Martin Tell, Joyce Borger, and John Witvliet. Grand Rapids, MI: Brazos Press, Faith Alive Resources, and Calvin Institute for Christian Worship.

Psalter Hymnal. 1959. Grand Rapids, MI: Publication Committee of the Christian Reformed Church.

Pseudo-Dionysius: The Complete Works. 1987. Tr. Colin Luibheid, ed. Paul Rorem. New York: Paulist Press.

Putnam, Hilary. 1975. *Language and Reality: Philosophical Papers, Vol. 2.* Cambridge: Cambridge University Press.

Rordorf, Willy, et al. 1978. *The Eucharist of the Early Christians.* Tr. Michael J. O'Connell. New York: Pueblo Publishing Co.

Ross, Melanie. 2014. *Evangelical or Liturgical: Defying a Dichotomy.* Grand Rapids, MI: William B. Eerdmans Publishing Co.

Rowthorn, Jeffrey. 2015. "Water in the Book of Common Prayer." *The Yale ISM Review* 2/1 (Fall): 1–11. Article online at <http://ismreviw.yale.edu/article/water-in-the-book-of-common-prayer/>.

Ruth, Lester, Steenwyk, Carrie, and Witvliet, John D. 2010. *Walking Where Jesus Walked: Worship in Fourth-Century Jerusalem.* Grand Rapids, MI: William B. Eerdmans Publishing Co.

Rutledge, Fleming. 2015. *The Crucifixion: Understanding the Death of Christ.* Grand Rapids, MI: William B. Eerdmans Publishing Co.

Schilbrack, Kevin, ed. 2004. *Thinking through Rituals: Philosophical Perspectives.* New York: Routledge.

Schmemann, Alexander. 1969. *Great Lent: Journey to Pascha.* Crestwood, NY: St Vladimir's Press.

Schmemann, Alexander. 1998. Sixth printing. *For the Life of the World.* Crestwood, NY: St Vladimir's Seminary Press.

Searle, John. 1969. *Speech Acts: An Essay in the Philosophy of Language*. Cambridge: Cambridge University Press.

Searle, John. 1990. "Collective Intentions and Actions." In P. Cohen, J. Morgan, and M. E. Pollak, eds., *Intentions in Communication*. Cambridge, MA: MIT Press: 401–16.

Second Helvetic Confession. Text online at <http://www.sacred-texts.com/chr/2helvcnf.htm>. Translator not given.

Seligman, Adam, Weller, Robert, Puett, Michael, and Simon, Bennett. 2008. *An Essay on the Limits of Sincerity*. Oxford: Oxford University Press.

Smith, James K. A. 2013. *Imagining the Kingdom: How Worship Works*. Grand Rapids, MI: Baker Academic.

Stookey, Laurence Hull. 1996. *Calendar; Christ's Time for the Church*. Nashville: Abingdon Press.

Stowe, Harriet Beecher. 2005. *Uncle Tom's Cabin*. Mineola, NY: Dover Publications.

Stump, Eleonore. 2003. *Aquinas*. New York and London: Routledge.

Stump, Eleonore. 2016. *The God of the Bible and the God of the Philosophers: The Aquinas Lecture 2016*. Milwaukee: Marquette University Press.

Sunday Missal: The Complete Masses for Sundays, Holydays, and the Sacred Paschal Triduum. 2011. Totowa, NJ: Catholic Book Publishing Corp.

Taft, Robert. 1984. *Beyond East and West: Problems in Liturgical Understanding*. Washington, DC: The Pastoral Press.

Taliaferro, Charles. 2004. "Ritual and Christian Philosophy." In Kevin Schilbrack, ed., *Thinking through Rituals*. New York: Routledge: 238–50.

Thompson, Bard. 1962. *Liturgies of the Western Church*. Cleveland and New York: Meridian Books.

Thurian, Max. 1960. *The Eucharistic Memorial*, 2 vols. Richmond, VA: John Knox Press.

Trilling, Lionel. 1972. *Sincerity and Authenticity*. Cambridge, MA: Harvard University Press.

Von Allmen, Jean-Jacques. 1965. *Worship: Its Theology and Practice*. Tr. Harold Knight and W. Fletcher Fleet. London: Lutterworth Press.

Von Allmen, Jean-Jacques. 1969. *The Lord's Supper*. Richmond, VA: John Knox Press.

Von Balthasar, Hans Urs. 1982. *The Glory of the Lord*. Tr. Erasmo Leiva-Merikakis. San Francisco: Ignatius Press.

Wettstein, Howard. 2014. "The Stone." Interview of Wettstein by Gary Gutting. In *New York Times*: March 30, 2014.

Wettstein, Howard. n.d. "The Fabric of Faith." Unpublished.

Witvliet, John. 2015. " 'Planting' and 'Harvesting' Godly Sincerity: Pastoral Wisdom in the Practice of Public Worship." *Evangelical Quarterly* 87/4 (October): 291–309.

Wolterstorff, Nicholas. 1980. *Works and Worlds of Art*. Oxford: Clarendon Press.

Wolterstorff, Nicholas. 1983. *Until Justice and Peace Embrace*. Grand Rapids, MI: William B. Eerdmans Publishing Co.

Wolterstorff, Nicholas. 1990. "The Remembrance of Things (Not) Past." In Thomas V. Flint, ed., *Christian Philosophy*. Notre Dame, IN: University of Notre Dame Press: 118–61.

Wolterstorff, Nicholas. 1995. *Divine Discourse: Philosophical Reflections on the Claim that God Speaks.* Cambridge: Cambridge University Press.

Wolterstorff, Nicholas. 1996. *John Locke and the Ethics of Belief.* Cambridge: Cambridge University Press.

Wolterstorff, Nicholas. 2008. *Justice: Rights and Wrongs.* Princeton: Princeton University Press.

Wolterstorff, Nicholas. 2010a. *Inquiring about God.* Ed. Terence Cuneo. Cambridge: Cambridge University Press.

Wolterstorff, Nicholas. 2010b. *Practices of Belief.* Ed. Terence Cuneo. Cambridge: Cambridge University Press.

Wolterstorff, Nicholas. 2011a. *Hearing the Call: Liturgy, Justice, Church, and World.* Grand Rapids, MI: William B. Eerdmans Publishing Co.

Wolterstorff, Nicholas. 2011b. *Justice in Love.* Grand Rapids, MI: William B. Eerdmans Publishing Co.

Wolterstorff, Nicholas. 2011c. "Reading Joshua." In Michael Bergmann, Michael J. Murray, and Michael E. Rea, eds., *Divine Evil: The Moral Character of the God of Abraham.* Oxford: Oxford University Press: 236–56.

Wolterstorff, Nicholas. 2012. *The Mighty and the Almighty.* Cambridge: Cambridge University Press.

Wolterstorff, Nicholas. 2013a. "John Calvin's Theology of the Eucharist." In Lee Palmer Wandel, ed., *A Companion to the Eucharist in the Reformation.* Leiden: Brill: 97–113.

Wolterstorff, Nicholas. 2013b. *Journey toward Justice.* Grand Rapids, MI: Baker Academic.

Wolterstorff, Nicholas. 2015a. *Art Rethought.* Oxford: Oxford University Press.

Wolterstorff, Nicholas. 2015b. *The God We Worship: An Exploration of Liturgical Theology.* Grand Rapids, MI: William B. Eerdmans Publishing Co.

Wolterstorff, Nicholas. 2015c. "Would You Stomp on a Picture of Your Mother? Would You Kiss an Icon?" *Faith and Philosophy* 32/1: 3–24.

Wolterstorff, Nicholas. 2016a. "The Liturgical Present Tense." In Michael Bergmann and Jeffrey E. Brower, eds., *Reason and Faith: Themes from Richard Swinburne.* Oxford: Oxford University Press: 171–93.

Wolterstorff, Nicholas. 2016b. "Why Animals Don't Speak." In Peter J. Weigel and Joseph G. Prud'homme, eds., *The Philosophy of Human Nature in Christian Perspective.* New York: Peter Lang: 17–38.

The Worship Book. 1975. Prepared by The Joint Committee on Worship for Cumberland Presbyterian Church, Presbyterian Church in the United States, The United Presbyterian Church in the United States. Philadelphia: The Westminster Press.

Young, James. 1993. *Holocaust Memorials and Meaning.* New Haven: Yale University Press.

Zahavi, Dan. 2014. *Self and Other: Exploring Subjectivity, Empathy, and Shame.* Oxford: Oxford University Press.

Zahavi, Dan. 2015. "Self and Other: From Pure Ego to Co-Constituted We." *Continental Philosophy Review* 48/2: 143–60.

Index

INDEX OF FIRST LINES OF
HYMNS, SPIRITUALS, AND
METRICAL PSALMS